Warning: This volume contains depictions of suicide, suicide attempts and/or suicidal ideation. If you are experiencing suicidal thoughts or feelings, you are not alone, and there is help. In the United States, call the Suicide & Crisis Lifeline by dialing 988 or go to suicidepreventionlifeline.org. Otherwise, visit findahelpline.com to find support.

Grand Blue Dreaming 19

PRESENTED BY KENJI INOUE & KIMITAKE YOSHIOKA

P9-ASE-868

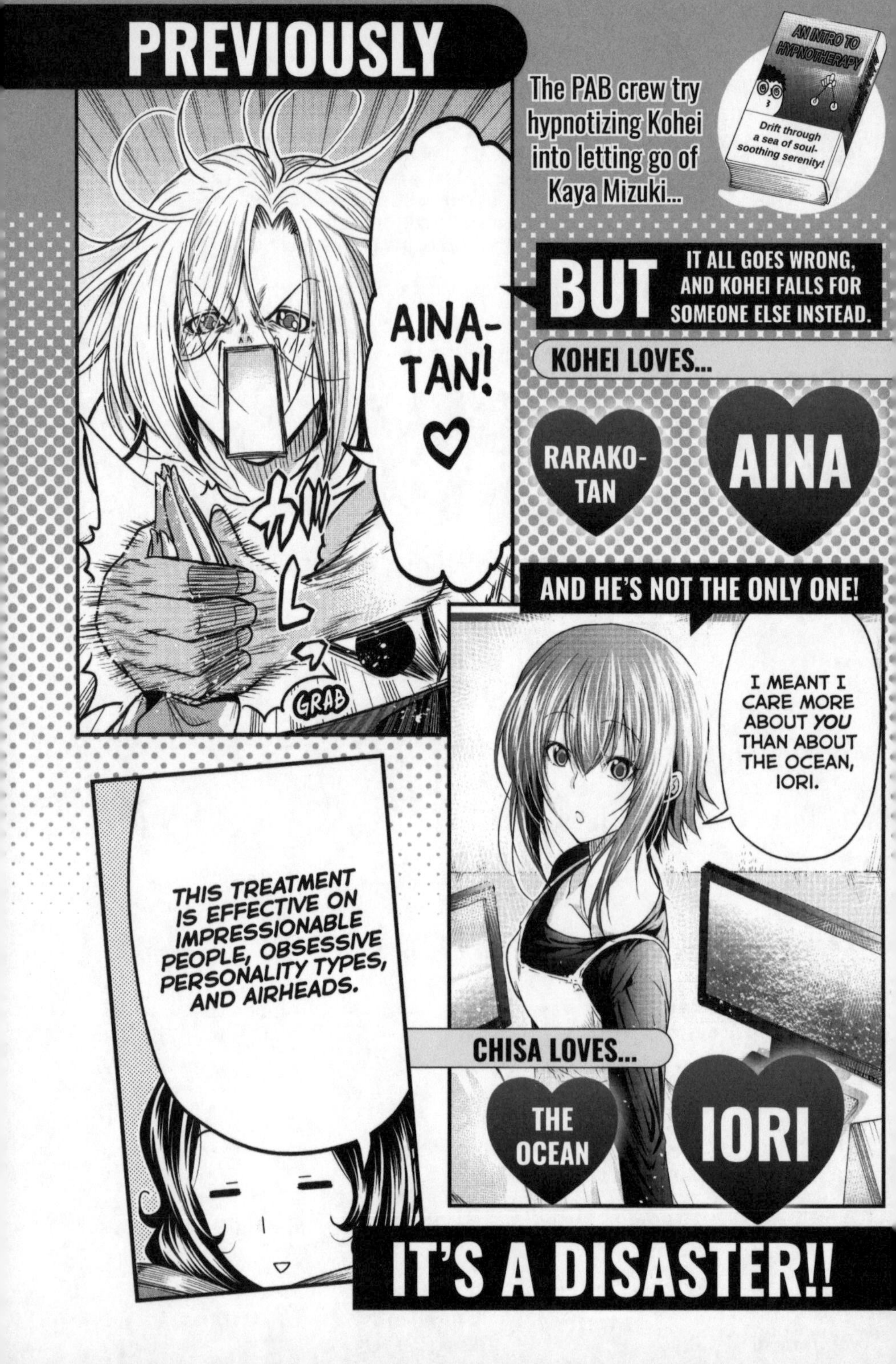
PREVIOUSLY
The PAB crew try hypnotizing Kohei into letting go of Kaya Mizuki...
AN INTRO TO HYPNOTHERAPY
Drift through a sea of soul-soothing serenity!
BUT IT ALL GOES WRONG, AND KOHEI FALLS FOR SOMEONE ELSE INSTEAD.
AINA-TAN! ♡
GRAB
KOHEI LOVES...
RARAKO-TAN
AINA
AND HE'S NOT THE ONLY ONE!
I MEANT I CARE MORE ABOUT *YOU* THAN ABOUT THE OCEAN, IORI.
CHISA LOVES...
THE OCEAN
IORI
THIS TREATMENT IS EFFECTIVE ON IMPRESSIONABLE PEOPLE, OBSESSIVE PERSONALITY TYPES, AND AIRHEADS.
IT'S A DISASTER!!

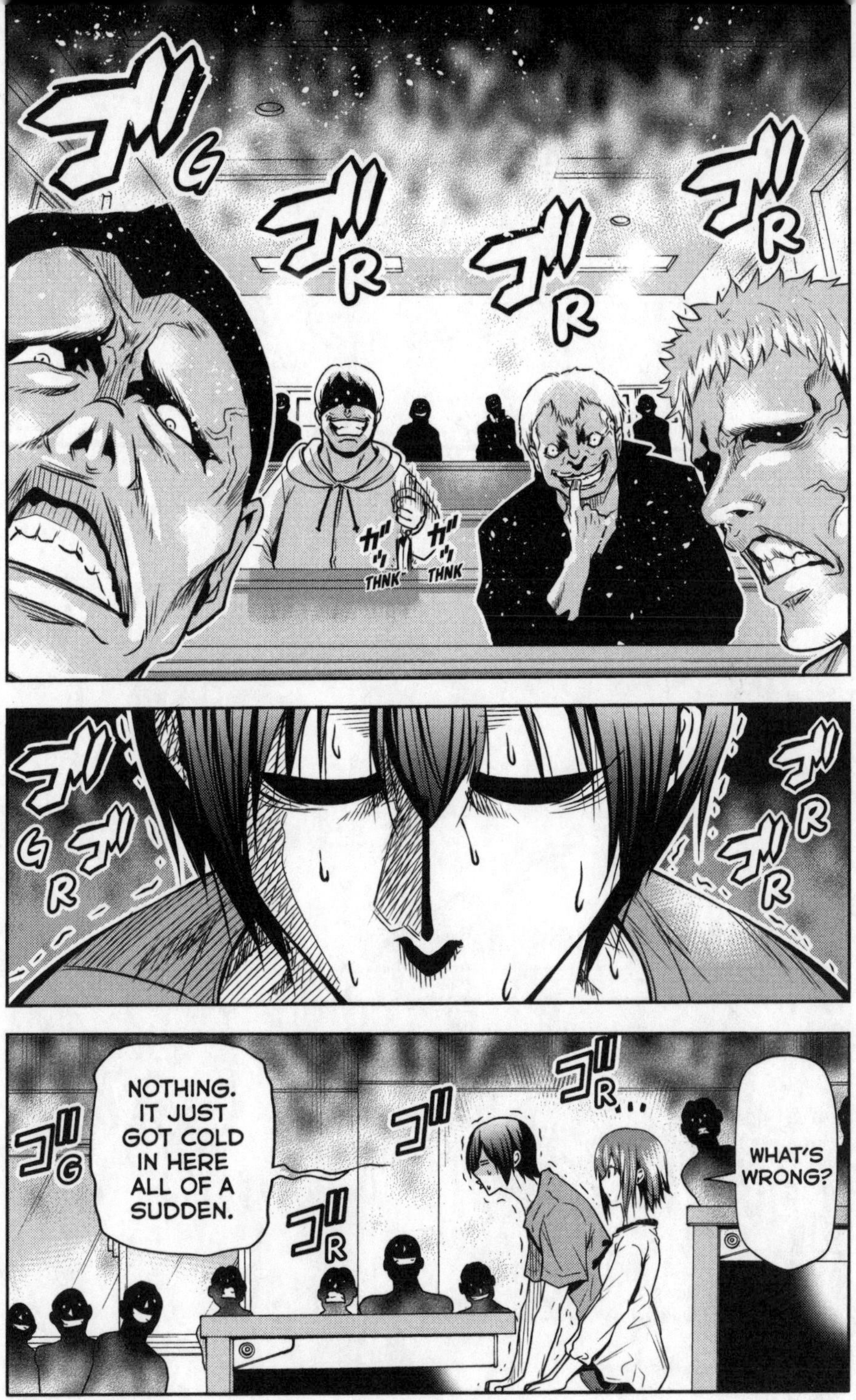
R
R
R
G
THNK
THNK
R
R
G
R
WHAT'S WRONG?
R...
NOTHING. IT JUST GOT COLD IN HERE ALL OF A SUDDEN.
G
R

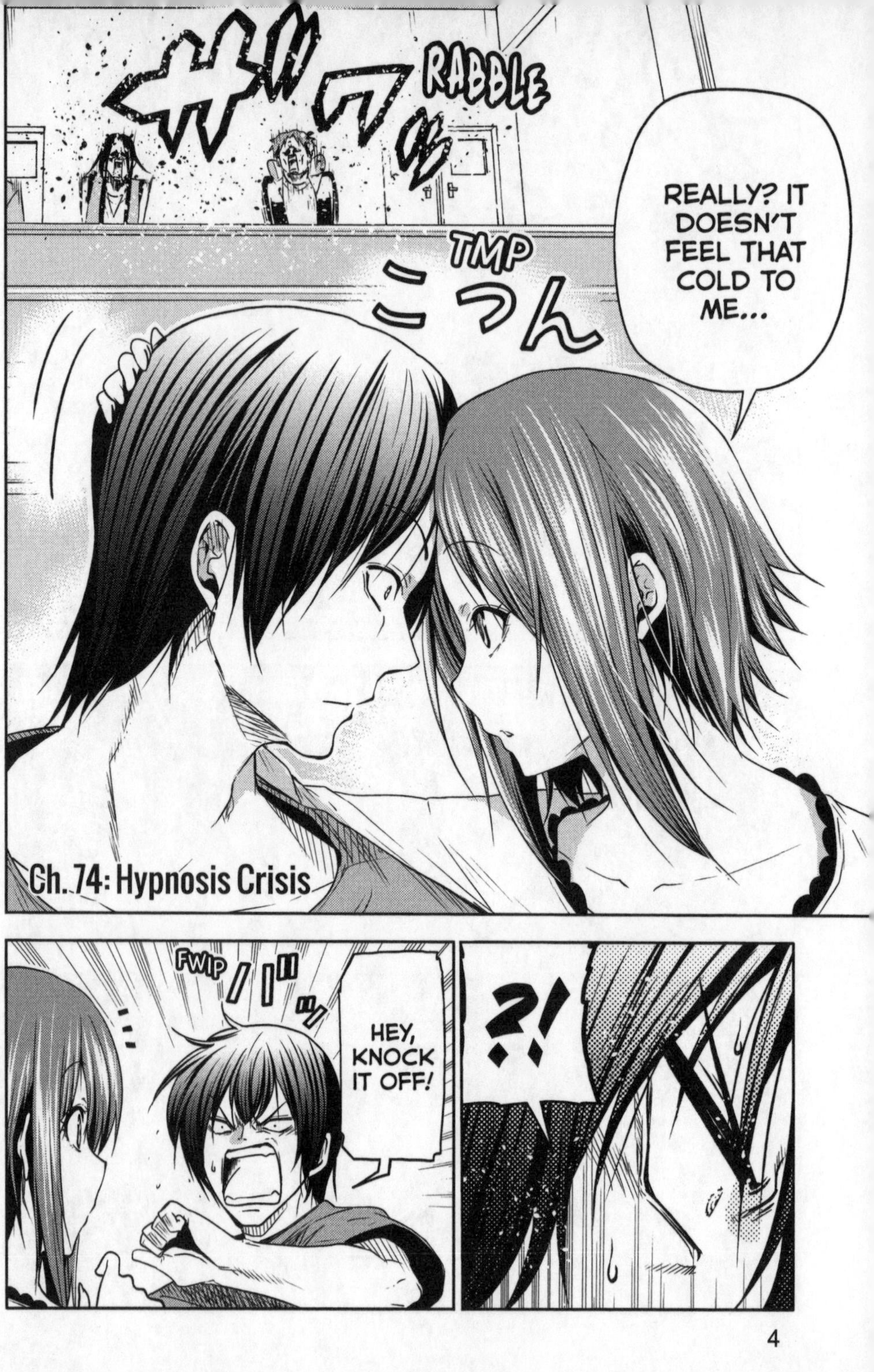
RABBLE
TMP
こつん
REALLY? IT DOESN'T FEEL THAT COLD TO ME...
Ch. 74: Hypnosis Crisis
?!
FWIP
HEY, KNOCK IT OFF!

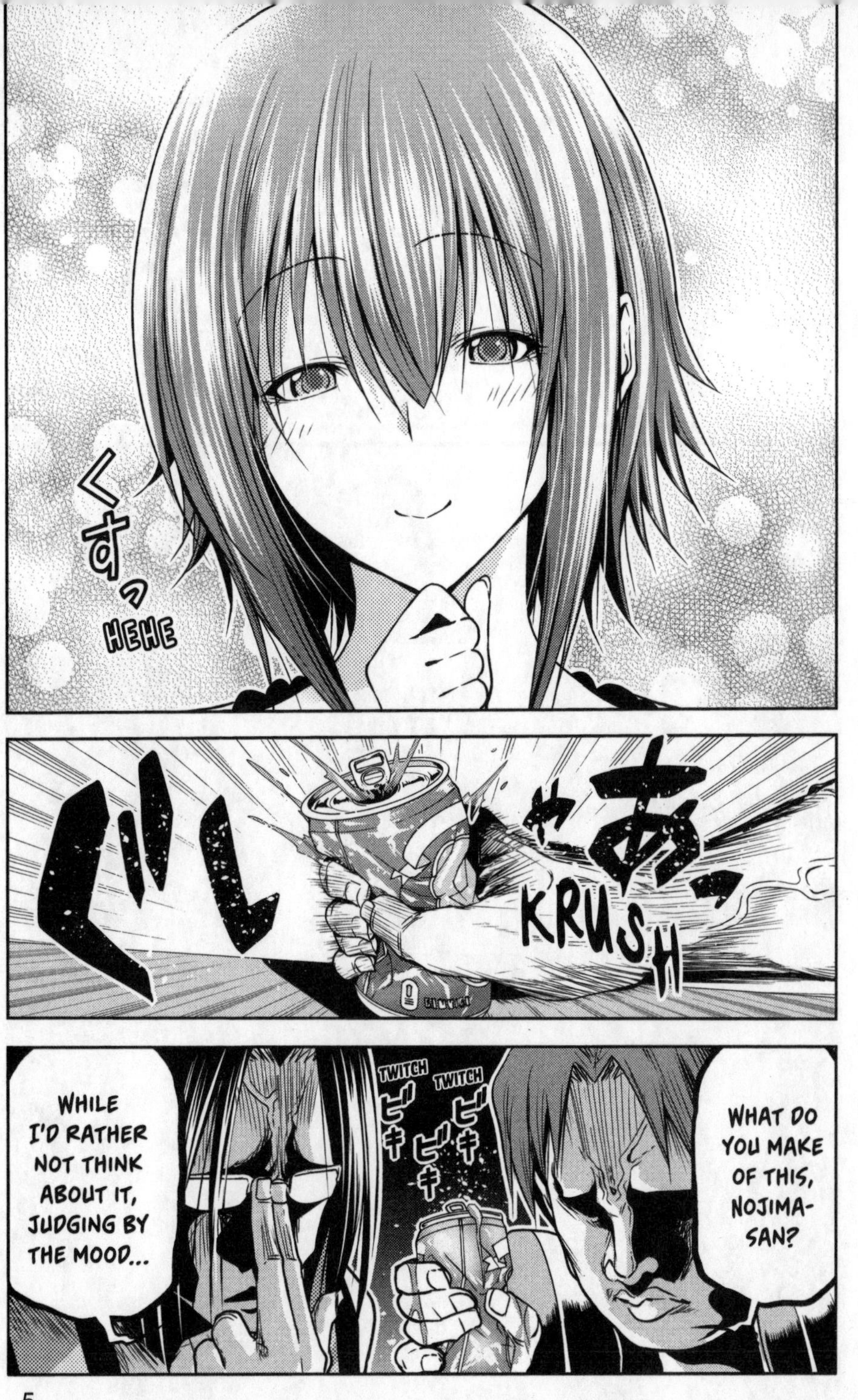
くすっ
HEHE
ぐしゃっ
KRUSH
WHAT DO YOU MAKE OF THIS, NOJIMA-SAN?
TWITCH TWITCH
ビキビキ
WHILE I'D RATHER NOT THINK ABOUT IT, JUDGING BY THE MOOD...

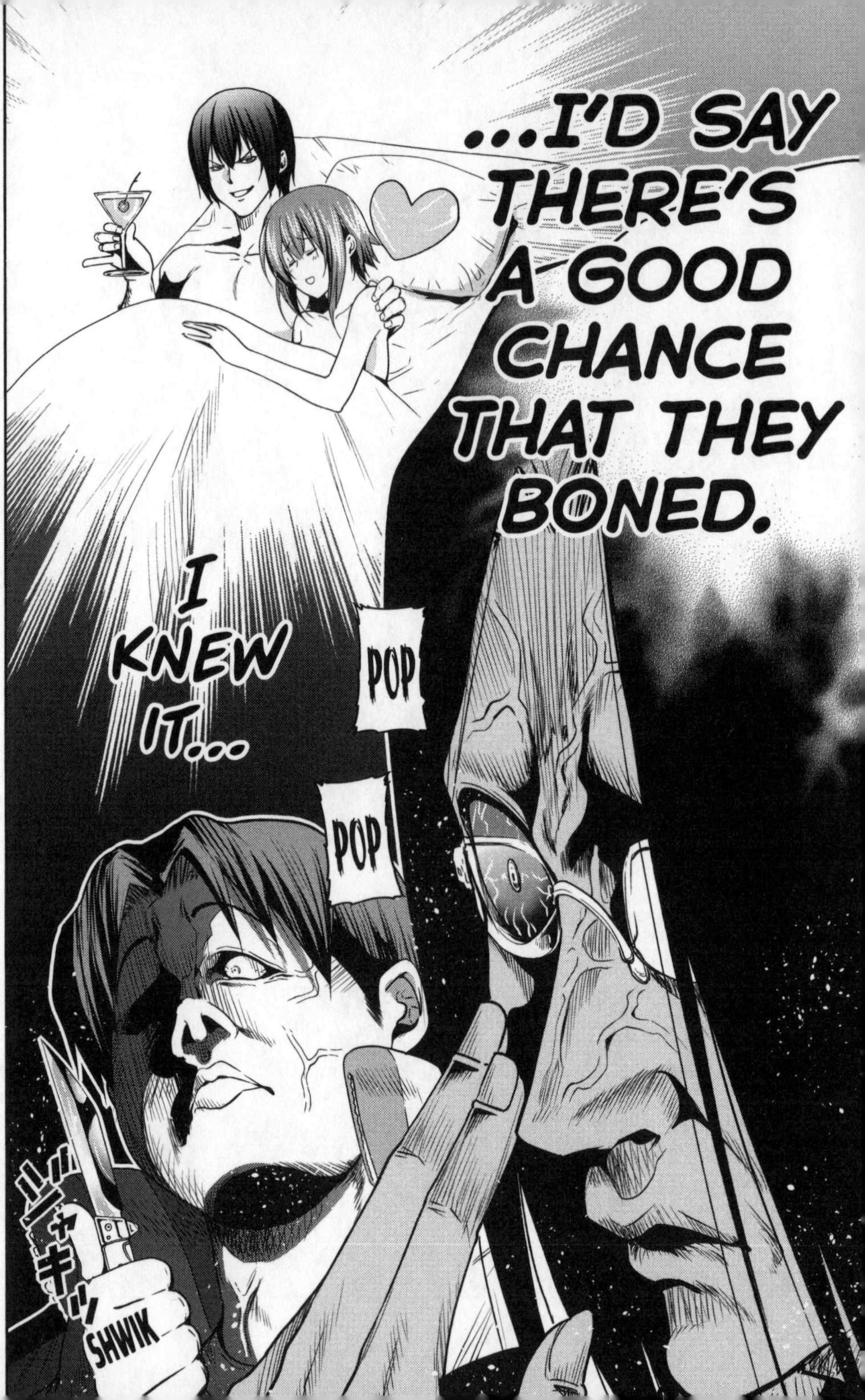
...I'D SAY THERE'S A GOOD CHANCE THAT THEY BONED.
POP
I KNEW IT...
POP
ジャキッ
SHWIK

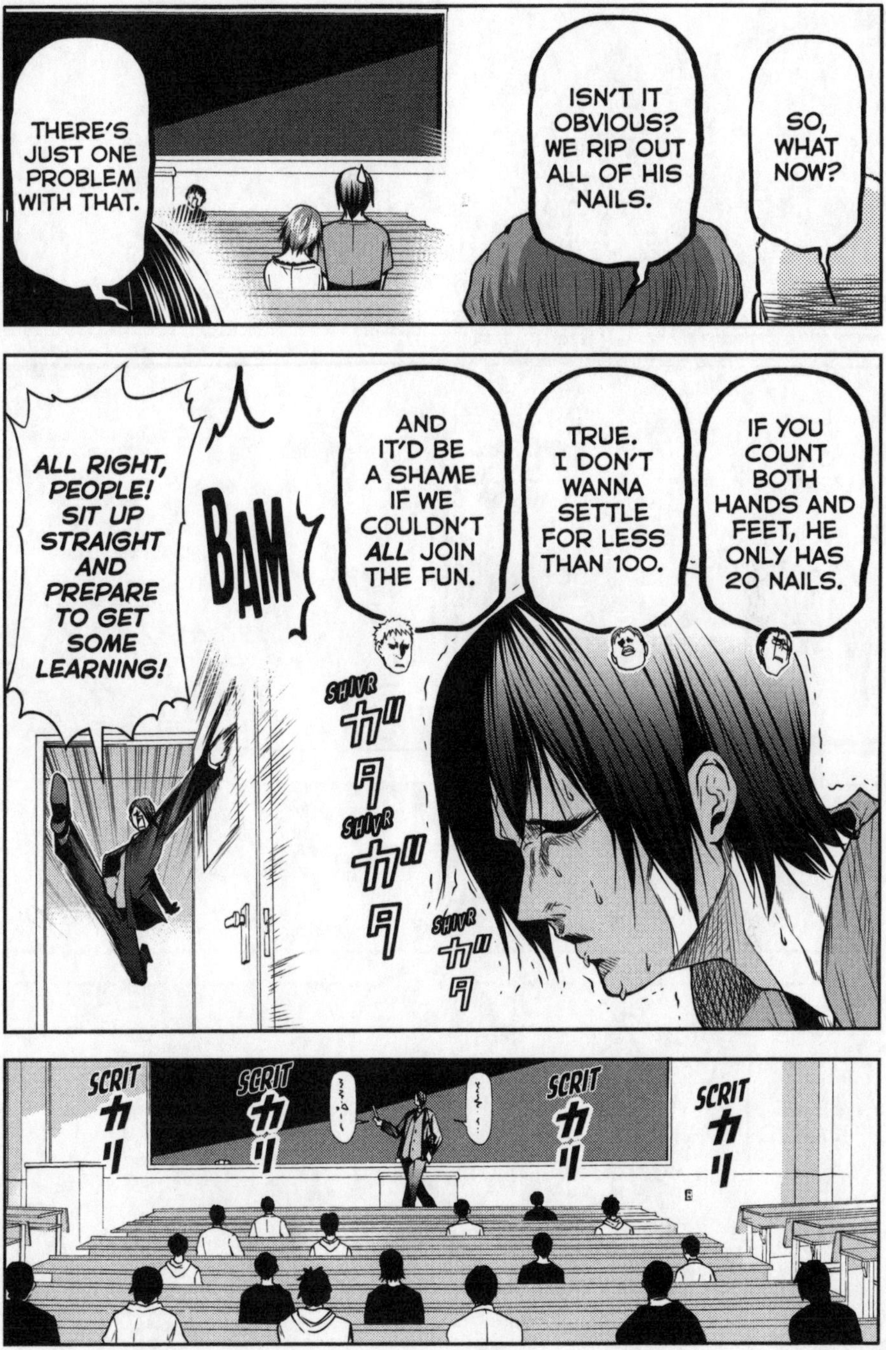

SO, WHAT NOW?
ISN'T IT OBVIOUS? WE RIP OUT ALL OF HIS NAILS.
THERE'S JUST ONE PROBLEM WITH THAT.
IF YOU COUNT BOTH HANDS AND FEET, HE ONLY HAS 20 NAILS.
TRUE. I DON'T WANNA SETTLE FOR LESS THAN 100.
AND IT'D BE A SHAME IF WE COULDN'T *ALL* JOIN THE FUN.
SHIVR ガタ
SHIVR ガタ
SHIVR ガタ
BAM
ALL RIGHT, PEOPLE! SIT UP STRAIGHT AND PREPARE TO GET SOME LEARNING!
SCRIT カリ
SCRIT カリ
SCRIT カリ
SCRIT カリ

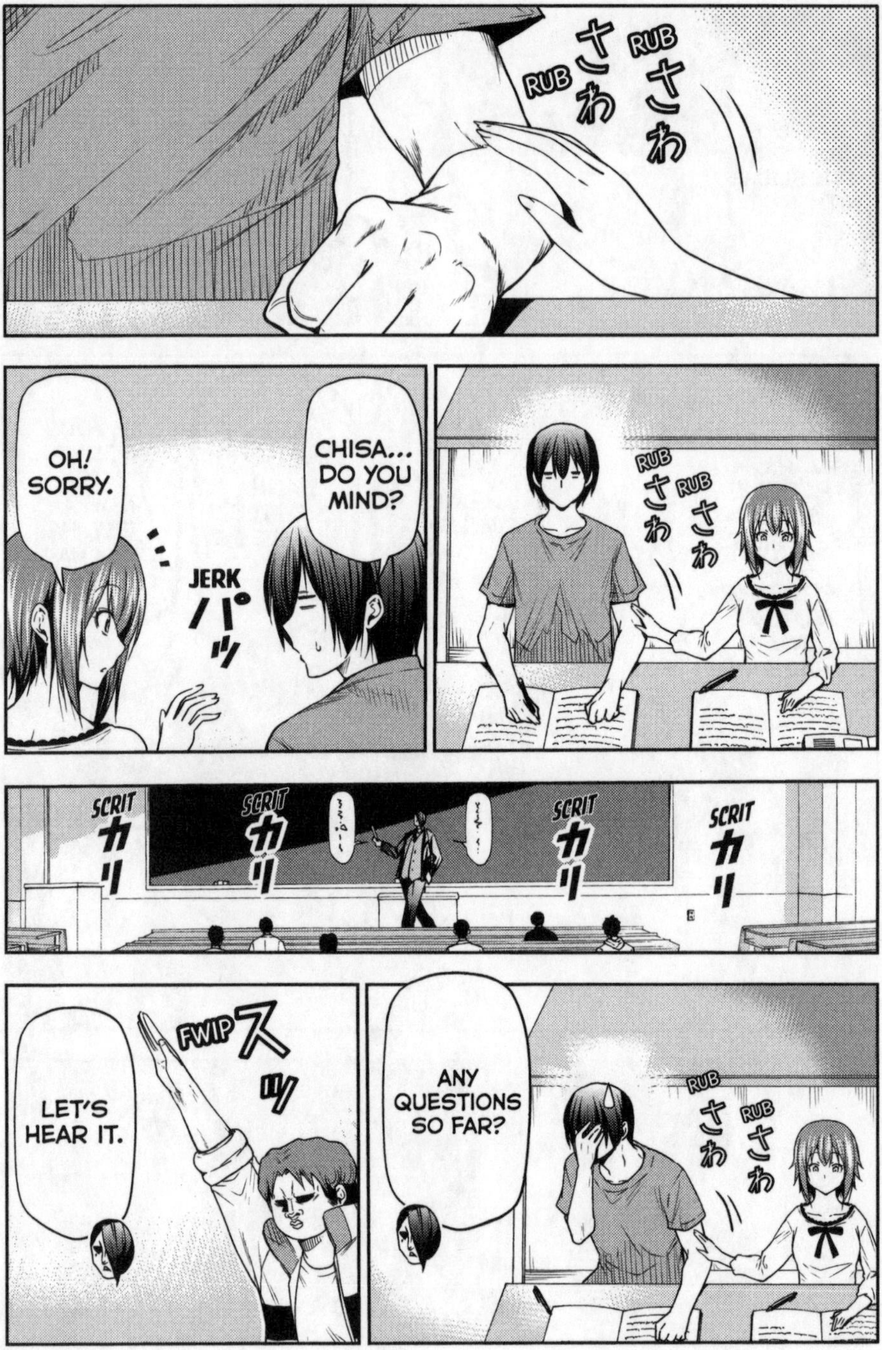
RUB さわ
RUB さわ
RUB さわ
RUB さわ
CHISA... DO YOU MIND?
JERK パッ
OH! SORRY.
SCRIT カリ
SCRIT カリ
SCRIT カリ
SCRIT カリ
ANY QUESTIONS SO FAR?
RUB さわ
RUB さわ
FWIP スッ
LET'S HEAR IT.

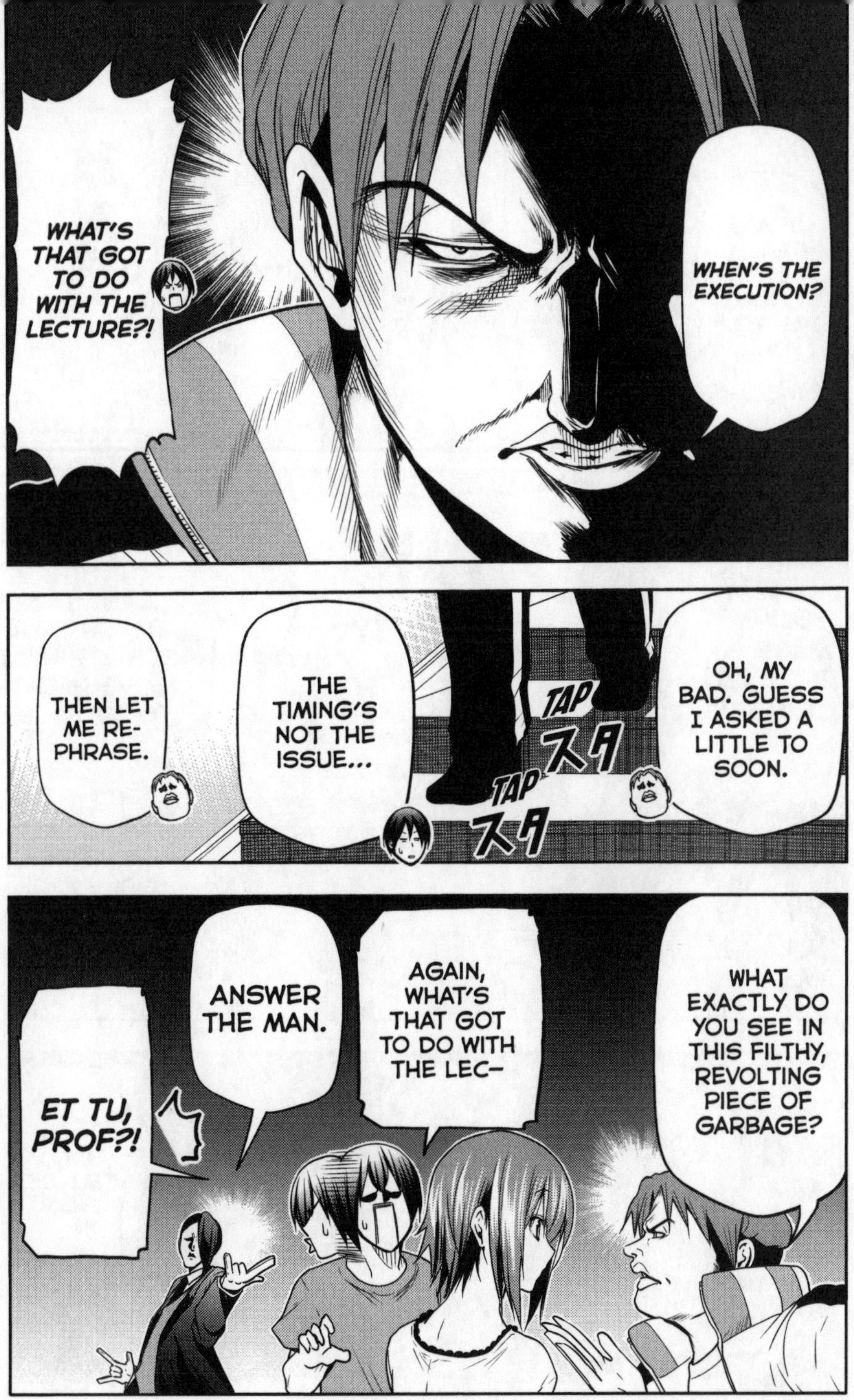
WHEN'S THE EXECUTION?
WHAT'S THAT GOT TO DO WITH THE LECTURE?!
OH, MY BAD. GUESS I ASKED A LITTLE TO SOON.
TAP スタ
TAP スタ
THE TIMING'S NOT THE ISSUE...
THEN LET ME RE-PHRASE.
WHAT EXACTLY DO YOU SEE IN THIS FILTHY, REVOLTING PIECE OF GARBAGE?
AGAIN, WHAT'S THAT GOT TO DO WITH THE LEC—
ANSWER THE MAN.
ET TU, PROF?!

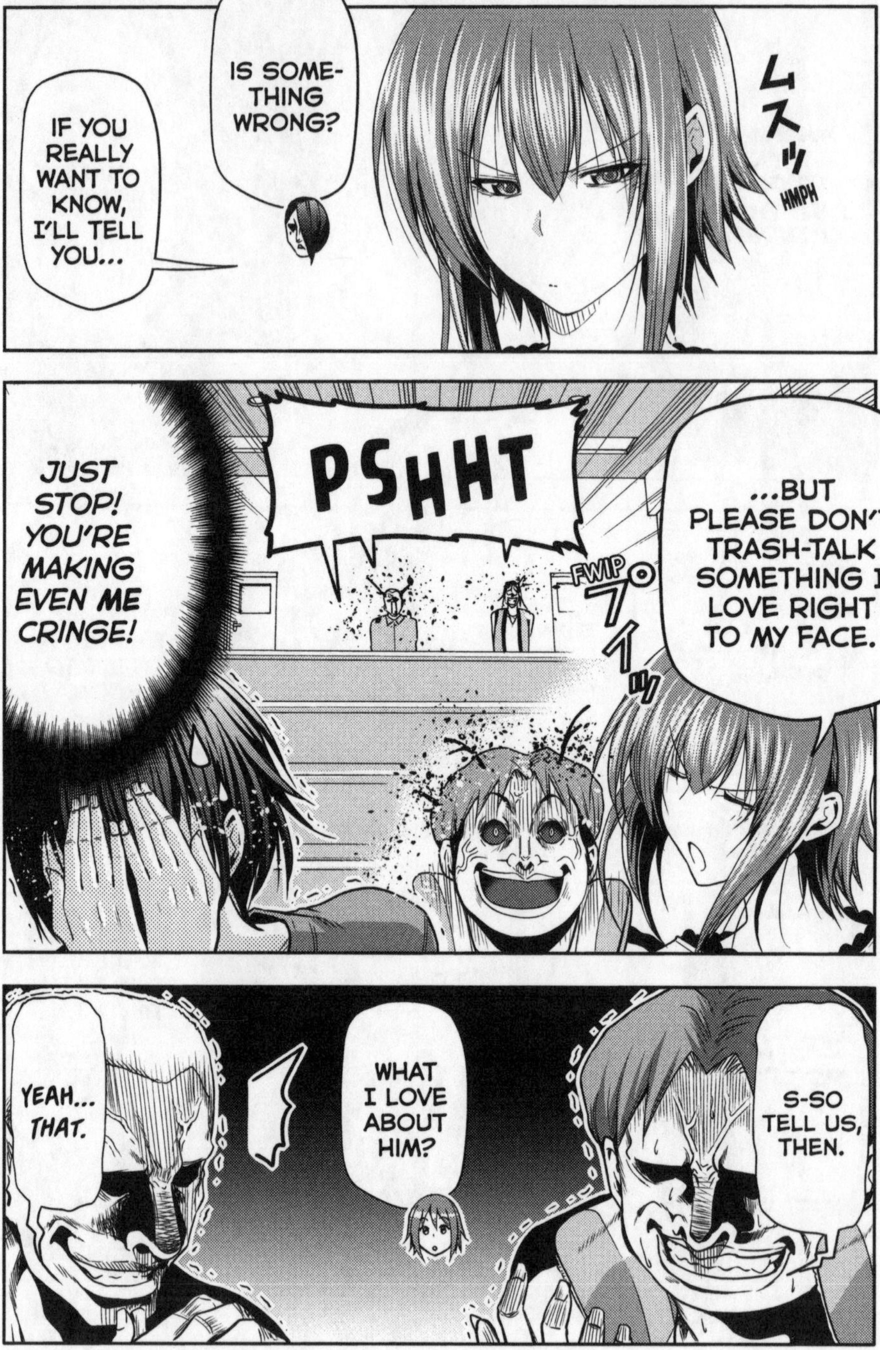

ムスッ
HMPH
IS SOME-THING WRONG?
IF YOU REALLY WANT TO KNOW, I'LL TELL YOU...
...BUT PLEASE DON'T TRASH-TALK SOMETHING I LOVE RIGHT TO MY FACE.
FWIP
プイッ
PSHHT
JUST STOP! YOU'RE MAKING EVEN ME CRINGE!
S-SO TELL US, THEN.
WHAT I LOVE ABOUT HIM?
YEAH... THAT.

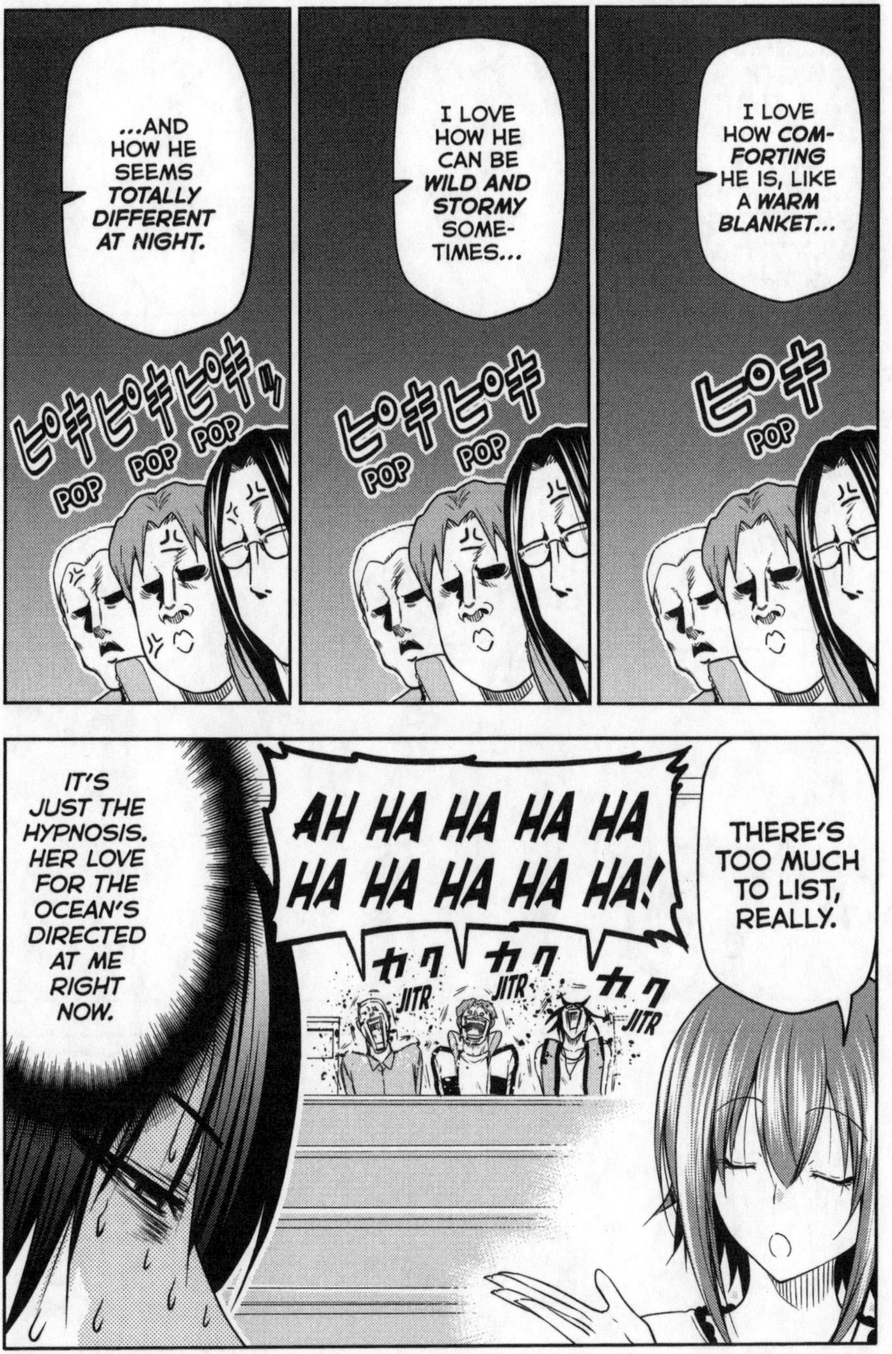
I LOVE HOW COMFORTING HE IS, LIKE A WARM BLANKET...
ピキ
POP
I LOVE HOW HE CAN BE WILD AND STORMY SOMETIMES...
ピキピキ
POP POP
...AND HOW HE SEEMS TOTALLY DIFFERENT AT NIGHT.
ピキピキピキッ
POP POP POP
THERE'S TOO MUCH TO LIST, REALLY.
AH HA HA HA HA HA HA HA HA HA!
カク カク カク
JITR JITR JITR
IT'S JUST THE HYPNOSIS. HER LOVE FOR THE OCEAN'S DIRECTED AT ME RIGHT NOW.

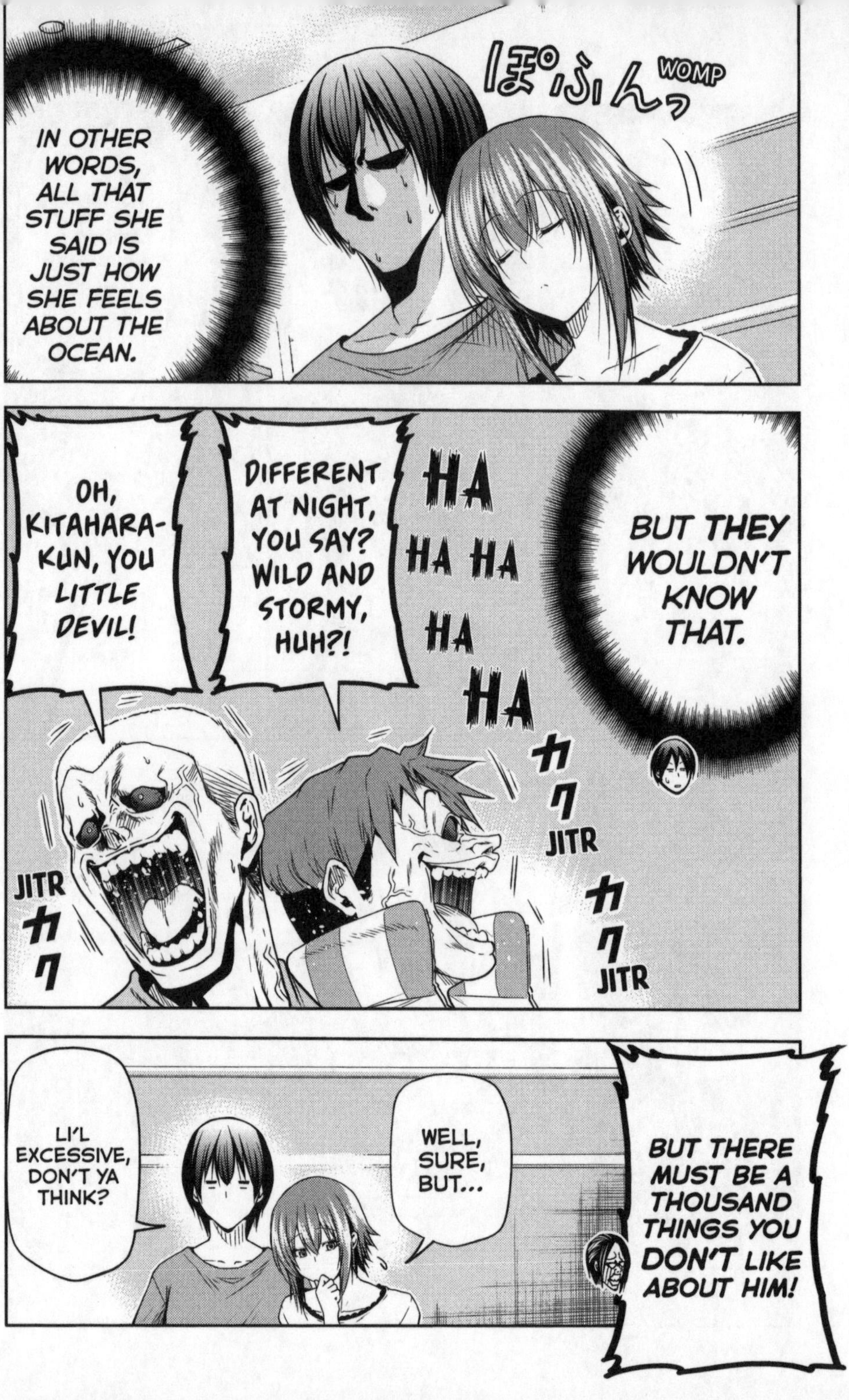
ぽふんっ
WOMP
IN OTHER WORDS, ALL THAT STUFF SHE SAID IS JUST HOW SHE FEELS ABOUT THE OCEAN.
BUT THEY WOULDN'T KNOW THAT.
HA HA HA HA HA
カク
JITR
カク
JITR
DIFFERENT AT NIGHT, YOU SAY? WILD AND STORMY, HUH?!
OH, KITAHARA-KUN, YOU LITTLE DEVIL!
JITR
カク
BUT THERE MUST BE A THOUSAND THINGS YOU DON'T LIKE ABOUT HIM!
WELL, SURE, BUT...
LI'L EXCESSIVE, DON'T YA THINK?

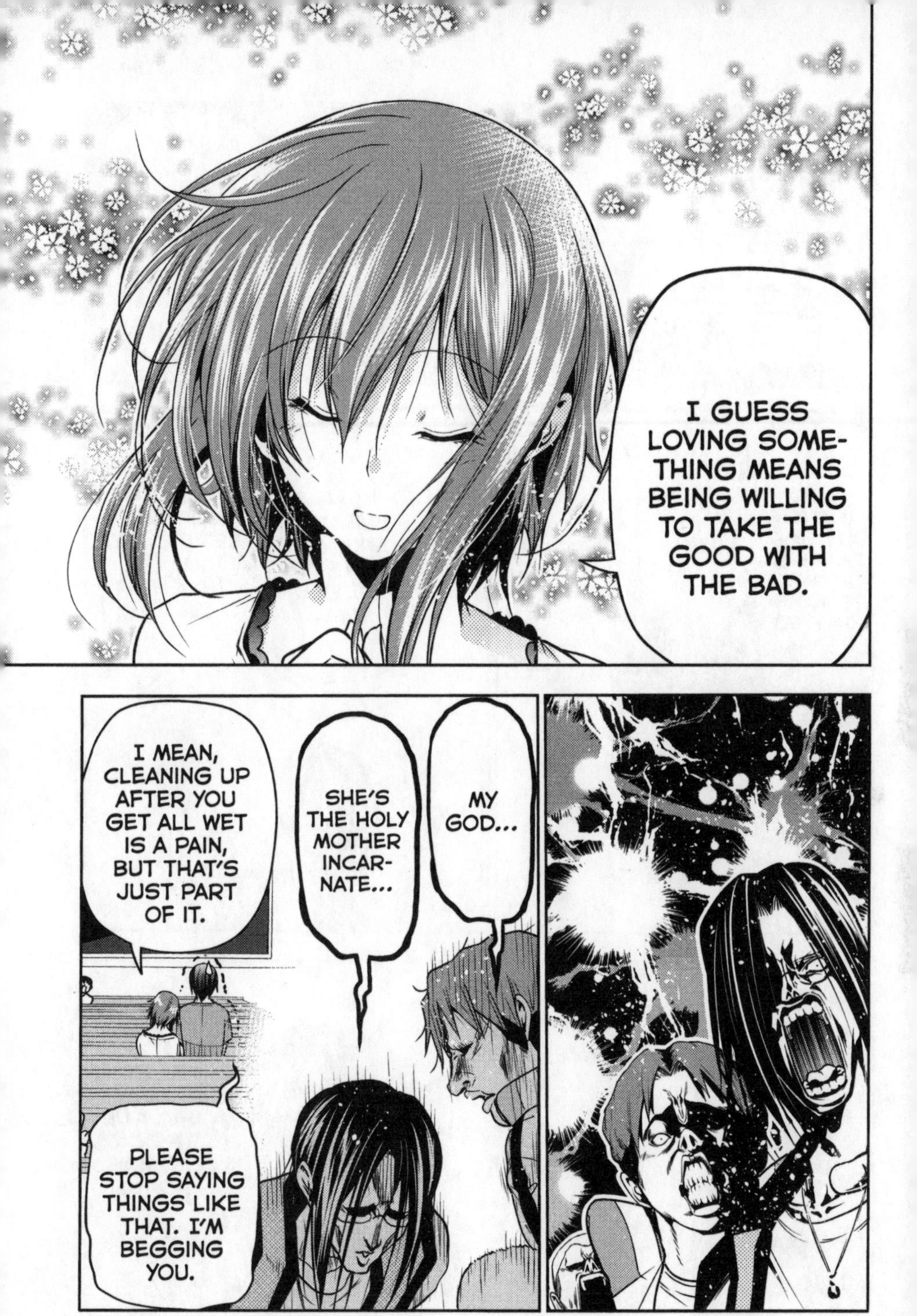
I GUESS LOVING SOME-THING MEANS BEING WILLING TO TAKE THE GOOD WITH THE BAD.
MY GOD...
SHE'S THE HOLY MOTHER INCAR-NATE...
I MEAN, CLEANING UP AFTER YOU GET ALL WET IS A PAIN, BUT THAT'S JUST PART OF IT.
PLEASE STOP SAYING THINGS LIKE THAT. I'M BEGGING YOU.

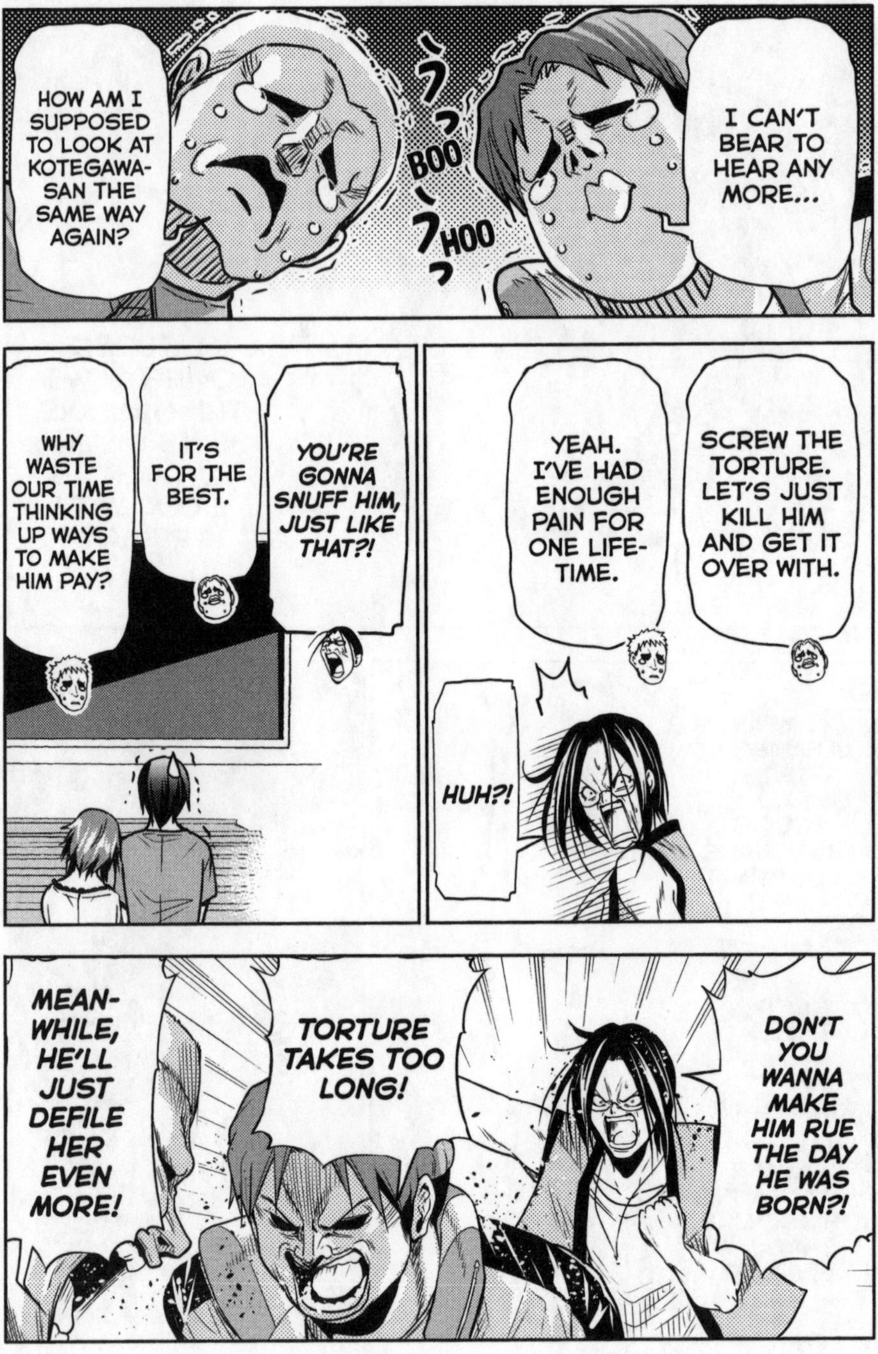
I CAN'T BEAR TO HEAR ANY MORE...
BOO HOO
HOW AM I SUPPOSED TO LOOK AT KOTEGAWA-SAN THE SAME WAY AGAIN?
SCREW THE TORTURE. LET'S JUST KILL HIM AND GET IT OVER WITH.
YEAH. I'VE HAD ENOUGH PAIN FOR ONE LIFE-TIME.
HUH?!
YOU'RE GONNA SNUFF HIM, JUST LIKE THAT?!
IT'S FOR THE BEST.
WHY WASTE OUR TIME THINKING UP WAYS TO MAKE HIM PAY?
DON'T YOU WANNA MAKE HIM RUE THE DAY HE WAS BORN?!
TORTURE TAKES TOO LONG!
MEAN-WHILE, HE'LL JUST DEFILE HER EVEN MORE!

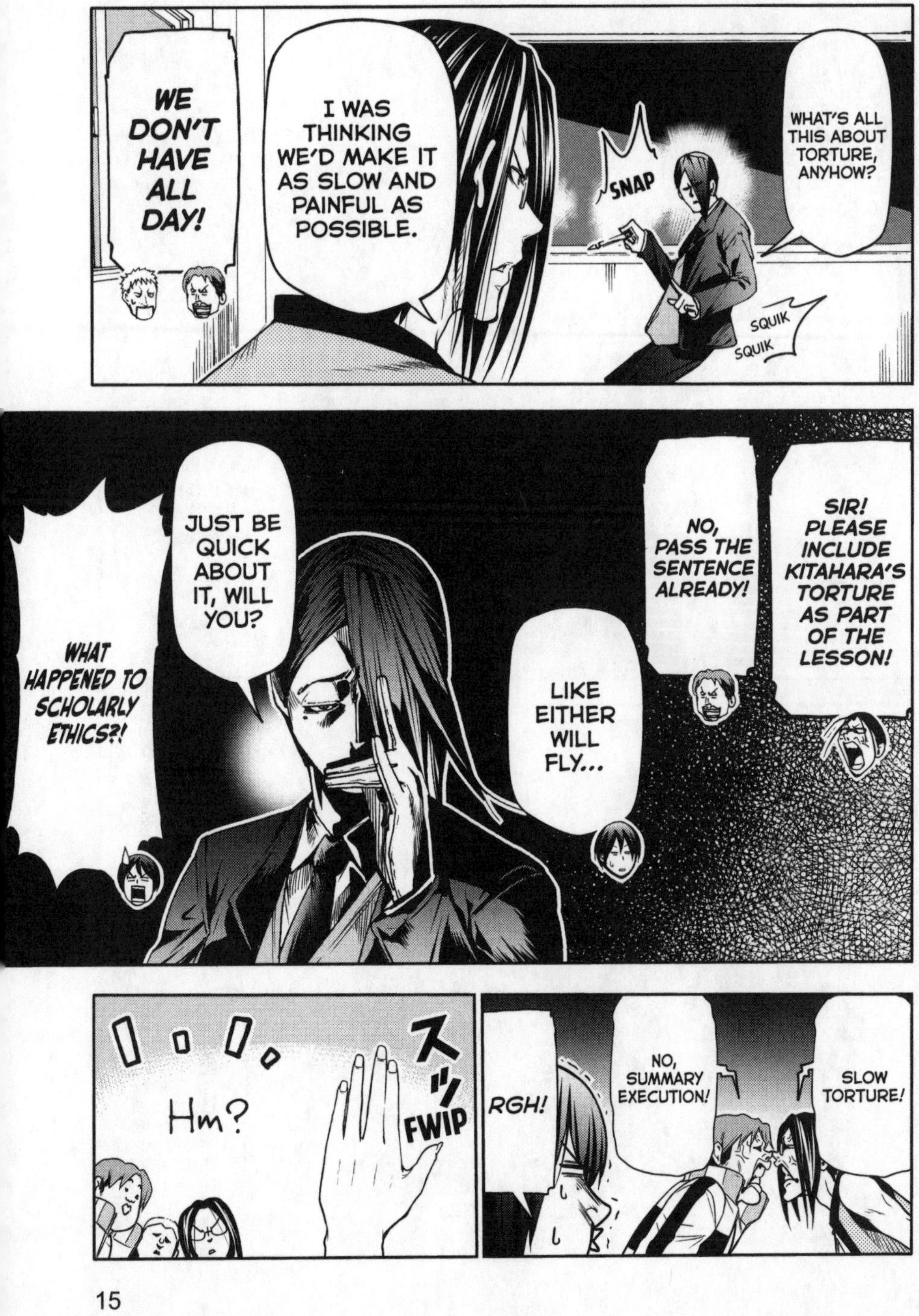
WHAT'S ALL THIS ABOUT TORTURE, ANYHOW?
SNAP
SQUIK SQUIK
I WAS THINKING WE'D MAKE IT AS SLOW AND PAINFUL AS POSSIBLE.
WE DON'T HAVE ALL DAY!
SIR! PLEASE INCLUDE KITAHARA'S TORTURE AS PART OF THE LESSON!
NO, PASS THE SENTENCE ALREADY!
LIKE EITHER WILL FLY...
JUST BE QUICK ABOUT IT, WILL YOU?
WHAT HAPPENED TO SCHOLARLY ETHICS?!
SLOW TORTURE!
NO, SUMMARY EXECUTION!
RGH!
スッ
FWIP
Hm?

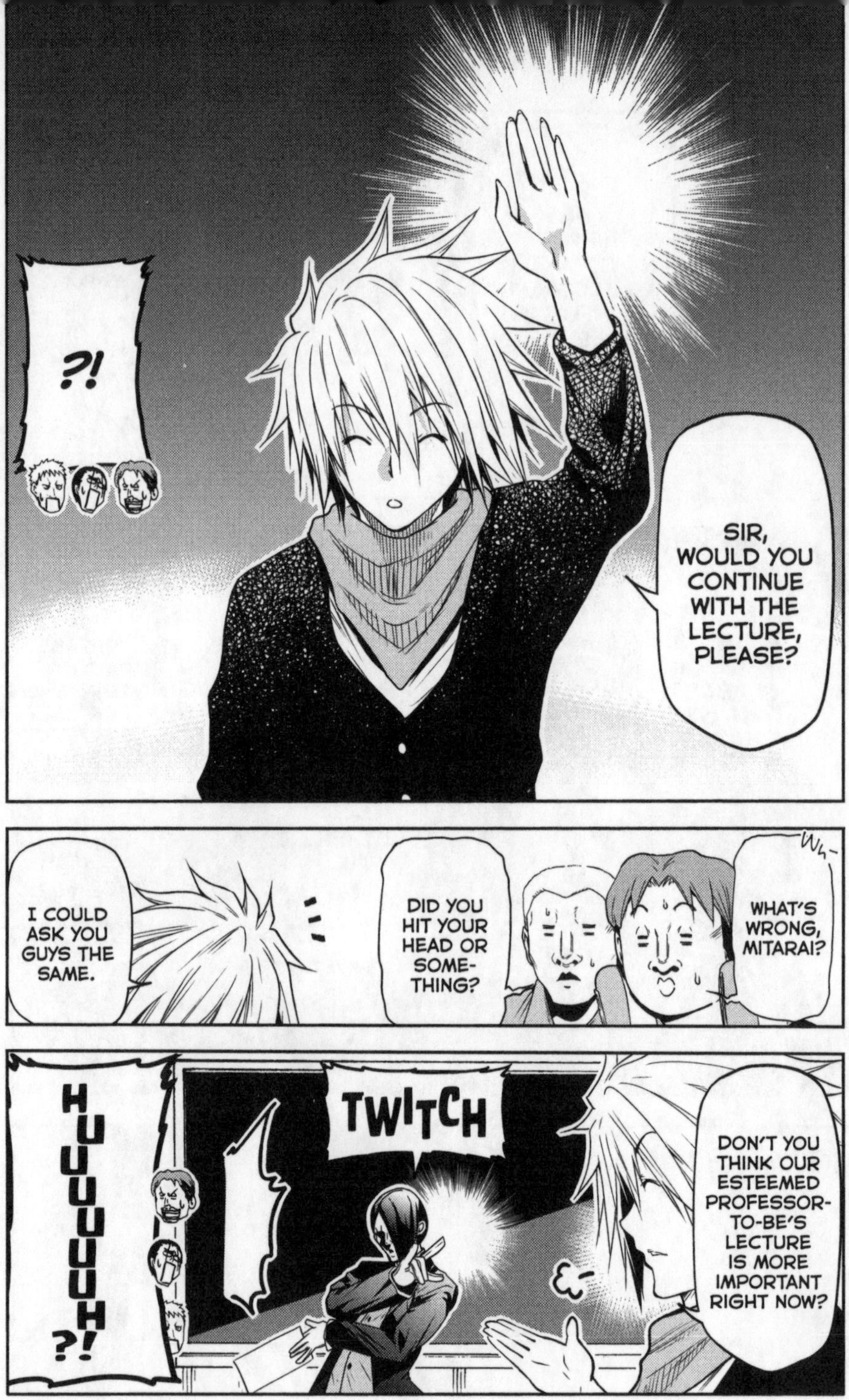
SIR, WOULD YOU CONTINUE WITH THE LECTURE, PLEASE?
?!
WHAT'S WRONG, MITARAI?
DID YOU HIT YOUR HEAD OR SOME-THING?
I COULD ASK YOU GUYS THE SAME.
DON'T YOU THINK OUR ESTEEMED PROFESSOR-TO-BE'S LECTURE IS MORE IMPORTANT RIGHT NOW?
TWITCH
HUUUUUUUH?!

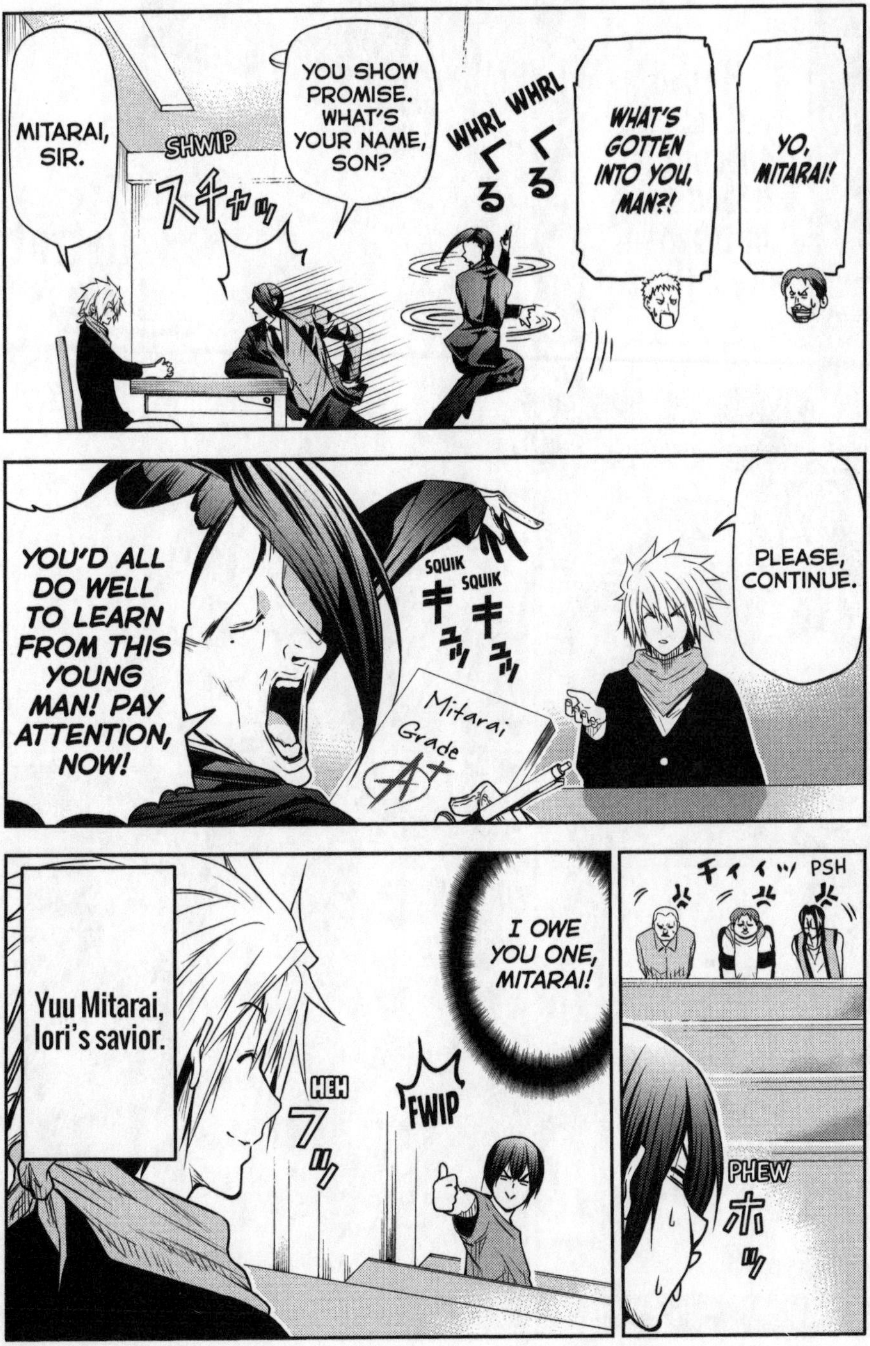
YO, MITARAI!
WHAT'S GOTTEN INTO YOU, MAN?!
WHRL WHRL
くるくる
YOU SHOW PROMISE. WHAT'S YOUR NAME, SON?
SHWIP
スチャッ
MITARAI, SIR.
PLEASE, CONTINUE.
SQUIK SQUIK
キュッキュッ
Mitarai
Grade
A+
YOU'D ALL DO WELL TO LEARN FROM THIS YOUNG MAN! PAY ATTENTION, NOW!
チィィッ
PSH
PHEW
ホッ
I OWE YOU ONE, MITARAI!
FWIP
HEH
フッ
Yuu Mitarai, Iori's savior.

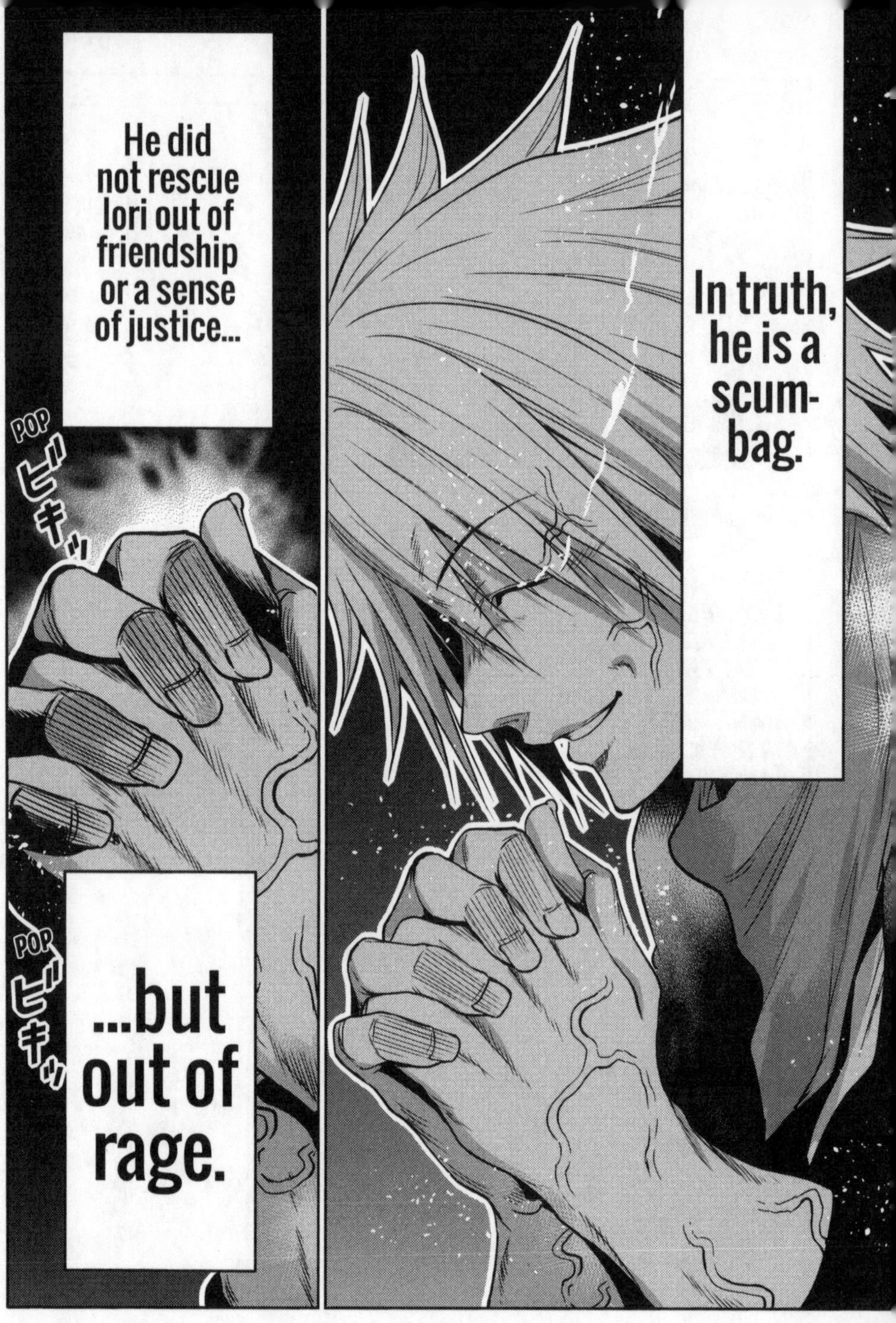
In truth, he is a scum-bag.
He did not rescue lori out of friendship or a sense of justice...
POP
ビキッ
...but out of rage.
POP
ビキッ

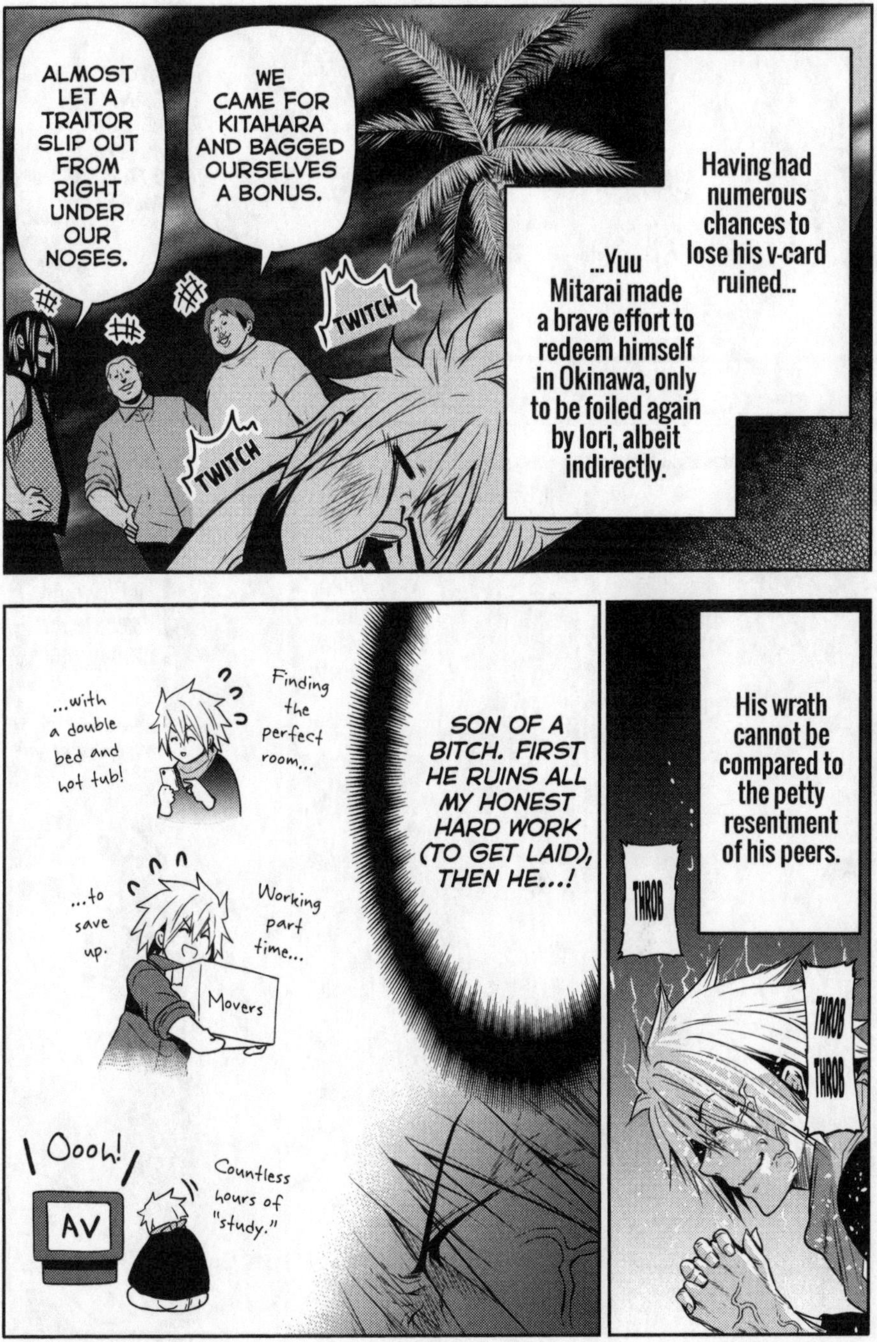

Having had numerous chances to lose his v-card ruined...
...Yuu Mitarai made a brave effort to redeem himself in Okinawa, only to be foiled again by Iori, albeit indirectly.
TWITCH
TWITCH
WE CAME FOR KITAHARA AND BAGGED OURSELVES A BONUS.
ALMOST LET A TRAITOR SLIP OUT FROM RIGHT UNDER OUR NOSES.
His wrath cannot be compared to the petty resentment of his peers.
THROB
THROB THROB
SON OF A BITCH. FIRST HE RUINS ALL MY HONEST HARD WORK (TO GET LAID), THEN HE...!
Finding the perfect room...
...with a double bed and hot tub!
Working part time...
...to save up.
Movers
Countless hours of "study."
Oooh!
AV

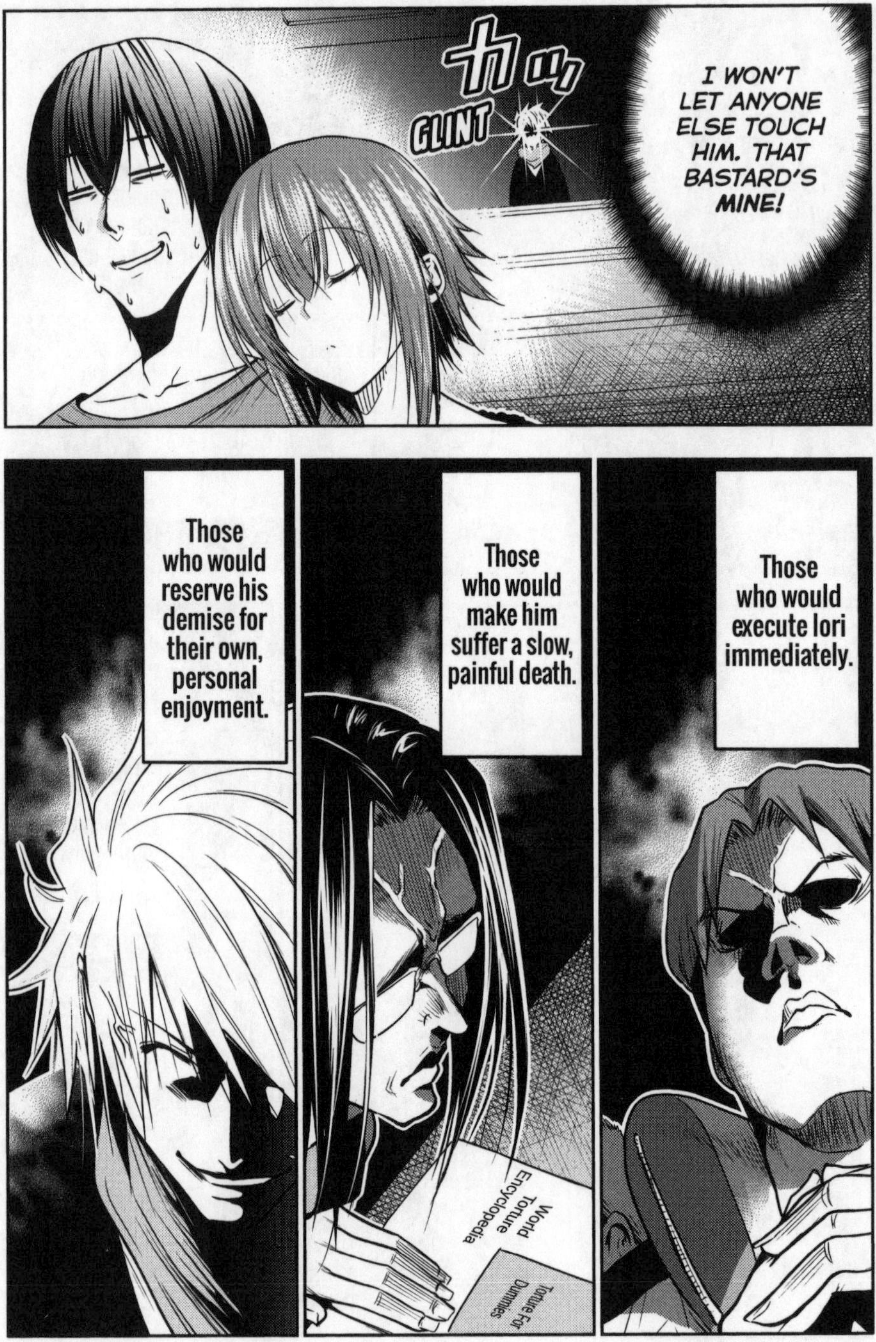
I WON'T LET ANYONE ELSE TOUCH HIM. THAT BASTARD'S MINE!
カッ
GLINT
Those who would execute Iori immediately.
Those who would make him suffer a slow, painful death.
World Torture Encyclopedia
Torture For Dummies
Those who would reserve his demise for their own, personal enjoyment.

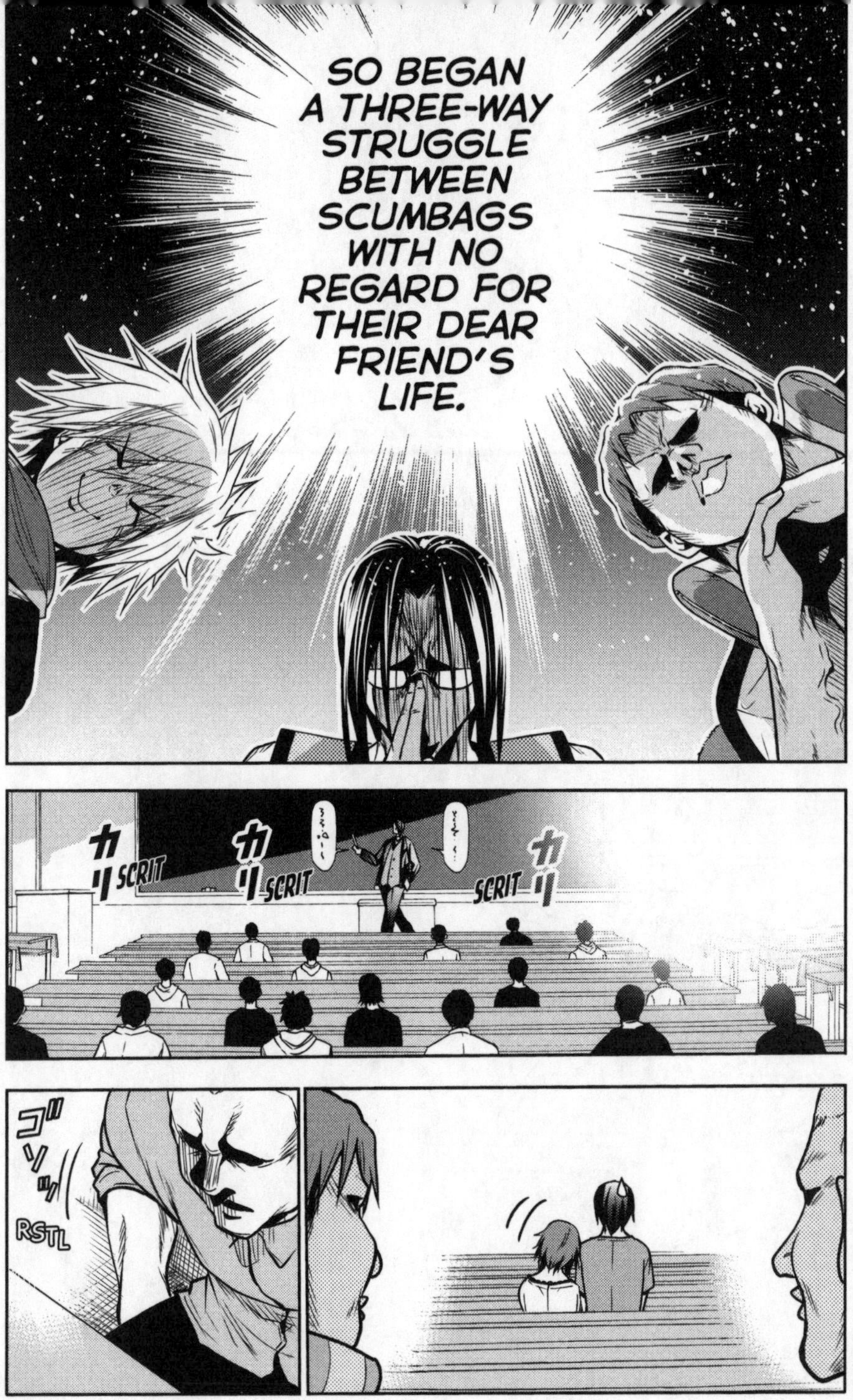
SO BEGAN A THREE-WAY STRUGGLE BETWEEN SCUMBAGS WITH NO REGARD FOR THEIR DEAR FRIEND'S LIFE.
カリ SCRIT
カリ SCRIT
カリ SCRIT
ゴソッ RSTL

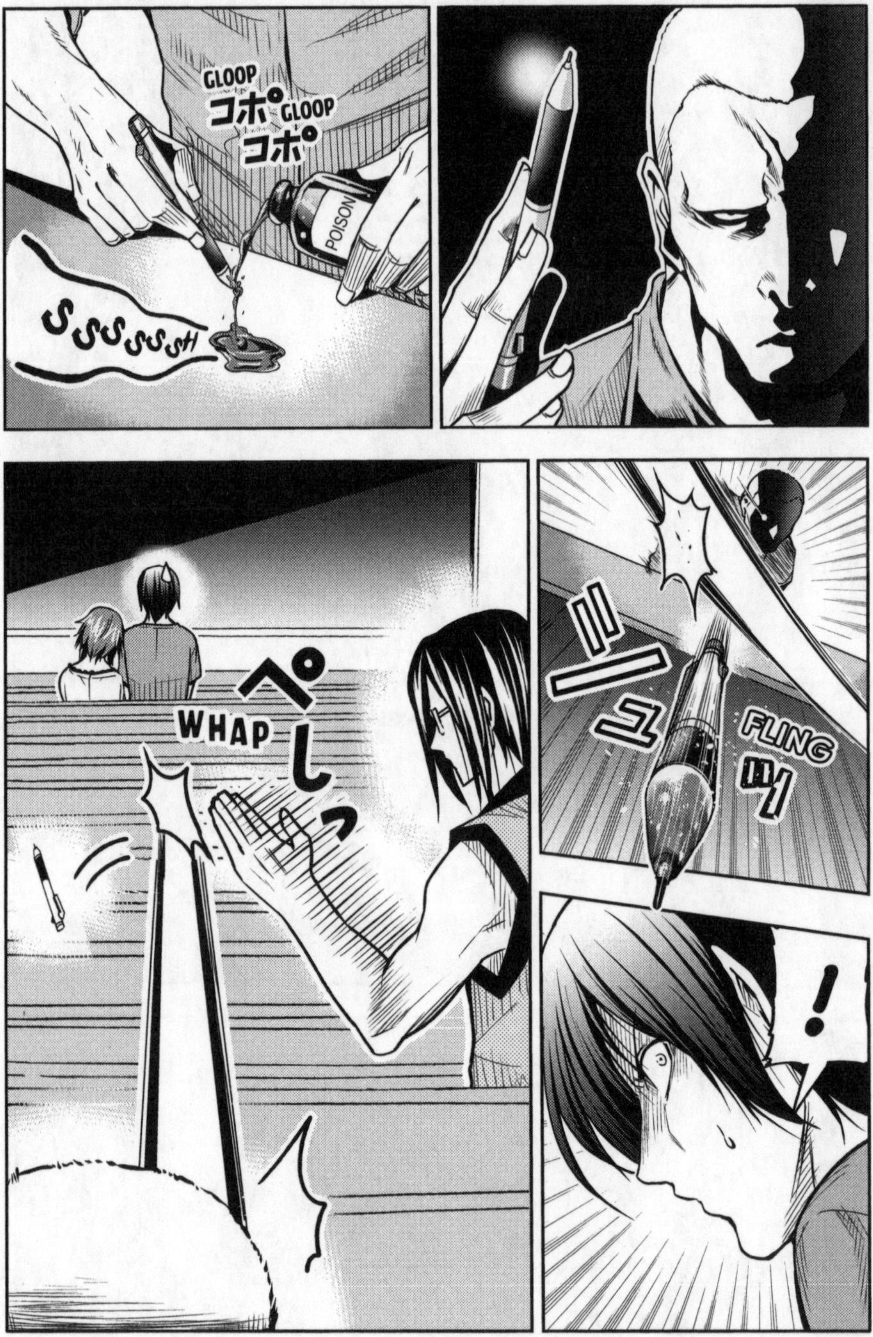
GLOOP
コポ
GLOOP
コポ
POISON
SSSSSSSH
FLING
!
WHAP
ぺしっ

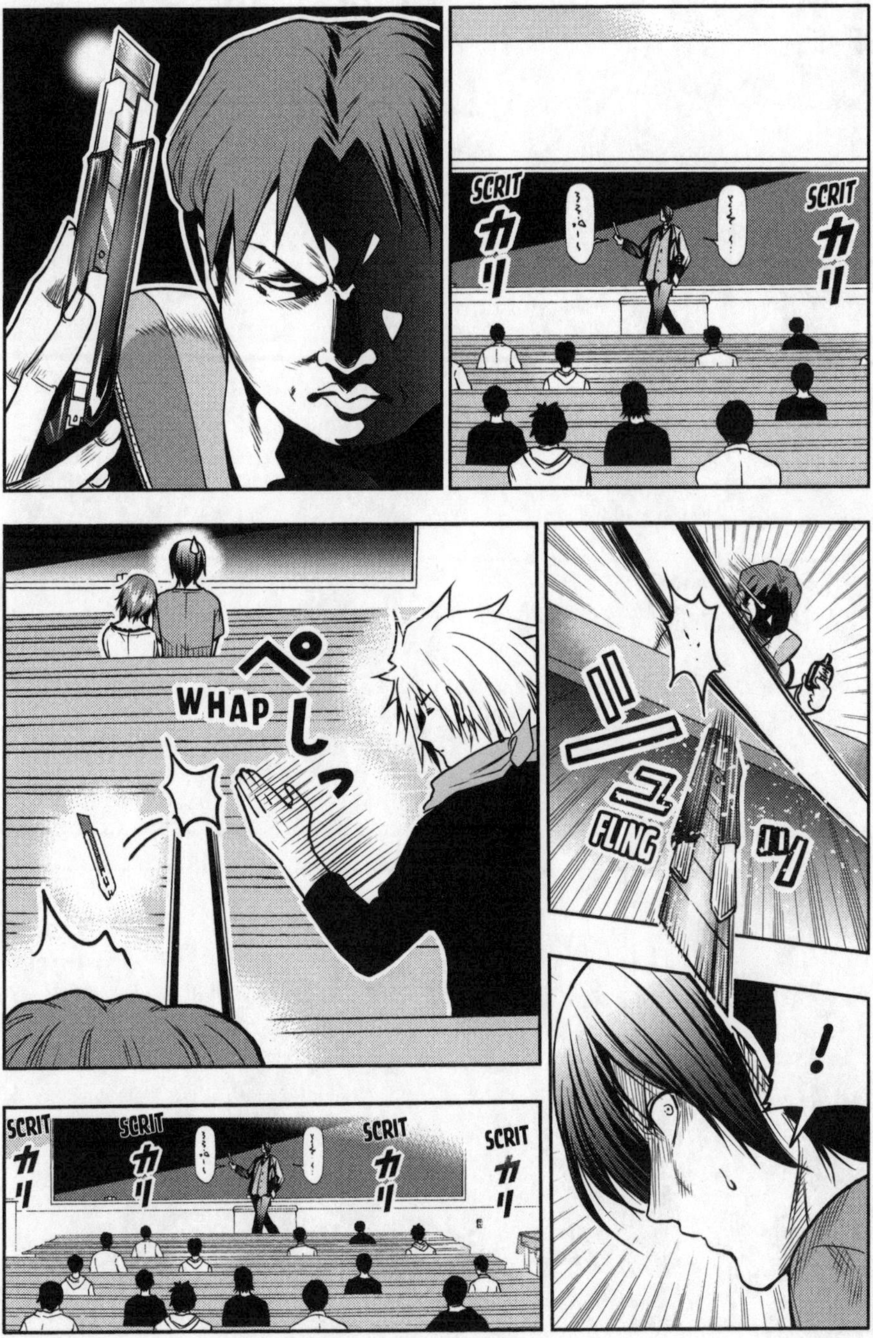
SCRIT カリ
SCRIT カリ
FLING
!
WHAP ぺしっ
SCRIT カリ
SCRIT カリ
SCRIT カリ
SCRIT カリ

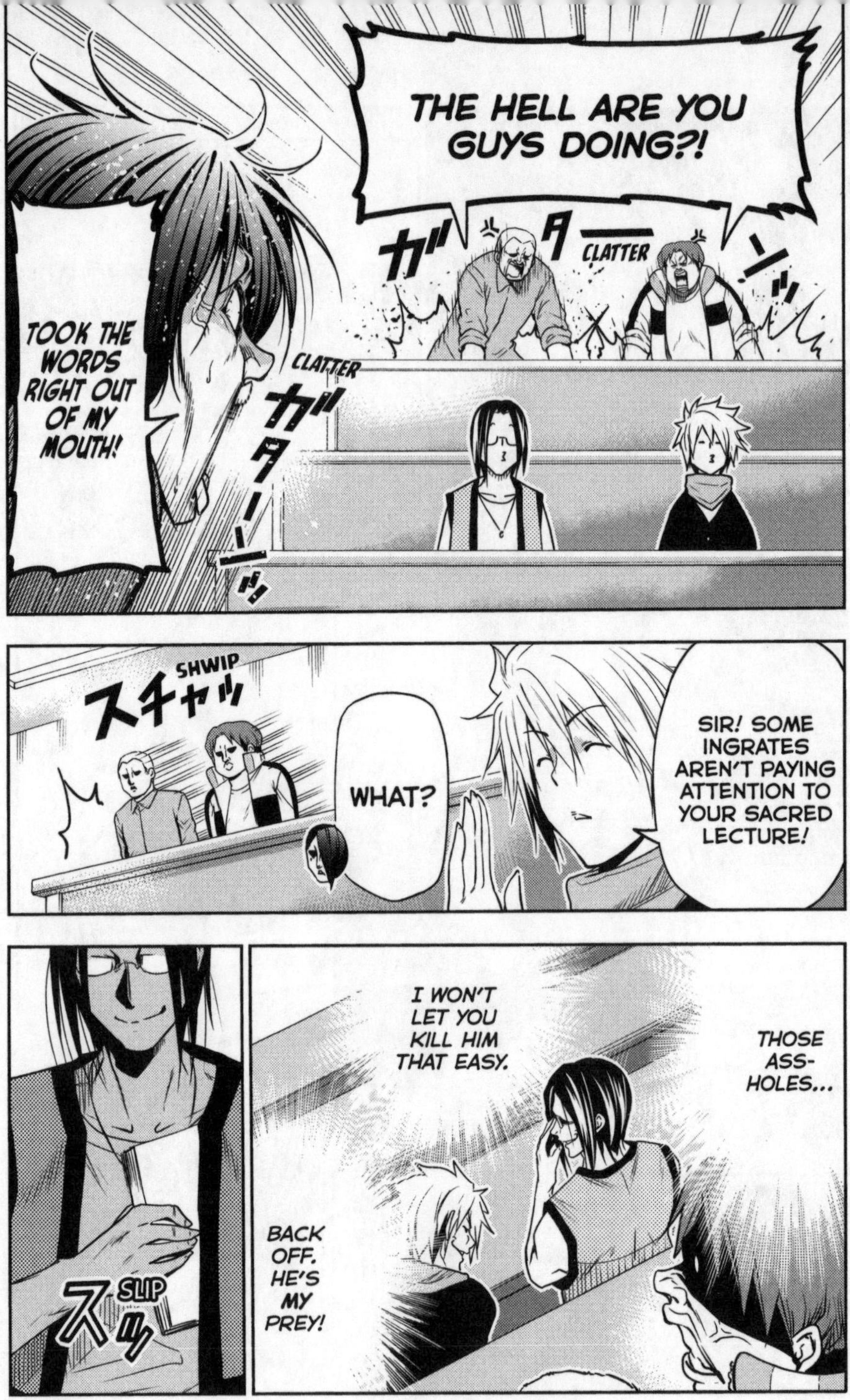
THE HELL ARE YOU GUYS DOING?!
ガタ—ンッ
CLATTER
CLATTER
ガタ—ンッ
TOOK THE WORDS RIGHT OUT OF MY MOUTH!
SIR! SOME INGRATES AREN'T PAYING ATTENTION TO YOUR SACRED LECTURE!
WHAT?
SHWIP
スチャッ
THOSE ASS-HOLES...
I WON'T LET YOU KILL HIM THAT EASY.
BACK OFF. HE'S MY PREY!
SLIP
スッ

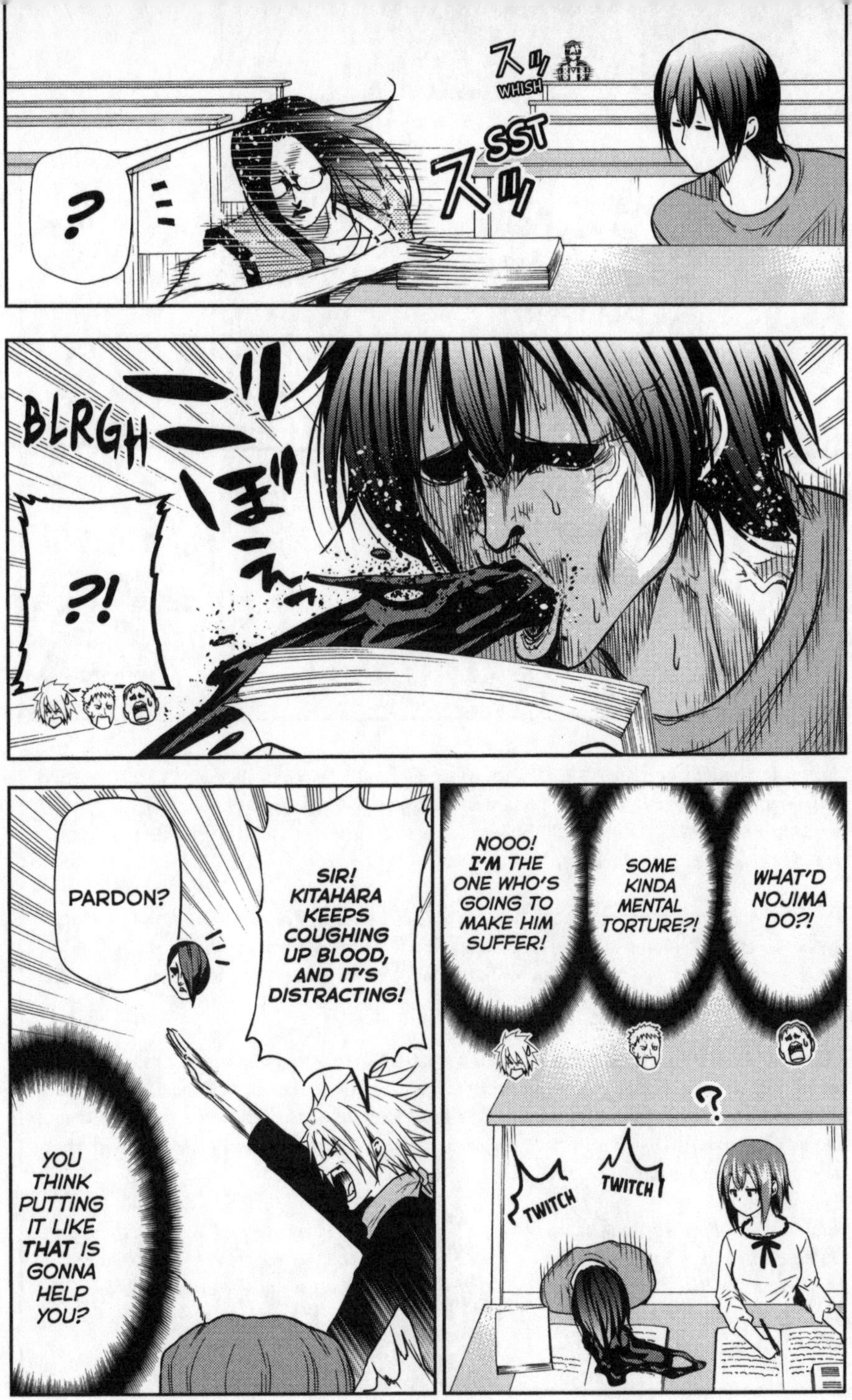
スッ
WHISH
SST
スッ
?
BLRGH
?!
WHAT'D NOJIMA DO?!
SOME KINDA MENTAL TORTURE?!
NOOO! I'M THE ONE WHO'S GOING TO MAKE HIM SUFFER!
?
TWITCH
TWITCH
SIR! KITAHARA KEEPS COUGHING UP BLOOD, AND IT'S DISTRACTING!
PARDON?
YOU THINK PUTTING IT LIKE THAT IS GONNA HELP YOU?

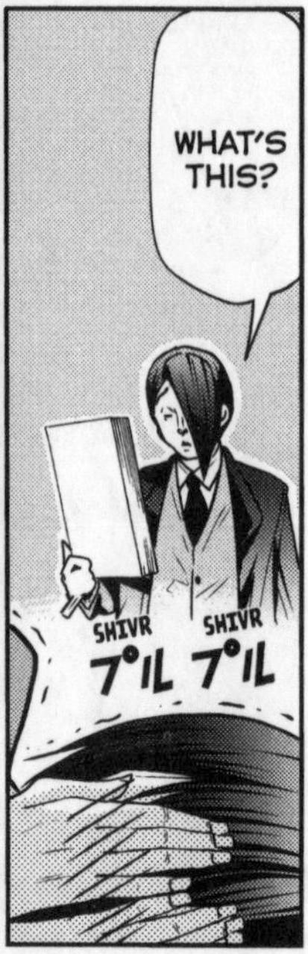
WHAT'S THIS?
SHIVR SHIVR

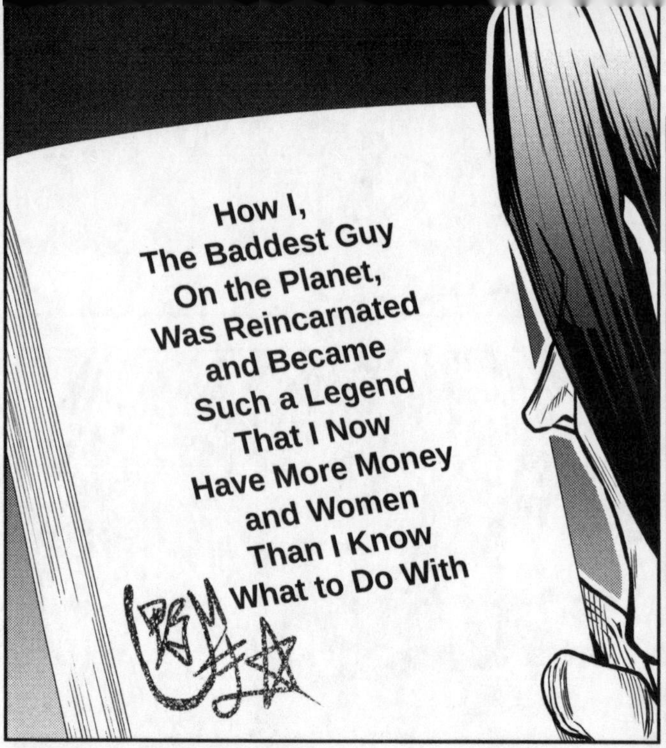
How I, The Baddest Guy On the Planet, Was Reincarnated and Became Such a Legend That I Now Have More Money and Women Than I Know What to Do With

"So, this is a parallel world, huh?" I mumbled under my breath. Before me stood over a hundred beautiful women, each with a look of pure rapture on their faces. Near the front of the crowd, one of them turned to me and said, "Behold. Surely he must be the legendary sage, Lord Lucifer, whose wisdom is said to be rivaled only by his beauty."

True enough, before I was reincarnated, I'd earned the nickname "Fallen Angel" due to my stunning good looks, and had spent most of my days being courted by women from all over the world. At this rate, I feared the same fate might befall me in this world. It was almost like I was destined to conquer the world with my chiseled visage.

Eventually, using my experience from my previous life and the powers I acquired in this world, I put out a CD of the song "Elena Phantom," a ballad I dedicated to my former love, Elena. Unsurprisingly, it was an international hit, and the name of Star Lucifer spread like wildfire across the parallel world. And yet, by merely existing, I attracted more money, women, and power than I could ever want. It seemed there was no defying fate, after all.

Needless to say, there was no way a would-be party of heroes would leave a hot commodity like me alone. With so many offers from so many parties, the only thing that kept me from taking to a life of adventure were the beauties waiting for me in Nojima City. But I knew I had to. The fate of this world rested on me. So, with a heavy heart, I visited the local adventurer's guild...

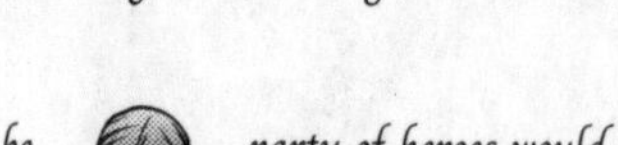

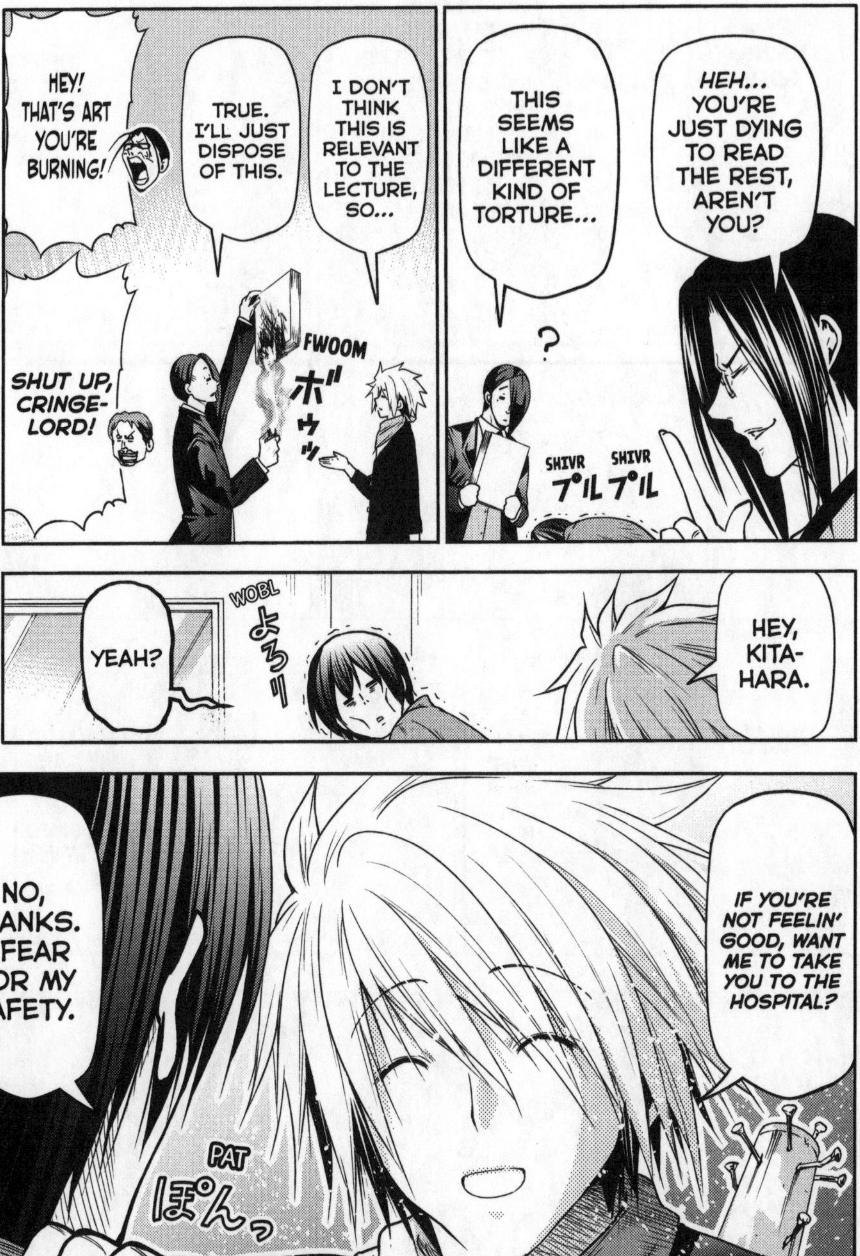
HEH... YOU'RE JUST DYING TO READ THE REST, AREN'T YOU?
THIS SEEMS LIKE A DIFFERENT KIND OF TORTURE...
?
SHIVR SHIVR
プルプル
I DON'T THINK THIS IS RELEVANT TO THE LECTURE, SO...
TRUE. I'LL JUST DISPOSE OF THIS.
HEY! THAT'S ART YOU'RE BURNING!
FWOOM
ボウッ
SHUT UP, CRINGE-LORD!
HEY, KITA-HARA.
WOBL
よろり
YEAH?
IF YOU'RE NOT FEELIN' GOOD, WANT ME TO TAKE YOU TO THE HOSPITAL?
NO, THANKS. I FEAR FOR MY SAFETY.
PAT
ぽんっ

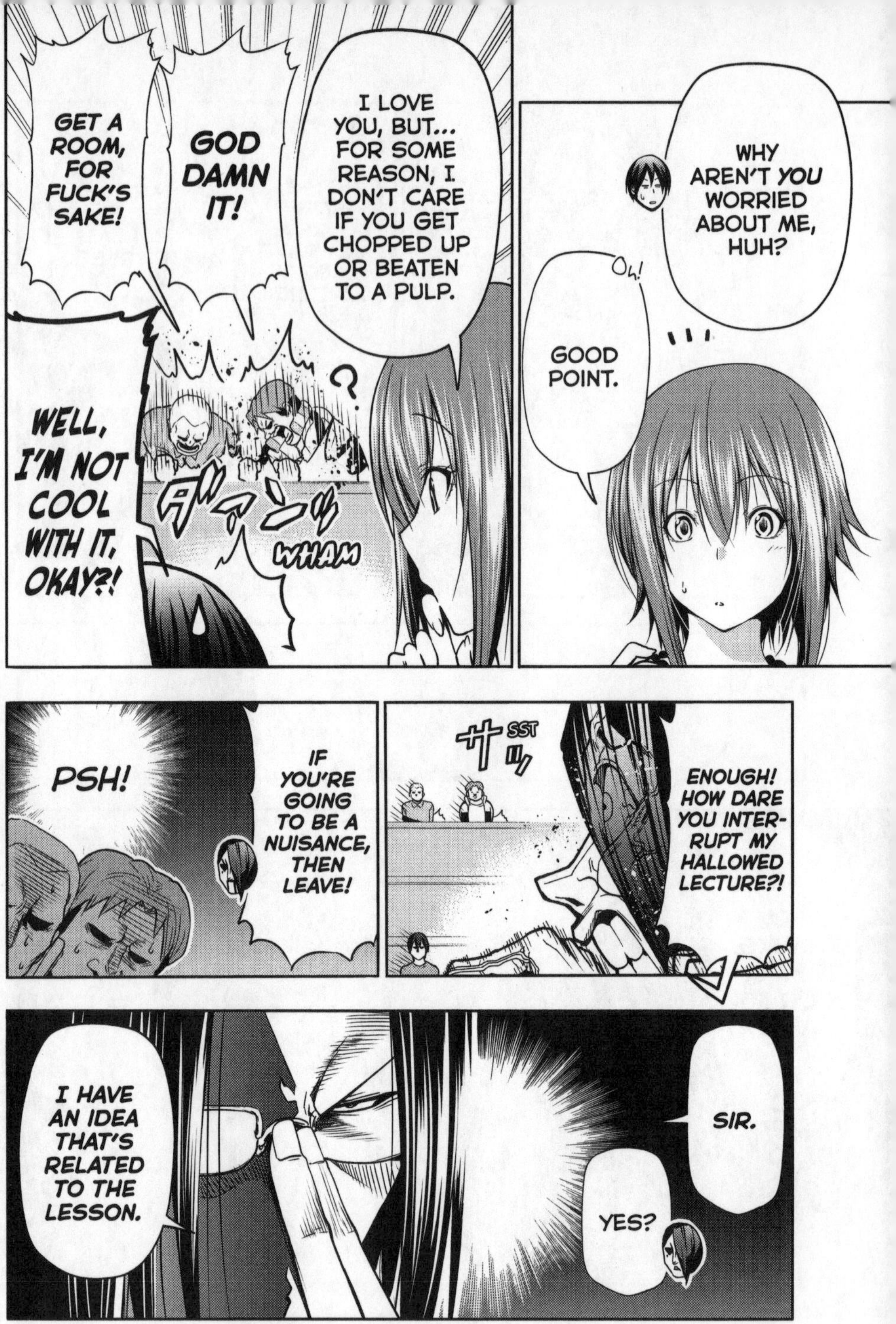
WHY AREN'T YOU WORRIED ABOUT ME, HUH?
Oh!
GOOD POINT.
I LOVE YOU, BUT... FOR SOME REASON, I DON'T CARE IF YOU GET CHOPPED UP OR BEATEN TO A PULP.
GOD DAMN IT!
GET A ROOM, FOR FUCK'S SAKE!
WHAM
WELL, I'M NOT COOL WITH IT, OKAY?!
SST
ENOUGH! HOW DARE YOU INTER-RUPT MY HALLOWED LECTURE?!
IF YOU'RE GOING TO BE A NUISANCE, THEN LEAVE!
PSH!
SIR.
YES?
I HAVE AN IDEA THAT'S RELATED TO THE LESSON.

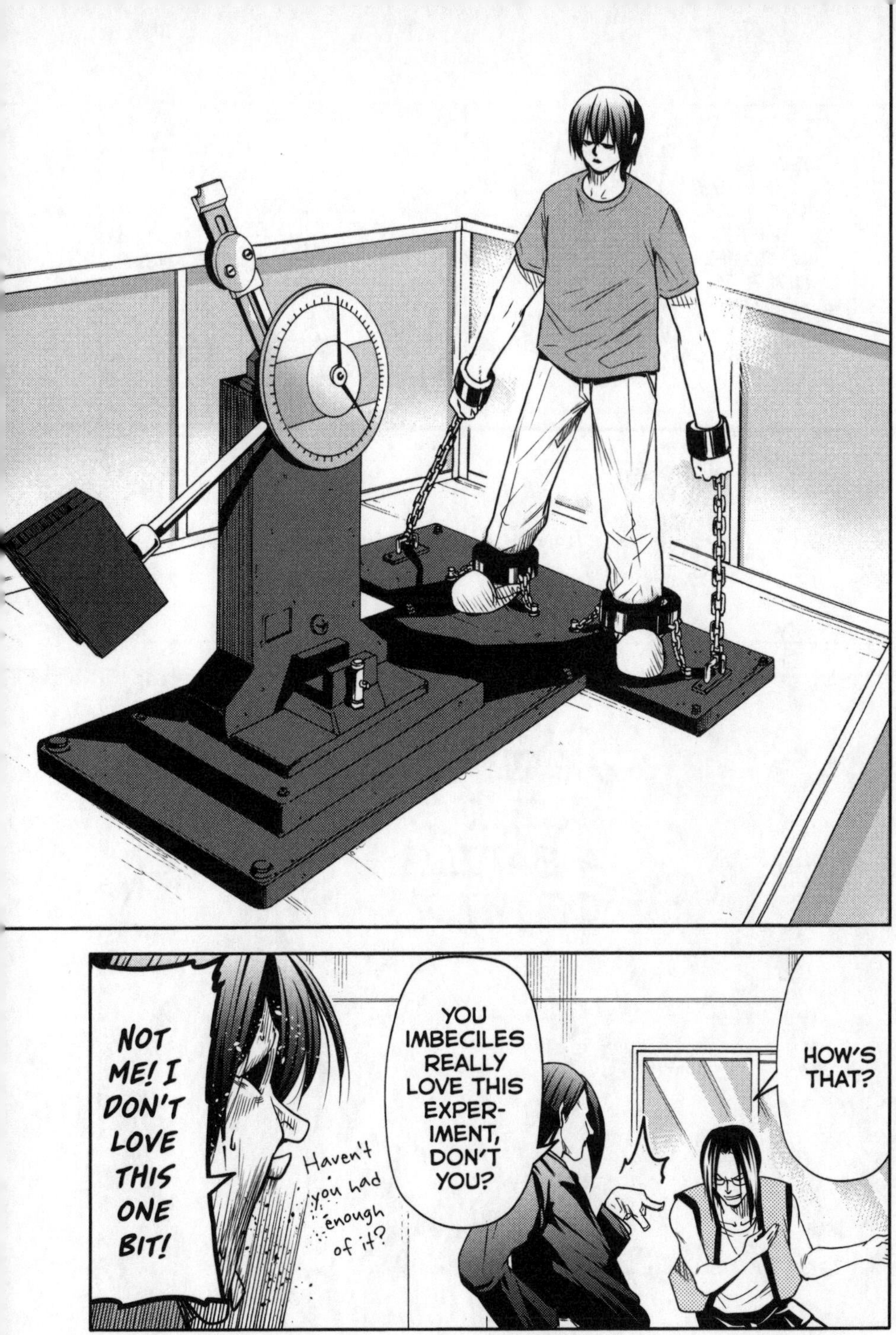
HOW'S THAT?
YOU IMBECILES REALLY LOVE THIS EXPERIMENT, DON'T YOU?
Haven't you had enough of it?
NOT ME! I DON'T LOVE THIS ONE BIT!

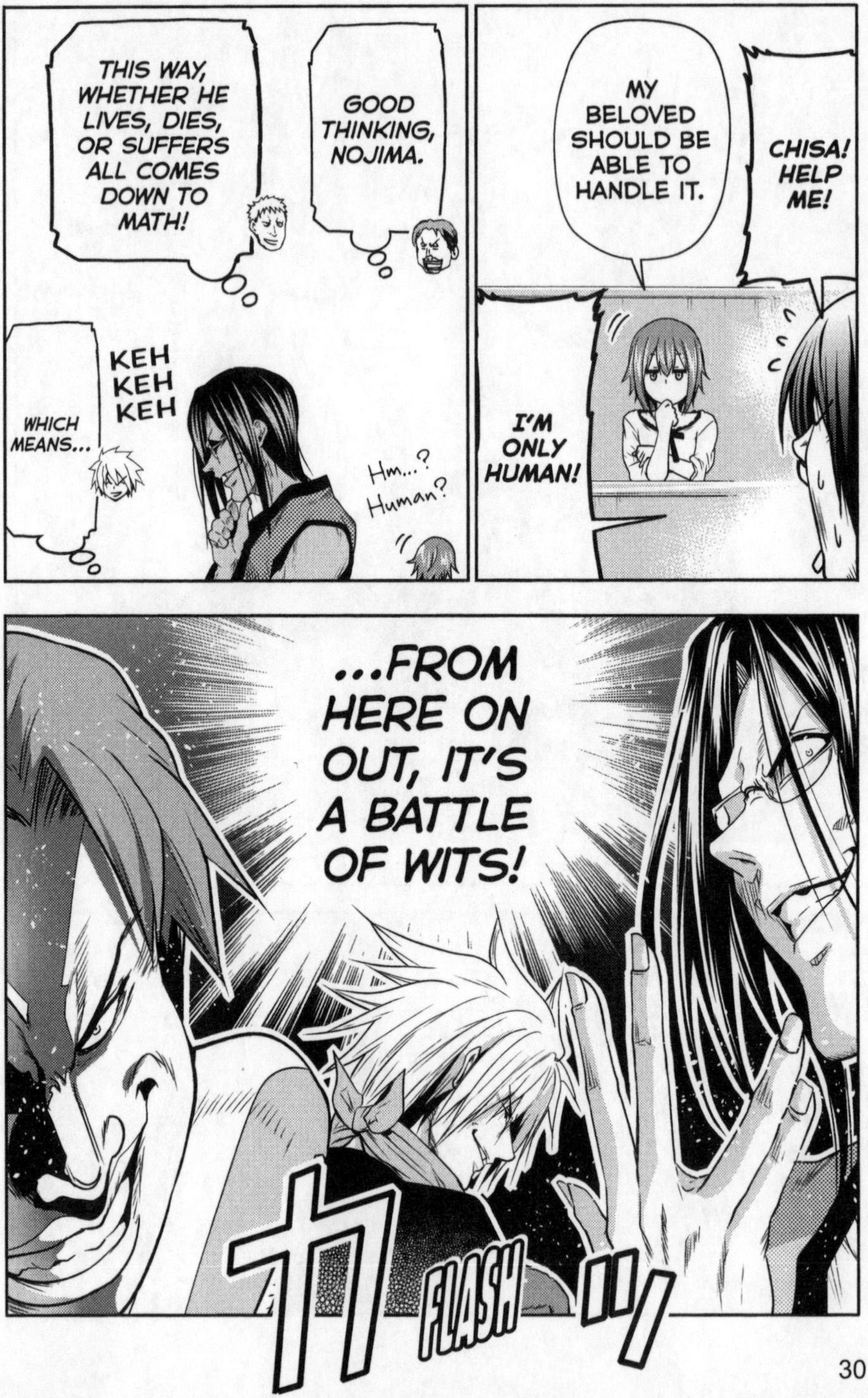
CHISA! HELP ME!
MY BELOVED SHOULD BE ABLE TO HANDLE IT.
I'M ONLY HUMAN!
GOOD THINKING, NOJIMA.
THIS WAY, WHETHER HE LIVES, DIES, OR SUFFERS ALL COMES DOWN TO MATH!
KEH KEH KEH
Hm...? Human?
WHICH MEANS...
...FROM HERE ON OUT, IT'S A BATTLE OF WITS!
FLASH

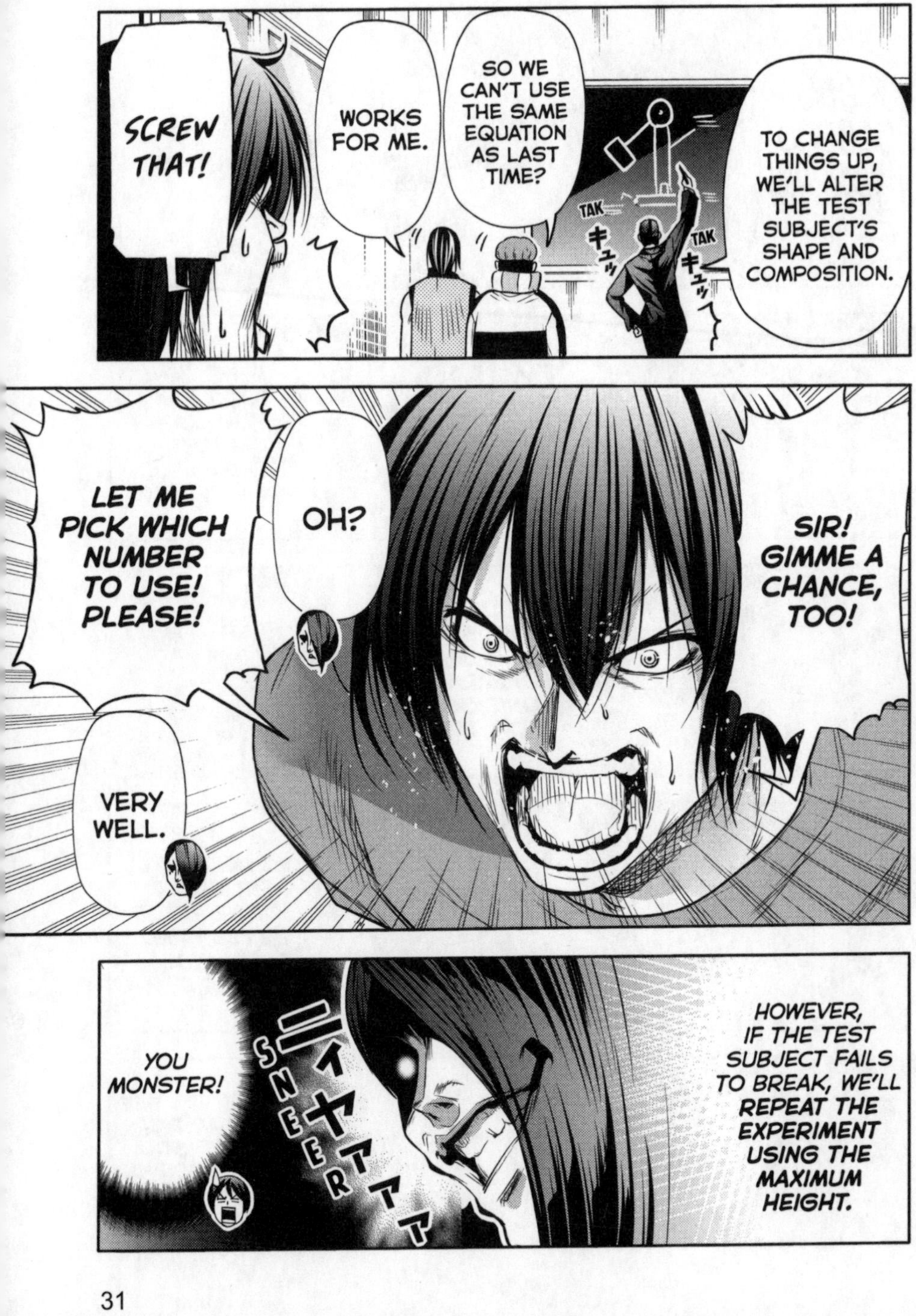
TO CHANGE THINGS UP, WE'LL ALTER THE TEST SUBJECT'S SHAPE AND COMPOSITION.
TAK
TAK
SO WE CAN'T USE THE SAME EQUATION AS LAST TIME?
WORKS FOR ME.
SCREW THAT!
SIR! GIMME A CHANCE, TOO!
OH?
LET ME PICK WHICH NUMBER TO USE! PLEASE!
VERY WELL.
HOWEVER, IF THE TEST SUBJECT FAILS TO BREAK, WE'LL REPEAT THE EXPERIMENT USING THE MAXIMUM HEIGHT.
SNEER
YOU MONSTER!

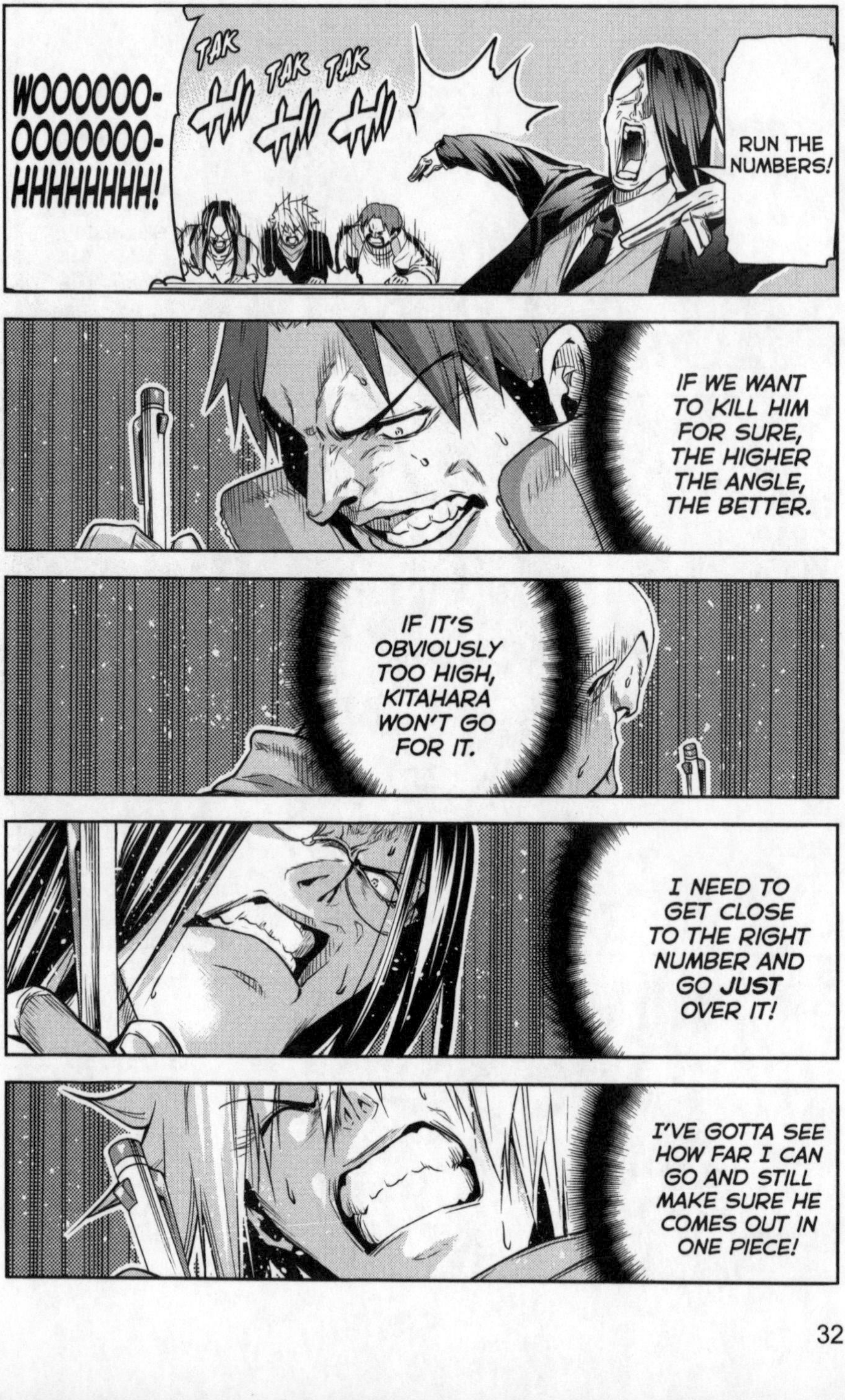
RUN THE NUMBERS!
TAK
TAK
TAK
WOOOOOO-OOOOOOO-HHHHHHHH!
IF WE WANT TO KILL HIM FOR SURE, THE HIGHER THE ANGLE, THE BETTER.
IF IT'S OBVIOUSLY TOO HIGH, KITAHARA WON'T GO FOR IT.
I NEED TO GET CLOSE TO THE RIGHT NUMBER AND GO JUST OVER IT!
I'VE GOTTA SEE HOW FAR I CAN GO AND STILL MAKE SURE HE COMES OUT IN ONE PIECE!

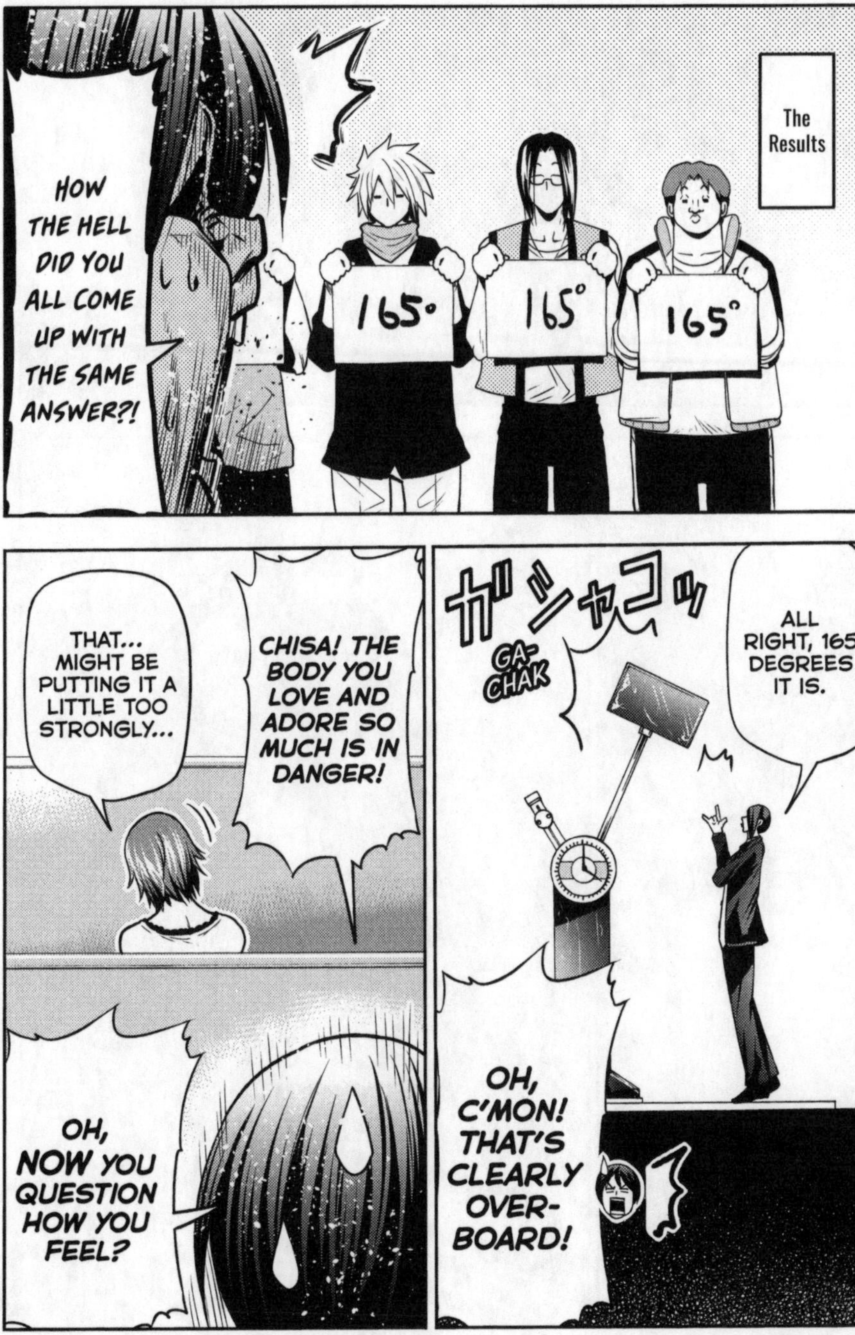
The Results
HOW THE HELL DID YOU ALL COME UP WITH THE SAME ANSWER?!
165°
165°
165°
ALL RIGHT, 165 DEGREES IT IS.
ガシャコッ
GA-CHAK
OH, C'MON! THAT'S CLEARLY OVER-BOARD!
CHISA! THE BODY YOU LOVE AND ADORE SO MUCH IS IN DANGER!
THAT... MIGHT BE PUTTING IT A LITTLE TOO STRONGLY...
OH, NOW YOU QUESTION HOW YOU FEEL?

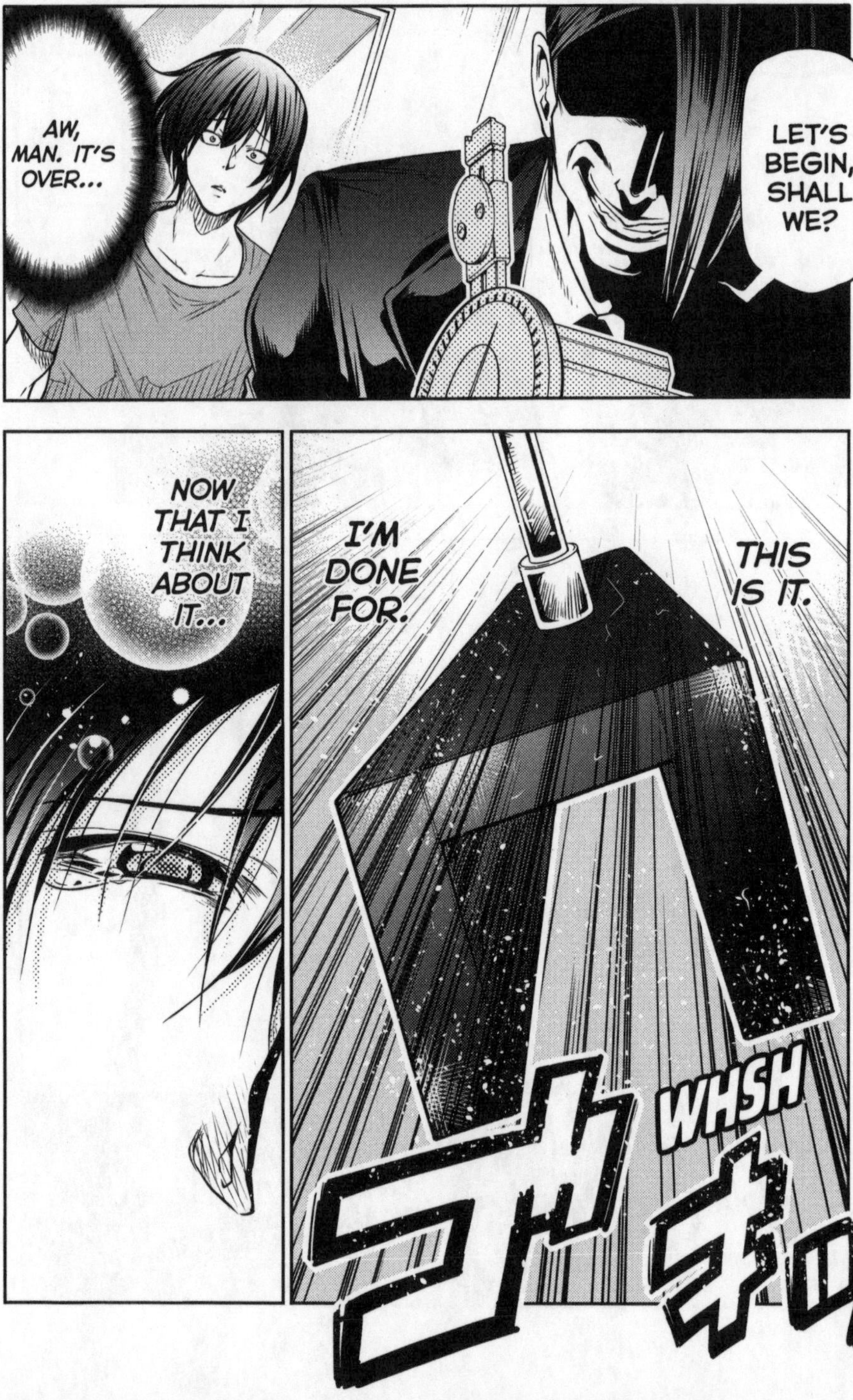
LET'S BEGIN, SHALL WE?
AW, MAN. IT'S OVER...
THIS IS IT.
I'M DONE FOR.
WHSH
NOW THAT I THINK ABOUT IT...

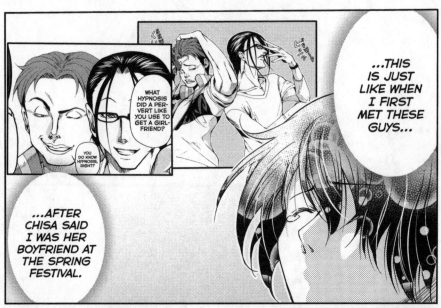

...THIS IS JUST LIKE WHEN I FIRST MET THESE GUYS...
...AFTER CHISA SAID I WAS HER BOYFRIEND AT THE SPRING FESTIVAL.
WHAT HYPNOSIS DID A PERVERT LIKE YOU USE TO GET A GIRLFRIEND?
YOU DO KNOW HYPNOSIS, RIGHT?
FLA ASH
GUYS, YOU GOTTA SAVE ME!
WUH?
LISTEN, I'VE FIGURED IT OUT!

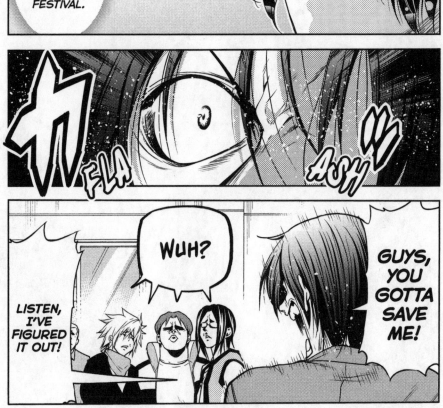

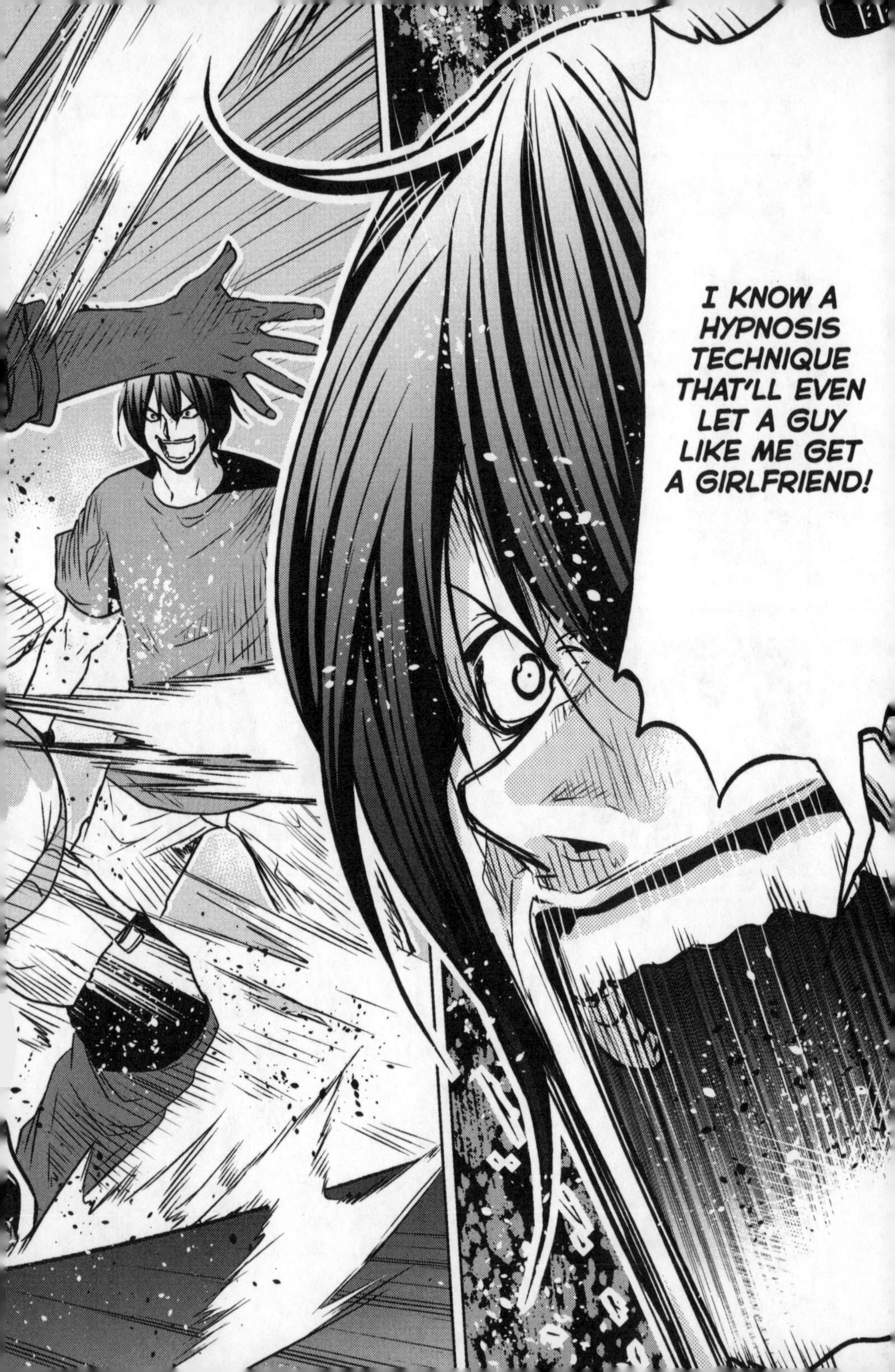
I KNOW A HYPNOSIS TECHNIQUE THAT'LL EVEN LET A GUY LIKE ME GET A GIRLFRIEND!

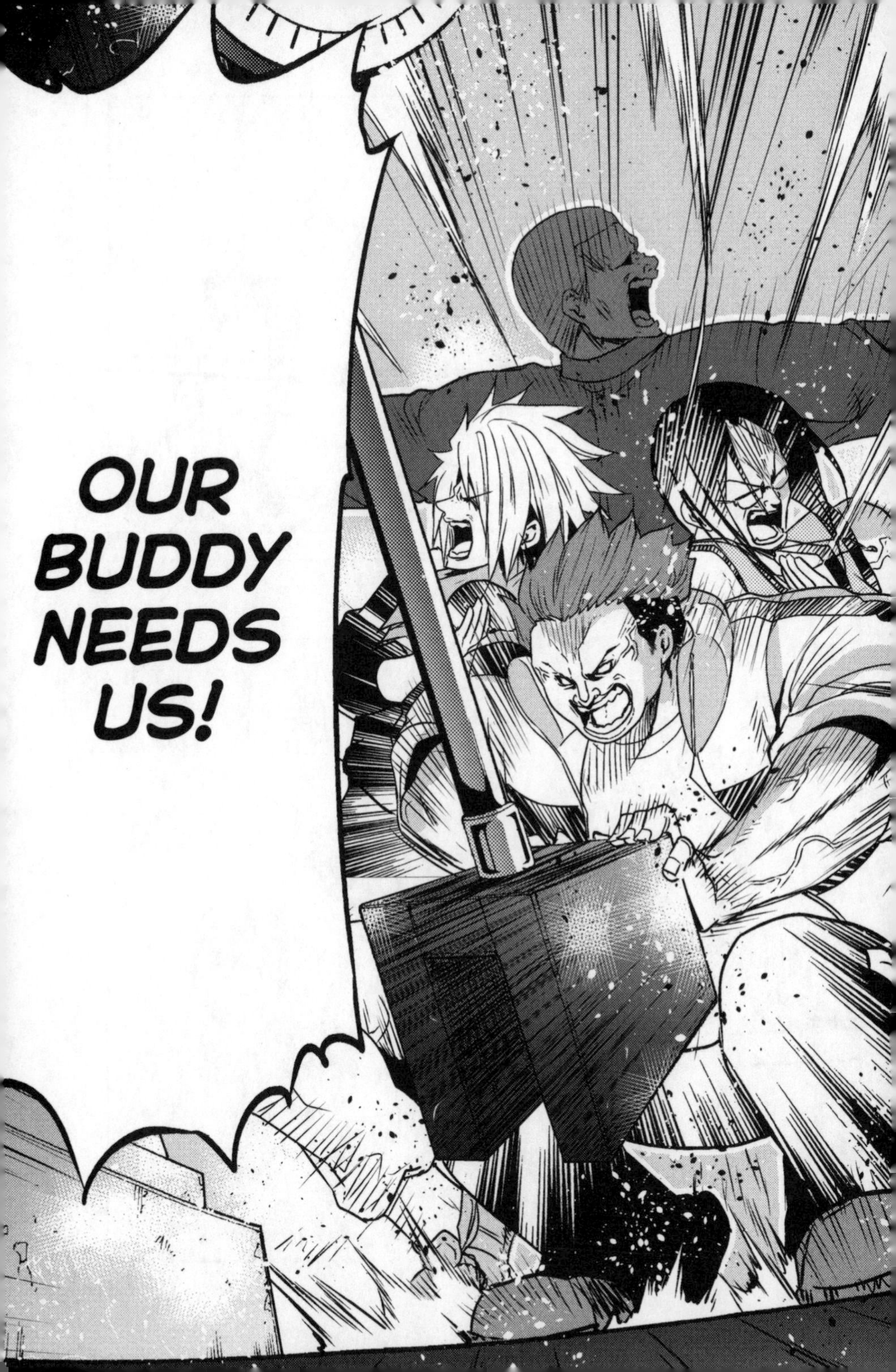
OUR BUDDY NEEDS US!

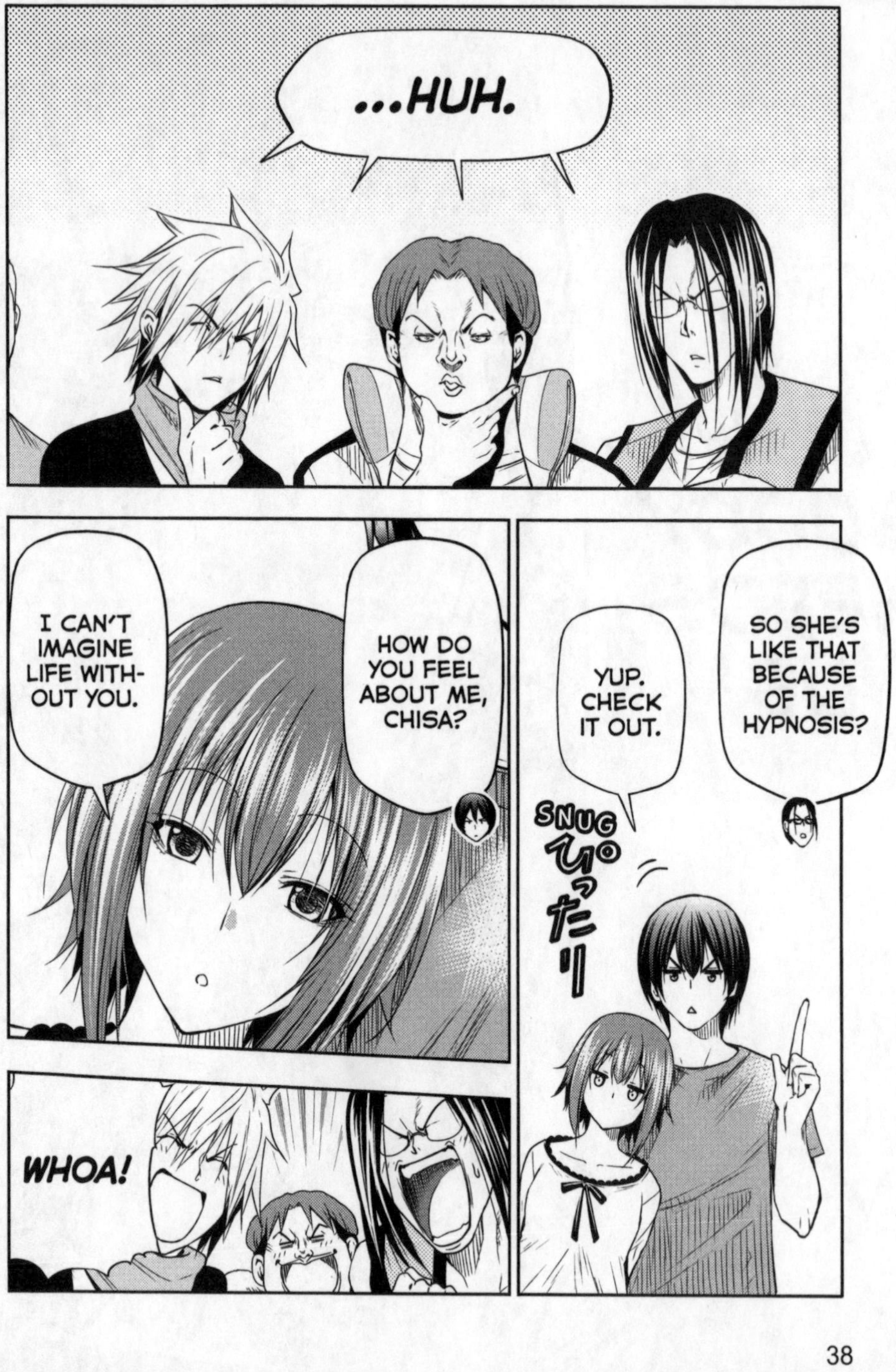
...HUH.
SO SHE'S LIKE THAT BECAUSE OF THE HYPNOSIS?
YUP. CHECK IT OUT.
SNUG
ぴったり
HOW DO YOU FEEL ABOUT ME, CHISA?
I CAN'T IMAGINE LIFE WITH-OUT YOU.
WHOA!

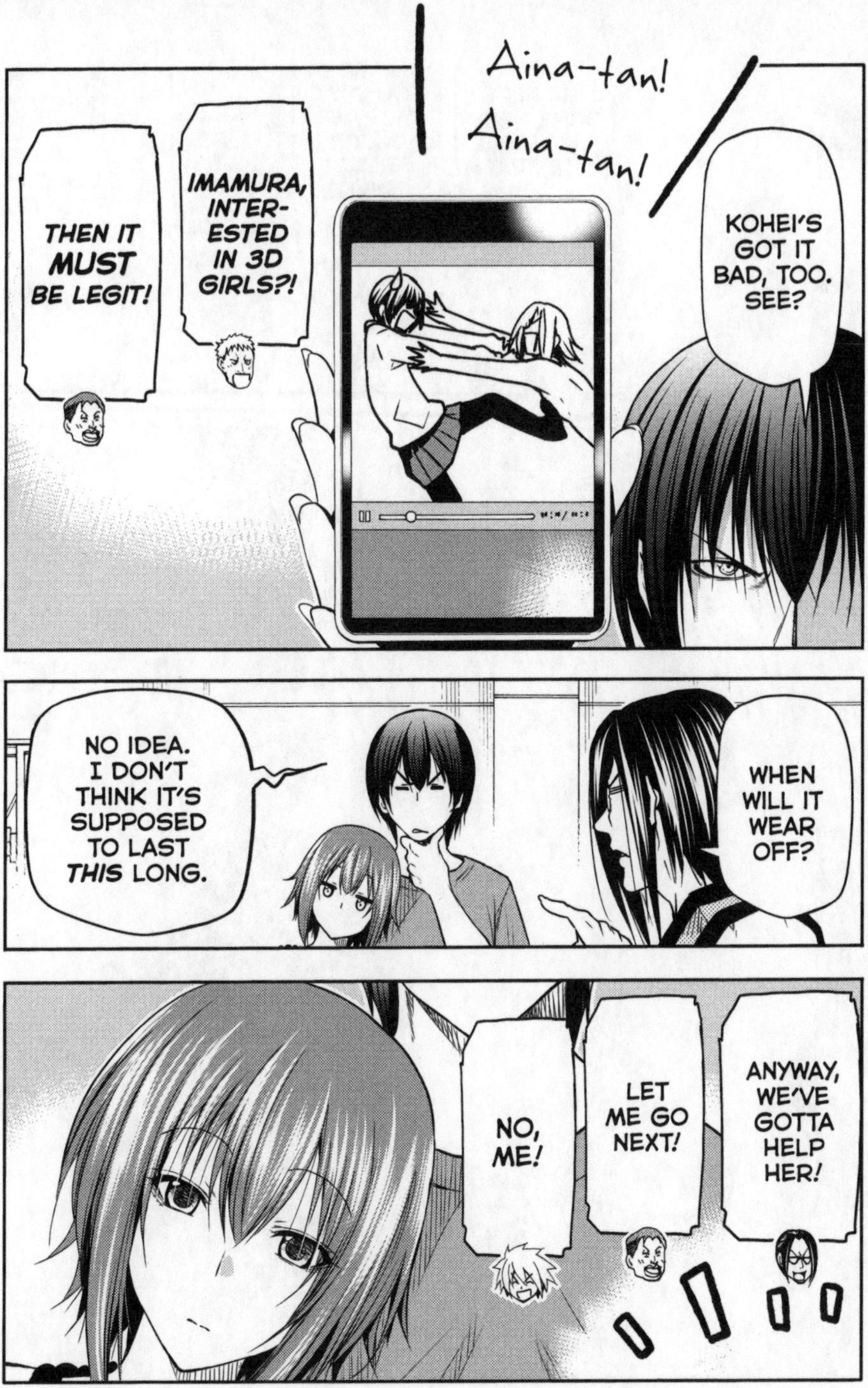
Aina-tan!
Aina-tan!
KOHEI'S GOT IT BAD, TOO. SEE?
IMAMURA, INTER-ESTED IN 3D GIRLS?!
THEN IT MUST BE LEGIT!
WHEN WILL IT WEAR OFF?
NO IDEA. I DON'T THINK IT'S SUPPOSED TO LAST THIS LONG.
ANYWAY, WE'VE GOTTA HELP HER!
LET ME GO NEXT!
NO, ME!

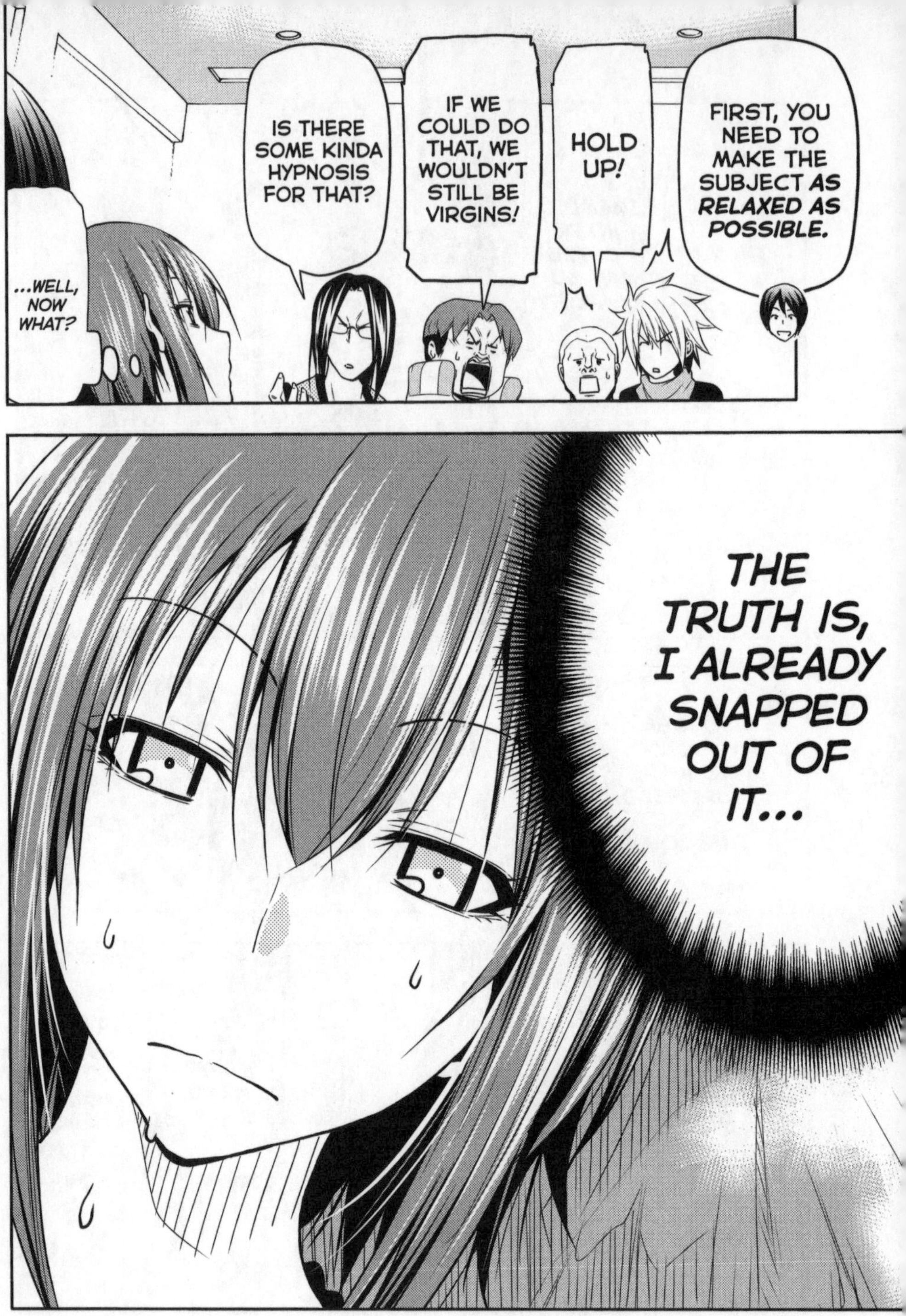
FIRST, YOU NEED TO MAKE THE SUBJECT AS RELAXED AS POSSIBLE.
HOLD UP!
IF WE COULD DO THAT, WE WOULDN'T STILL BE VIRGINS!
IS THERE SOME KINDA HYPNOSIS FOR THAT?
...WELL, NOW WHAT?
THE TRUTH IS, I ALREADY SNAPPED OUT OF IT...

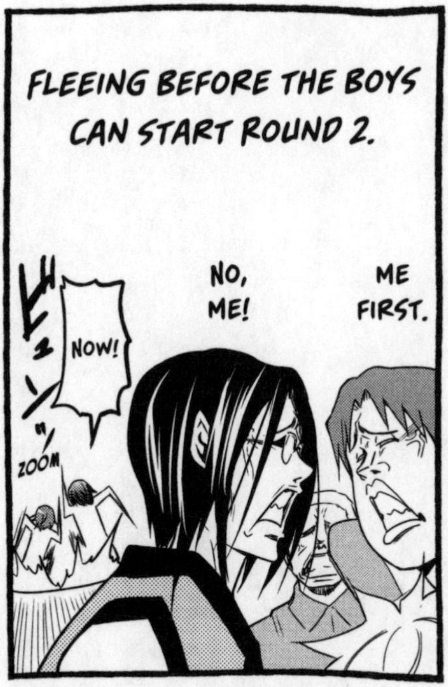
FLEEING BEFORE THE BOYS CAN START ROUND 2.
ME FIRST.
NO, ME!
NOW!
ZOOM

Grand Blue
Dreaming

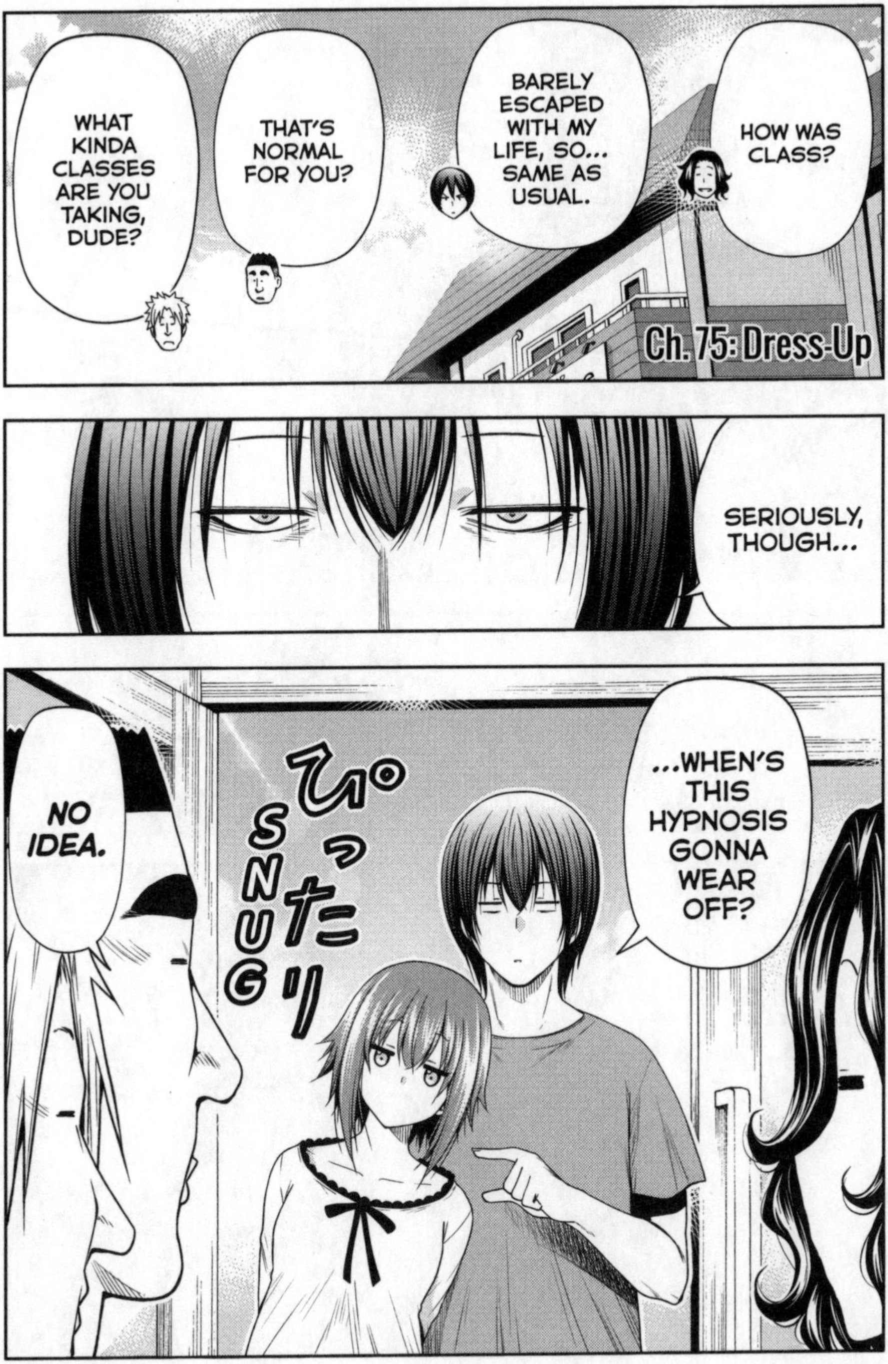
Ch. 75: Dress-Up
HOW WAS CLASS?
BARELY ESCAPED WITH MY LIFE, SO... SAME AS USUAL.
THAT'S NORMAL FOR YOU?
WHAT KINDA CLASSES ARE YOU TAKING, DUDE?
SERIOUSLY, THOUGH...
...WHEN'S THIS HYPNOSIS GONNA WEAR OFF?
ぴったり
SNUG
NO IDEA.

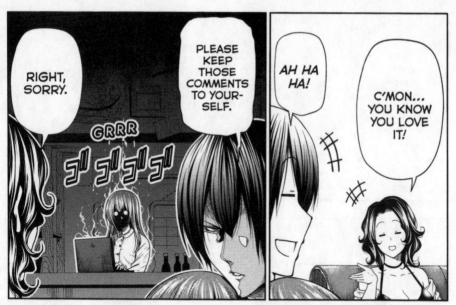

C'MON... YOU KNOW YOU LOVE IT!
AH HA HA!
PLEASE KEEP THOSE COMMENTS TO YOURSELF.
RIGHT, SORRY.
GRRR
ゴゴゴゴ
What if she stays like this forever?
Ha ha! Do you want me to die?
WHY...?
WHY DIDN'T I TELL HIM I SNAPPED OUT OF IT EARLIER?!
I'M ONLY HUMAN!
HM...? HUMAN?
?
NOW THAT I THINK ABOUT IT, WASN'T IT THE OCEAN THAT I LOVED THE MOST?

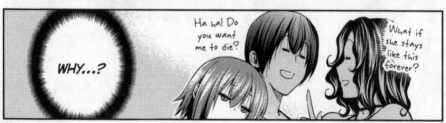

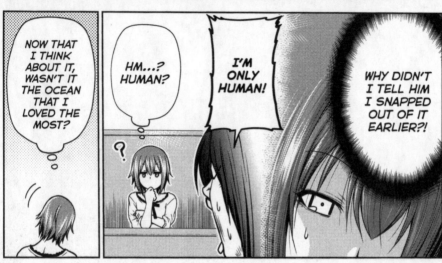

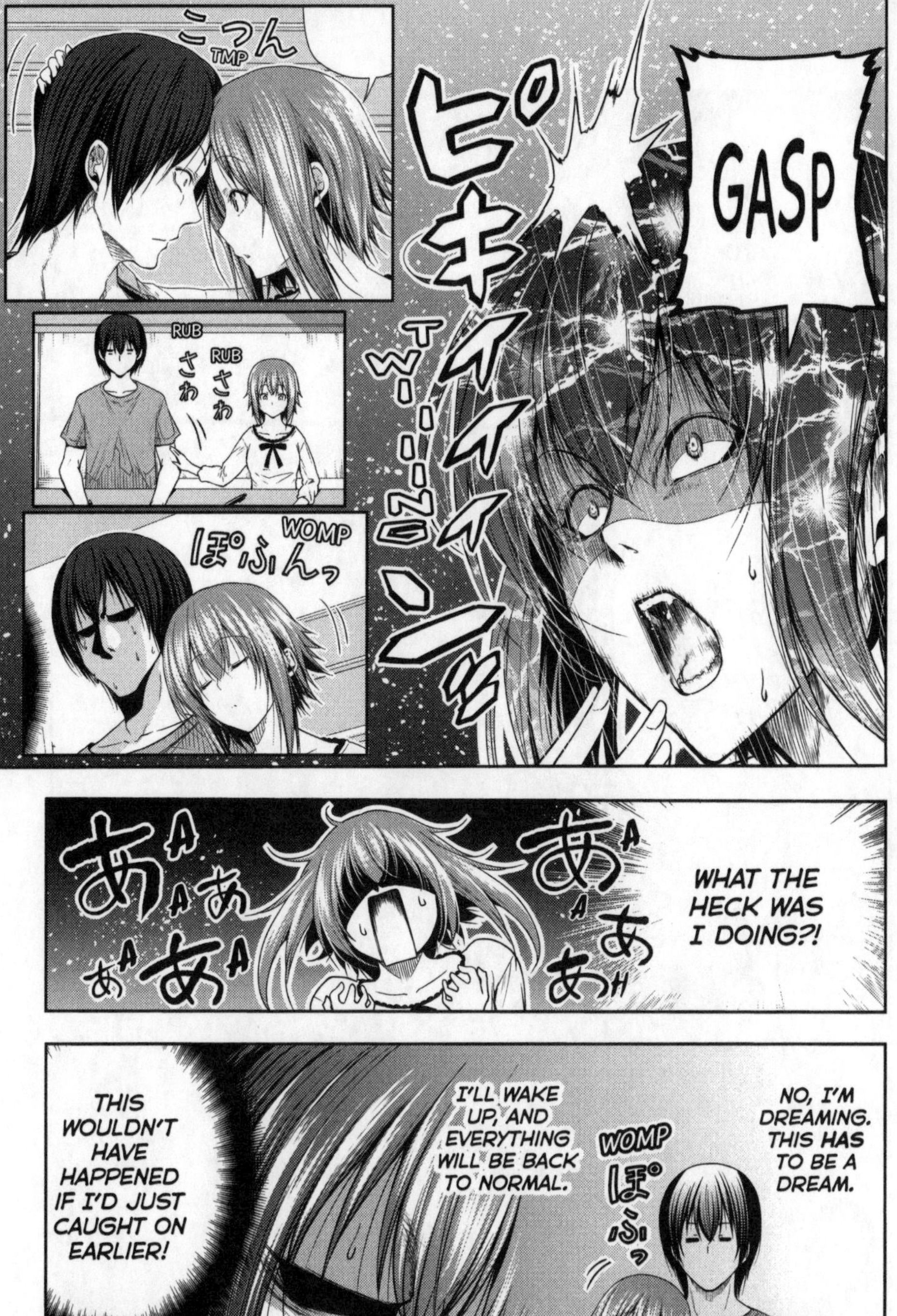
GASP
ピキイイイイン
WIIIING
こつん
TMP
RUB
RUB
さわ さわ
WOMP
ぽふんっ
WHAT THE HECK WAS I DOING?!
A A A A A A A H
ああああああああ
NO, I'M DREAMING. THIS HAS TO BE A DREAM.
WOMP
ぽふっ
I'LL WAKE UP, AND EVERYTHING WILL BE BACK TO NORMAL.
THIS WOULDN'T HAVE HAPPENED IF I'D JUST CAUGHT ON EARLIER!

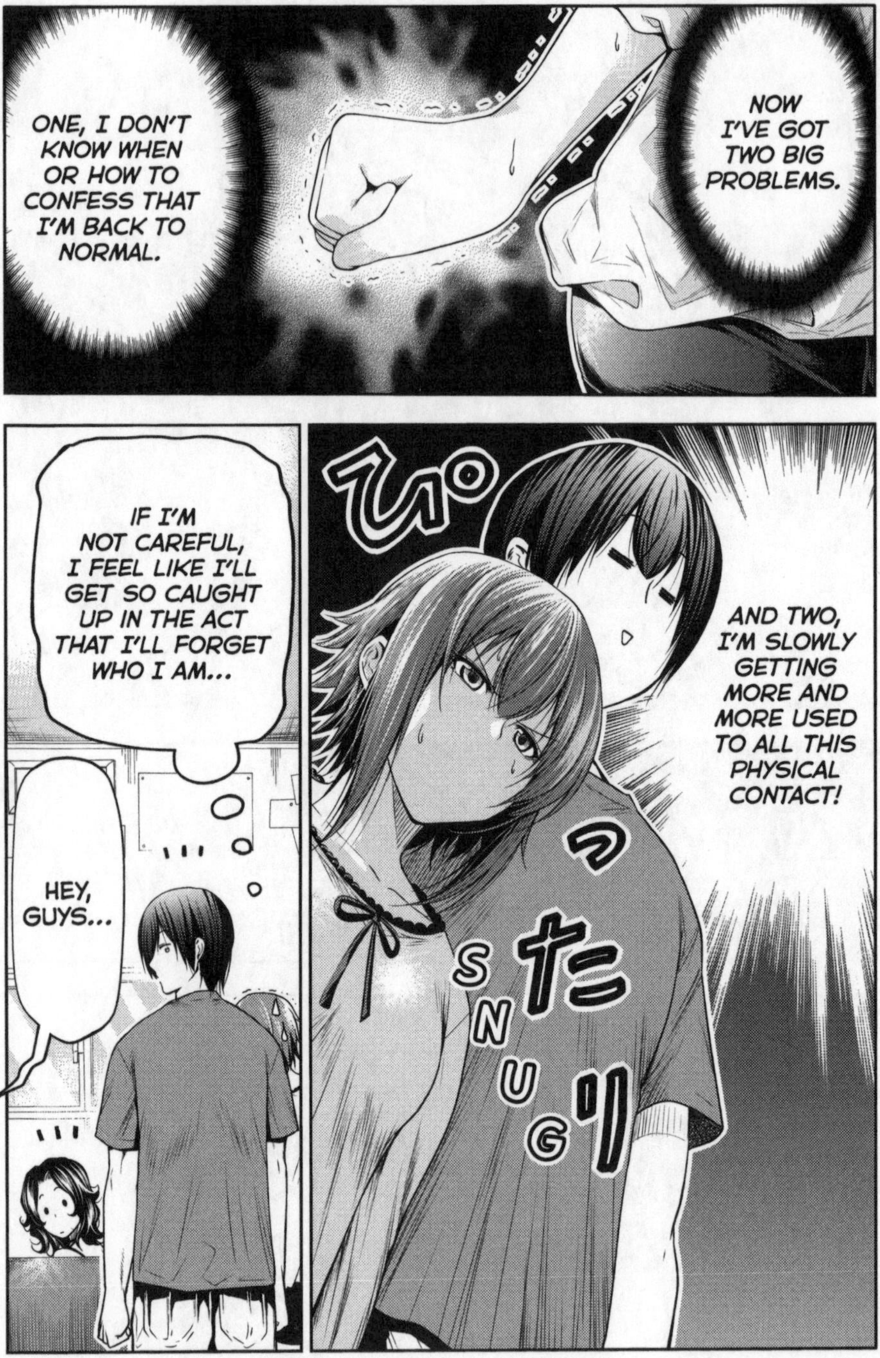
NOW I'VE GOT TWO BIG PROBLEMS.
ONE, I DON'T KNOW WHEN OR HOW TO CONFESS THAT I'M BACK TO NORMAL.
AND TWO, I'M SLOWLY GETTING MORE AND MORE USED TO ALL THIS PHYSICAL CONTACT!
ぴつたり
SNUG
IF I'M NOT CAREFUL, I FEEL LIKE I'LL GET SO CAUGHT UP IN THE ACT THAT I'LL FORGET WHO I AM...
HEY, GUYS...

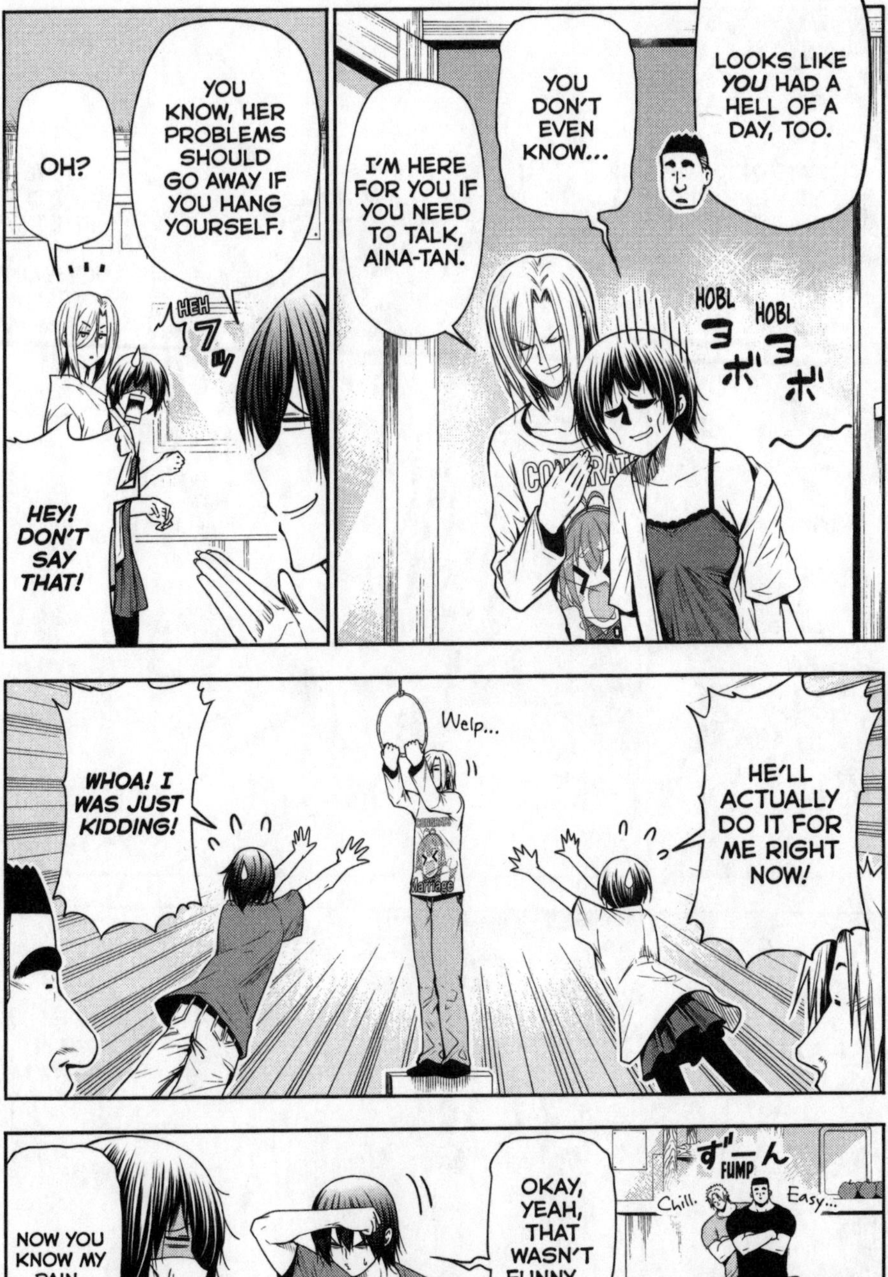
LOOKS LIKE YOU HAD A HELL OF A DAY, TOO.
YOU DON'T EVEN KNOW...
HOBL ヨボ HOBL ヨボ
I'M HERE FOR YOU IF YOU NEED TO TALK, AINA-TAN.
YOU KNOW, HER PROBLEMS SHOULD GO AWAY IF YOU HANG YOURSELF.
HEH フッ
OH?
HEY! DON'T SAY THAT!
HE'LL ACTUALLY DO IT FOR ME RIGHT NOW!
Welp...
WHOA! I WAS JUST KIDDING!
ずーん FUMP
Easy...
Chill.
OKAY, YEAH, THAT WASN'T FUNNY...
NOW YOU KNOW MY PAIN.

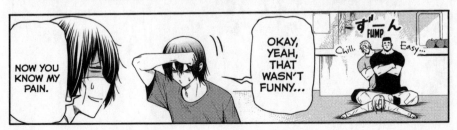

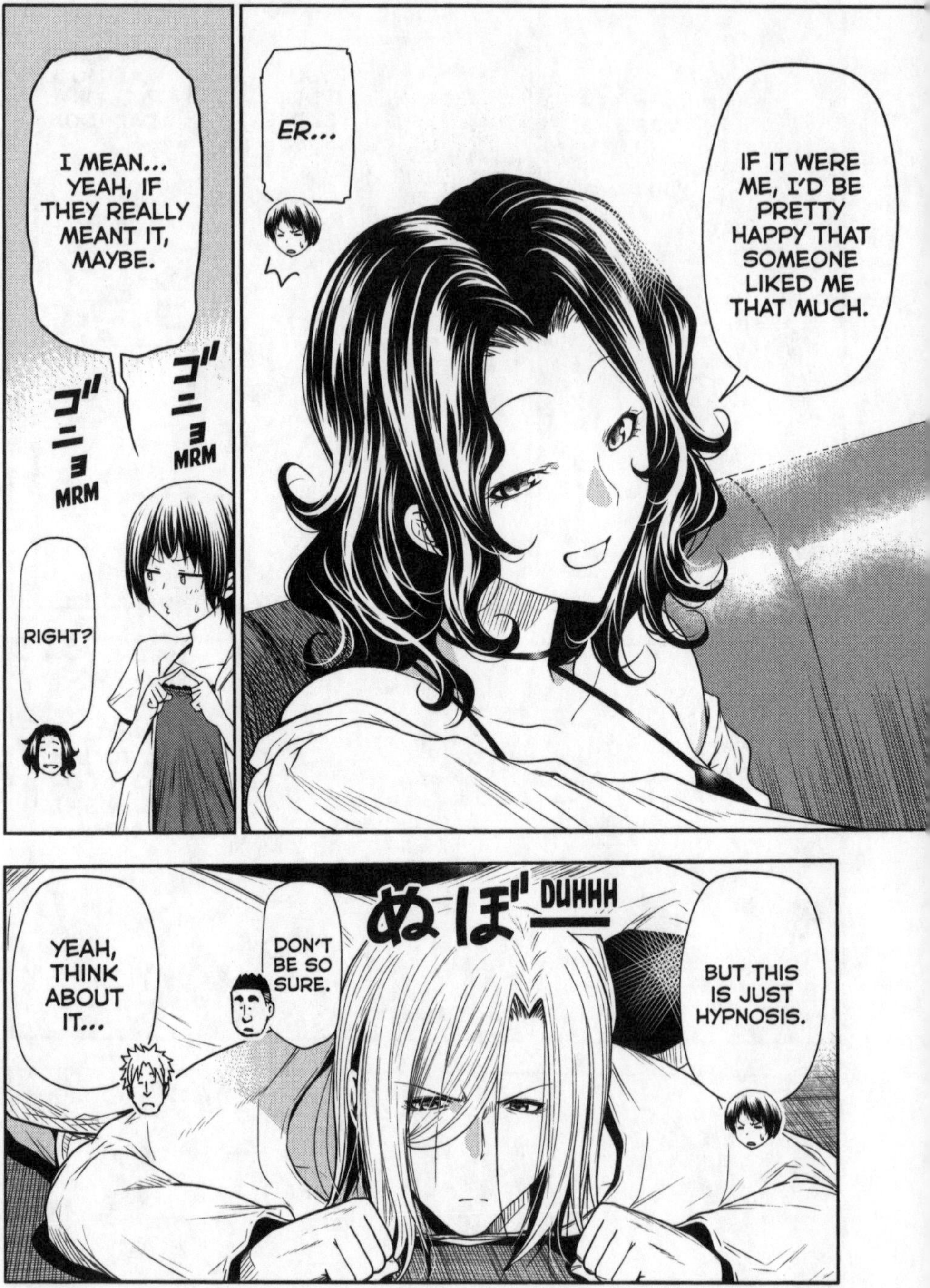
IF IT WERE ME, I'D BE PRETTY HAPPY THAT SOMEONE LIKED ME THAT MUCH.
ER...
I MEAN... YEAH, IF THEY REALLY MEANT IT, MAYBE.
ゴニョ MRM
ゴニョ MRM
RIGHT?
BUT THIS IS JUST HYPNOSIS.
ぬぼー DUHHH
DON'T BE SO SURE.
YEAH, THINK ABOUT IT...

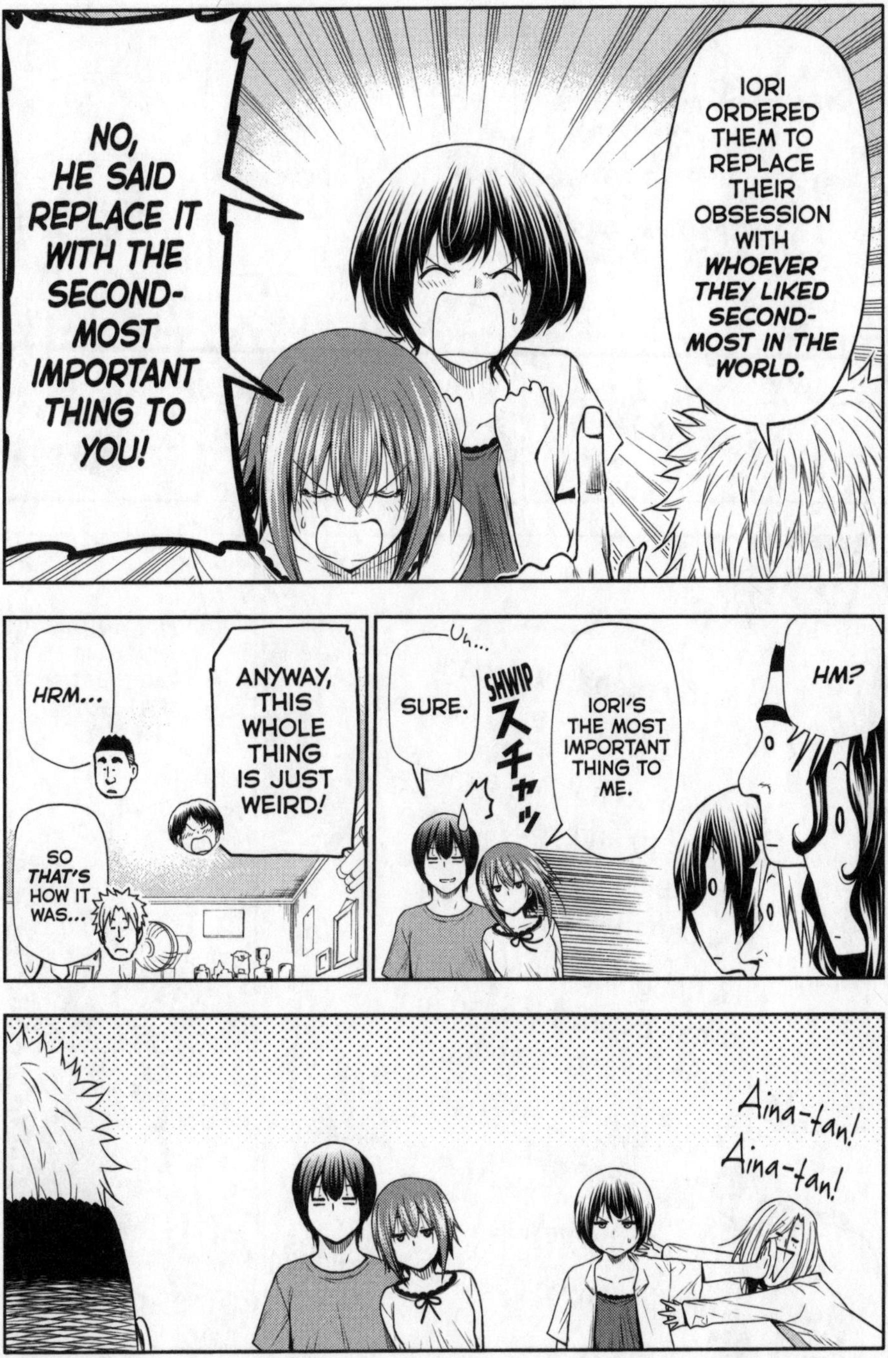
IORI ORDERED THEM TO REPLACE THEIR OBSESSION WITH WHOEVER THEY LIKED SECOND-MOST IN THE WORLD.
NO, HE SAID REPLACE IT WITH THE SECOND-MOST IMPORTANT THING TO YOU!
HM?
IORI'S THE MOST IMPORTANT THING TO ME.
SHWIP スチャッ
SURE.
Uh...
ANYWAY, THIS WHOLE THING IS JUST WEIRD!
HRM...
SO THAT'S HOW IT WAS...
Aina-tan!
Aina-tan!

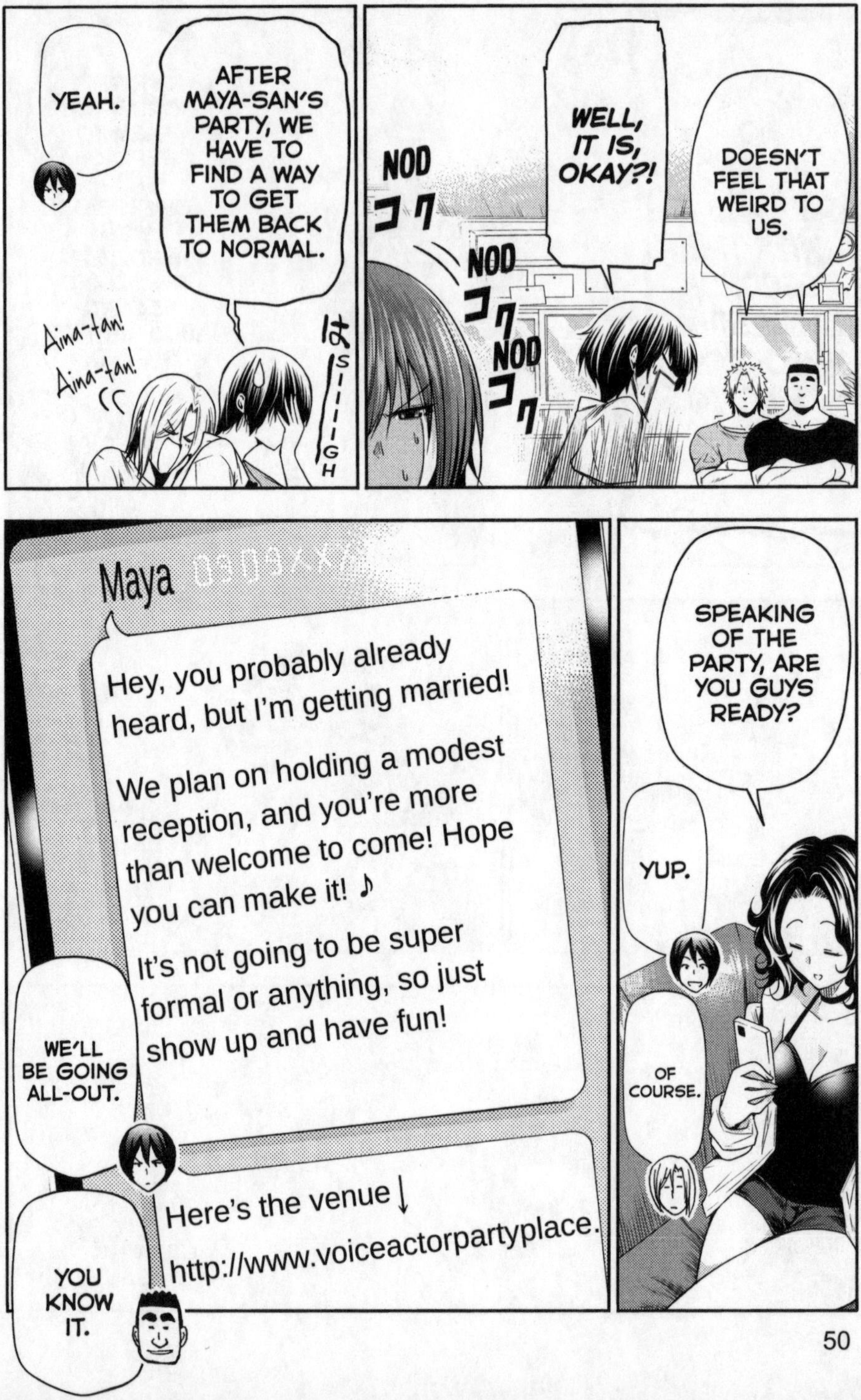
DOESN'T FEEL THAT WEIRD TO US.
WELL, IT IS, OKAY?!
NOD コク
NOD コク
NOD コク
AFTER MAYA-SAN'S PARTY, WE HAVE TO FIND A WAY TO GET THEM BACK TO NORMAL.
YEAH.
は SIIIIGH
Aina-tan! Aina-tan!
SPEAKING OF THE PARTY, ARE YOU GUYS READY?
YUP.
OF COURSE.
Maya
Hey, you probably already heard, but I'm getting married!
We plan on holding a modest reception, and you're more than welcome to come! Hope you can make it! ♪
It's not going to be super formal or anything, so just show up and have fun!
WE'LL BE GOING ALL-OUT.
Here's the venue↓
http://www.voiceactorpartyplace.
YOU KNOW IT.

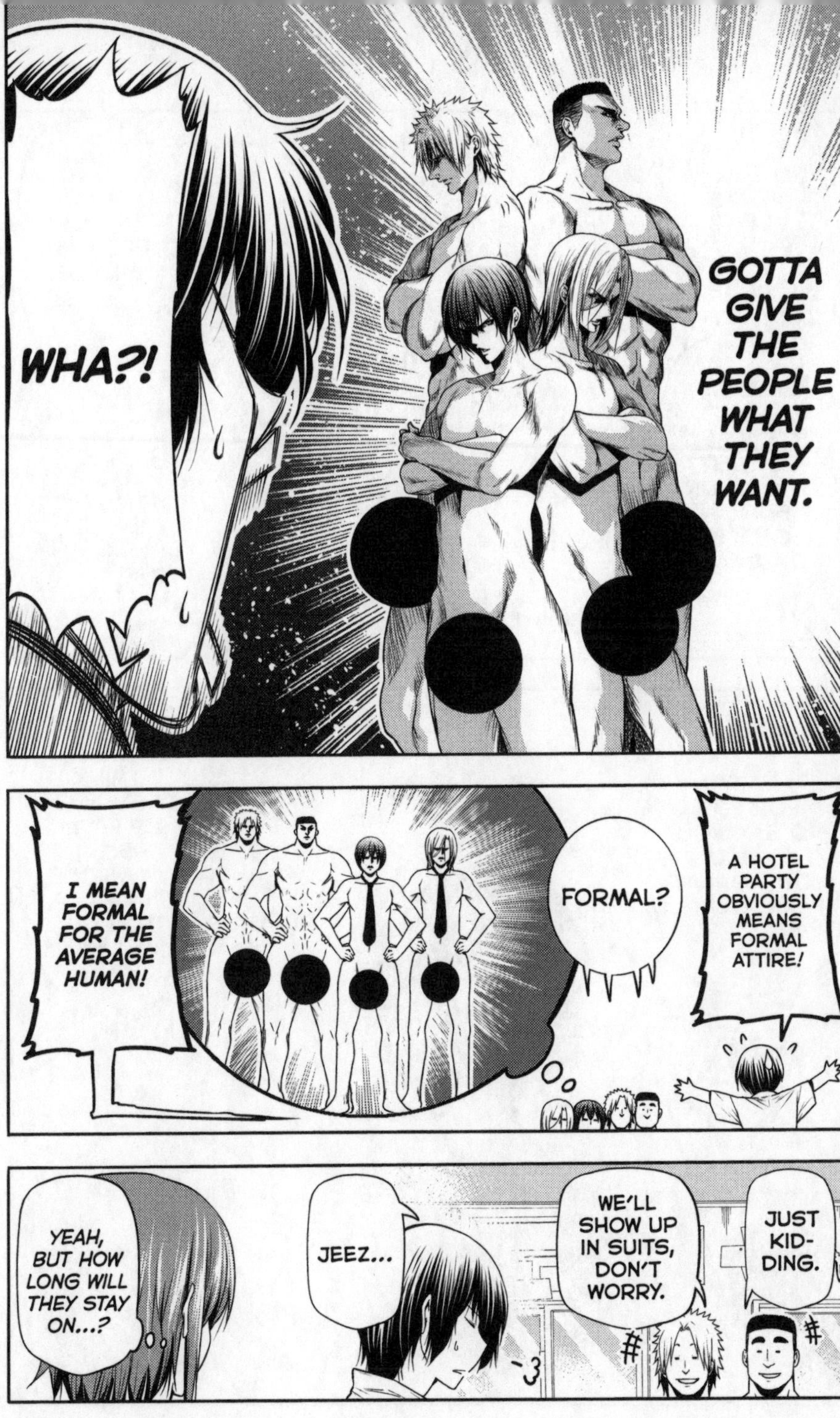
GOTTA GIVE THE PEOPLE WHAT THEY WANT.
WHA?!
A HOTEL PARTY OBVIOUSLY MEANS FORMAL ATTIRE!
FORMAL?
I MEAN FORMAL FOR THE AVERAGE HUMAN!
JUST KID-DING.
WE'LL SHOW UP IN SUITS, DON'T WORRY.
JEEZ...
YEAH, BUT HOW LONG WILL THEY STAY ON...?

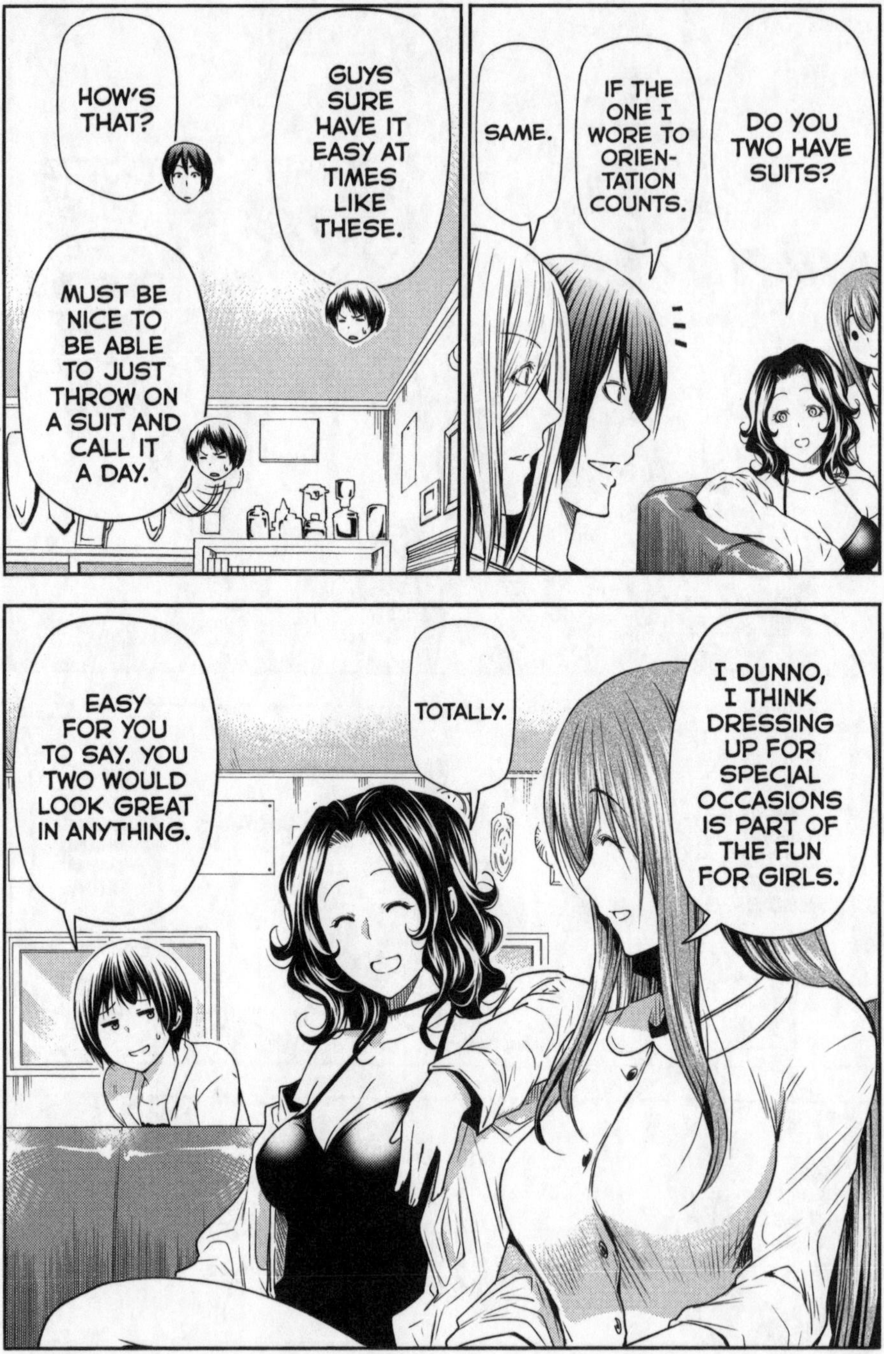
DO YOU TWO HAVE SUITS?
IF THE ONE I WORE TO ORIEN-TATION COUNTS.
SAME.
GUYS SURE HAVE IT EASY AT TIMES LIKE THESE.
HOW'S THAT?
MUST BE NICE TO BE ABLE TO JUST THROW ON A SUIT AND CALL IT A DAY.
I DUNNO, I THINK DRESSING UP FOR SPECIAL OCCASIONS IS PART OF THE FUN FOR GIRLS.
TOTALLY.
EASY FOR YOU TO SAY. YOU TWO WOULD LOOK GREAT IN ANYTHING.

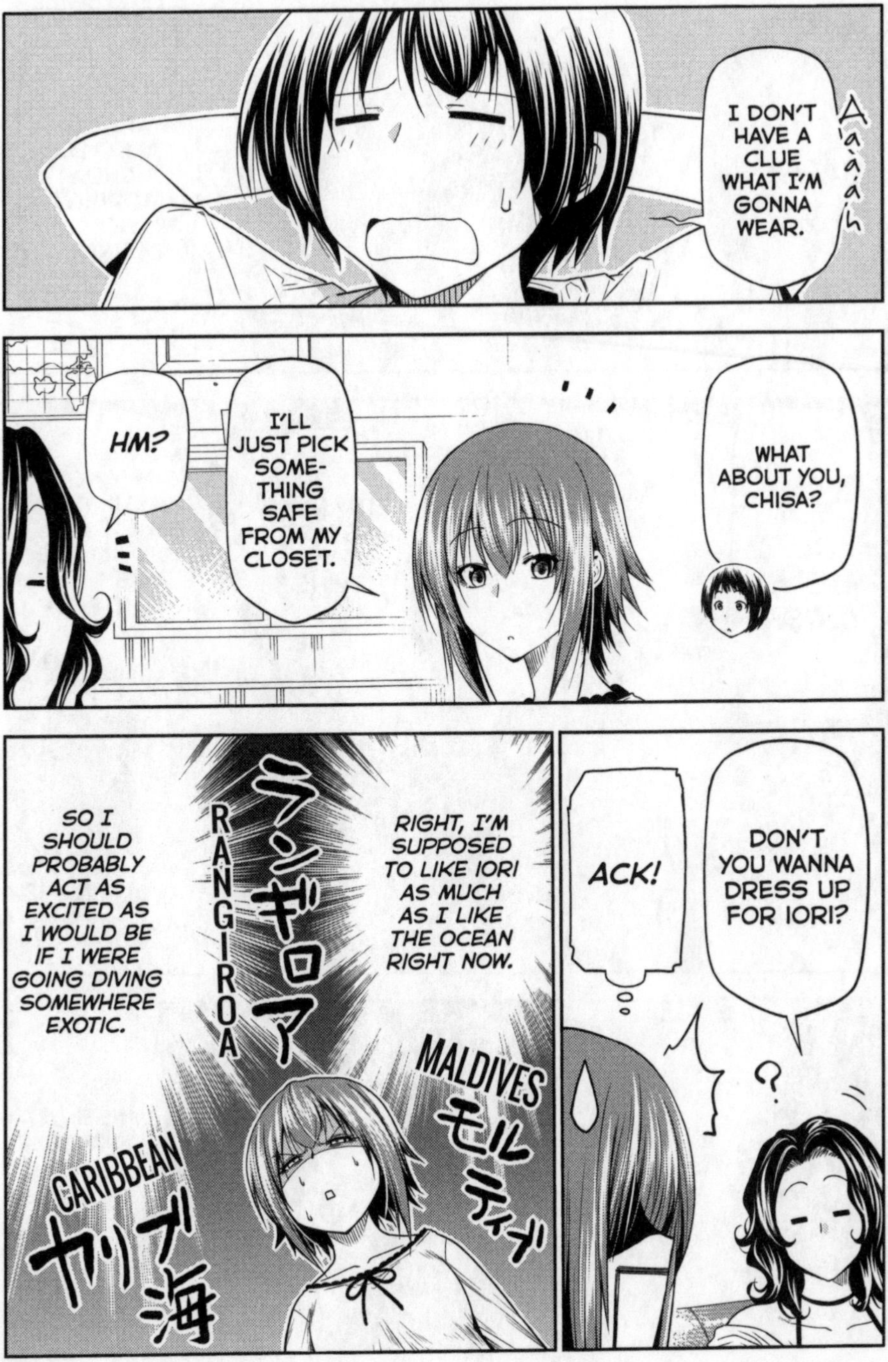
Aaaah
I DON'T HAVE A CLUE WHAT I'M GONNA WEAR.
WHAT ABOUT YOU, CHISA?
...
I'LL JUST PICK SOMETHING SAFE FROM MY CLOSET.
HM?
DON'T YOU WANNA DRESS UP FOR IORI?
ACK!
RIGHT, I'M SUPPOSED TO LIKE IORI AS MUCH AS I LIKE THE OCEAN RIGHT NOW.
SO I SHOULD PROBABLY ACT AS EXCITED AS I WOULD BE IF I WERE GOING DIVING SOMEWHERE EXOTIC.
ランギロア
RANGIROA
MALDIVES
モルディブ
CARIBBEAN
カリブ海

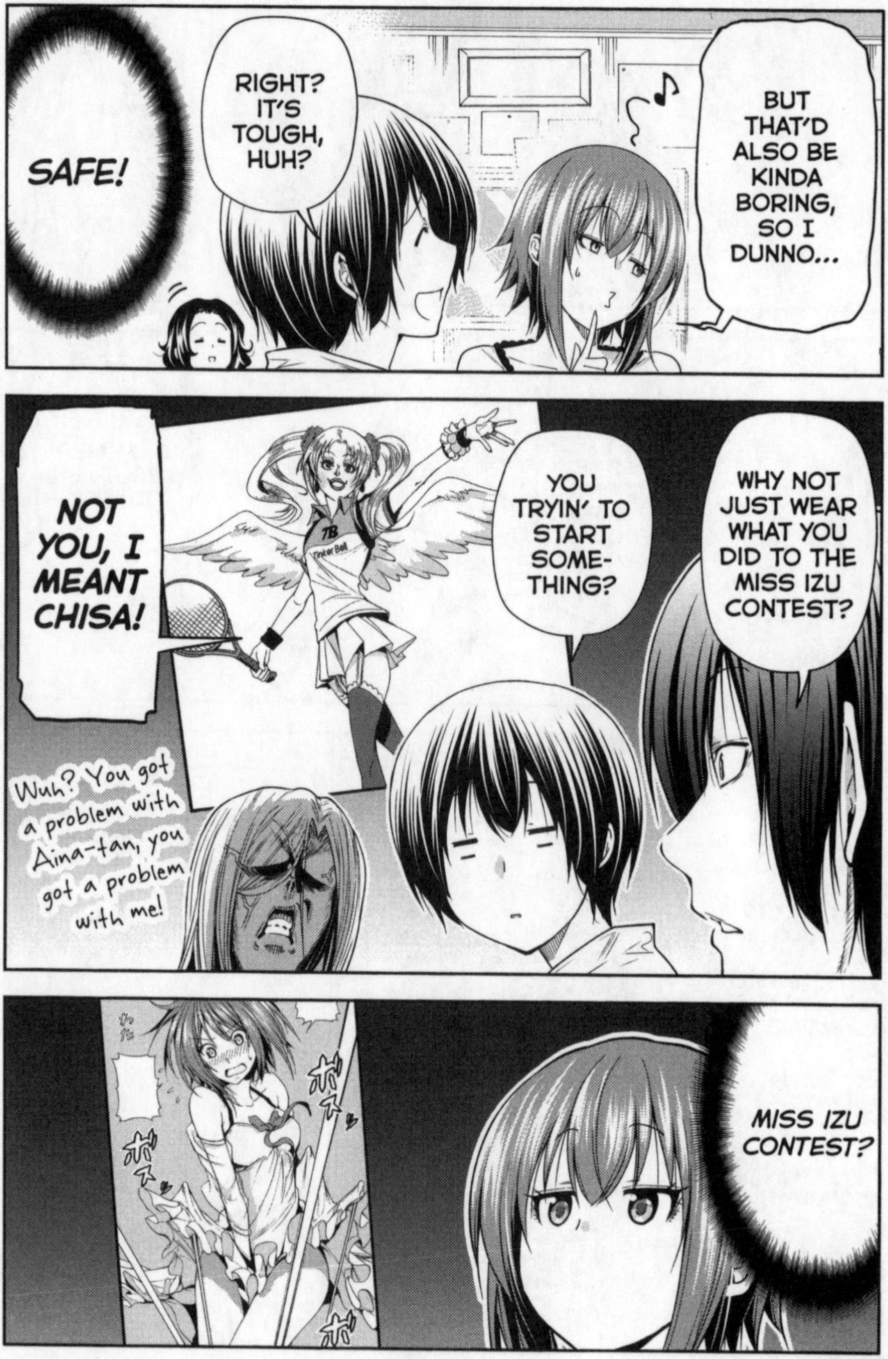
BUT THAT'D ALSO BE KINDA BORING, SO I DUNNO...
RIGHT? IT'S TOUGH, HUH?
SAFE!
WHY NOT JUST WEAR WHAT YOU DID TO THE MISS IZU CONTEST?
YOU TRYIN' TO START SOME-THING?
NOT YOU, I MEANT CHISA!
Wuh? You got a problem with Aina-tan, you got a problem with me!
MISS IZU CONTEST?

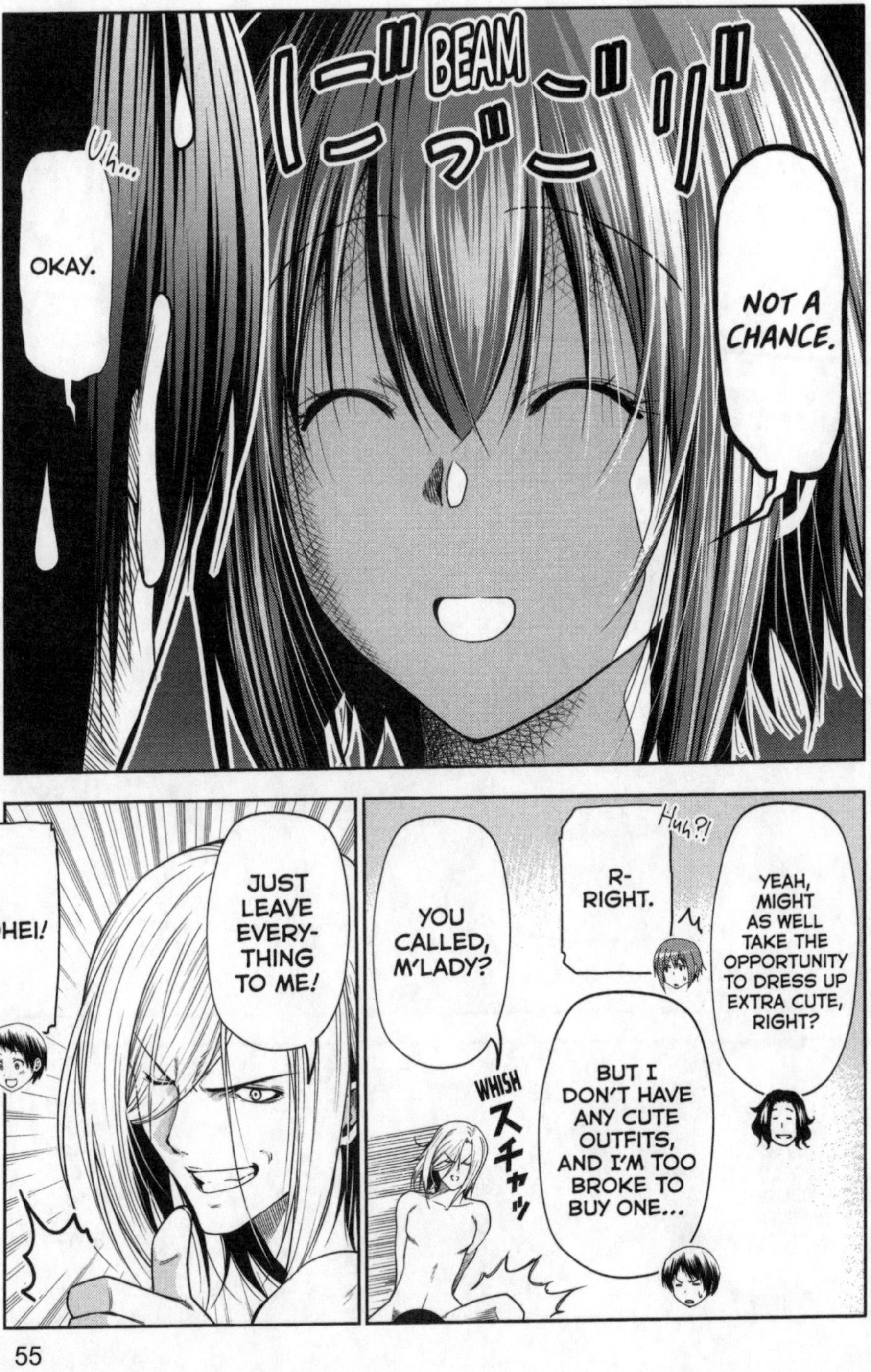
BEAM
NOT A CHANCE.
Uh...
OKAY.
YEAH, MIGHT AS WELL TAKE THE OPPORTUNITY TO DRESS UP EXTRA CUTE, RIGHT?
Huh?!
R-RIGHT.
BUT I DON'T HAVE ANY CUTE OUTFITS, AND I'M TOO BROKE TO BUY ONE...
YOU CALLED, M'LADY?
WHISH
JUST LEAVE EVERY-THING TO ME!
KOHEI!

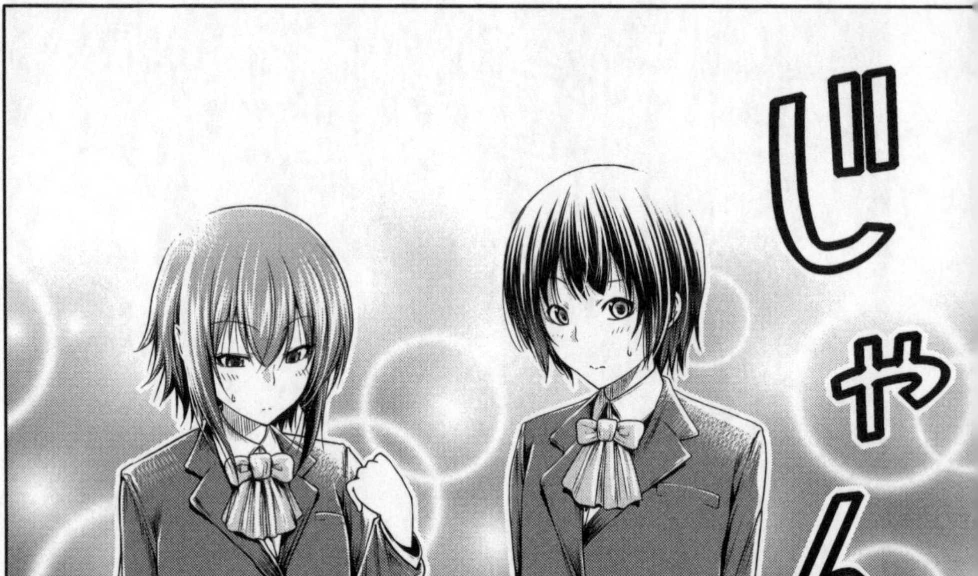
じゃんっ
TA-DA
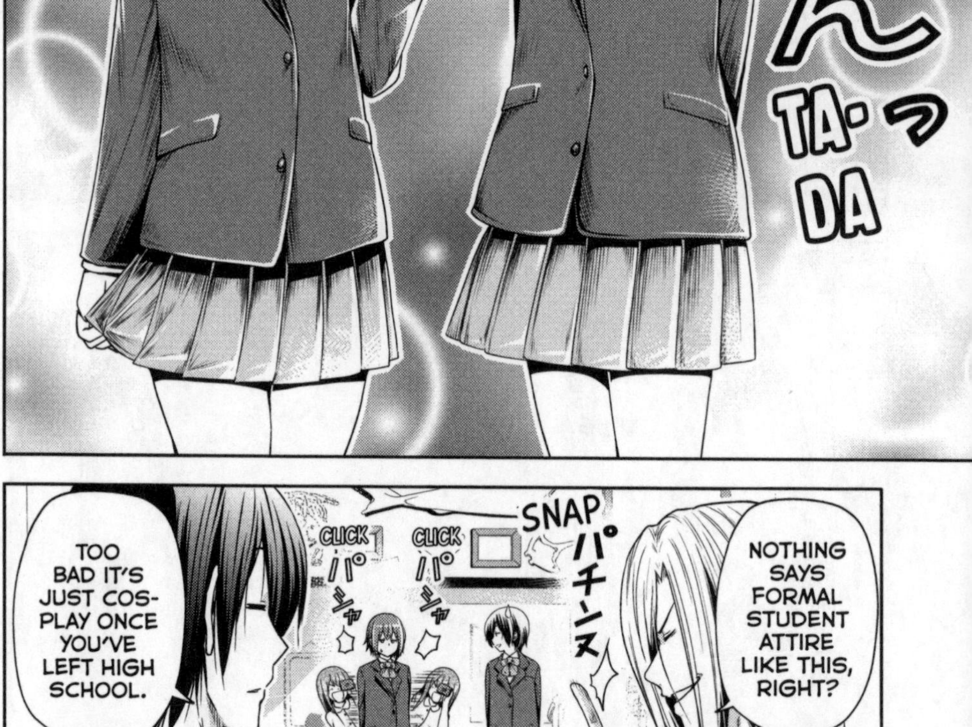
NOTHING SAYS FORMAL STUDENT ATTIRE LIKE THIS, RIGHT?
SNAP
CLICK
パシャ
CLICK
パシャ
TOO BAD IT'S JUST COS-PLAY ONCE YOU'VE LEFT HIGH SCHOOL.

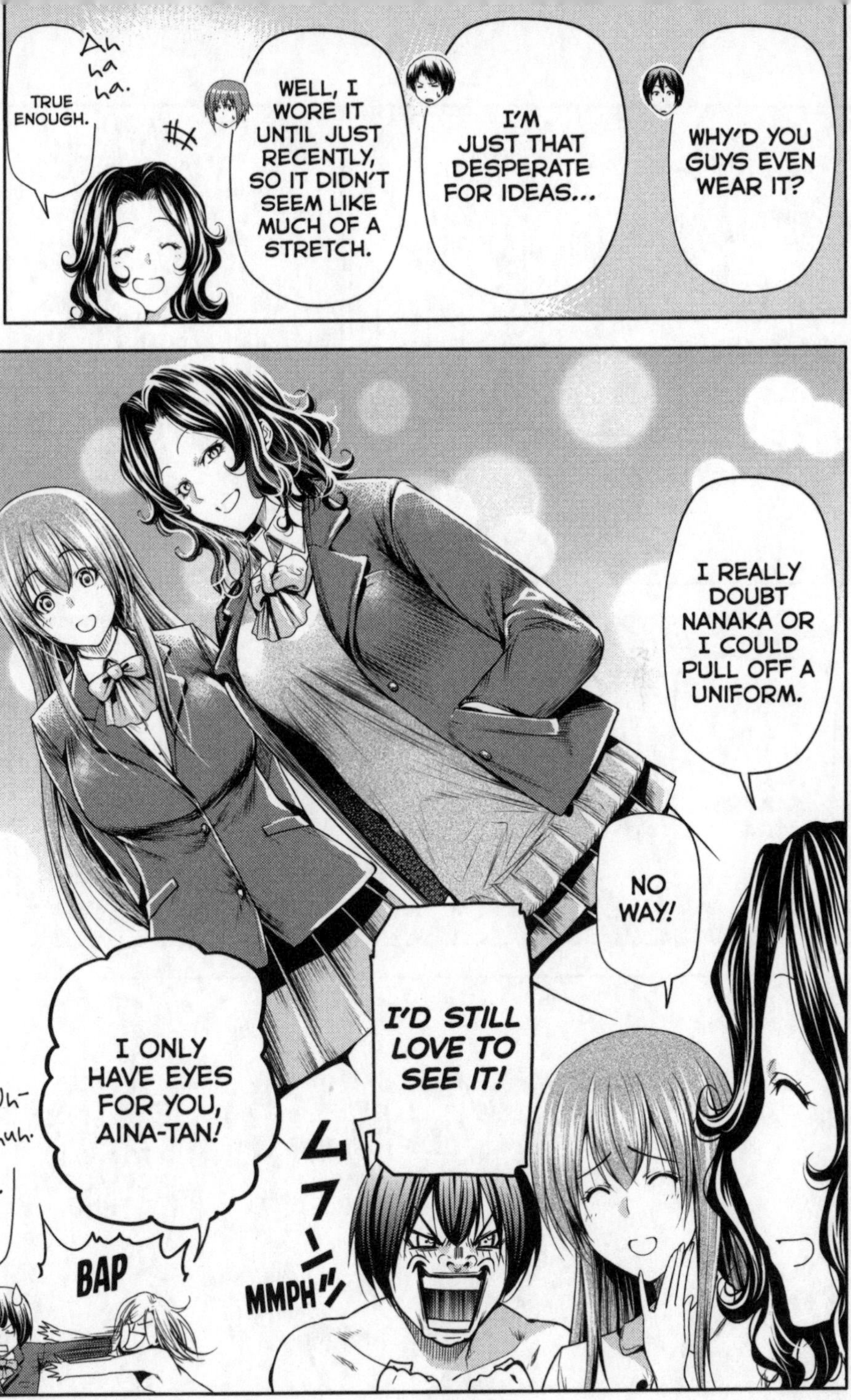
WHY'D YOU GUYS EVEN WEAR IT?
I'M JUST THAT DESPERATE FOR IDEAS...
WELL, I WORE IT UNTIL JUST RECENTLY, SO IT DIDN'T SEEM LIKE MUCH OF A STRETCH.
Ah ha ha.
TRUE ENOUGH.
I REALLY DOUBT NANAKA OR I COULD PULL OFF A UNIFORM.
NO WAY!
I'D STILL LOVE TO SEE IT!
MMPH
I ONLY HAVE EYES FOR YOU, AINA-TAN!
BAP
Uh-huh.
SURE...

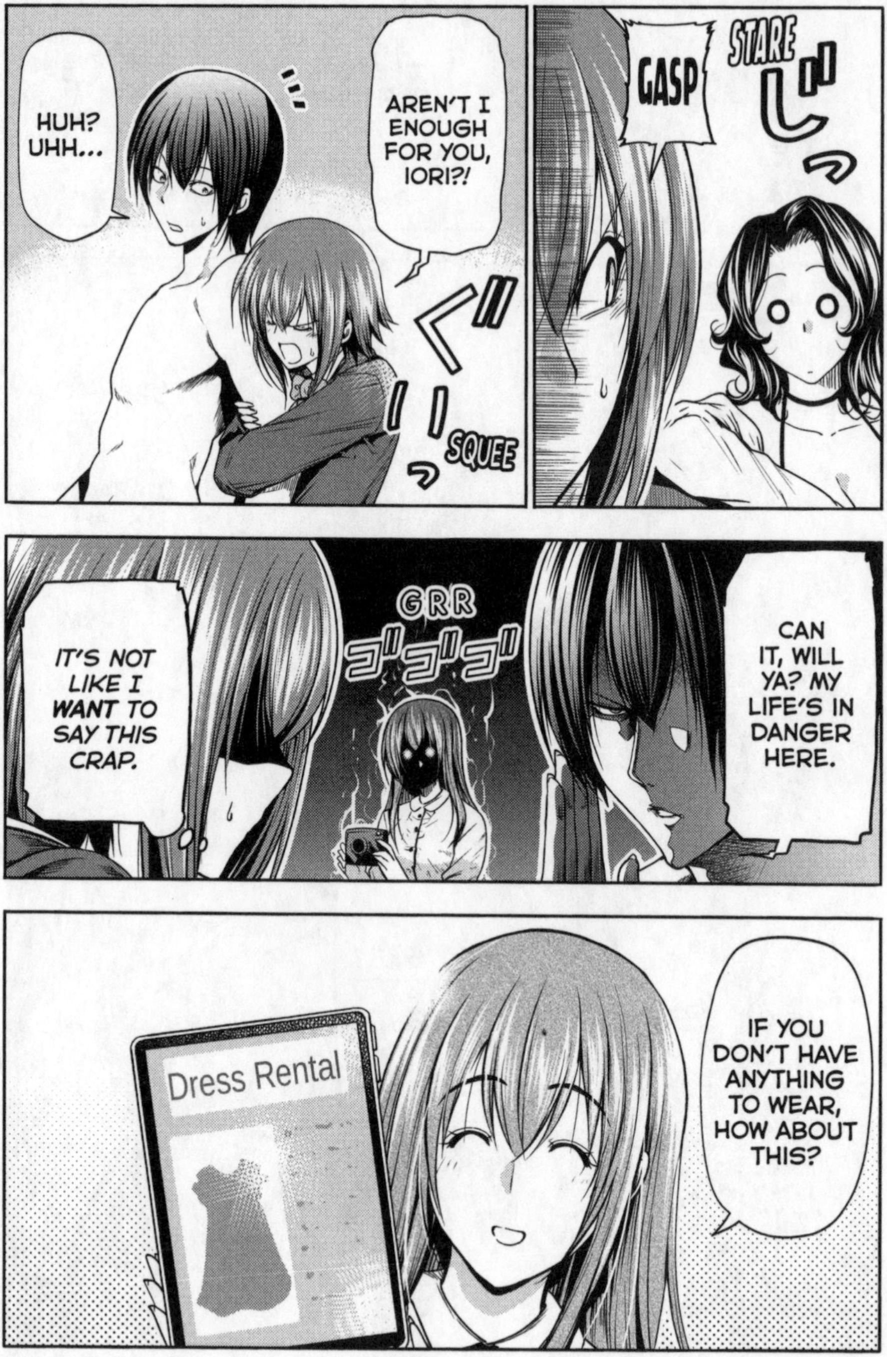
GASP
STARE
AREN'T I ENOUGH FOR YOU, IORI?!
SQUEE
HUH? UHH...
CAN IT, WILL YA? MY LIFE'S IN DANGER HERE.
GRR
IT'S NOT LIKE I *WANT* TO SAY THIS CRAP.
IF YOU DON'T HAVE ANYTHING TO WEAR, HOW ABOUT THIS?
Dress Rental

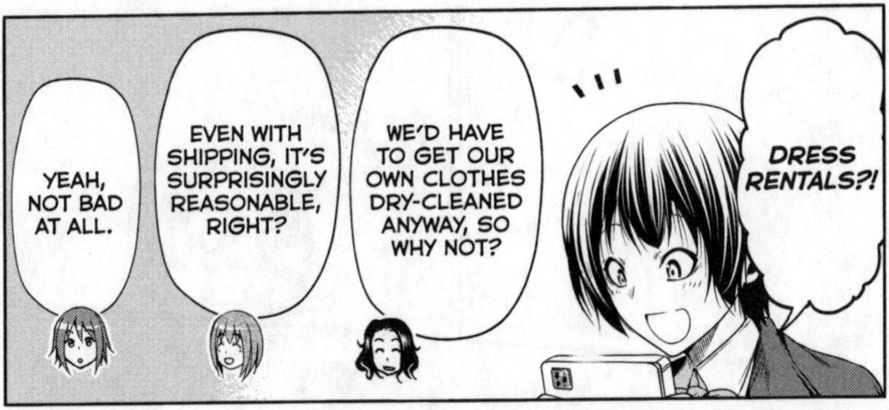
DRESS RENTALS?!
WE'D HAVE TO GET OUR OWN CLOTHES DRY-CLEANED ANYWAY, SO WHY NOT?
EVEN WITH SHIPPING, IT'S SURPRISINGLY REASONABLE, RIGHT?
YEAH, NOT BAD AT ALL.

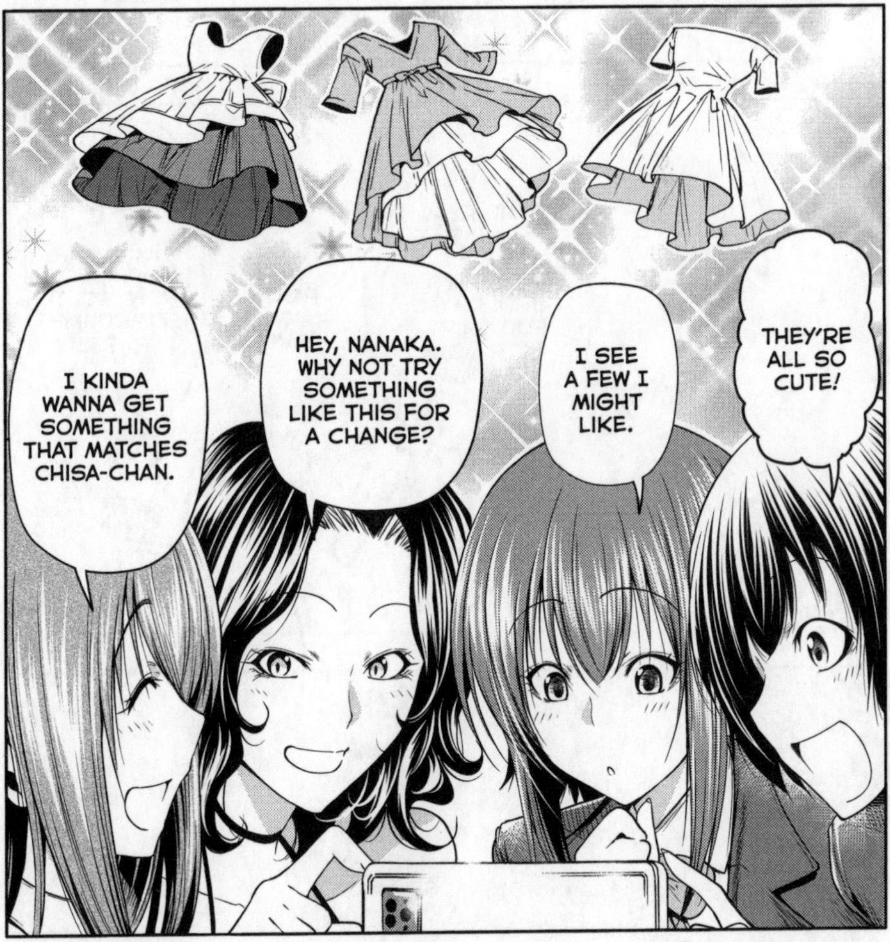
THEY'RE ALL SO CUTE!
I SEE A FEW I MIGHT LIKE.
HEY, NANAKA. WHY NOT TRY SOMETHING LIKE THIS FOR A CHANGE?
I KINDA WANNA GET SOMETHING THAT MATCHES CHISA-CHAN.

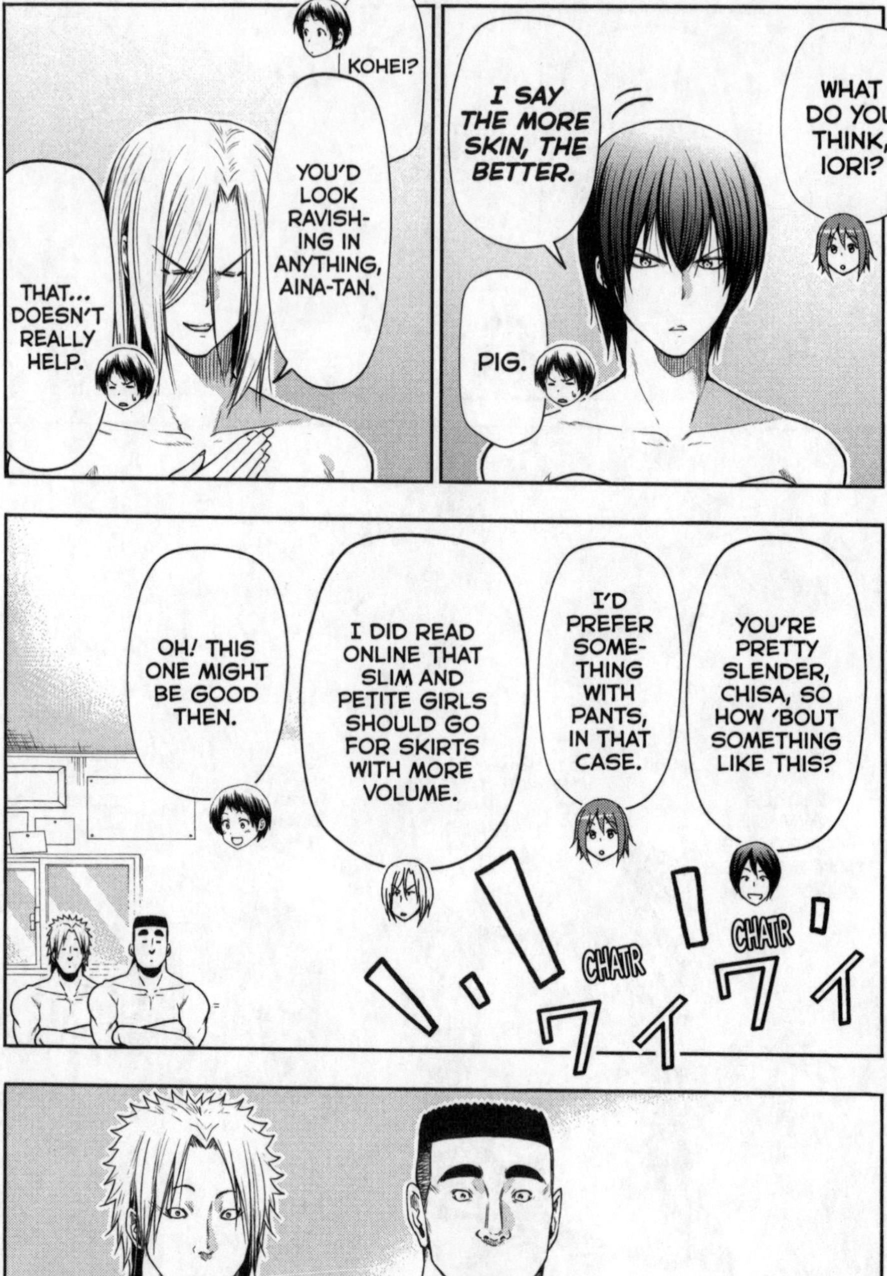
WHAT DO YOU THINK, IORI?
I SAY THE MORE SKIN, THE BETTER.
PIG.
KOHEI?
YOU'D LOOK RAVISH-ING IN ANYTHING, AINA-TAN.
THAT... DOESN'T REALLY HELP.
YOU'RE PRETTY SLENDER, CHISA, SO HOW 'BOUT SOMETHING LIKE THIS?
I'D PREFER SOME-THING WITH PANTS, IN THAT CASE.
I DID READ ONLINE THAT SLIM AND PETITE GIRLS SHOULD GO FOR SKIRTS WITH MORE VOLUME.
OH! THIS ONE MIGHT BE GOOD THEN.
CHATR
CHATR
ワイワイ

MM-HM.

CHATR

CHATR

STILL DOESN'T FEEL THAT WEIRD TO ME, REALLY.

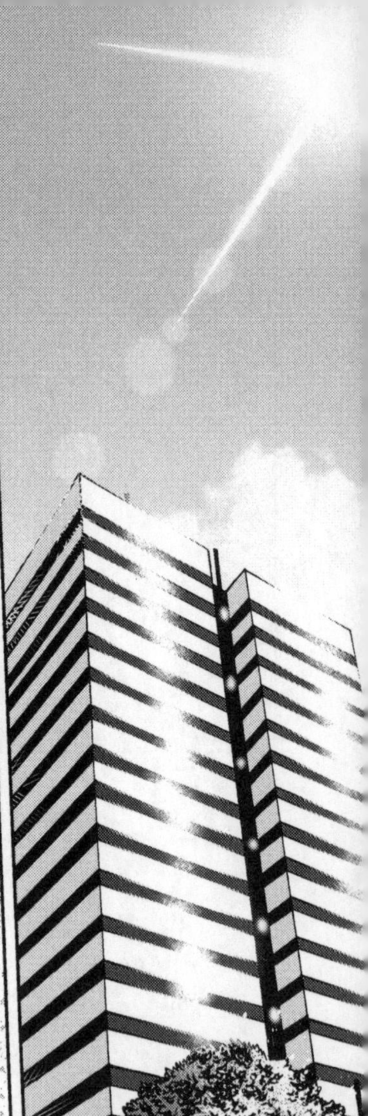

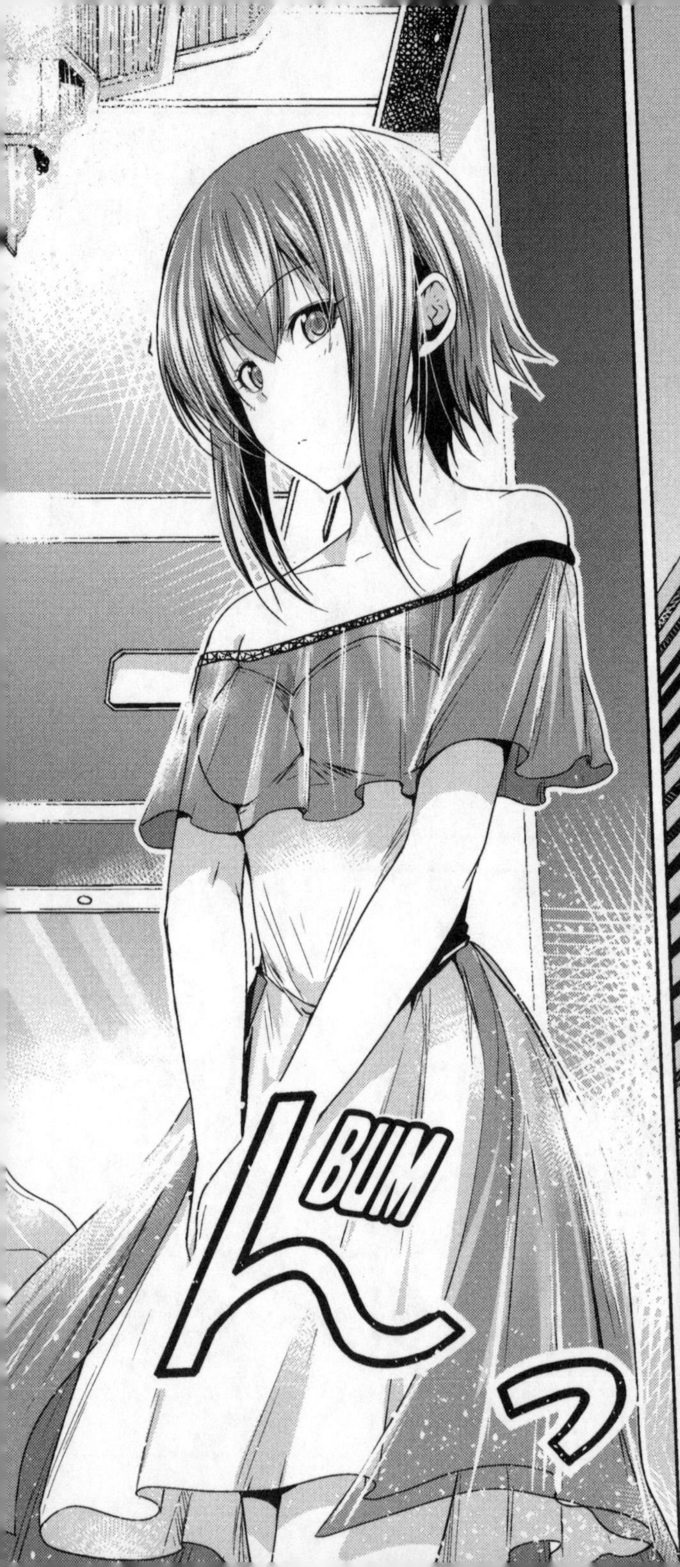

BUIM
んっ

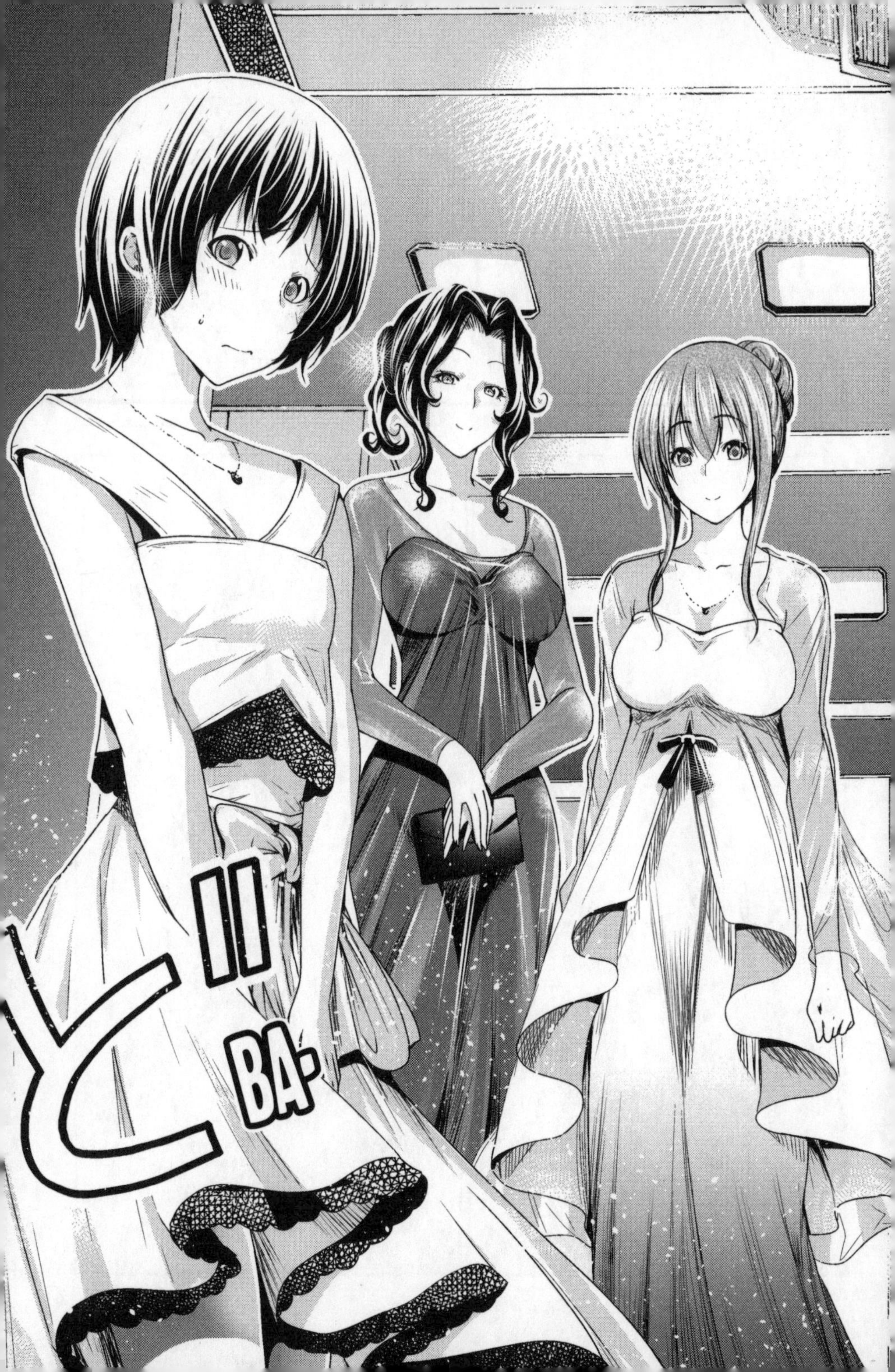
ドン
BA-

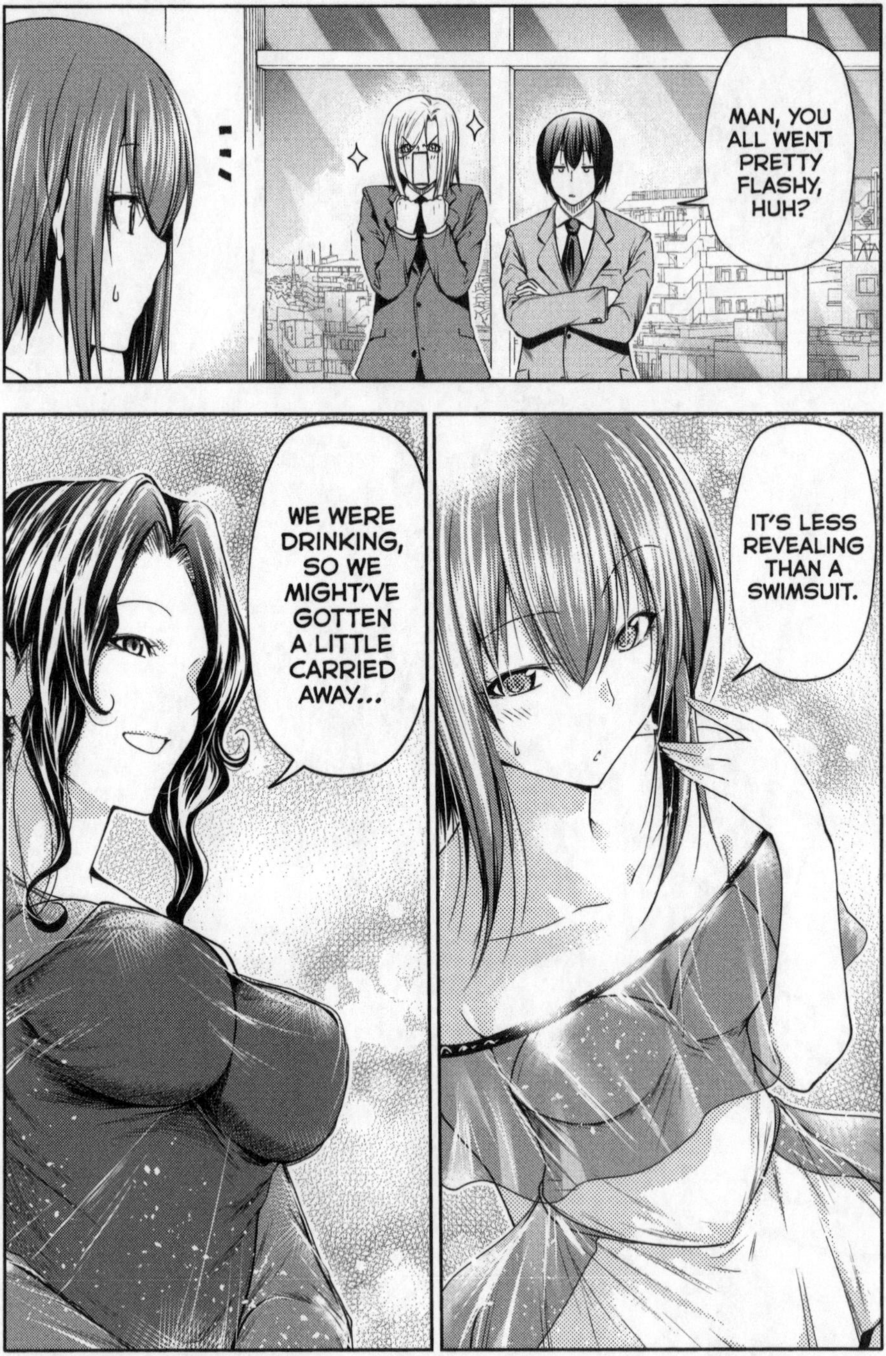
MAN, YOU ALL WENT PRETTY FLASHY, HUH?
IT'S LESS REVEALING THAN A SWIMSUIT.
WE WERE DRINKING, SO WE MIGHT'VE GOTTEN A LITTLE CARRIED AWAY...

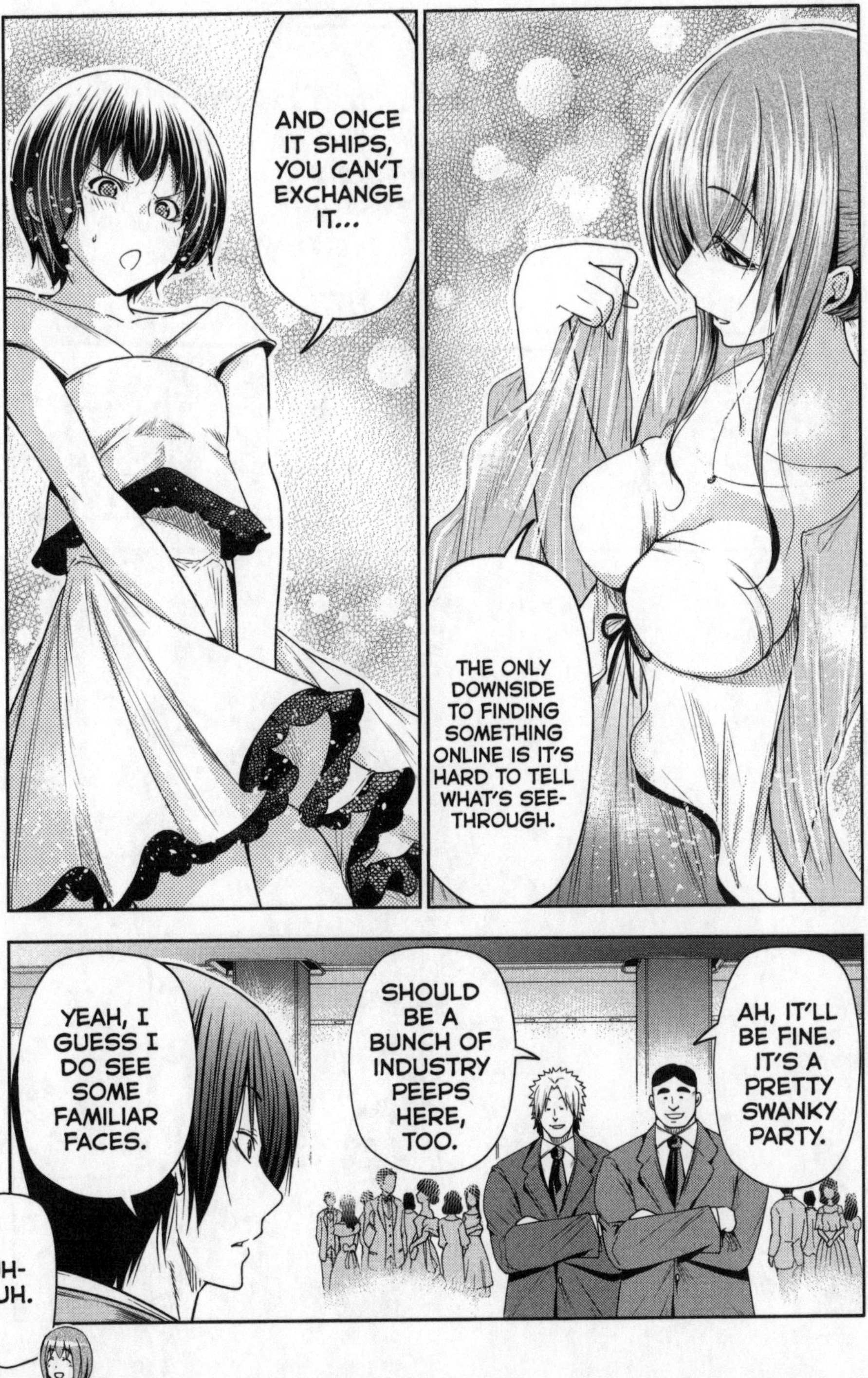
THE ONLY DOWNSIDE TO FINDING SOMETHING ONLINE IS IT'S HARD TO TELL WHAT'S SEE-THROUGH.
AND ONCE IT SHIPS, YOU CAN'T EXCHANGE IT...
AH, IT'LL BE FINE. IT'S A PRETTY SWANKY PARTY.
SHOULD BE A BUNCH OF INDUSTRY PEEPS HERE, TOO.
YEAH, I GUESS I DO SEE SOME FAMILIAR FACES.
UH-HUH.

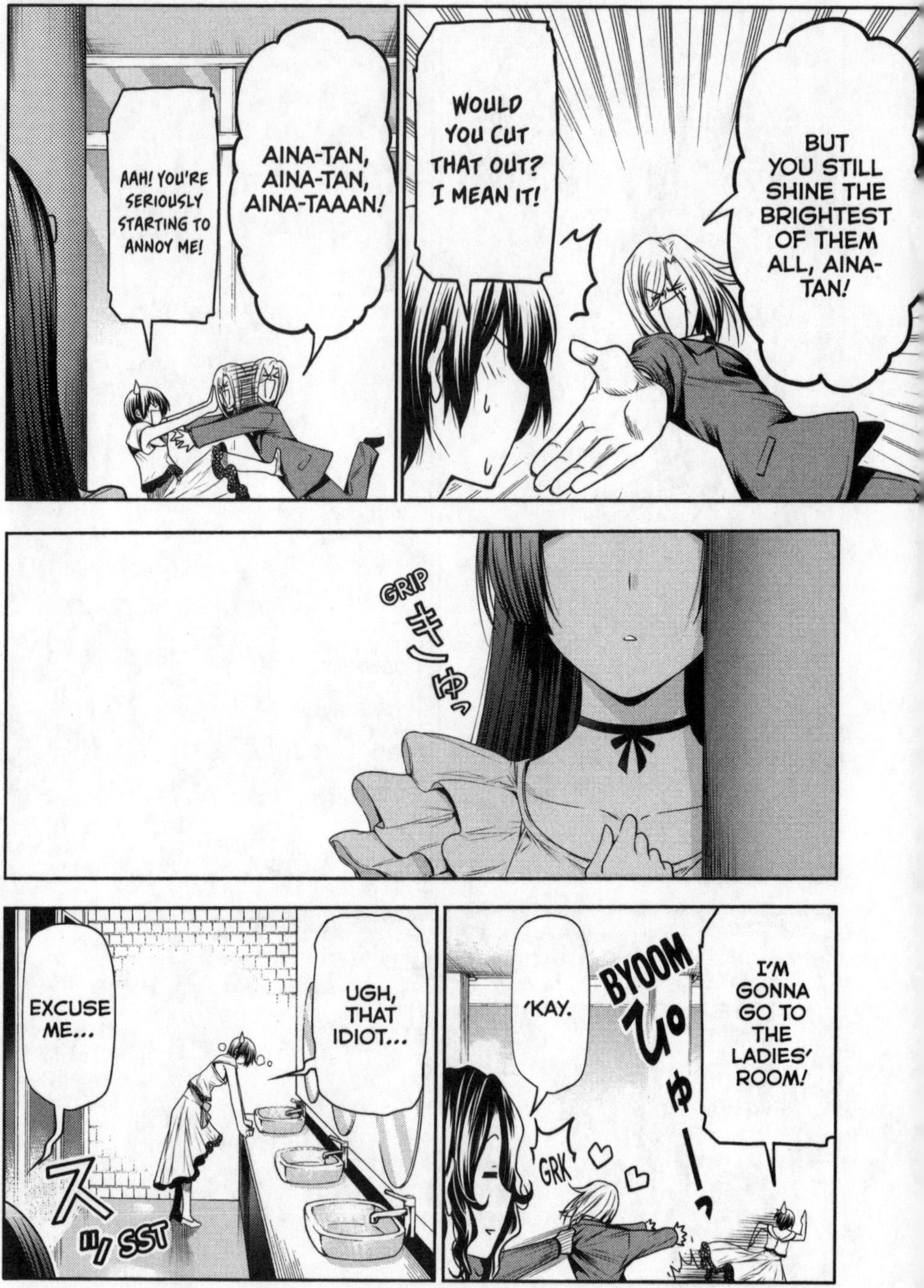
BUT YOU STILL SHINE THE BRIGHTEST OF THEM ALL, AINA-TAN!
WOULD YOU CUT THAT OUT? I MEAN IT!
AINA-TAN, AINA-TAN, AINA-TAAAN!
AAH! YOU'RE SERIOUSLY STARTING TO ANNOY ME!
GRIP
I'M GONNA GO TO THE LADIES' ROOM!
BYOOM
'KAY.
GRK
UGH, THAT IDIOT...
EXCUSE ME...
SST

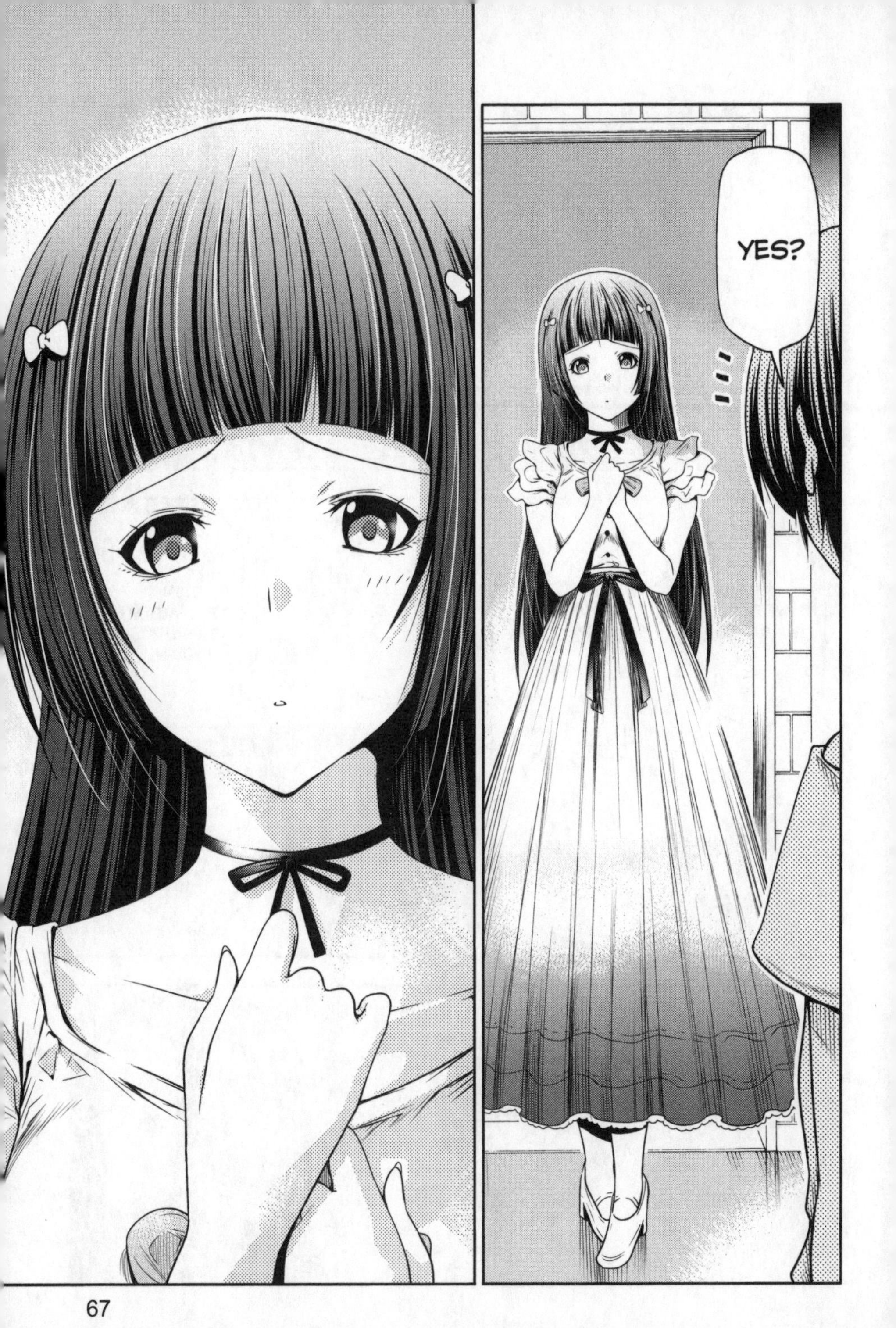
YES?

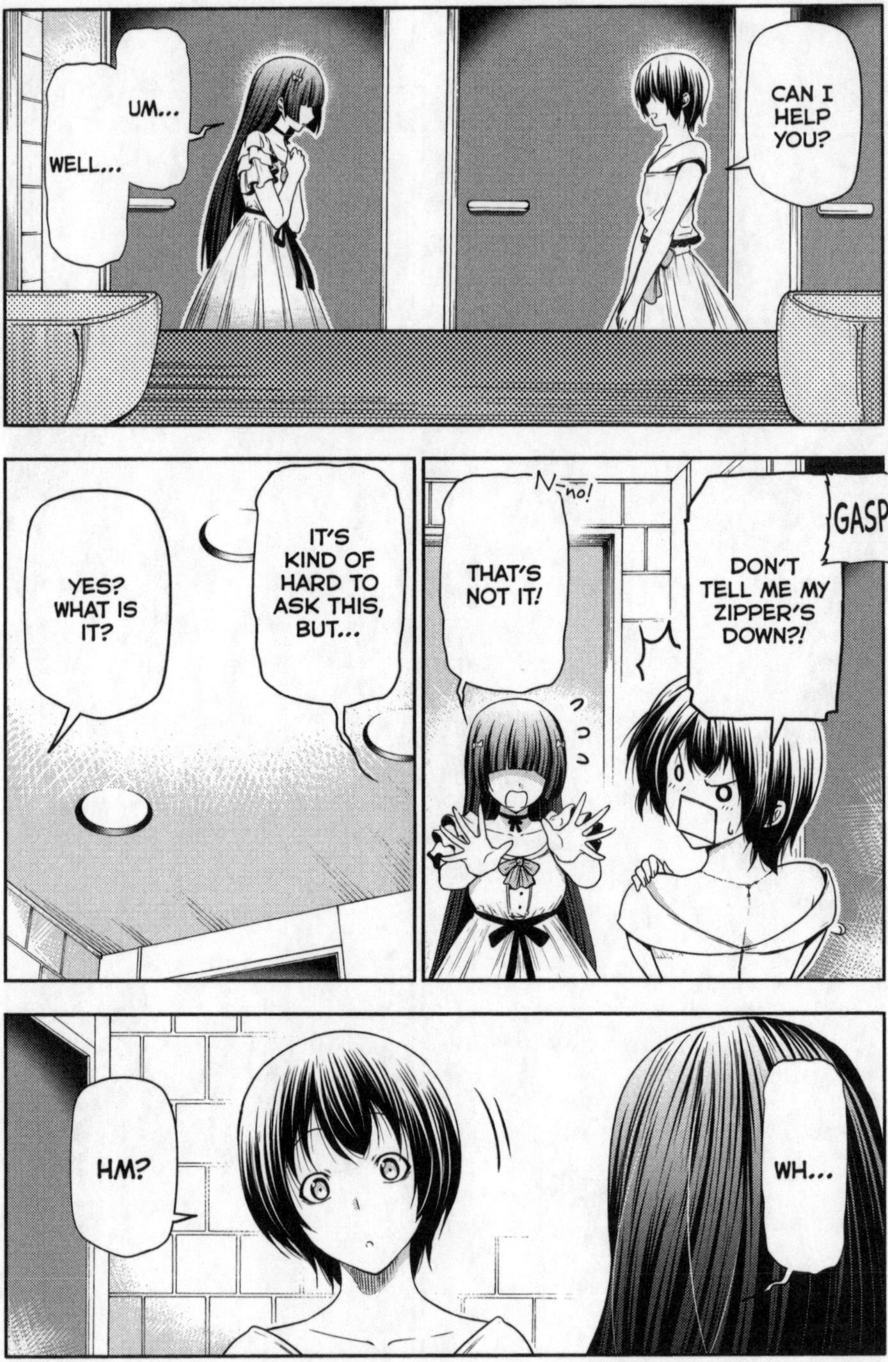
CAN I HELP YOU?
UM... WELL...
GASP
DON'T TELL ME MY ZIPPER'S DOWN?!
N-no!
THAT'S NOT IT!
IT'S KIND OF HARD TO ASK THIS, BUT...
YES? WHAT IS IT?
WH...
HM?

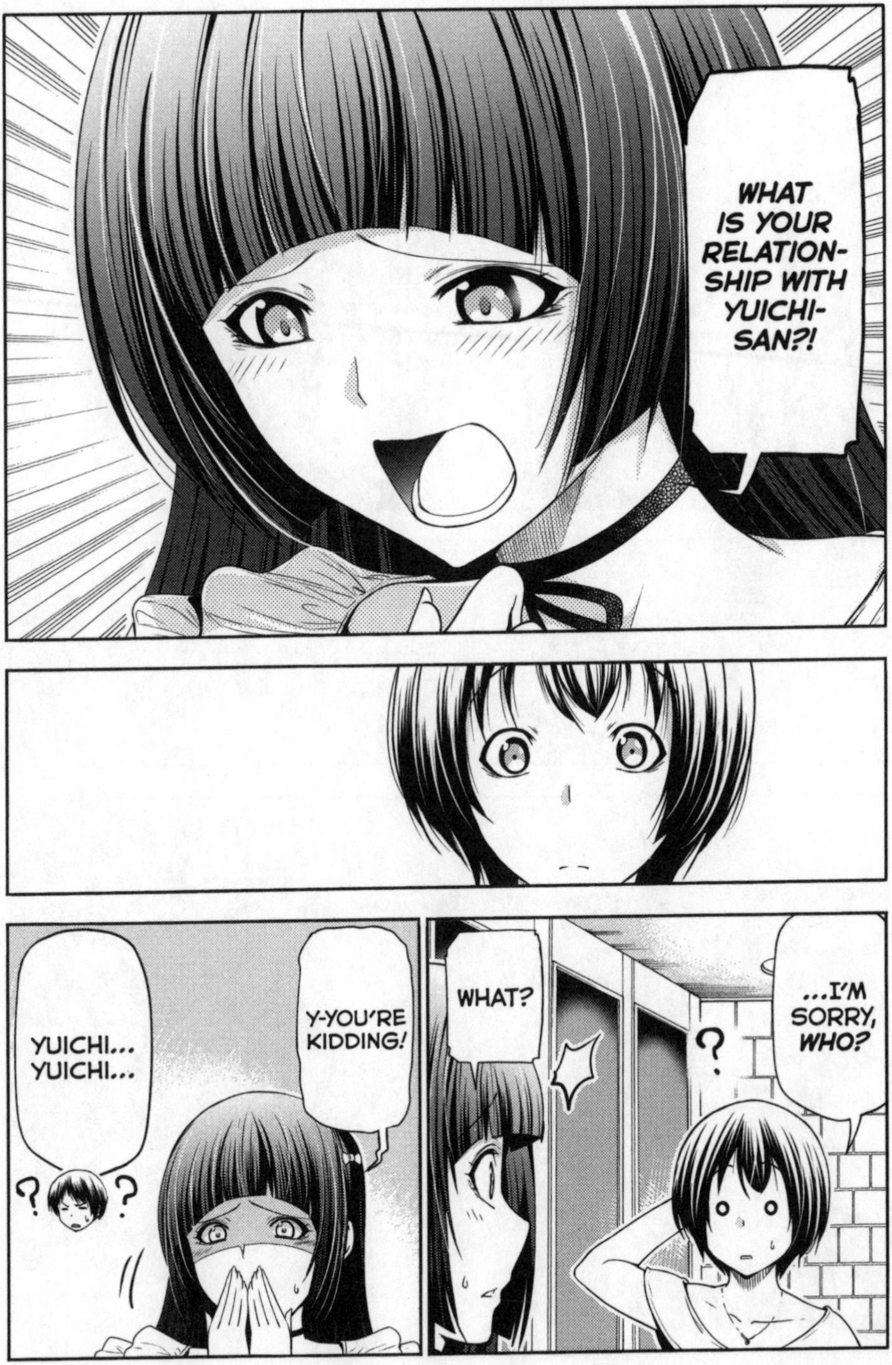
WHAT IS YOUR RELATIONSHIP WITH YUICHI-SAN?!
...I'M SORRY, WHO?
WHAT?
Y-YOU'RE KIDDING!
YUICHI... YUICHI...

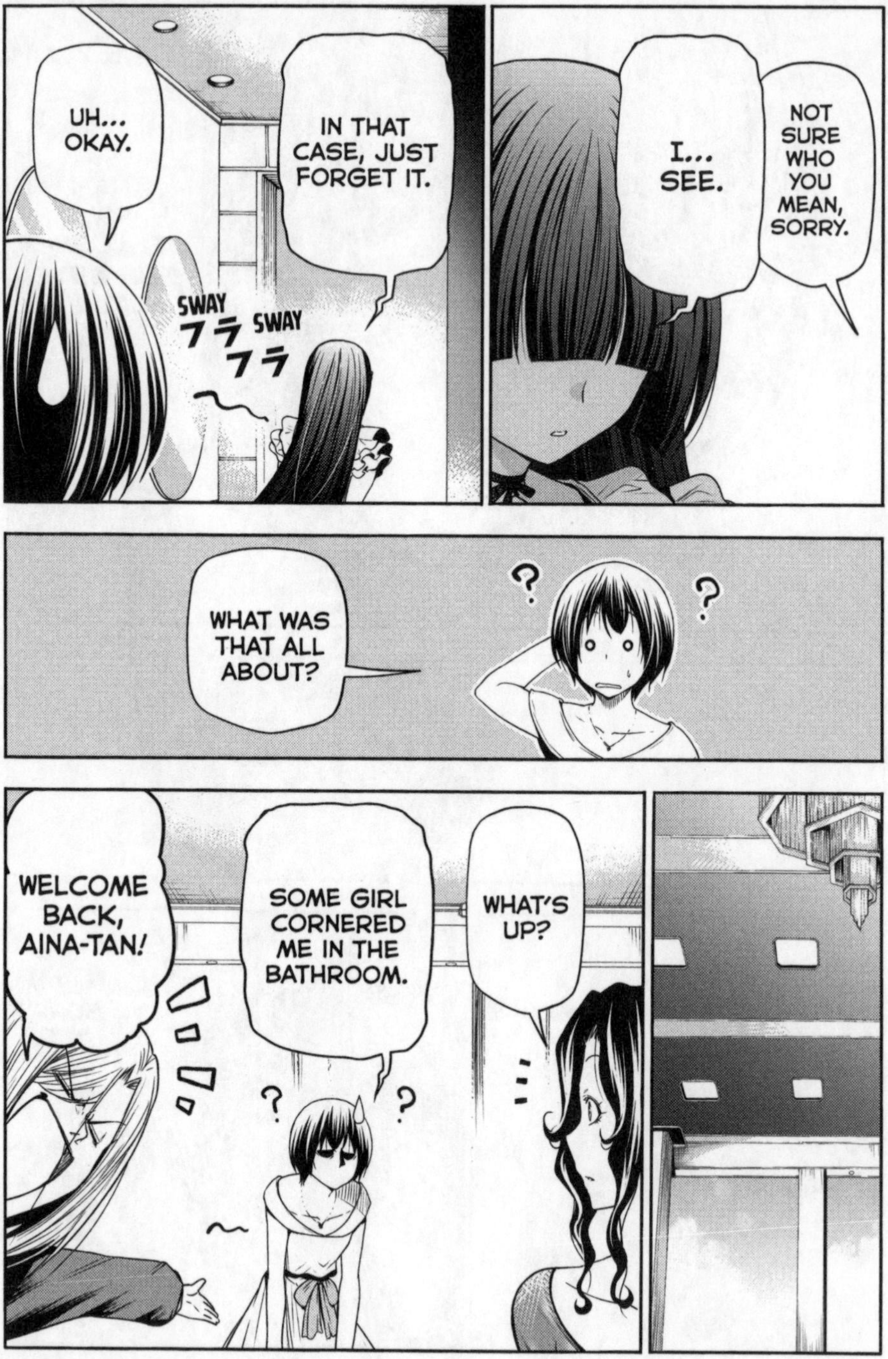
NOT SURE WHO YOU MEAN, SORRY.
I... SEE.
IN THAT CASE, JUST FORGET IT.
SWAY フラ
SWAY フラ
UH... OKAY.
WHAT WAS THAT ALL ABOUT?
WHAT'S UP?
SOME GIRL CORNERED ME IN THE BATHROOM.
WELCOME BACK, AINA-TAN!

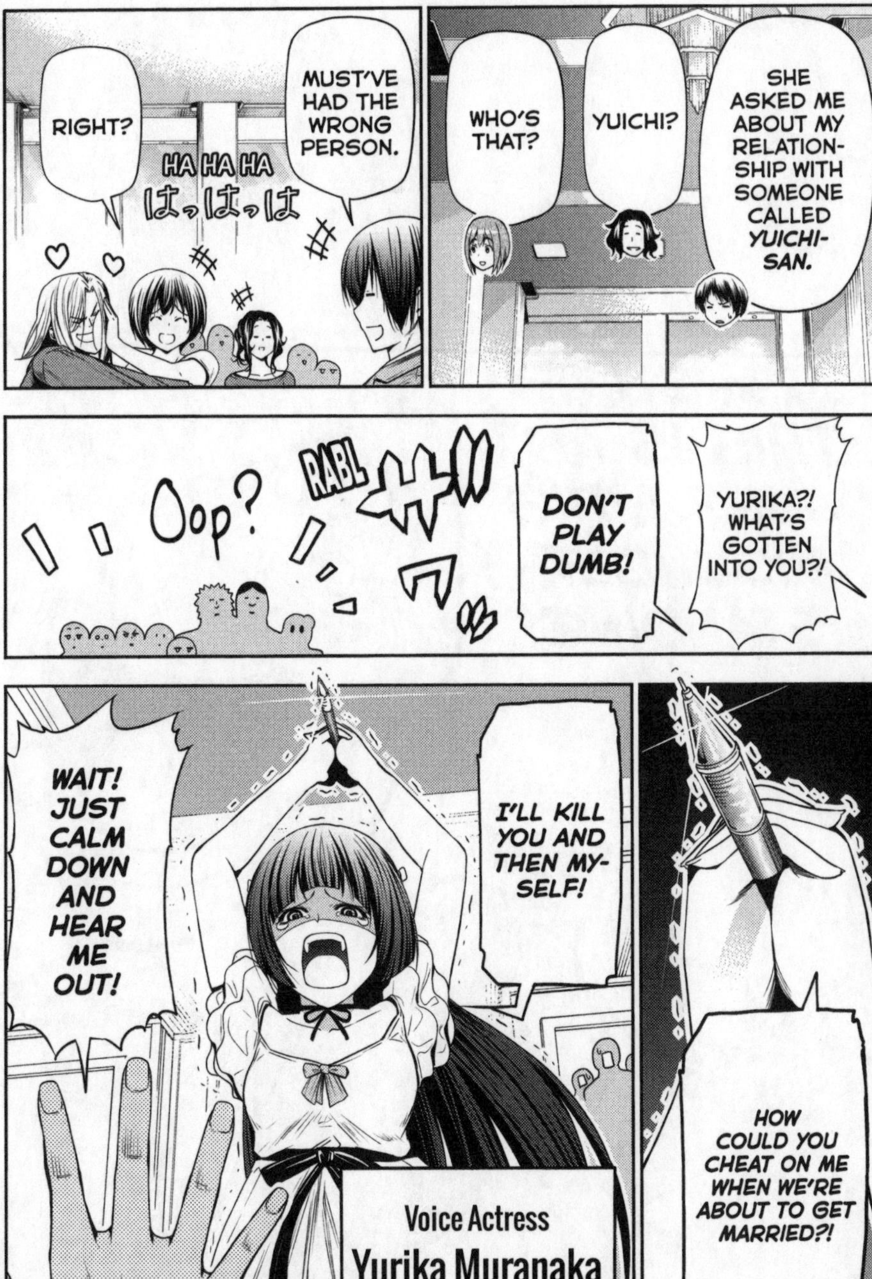
SHE ASKED ME ABOUT MY RELATION-SHIP WITH SOMEONE CALLED YUICHI-SAN.
YUICHI?
WHO'S THAT?
MUST'VE HAD THE WRONG PERSON.
HA HA HA
はっはっは
RIGHT?
YURIKA?! WHAT'S GOTTEN INTO YOU?!
DON'T PLAY DUMB!
RABL
Oop?
HOW COULD YOU CHEAT ON ME WHEN WE'RE ABOUT TO GET MARRIED?!
I'LL KILL YOU AND THEN MY-SELF!
WAIT! JUST CALM DOWN AND HEAR ME OUT!
Voice Actress
Yurika Muranaka

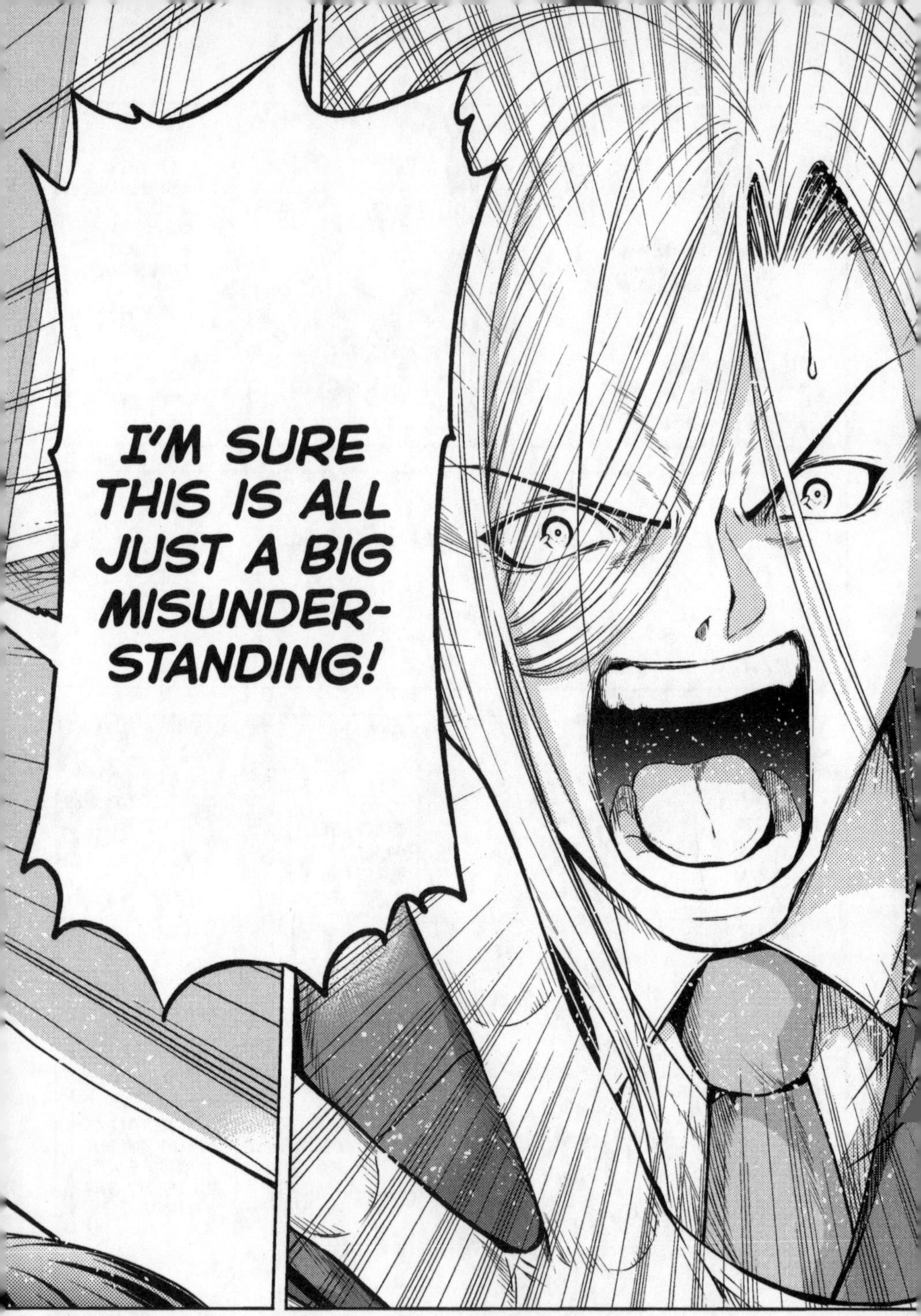
I'M SURE THIS IS ALL JUST A BIG MISUNDER-STANDING!

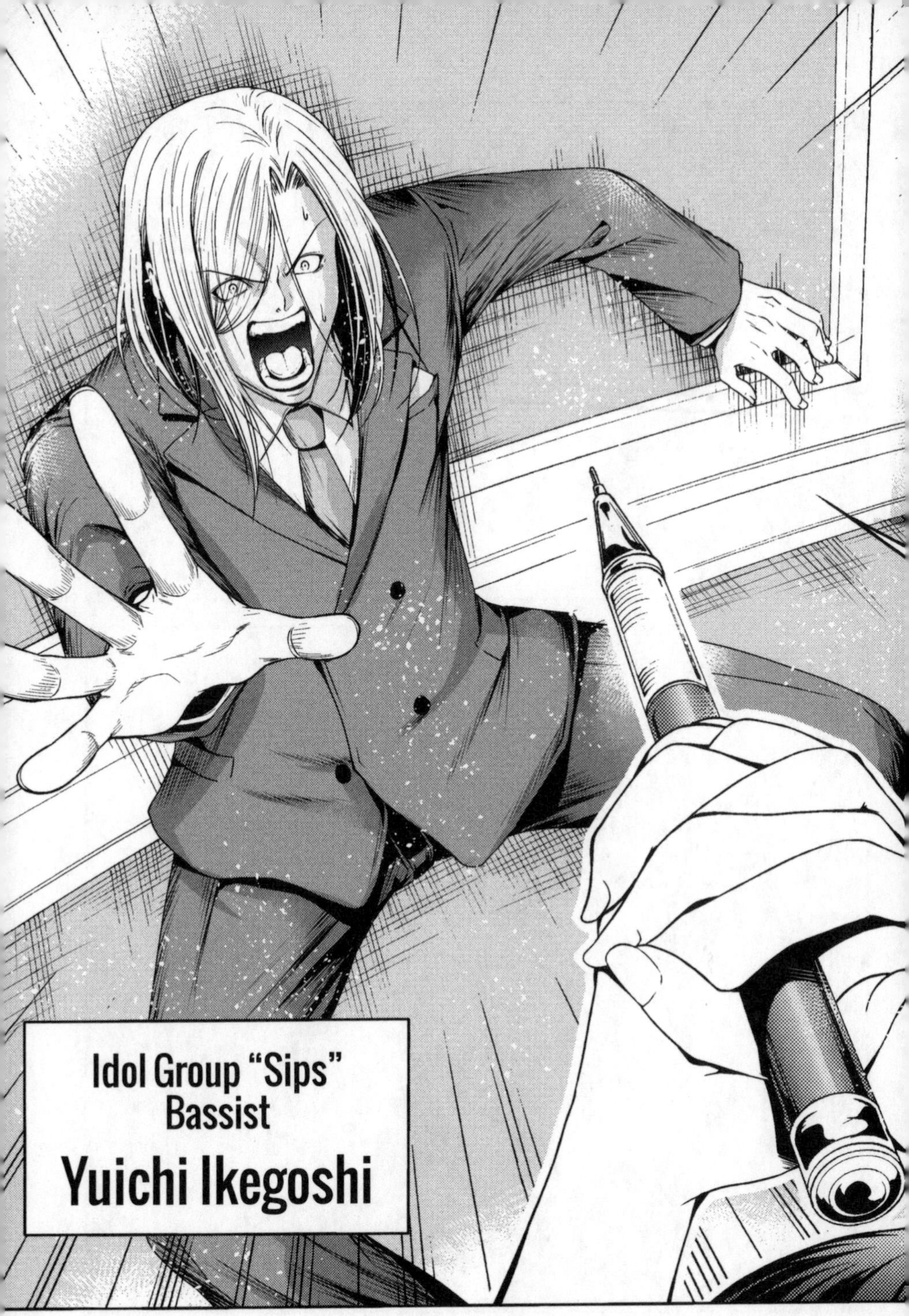
Idol Group "Sips"
Bassist
Yuichi Ikegoshi

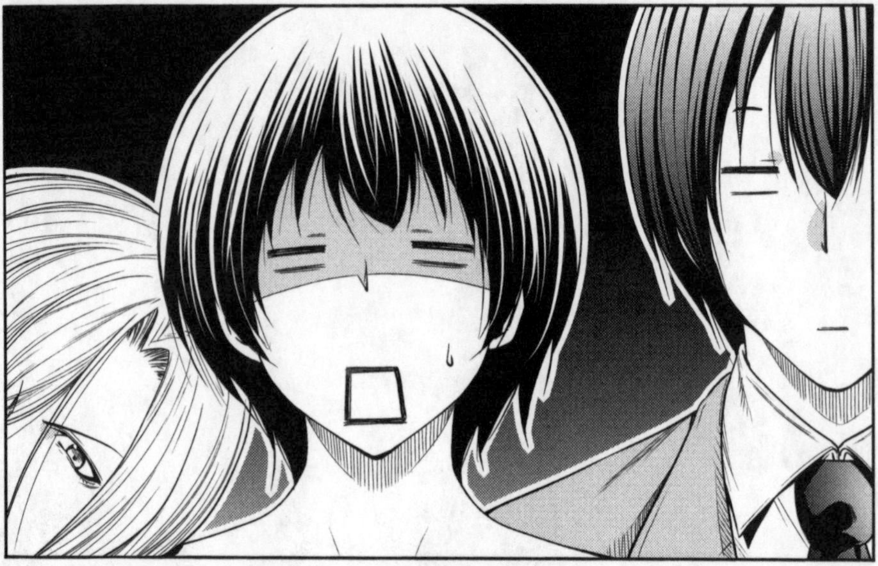

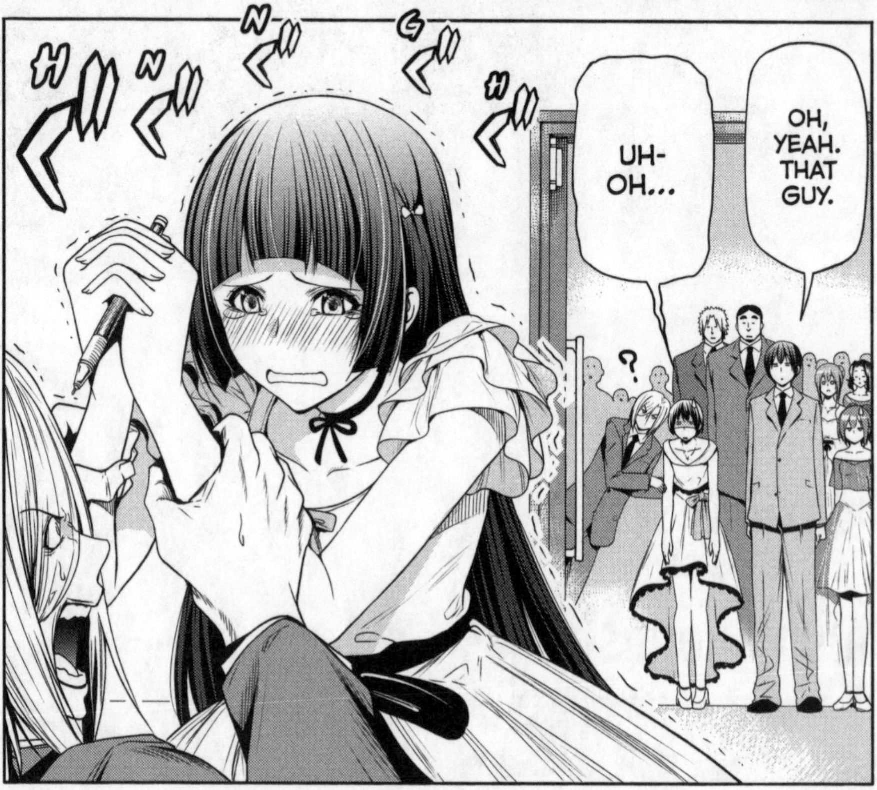
OH, YEAH. THAT GUY.
UH-OH...
HNNGH
?

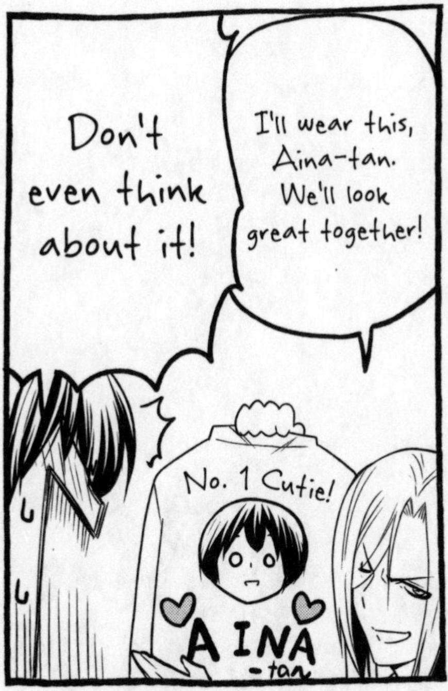
I'll wear this, Aina-tan. We'll look great together!
Don't even think about it!
No. 1 Cutie!
AINA
-tan

Grand Blue Dreaming

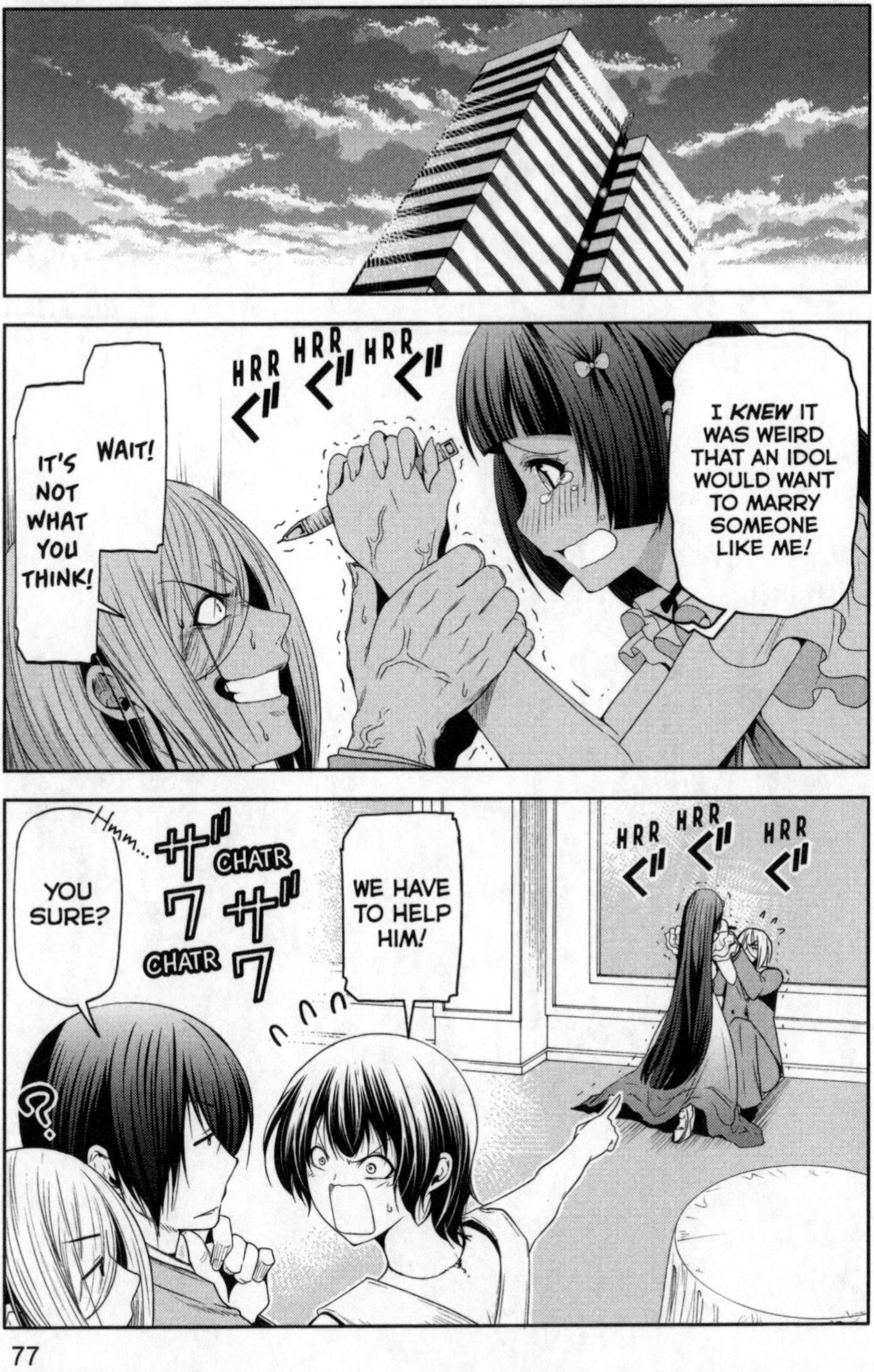
I KNEW IT WAS WEIRD THAT AN IDOL WOULD WANT TO MARRY SOMEONE LIKE ME!
HRR ぐ HRR ぐ HRR ぐ
WAIT! IT'S NOT WHAT YOU THINK!
HRR ぐ HRR ぐ HRR ぐ
WE HAVE TO HELP HIM!
ザワ CHATR ザワ CHATR
Hmm...
YOU SURE?

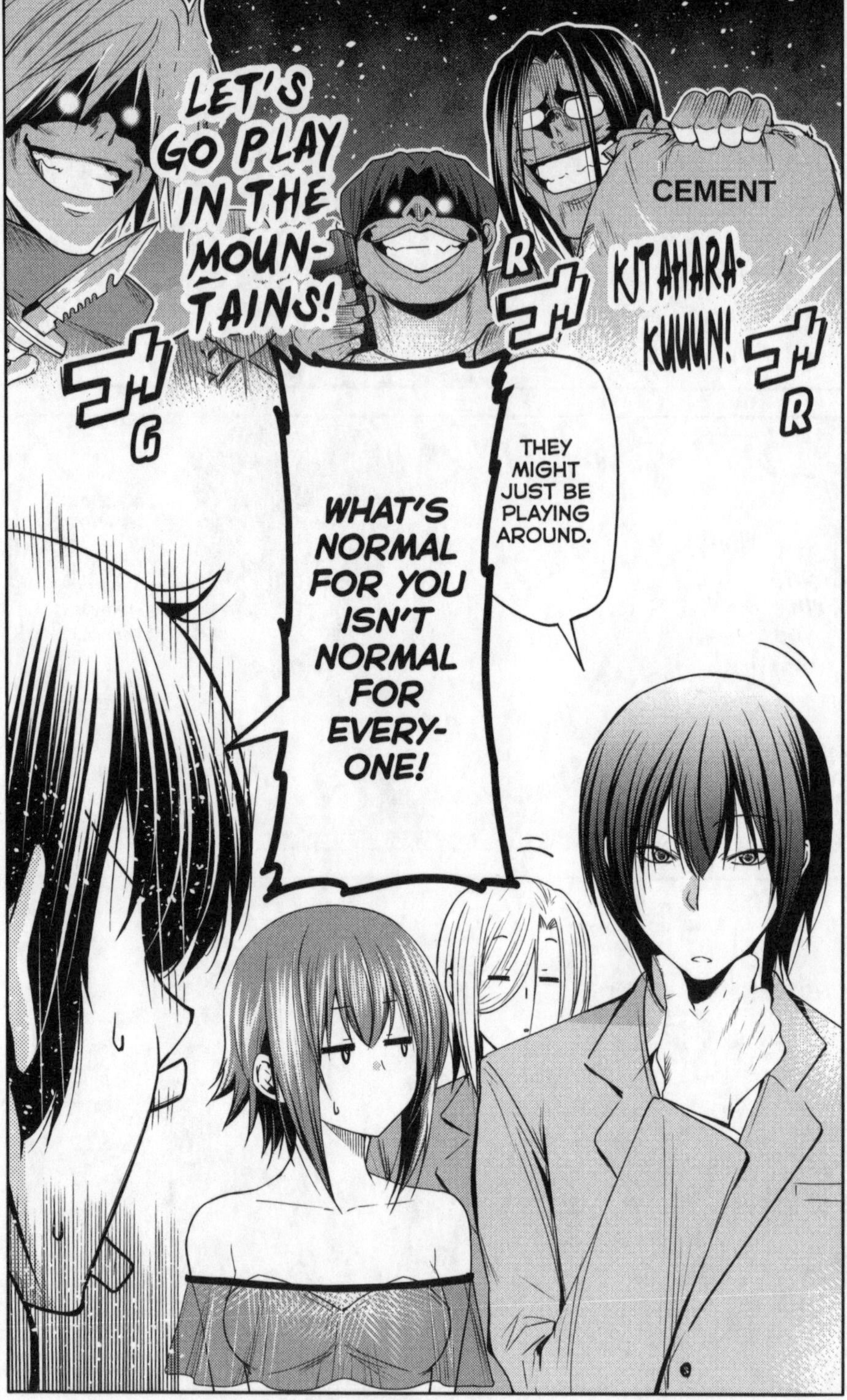
CEMENT
KITAHARA-KUUUN!
R
R
LET'S GO PLAY IN THE MOUN-TAINS!
G
THEY MIGHT JUST BE PLAYING AROUND.
WHAT'S NORMAL FOR YOU ISN'T NORMAL FOR EVERY-ONE!

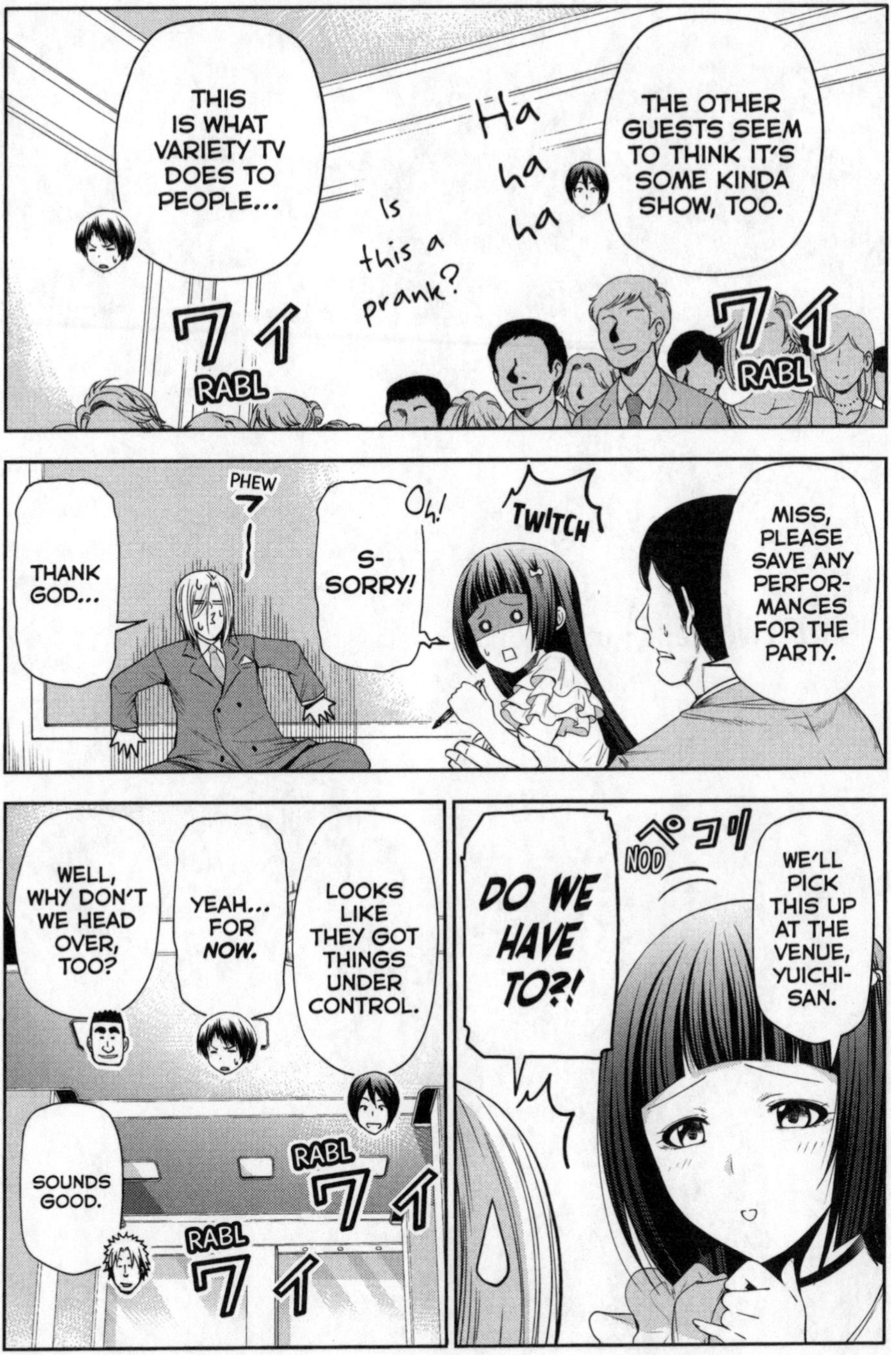
THE OTHER GUESTS SEEM TO THINK IT'S SOME KINDA SHOW, TOO.
Ha ha ha
Is this a prank?
THIS IS WHAT VARIETY TV DOES TO PEOPLE...
RABL
RABL
MISS, PLEASE SAVE ANY PERFORMANCES FOR THE PARTY.
TWITCH
Oh!
S-SORRY!
PHEW
THANK GOD...
NOD
WE'LL PICK THIS UP AT THE VENUE, YUICHI-SAN.
DO WE HAVE TO?!
LOOKS LIKE THEY GOT THINGS UNDER CONTROL.
YEAH... FOR NOW.
WELL, WHY DON'T WE HEAD OVER, TOO?
RABL
SOUNDS GOOD.
RABL

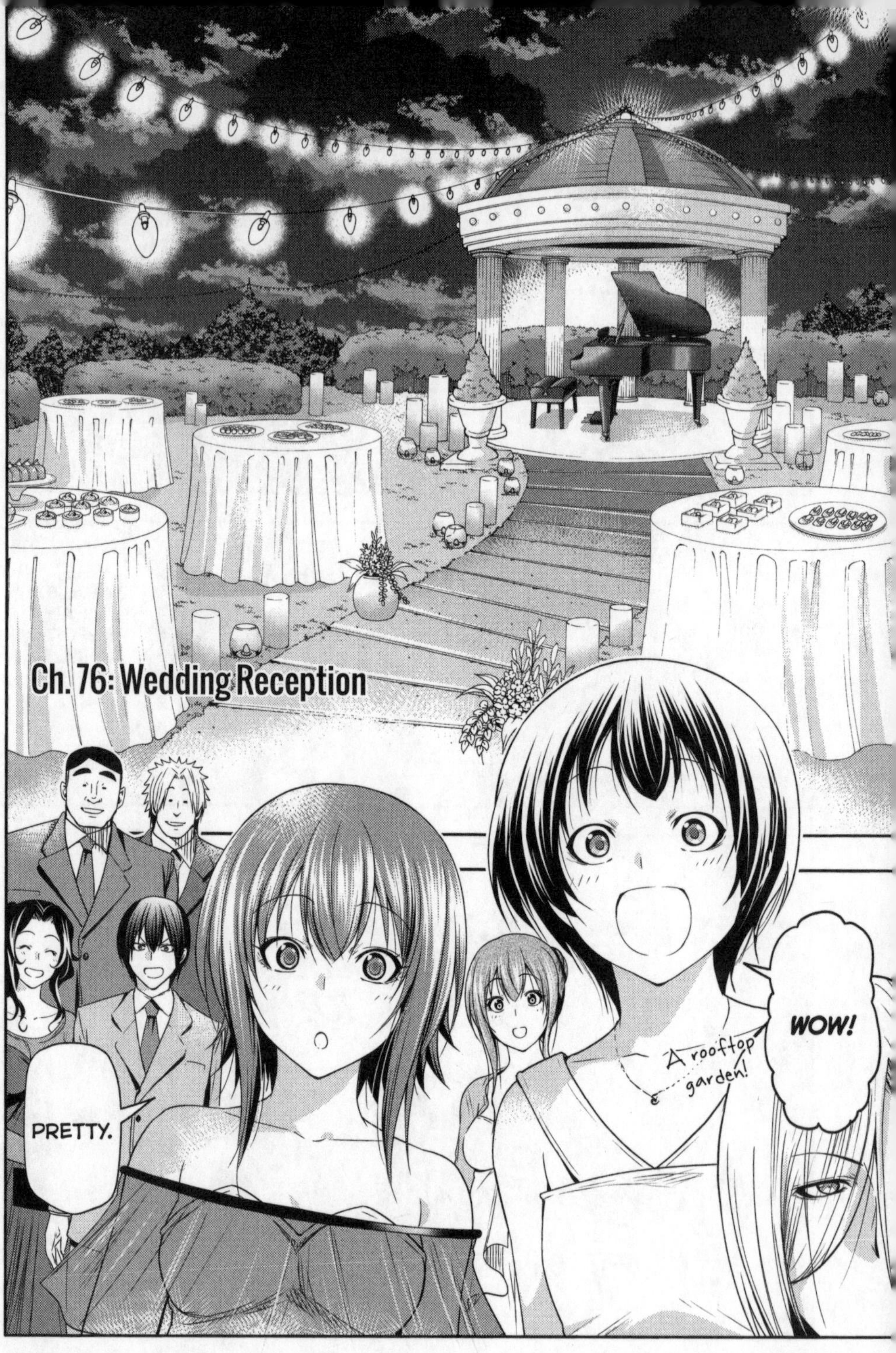
Ch. 76: Wedding Reception
WOW!
A rooftop garden!
PRETTY.

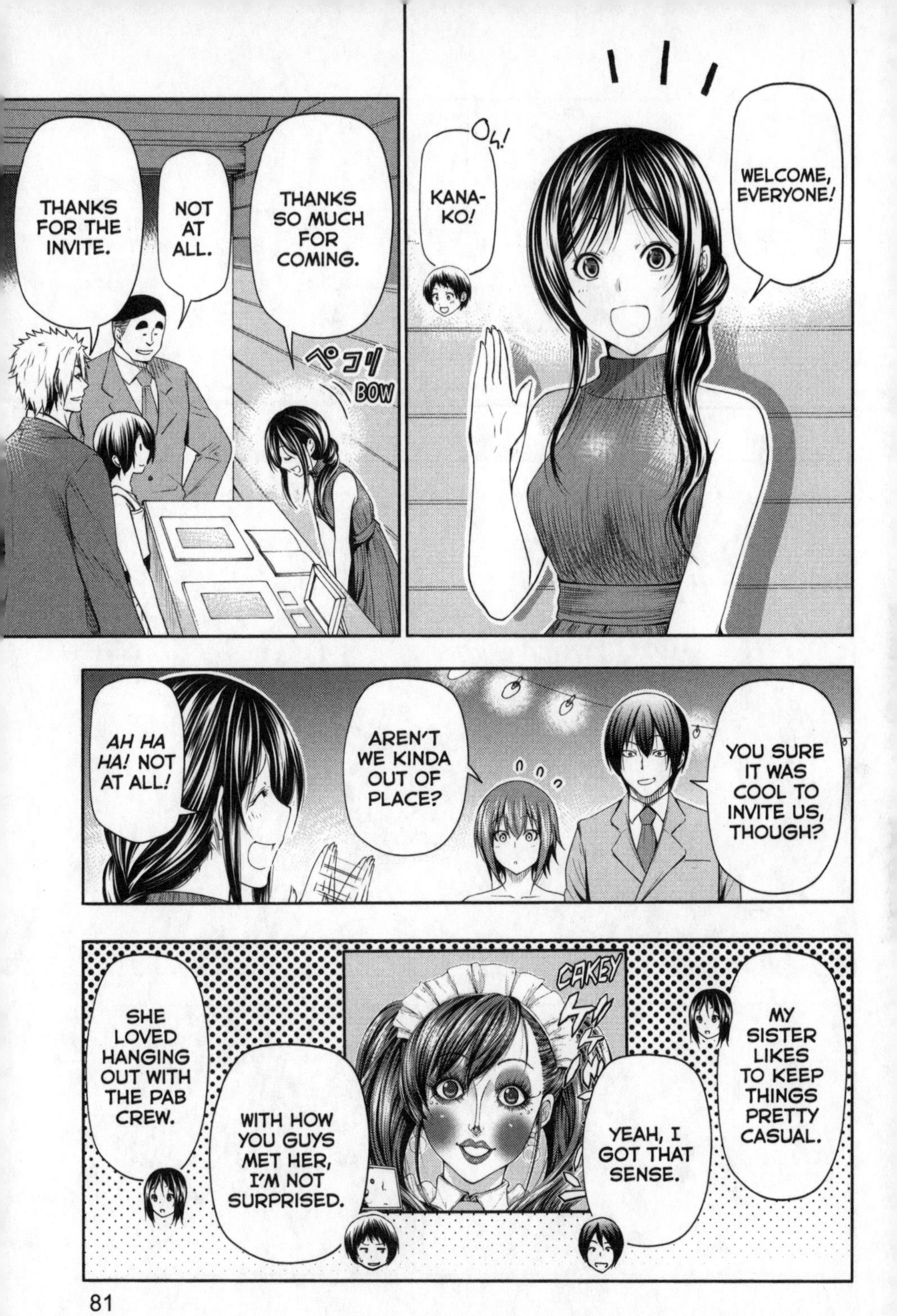
WELCOME, EVERYONE!
Oh!
KANA-KO!
THANKS SO MUCH FOR COMING.
ペコリ
BOW
NOT AT ALL.
THANKS FOR THE INVITE.
YOU SURE IT WAS COOL TO INVITE US, THOUGH?
AREN'T WE KINDA OUT OF PLACE?
AH HA HA! NOT AT ALL!
MY SISTER LIKES TO KEEP THINGS PRETTY CASUAL.
YEAH, I GOT THAT SENSE.
CAKEY
WITH HOW YOU GUYS MET HER, I'M NOT SURPRISED.
SHE LOVED HANGING OUT WITH THE PAB CREW.

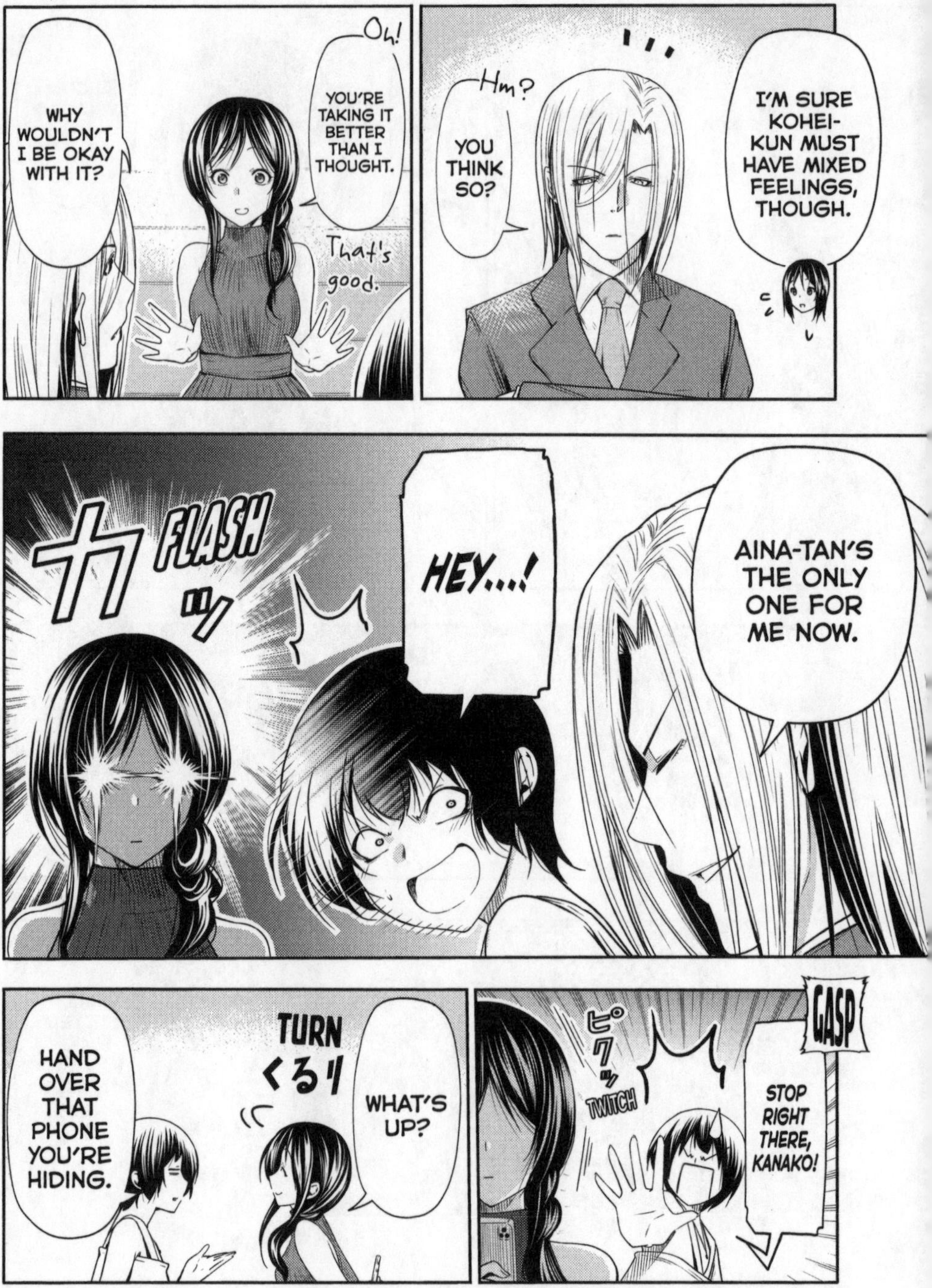
I'M SURE KOHEI-KUN MUST HAVE MIXED FEELINGS, THOUGH.
Hm?
YOU THINK SO?
Oh!
YOU'RE TAKING IT BETTER THAN I THOUGHT.
That's good.
WHY WOULDN'T I BE OKAY WITH IT?
AINA-TAN'S THE ONLY ONE FOR ME NOW.
HEY...!
カッ
FLASH
GASP
STOP RIGHT THERE, KANAKO!
ピクッ
TWITCH
WHAT'S UP?
くるり
TURN
HAND OVER THAT PHONE YOU'RE HIDING.

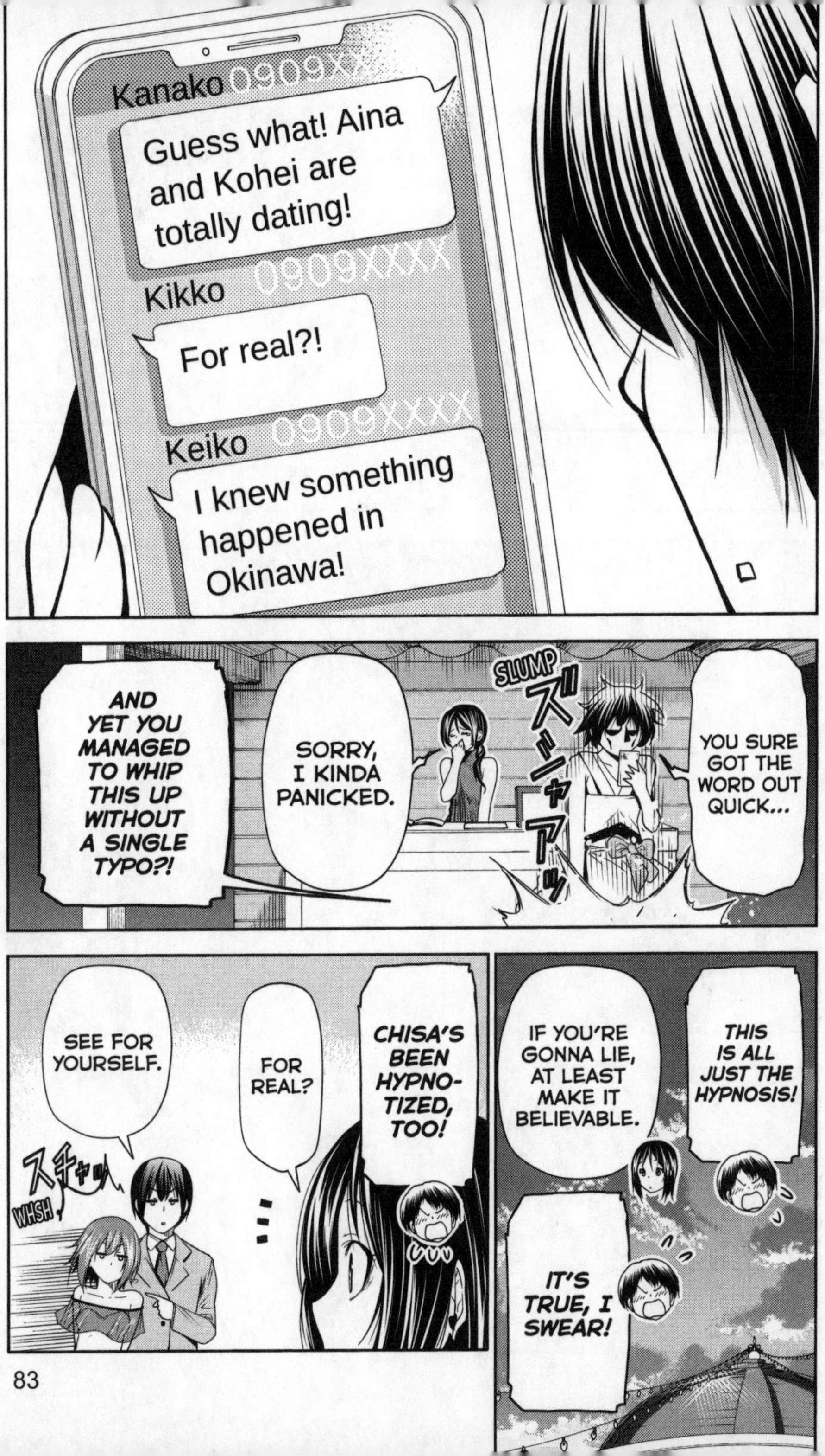
Kanako
Guess what! Aina and Kohei are totally dating!
Kikko 0909XXXX
For real?!
Keiko 0909XXXX
I knew something happened in Okinawa!
YOU SURE GOT THE WORD OUT QUICK...
SLUMP
SORRY, I KINDA PANICKED.
AND YET YOU MANAGED TO WHIP THIS UP WITHOUT A SINGLE TYPO?!
THIS IS ALL JUST THE HYPNOSIS!
IF YOU'RE GONNA LIE, AT LEAST MAKE IT BELIEVABLE.
IT'S TRUE, I SWEAR!
CHISA'S BEEN HYPNO-TIZED, TOO!
FOR REAL?
SEE FOR YOURSELF.
WHSH

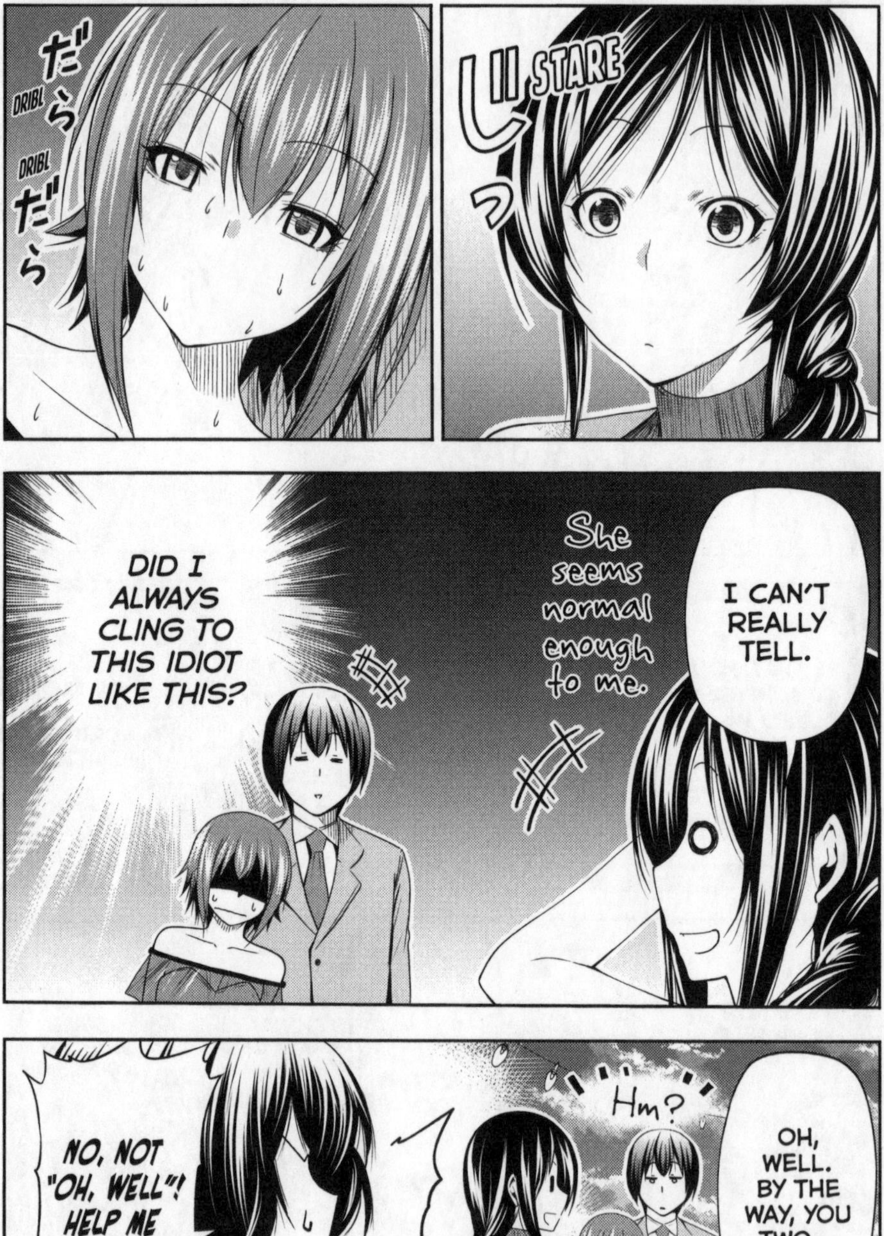
じっ
STARE
だらだら
DRIBL DRIBL
I CAN'T REALLY TELL.
She seems normal enough to me.
DID I ALWAYS CLING TO THIS IDIOT LIKE THIS?
OH, WELL. BY THE WAY, YOU TWO...
Hm?
...
NO, NOT "OH, WELL"! HELP ME FIX THIS!

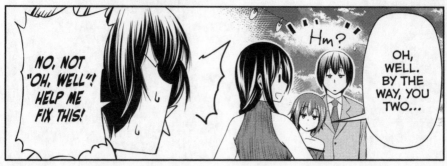

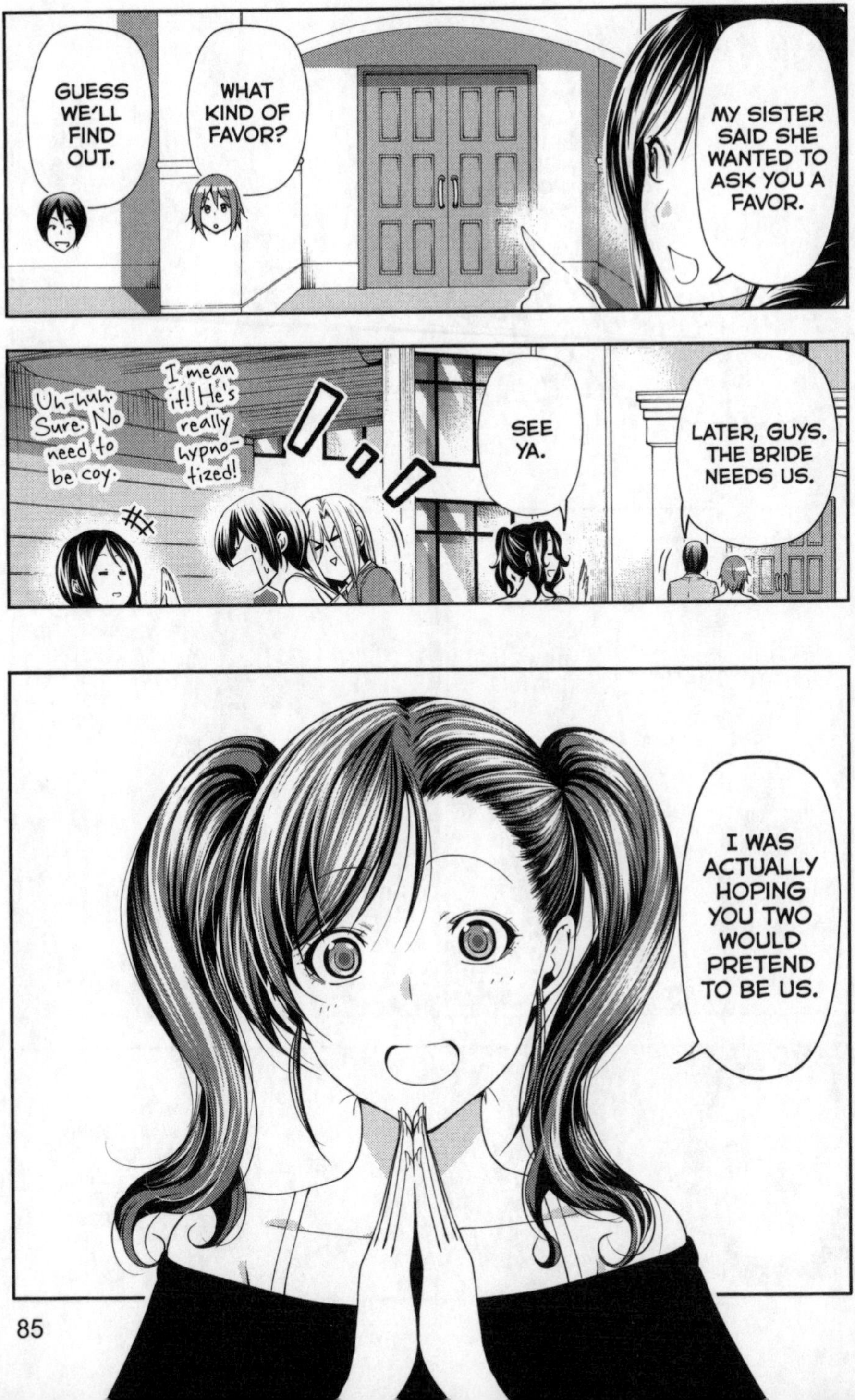
MY SISTER SAID SHE WANTED TO ASK YOU A FAVOR.
WHAT KIND OF FAVOR?
GUESS WE'LL FIND OUT.
LATER, GUYS. THE BRIDE NEEDS US.
SEE YA.
I mean it! He's really hypno-tized!
Uh-huh. Sure. No need to be coy.
I WAS ACTUALLY HOPING YOU TWO WOULD PRETEND TO BE US.

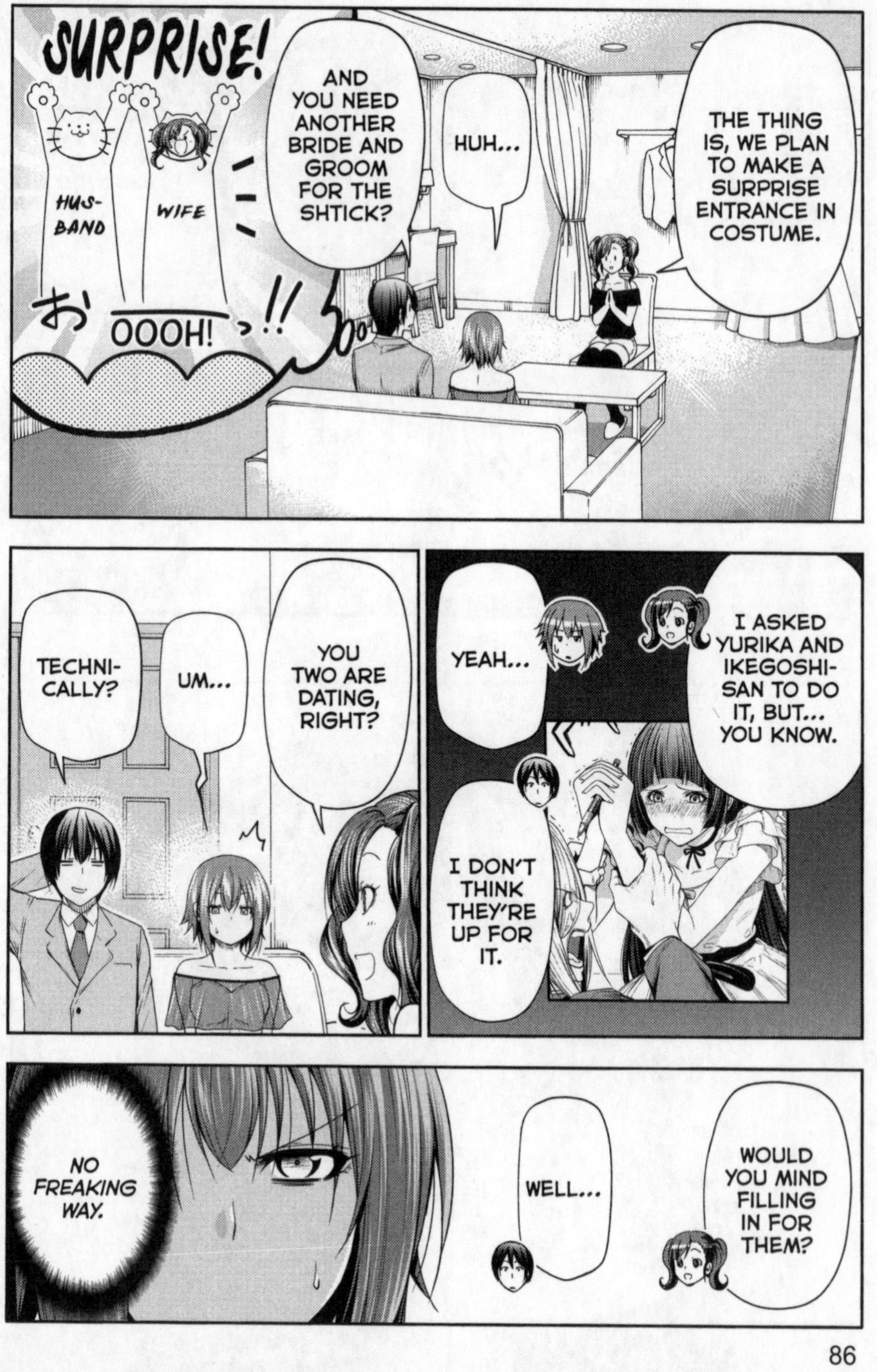
THE THING IS, WE PLAN TO MAKE A SURPRISE ENTRANCE IN COSTUME.
HUH...
AND YOU NEED ANOTHER BRIDE AND GROOM FOR THE SHTICK?
SURPRISE!
HUS-BAND
WIFE
お OOOH! っ!!
I ASKED YURIKA AND IKEGOSHI-SAN TO DO IT, BUT... YOU KNOW.
YEAH...
I DON'T THINK THEY'RE UP FOR IT.
YOU TWO ARE DATING, RIGHT?
UM...
TECHNI-CALLY?
WOULD YOU MIND FILLING IN FOR THEM?
WELL...
NO FREAKING WAY.

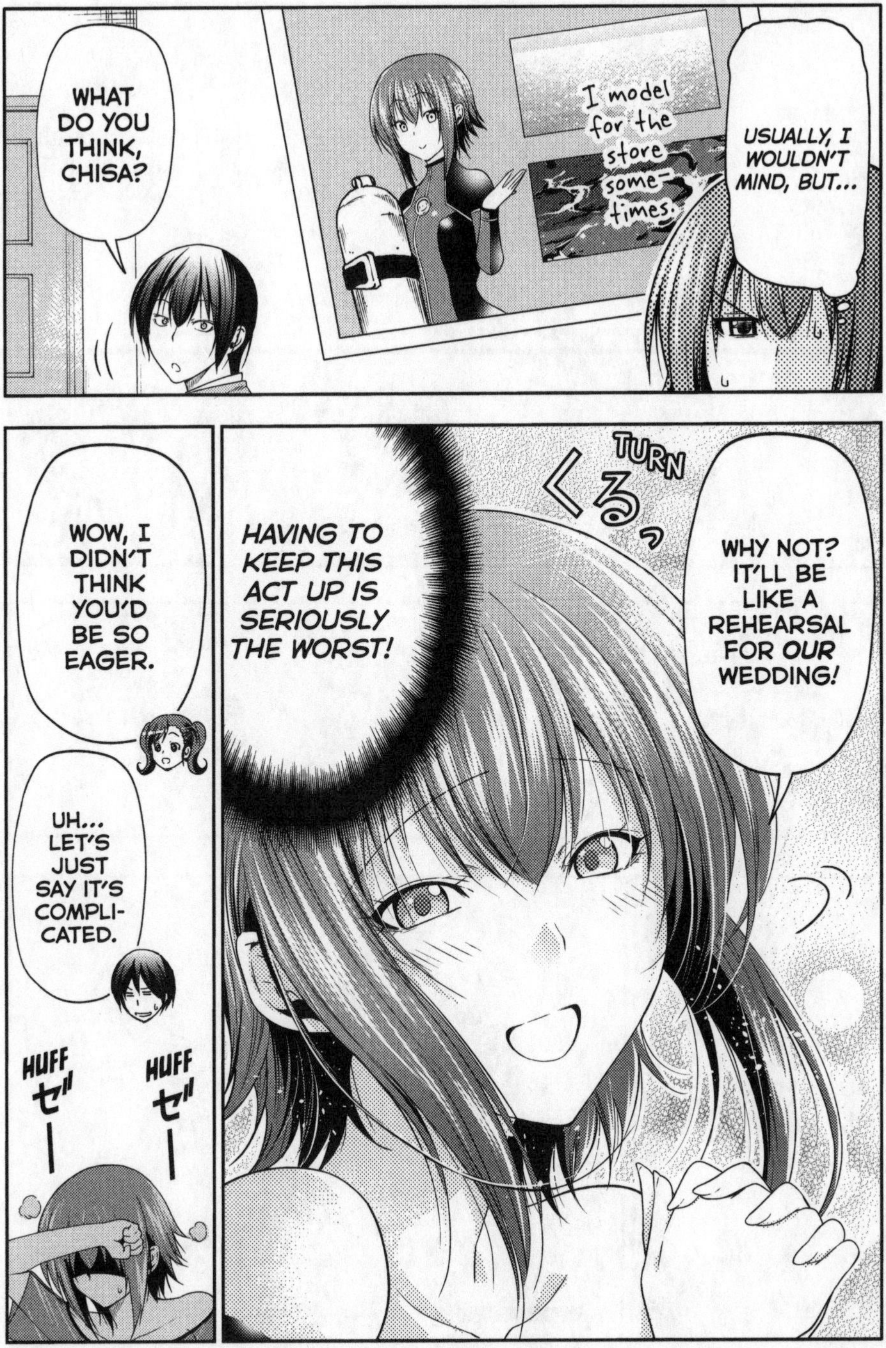
USUALLY, I WOULDN'T MIND, BUT...
I model for the store some-times.
WHAT DO YOU THINK, CHISA?
TURN
くるっ
WHY NOT? IT'LL BE LIKE A REHEARSAL FOR *OUR* WEDDING!
HAVING TO KEEP THIS ACT UP IS SERIOUSLY THE WORST!
WOW, I DIDN'T THINK YOU'D BE SO EAGER.
UH... LET'S JUST SAY IT'S COMPLICATED.
HUFF
ゼー
HUFF
ゼー

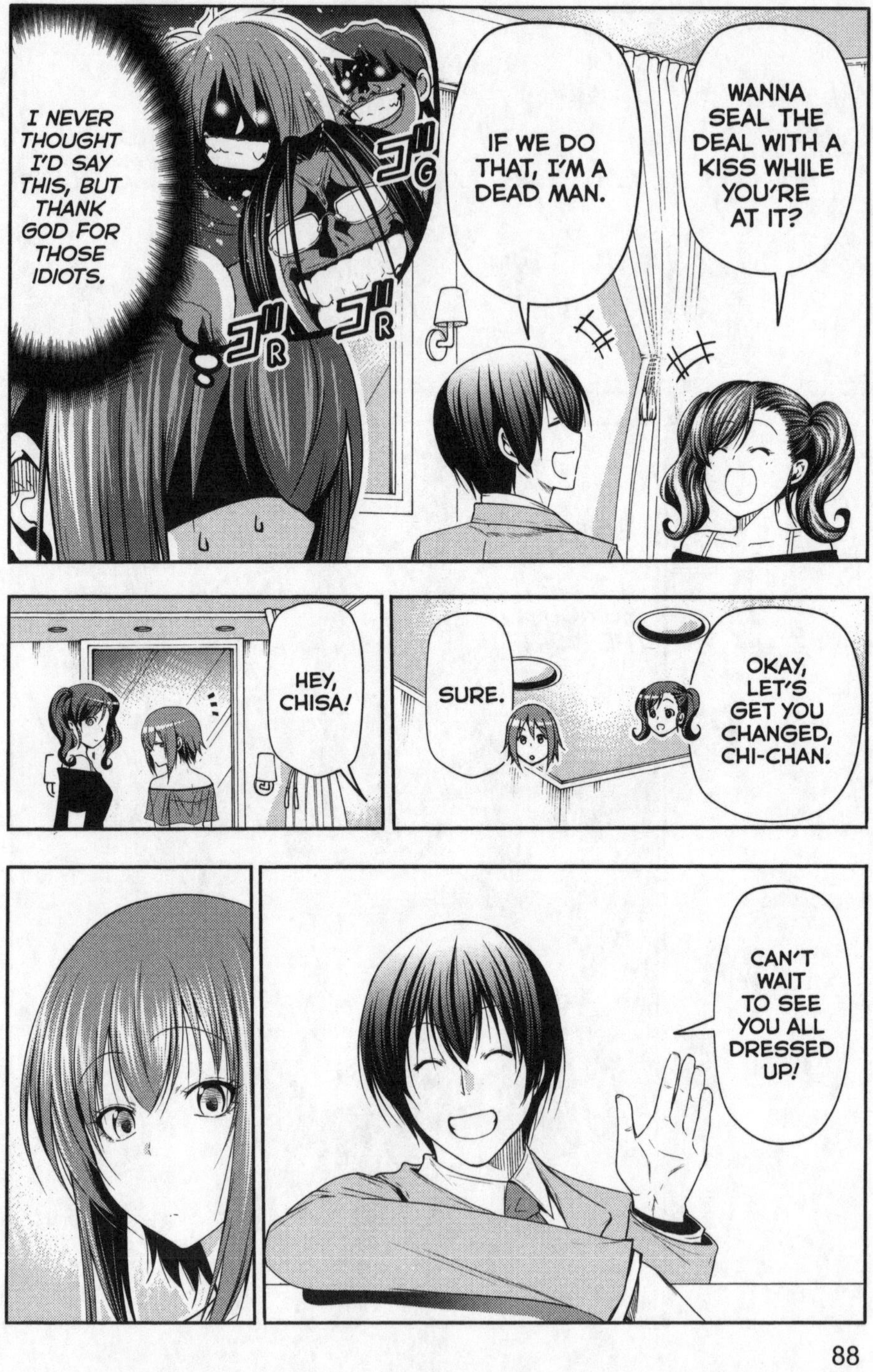
WANNA SEAL THE DEAL WITH A KISS WHILE YOU'RE AT IT?
IF WE DO THAT, I'M A DEAD MAN.
I NEVER THOUGHT I'D SAY THIS, BUT THANK GOD FOR THOSE IDIOTS.
OKAY, LET'S GET YOU CHANGED, CHI-CHAN.
SURE.
HEY, CHISA!
CAN'T WAIT TO SEE YOU ALL DRESSED UP!

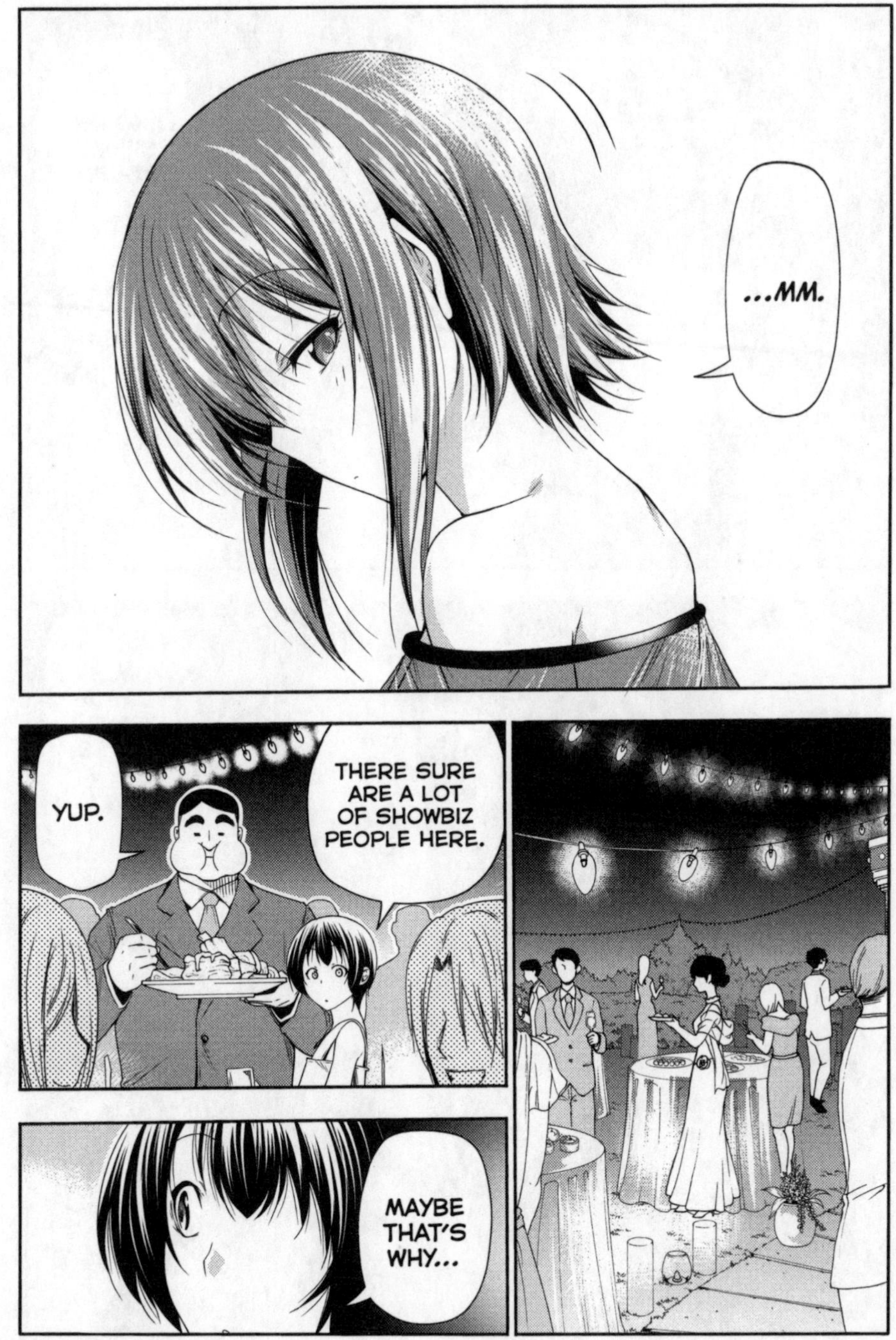
...MM.
THERE SURE ARE A LOT OF SHOWBIZ PEOPLE HERE.
YUP.
MAYBE THAT'S WHY...

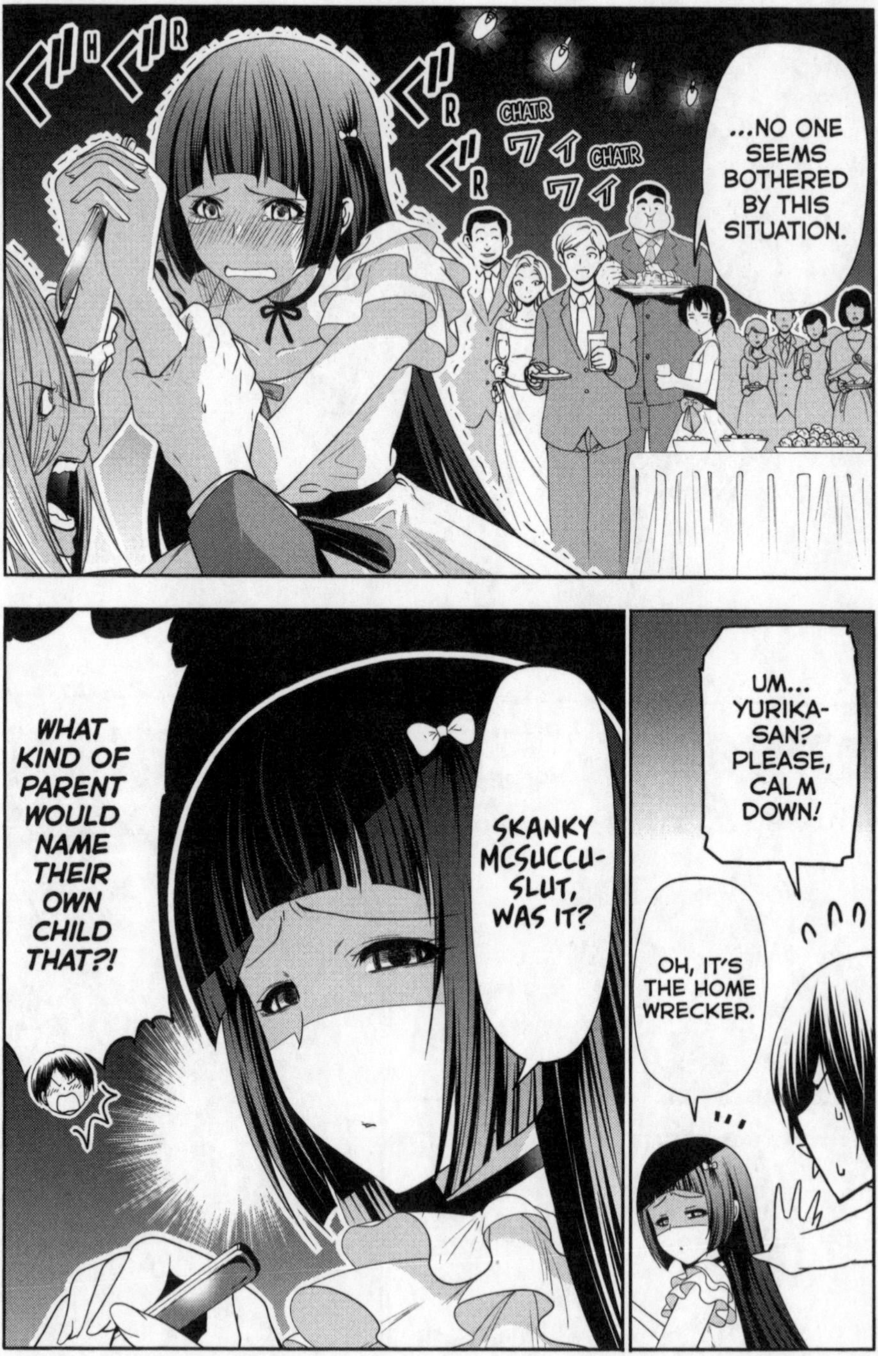
...NO ONE SEEMS BOTHERED BY THIS SITUATION.
CHATR
ワイ
CHATR
ワイ
UM... YURIKA-SAN? PLEASE, CALM DOWN!
OH, IT'S THE HOME WRECKER.
SKANKY MCSUCCU-SLUT, WAS IT?
WHAT KIND OF PARENT WOULD NAME THEIR OWN CHILD THAT?!

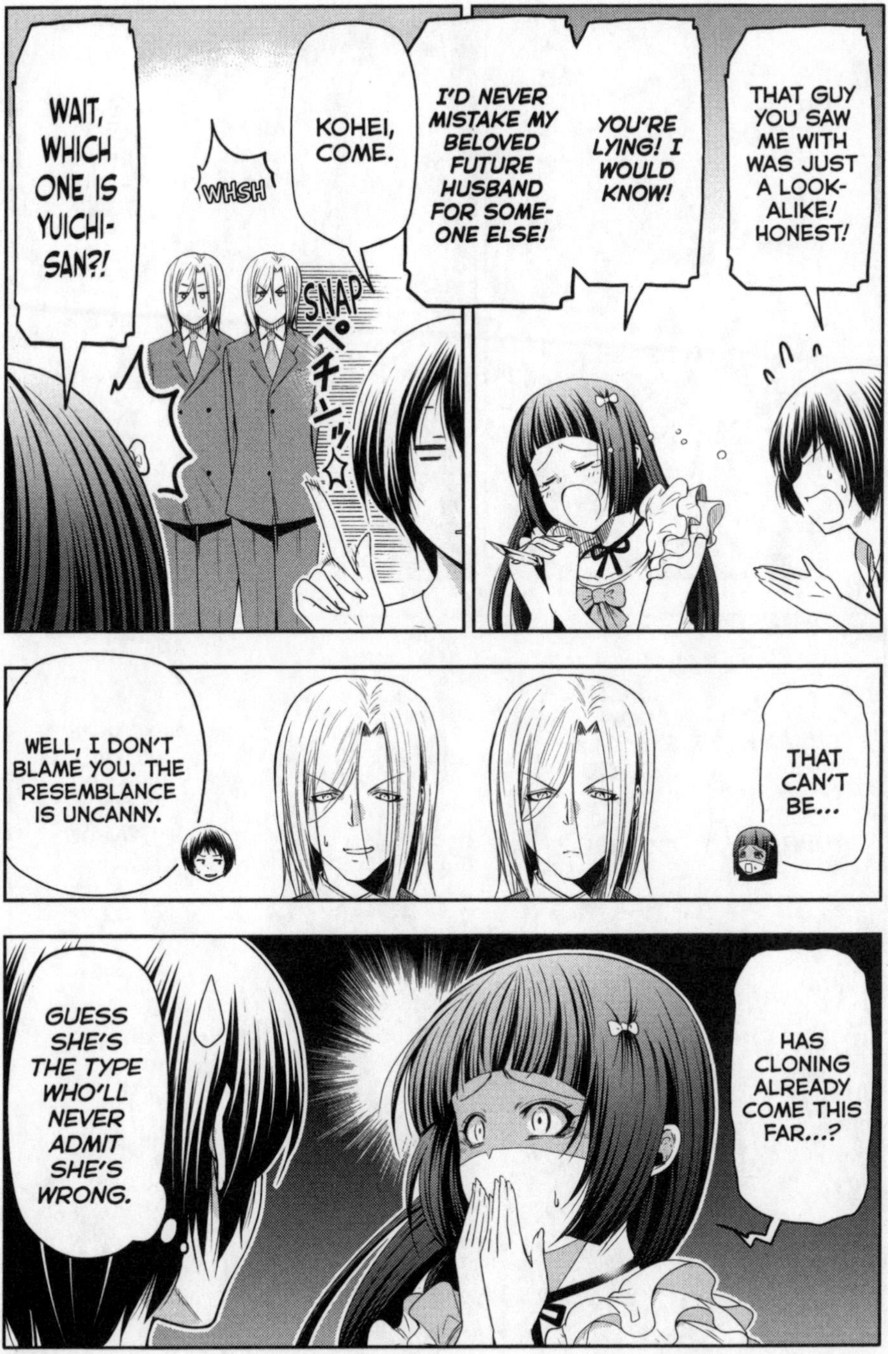
THAT GUY YOU SAW ME WITH WAS JUST A LOOK-ALIKE! HONEST!
YOU'RE LYING! I WOULD KNOW!
I'D NEVER MISTAKE MY BELOVED FUTURE HUSBAND FOR SOME-ONE ELSE!
KOHEI, COME.
SNAP
ペチンッ
WHSH
WAIT, WHICH ONE IS YUICHI-SAN?!
THAT CAN'T BE...
WELL, I DON'T BLAME YOU. THE RESEMBLANCE IS UNCANNY.
HAS CLONING ALREADY COME THIS FAR...?
GUESS SHE'S THE TYPE WHO'LL NEVER ADMIT SHE'S WRONG.

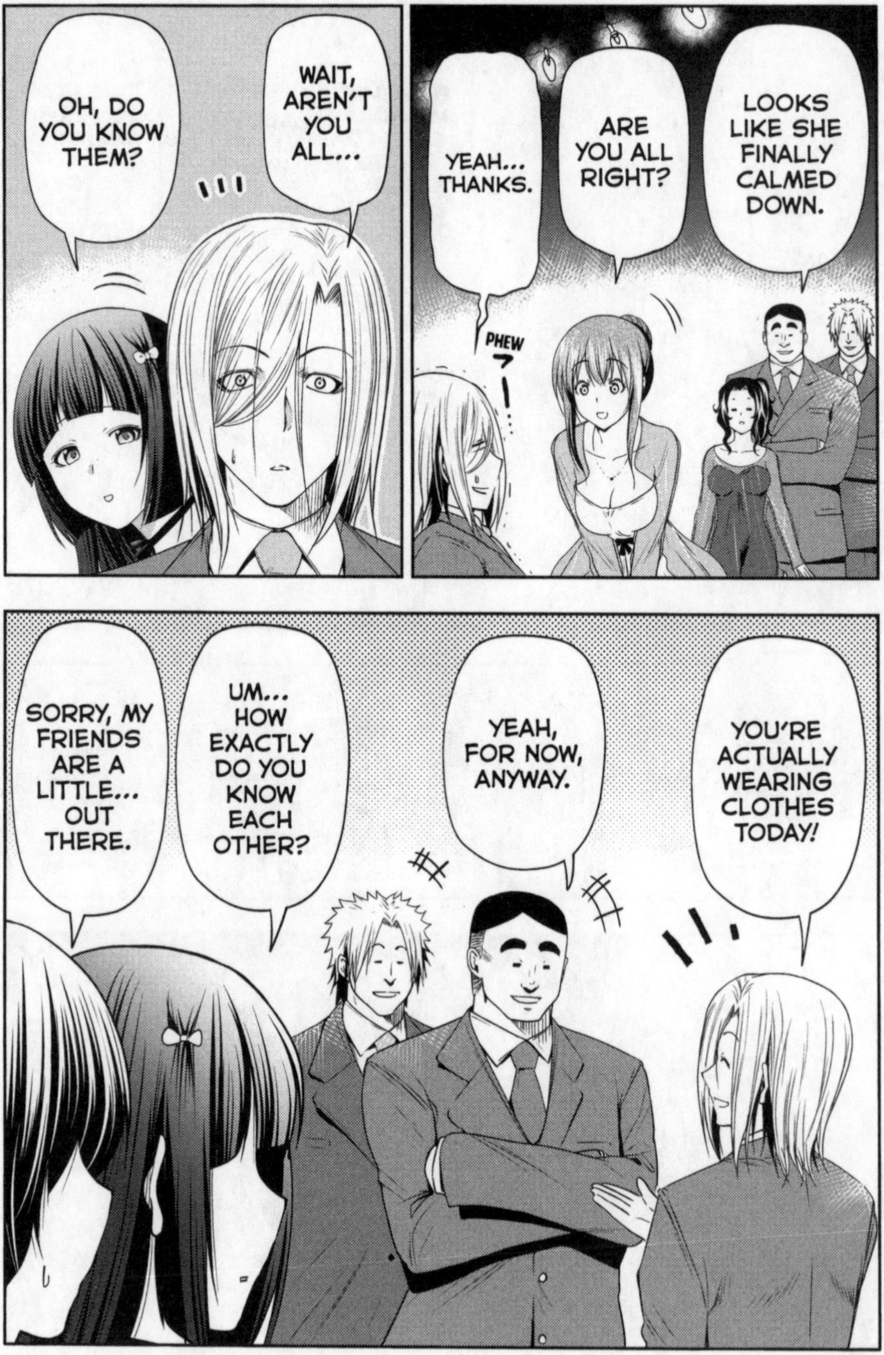
LOOKS LIKE SHE FINALLY CALMED DOWN.
ARE YOU ALL RIGHT?
YEAH... THANKS.
PHEW
WAIT, AREN'T YOU ALL...
OH, DO YOU KNOW THEM?
YOU'RE ACTUALLY WEARING CLOTHES TODAY!
YEAH, FOR NOW, ANYWAY.
UM... HOW EXACTLY DO YOU KNOW EACH OTHER?
SORRY, MY FRIENDS ARE A LITTLE... OUT THERE.

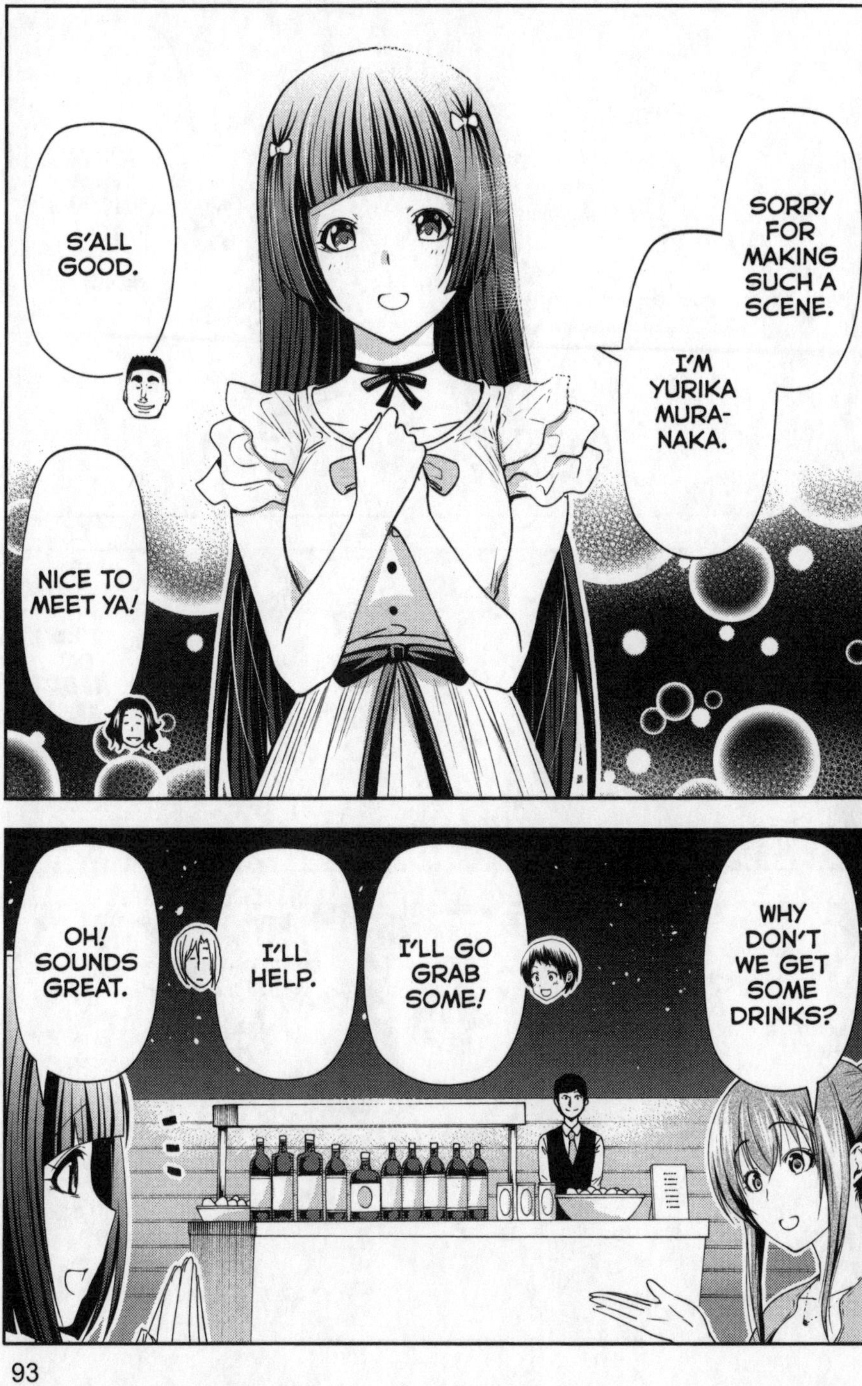
SORRY FOR MAKING SUCH A SCENE.
I'M YURIKA MURA-NAKA.
S'ALL GOOD.
NICE TO MEET YA!
WHY DON'T WE GET SOME DRINKS?
I'LL GO GRAB SOME!
I'LL HELP.
OH! SOUNDS GREAT.

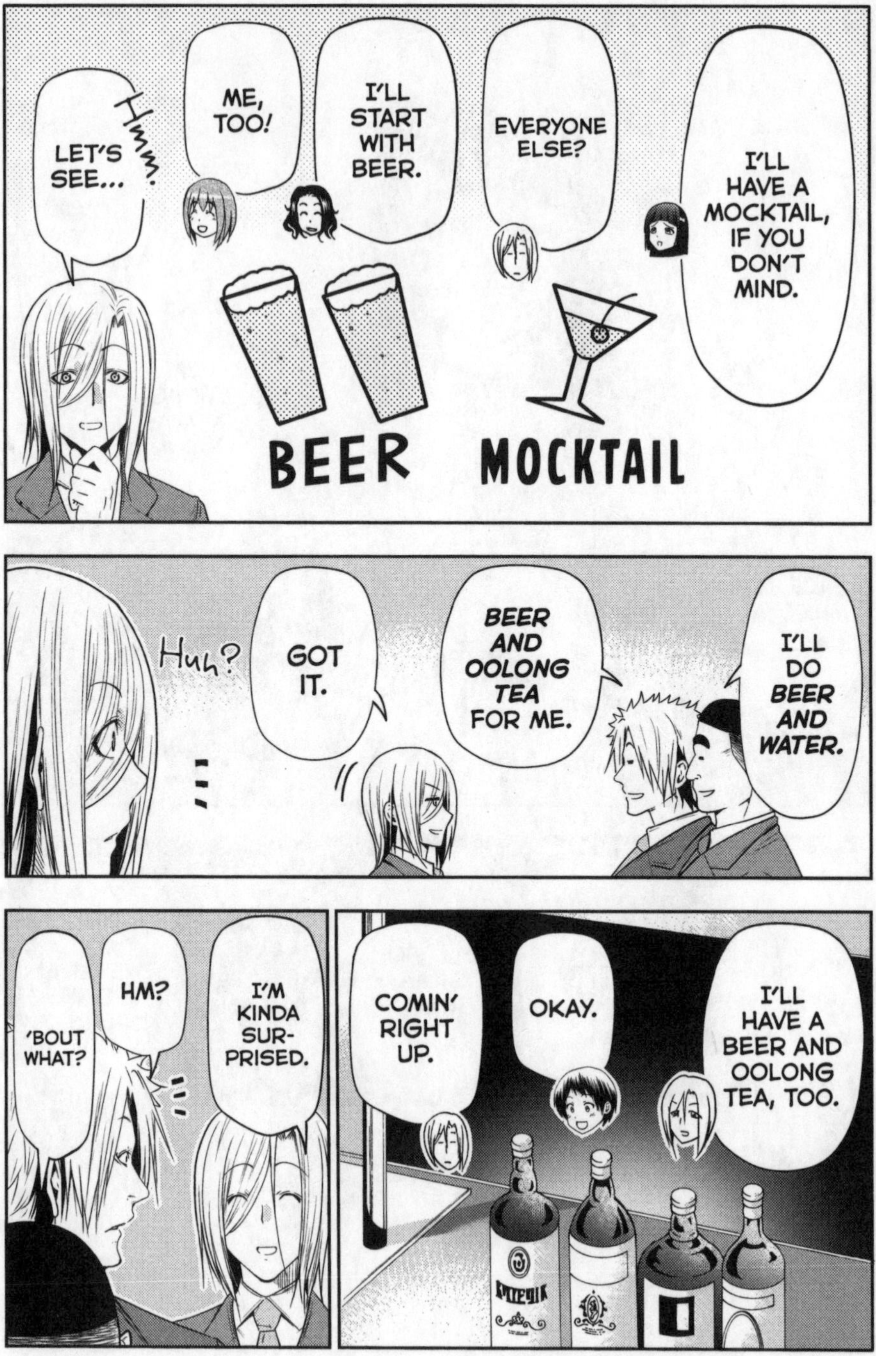
I'LL HAVE A MOCKTAIL, IF YOU DON'T MIND.
EVERYONE ELSE?
I'LL START WITH BEER.
ME, TOO!
Hmm.
LET'S SEE...
MOCKTAIL
BEER
I'LL DO BEER AND WATER.
BEER AND OOLONG TEA FOR ME.
GOT IT.
Huh?
I'LL HAVE A BEER AND OOLONG TEA, TOO.
OKAY.
COMIN' RIGHT UP.
I'M KINDA SURPRISED.
HM?
'BOUT WHAT?

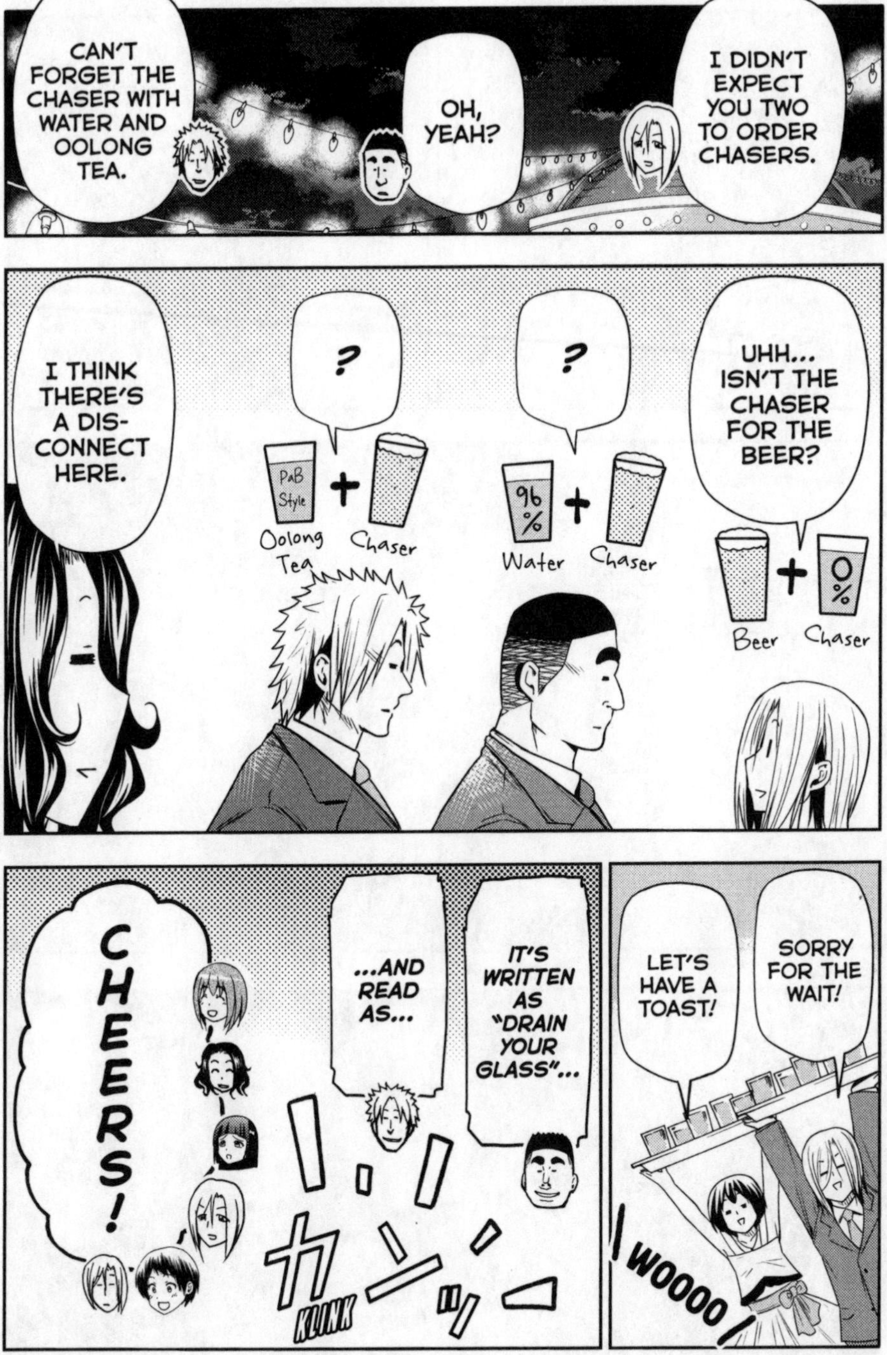
I DIDN'T EXPECT YOU TWO TO ORDER CHASERS.
OH, YEAH?
CAN'T FORGET THE CHASER WITH WATER AND OOLONG TEA.
UHH... ISN'T THE CHASER FOR THE BEER?
Beer
0%
Chaser
?
96 %
Water
Chaser
?
PaB Style
Oolong Tea
Chaser
I THINK THERE'S A DIS-CONNECT HERE.
SORRY FOR THE WAIT!
LET'S HAVE A TOAST!
WOOOO!
IT'S WRITTEN AS "DRAIN YOUR GLASS"...
...AND READ AS...
CHEERS!
カンッ
KLINK

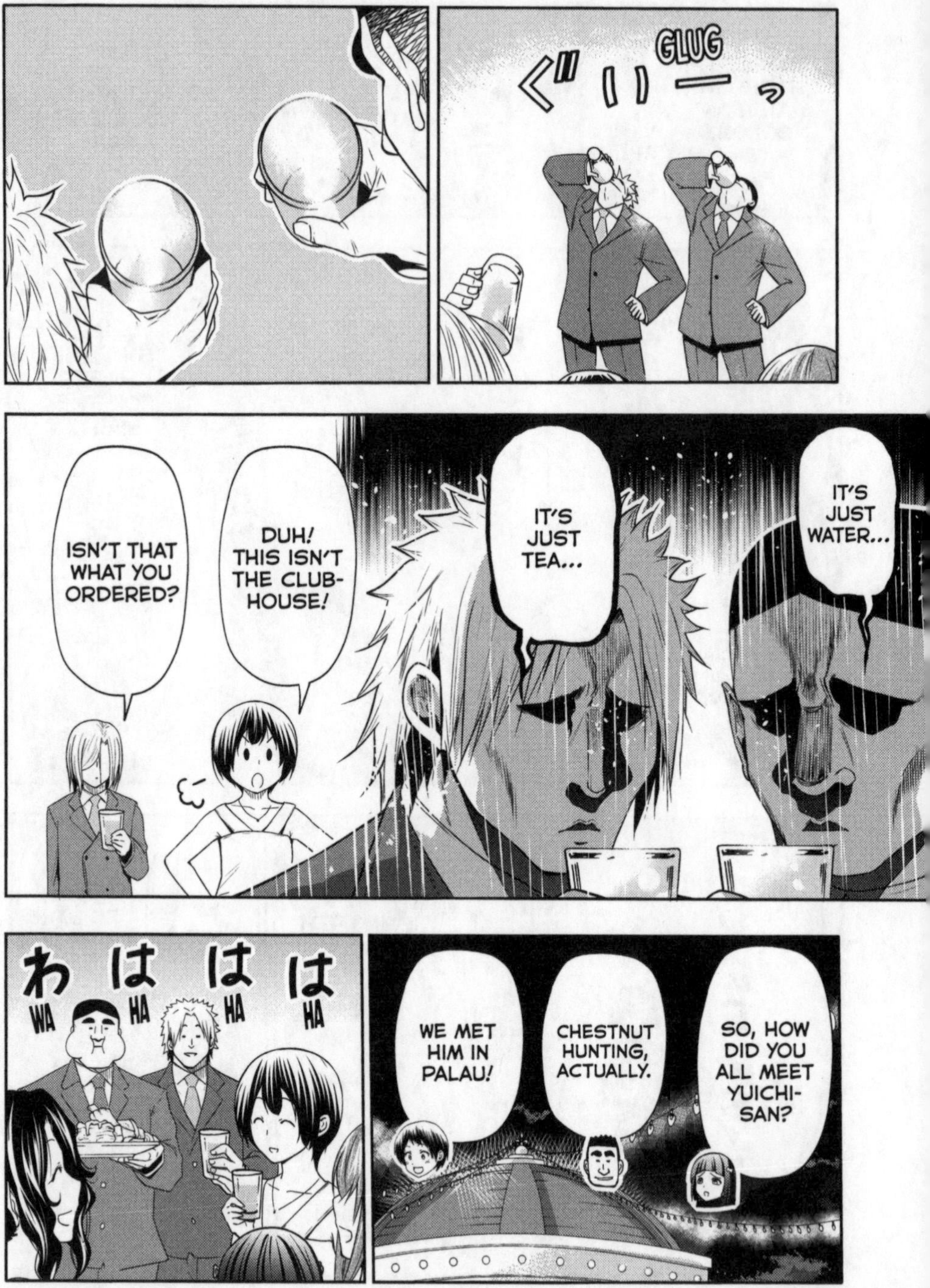
GLUG
ぐいーっ
IT'S JUST WATER...
IT'S JUST TEA...
DUH! THIS ISN'T THE CLUB-HOUSE!
ISN'T THAT WHAT YOU ORDERED?
SO, HOW DID YOU ALL MEET YUICHI-SAN?
CHESTNUT HUNTING, ACTUALLY.
WE MET HIM IN PALAU!
わははは
WA HA HA HA

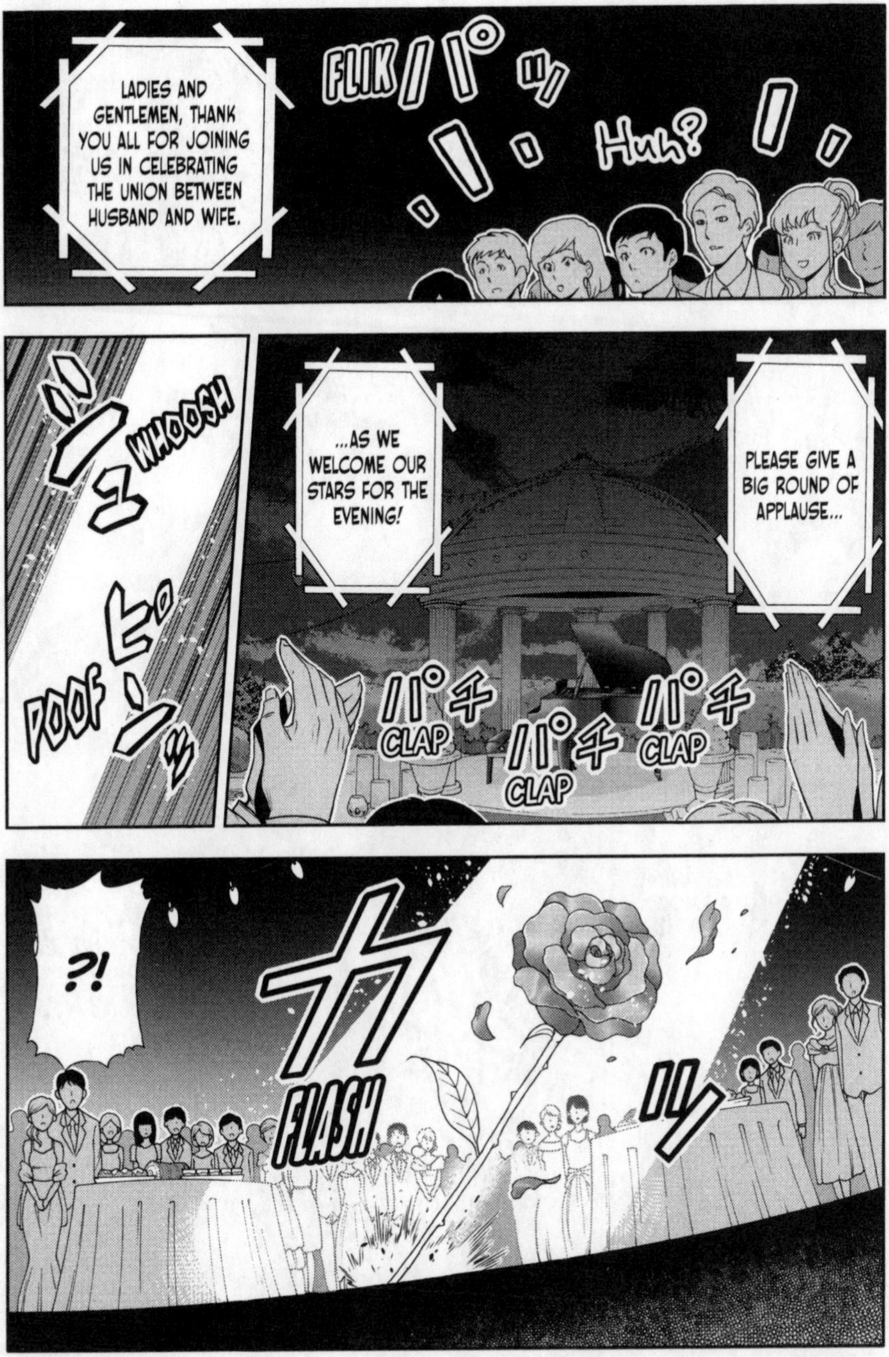
FLIK
Huh?
LADIES AND GENTLEMEN, THANK YOU ALL FOR JOINING US IN CELEBRATING THE UNION BETWEEN HUSBAND AND WIFE.
PLEASE GIVE A BIG ROUND OF APPLAUSE...
...AS WE WELCOME OUR STARS FOR THE EVENING!
CLAP
CLAP
CLAP
WHOOSH
POOF
FLASH
?!

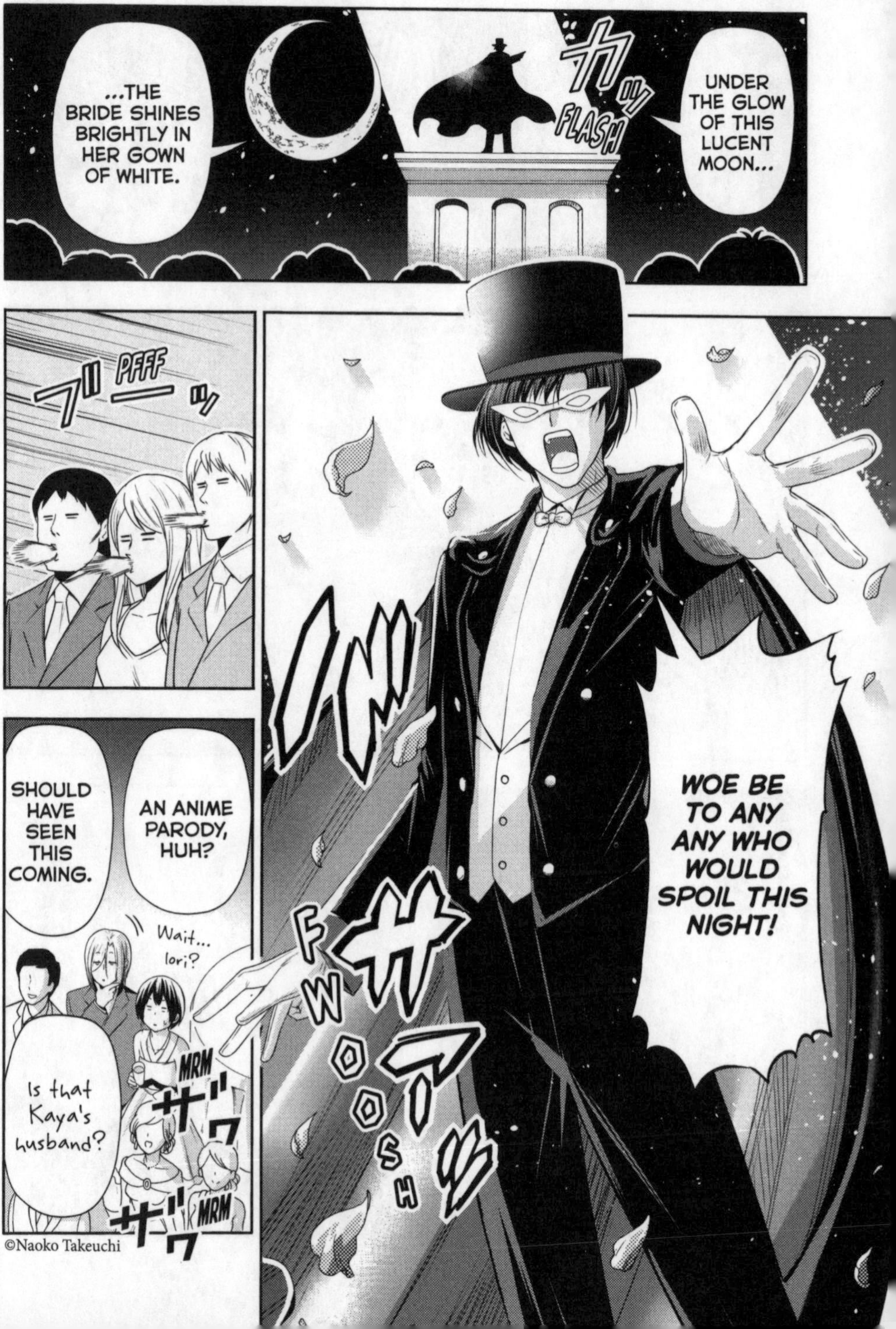
UNDER THE GLOW OF THIS LUCENT MOON...
FLASH
...THE BRIDE SHINES BRIGHTLY IN HER GOWN OF WHITE.
WOE BE TO ANY ANY WHO WOULD SPOIL THIS NIGHT!
FWOOSH
PFFF
AN ANIME PARODY, HUH?
SHOULD HAVE SEEN THIS COMING.
Wait... Iori?
Is that Kaya's husband?
MRM
MRM

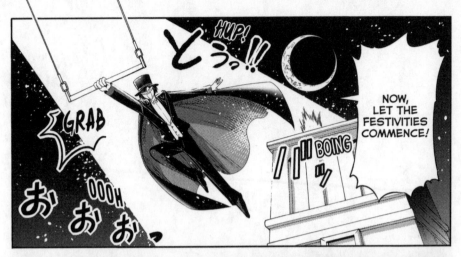

NOW, LET THE FESTIVITIES COMMENCE!
とうっ!!
HUP!
BOING
GRAB
おおおっ
OOOH
AAH-EE-AAH!
EE-AH-EE-AAH!
カッ
FLASH
I KNOW THAT OUTLINE!
SAILOR UNIFORMS ARE FINE AND ALL...
...BUT TONIGHT, I'M FEELING BRIDAL!

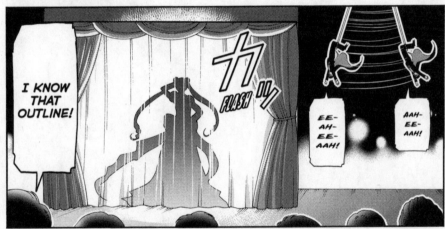

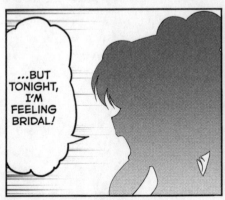

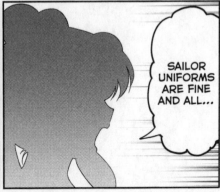

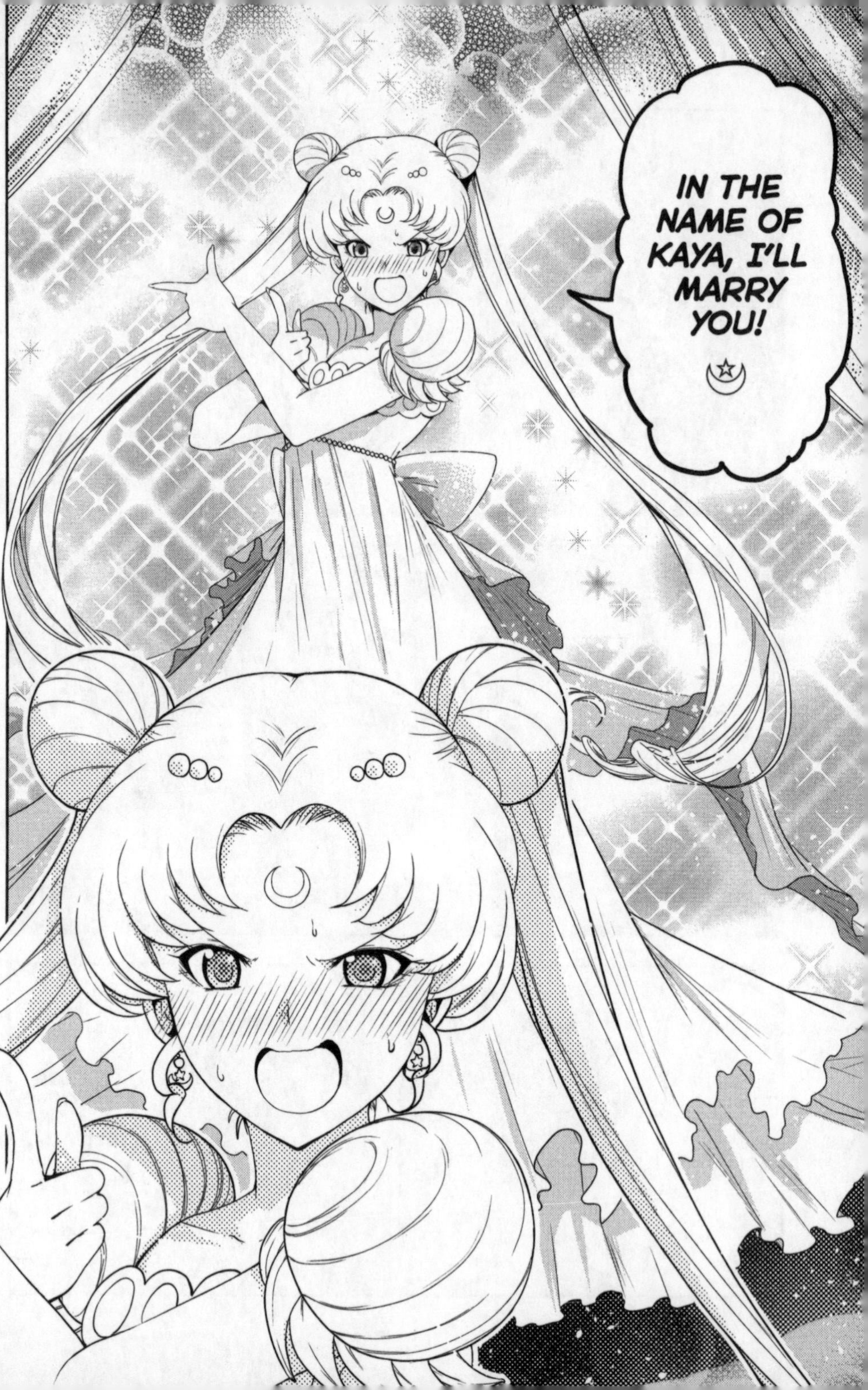
IN THE NAME OF KAYA, I'LL MARRY YOU!

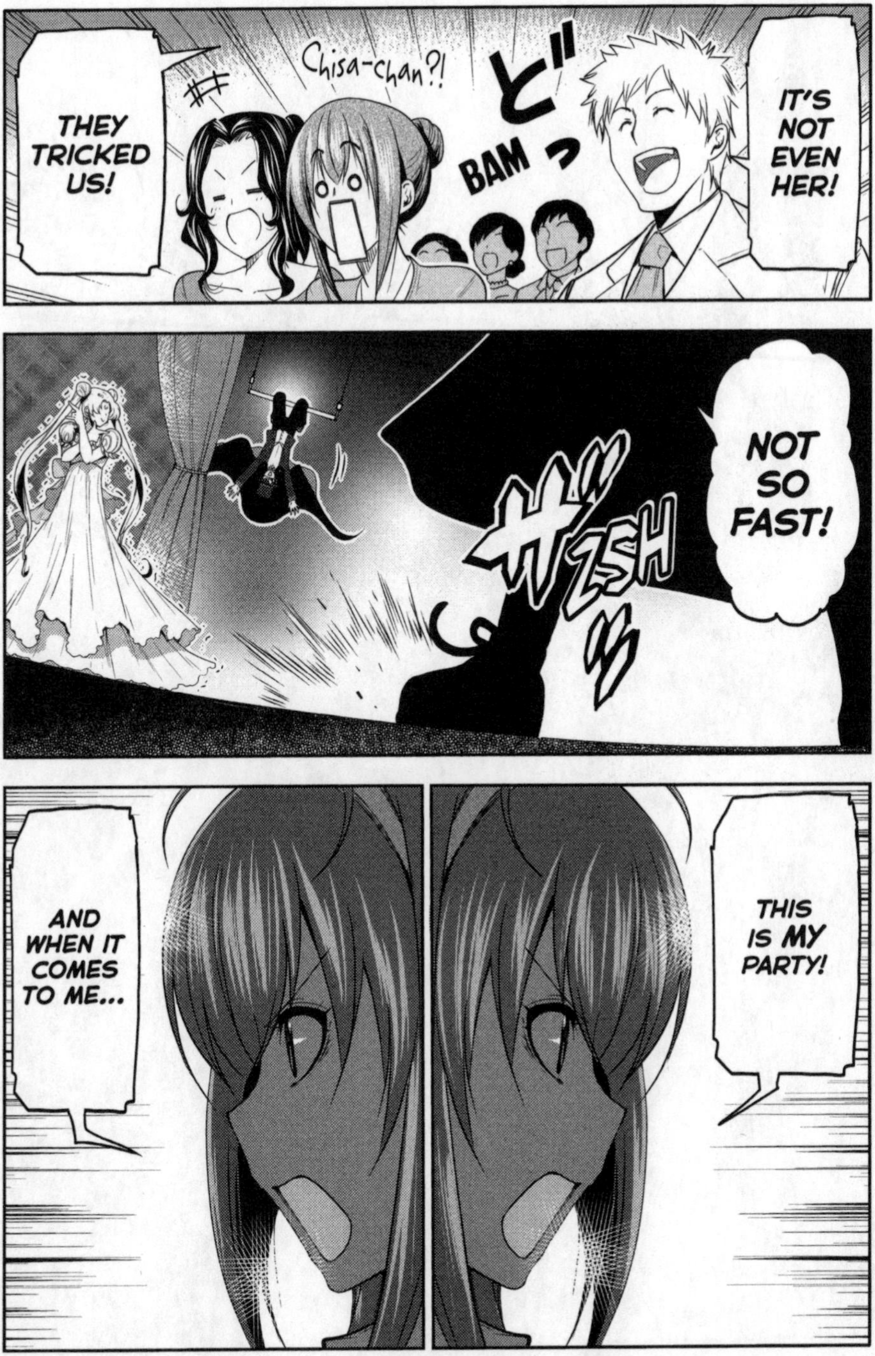
IT'S NOT EVEN HER!
BAM
Chisa-chan?!
THEY TRICKED US!
NOT SO FAST!
ZSH
THIS IS MY PARTY!
AND WHEN IT COMES TO ME...

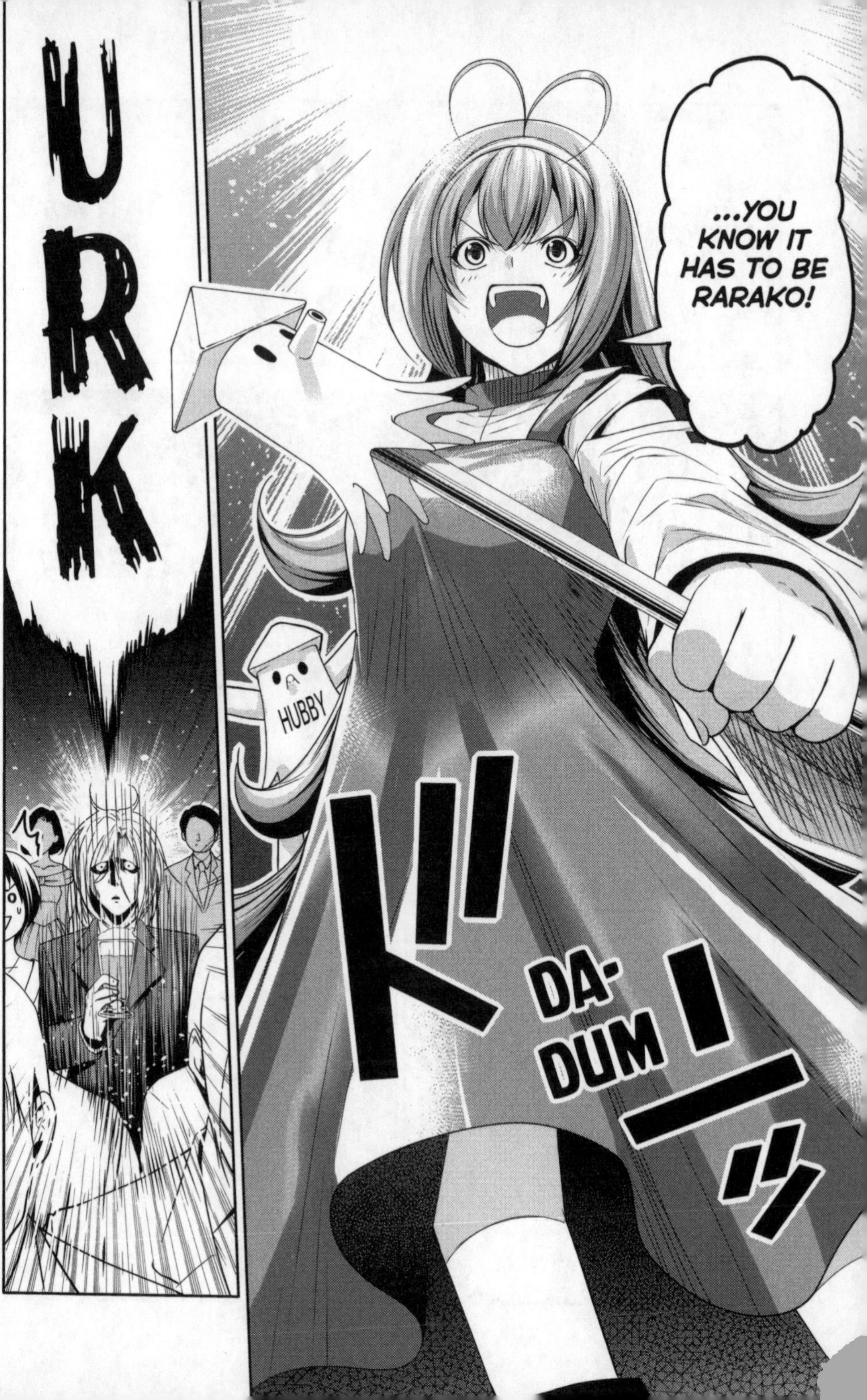
...YOU KNOW IT HAS TO BE RARAKO!
HUBBY
DA-DUM
URK

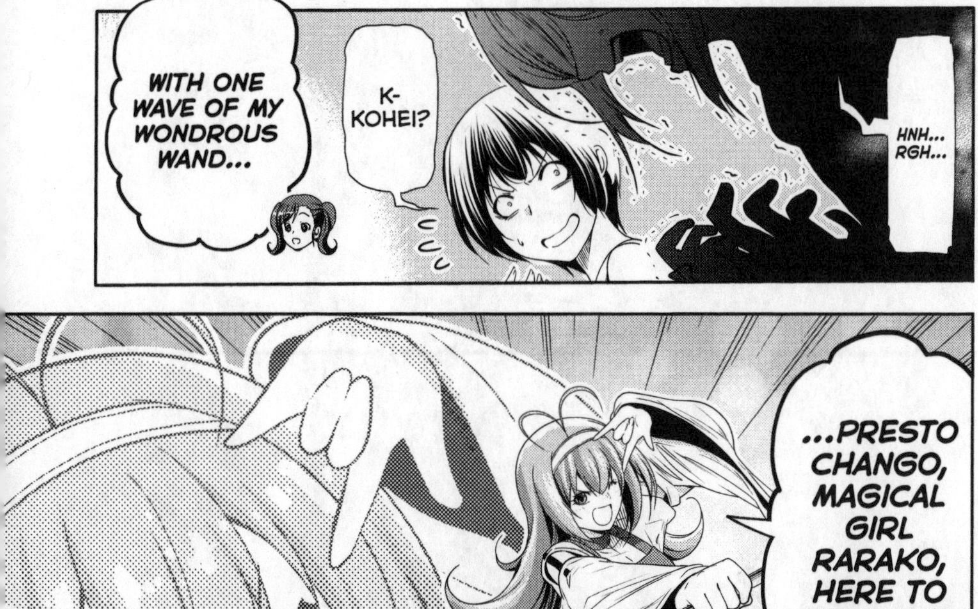
HNH... RGH...
K-KOHEI?
WITH ONE WAVE OF MY WONDROUS WAND...
...PRESTO CHANGO, MAGICAL GIRL RARAKO, HERE TO SAVE THE DAY! ☆
きらんっ☆
TWINKLE
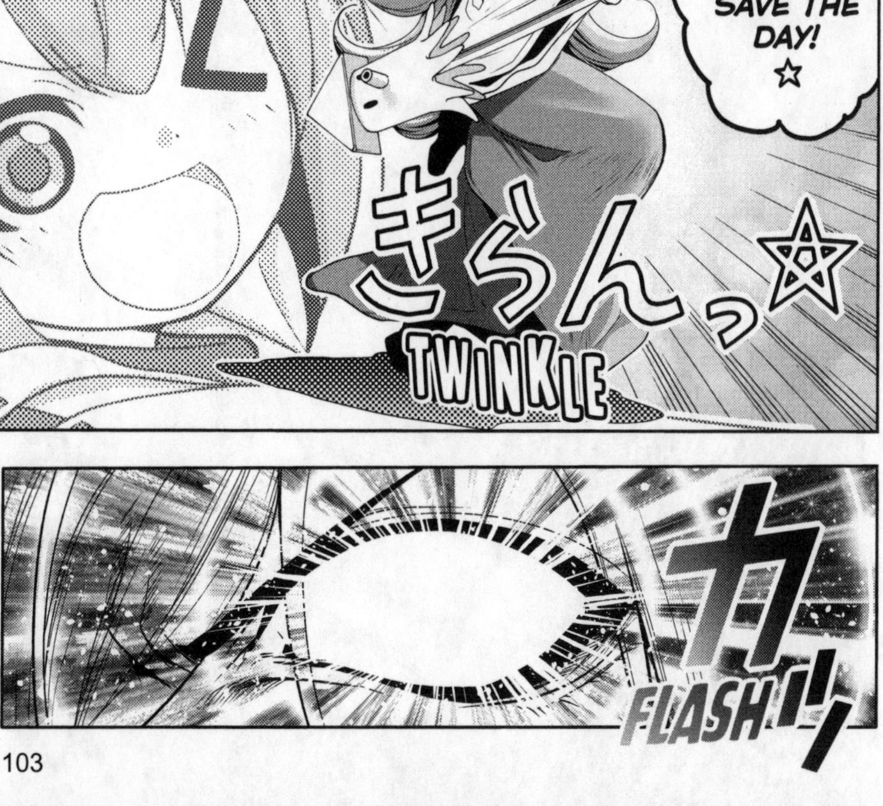
カッ!!
FLASH

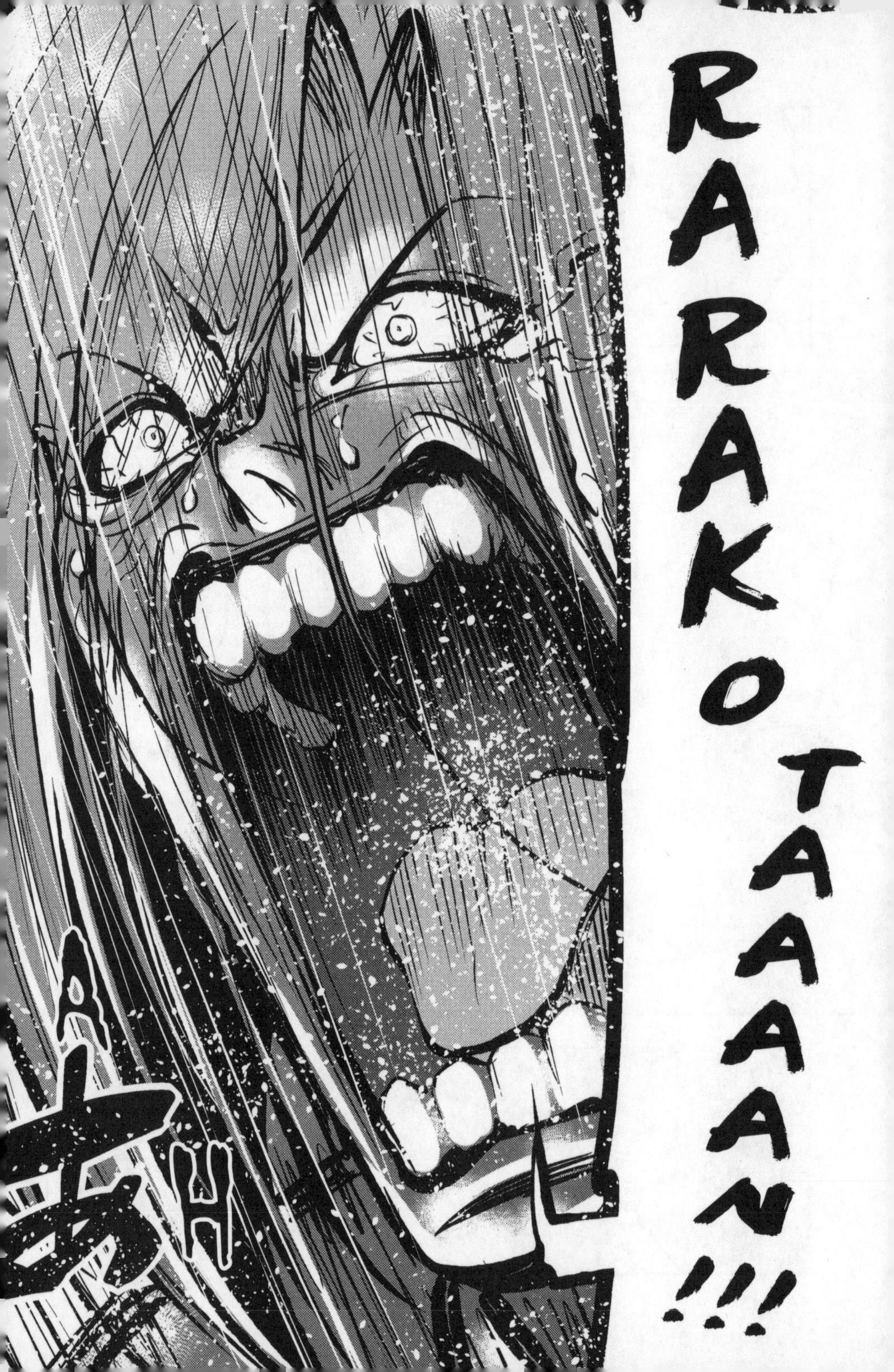
RARAKOTAAAAAN!!!
AH

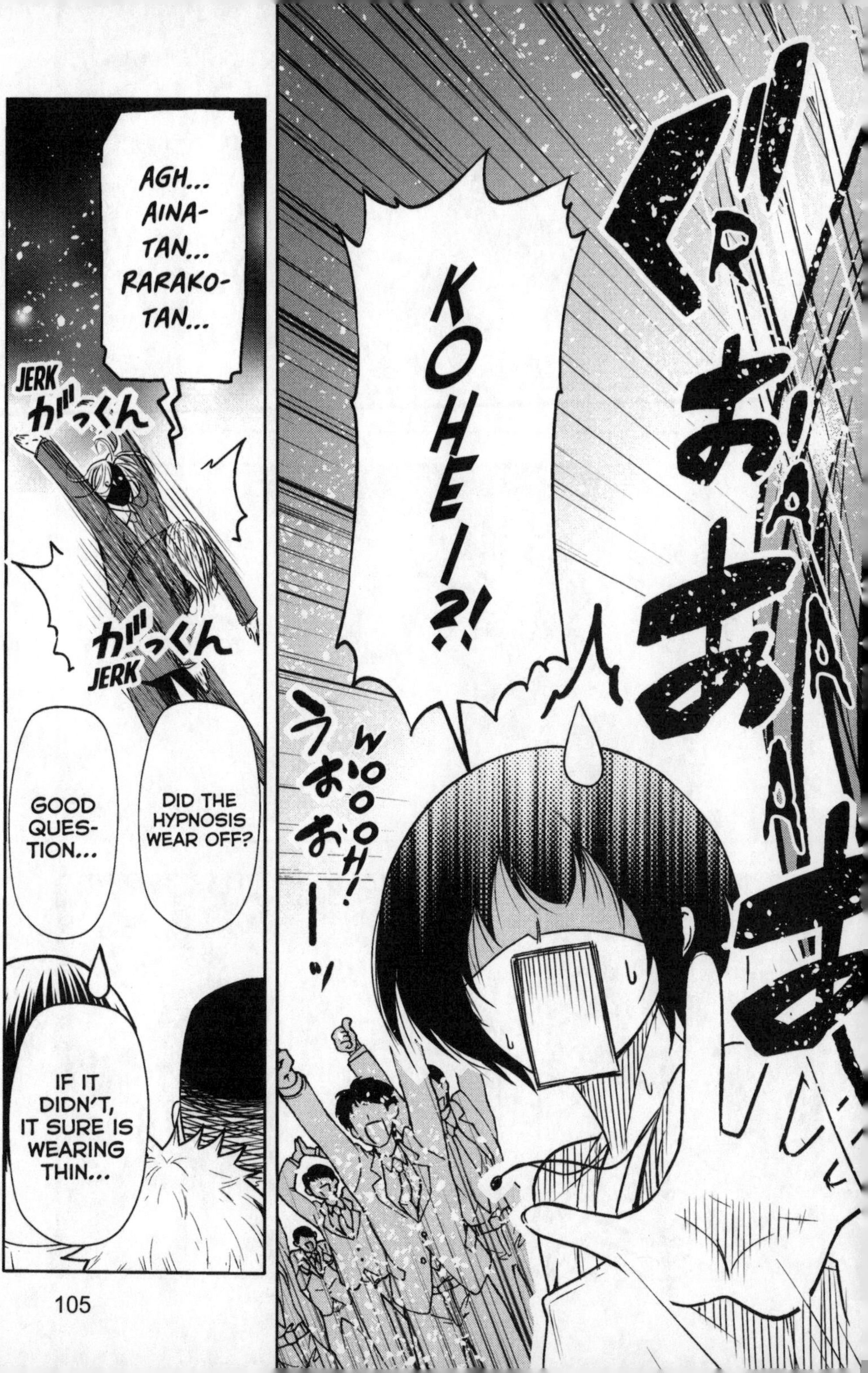
ぐおお
RAAAA
KOHEI?!
うおおおー
WOOOOH!
AGH... AINA-TAN... RARAKO-TAN...
がっくん
JERK
がっくん
JERK
DID THE HYPNOSIS WEAR OFF?
GOOD QUES-TION...
IF IT DIDN'T, IT SURE IS WEARING THIN...

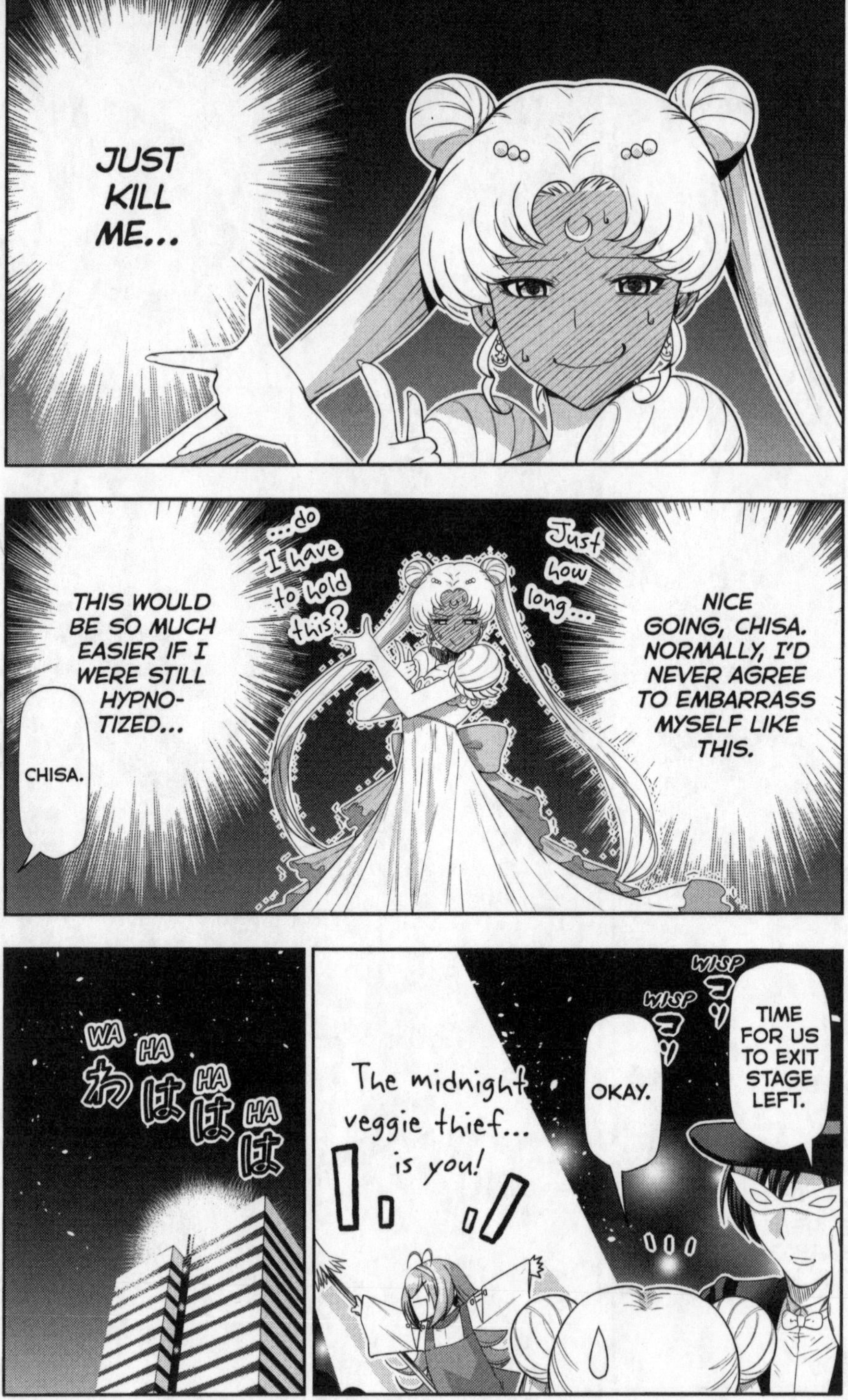

JUST KILL ME...
NICE GOING, CHISA. NORMALLY, I'D NEVER AGREE TO EMBARRASS MYSELF LIKE THIS.
Just how long...
...do I have to hold this?
THIS WOULD BE SO MUCH EASIER IF I WERE STILL HYPNO-TIZED...
CHISA.
WISP コソ
WISP コソ
TIME FOR US TO EXIT STAGE LEFT.
OKAY.
The midnight veggie thief... is you!
WA HA HA HA
わははは

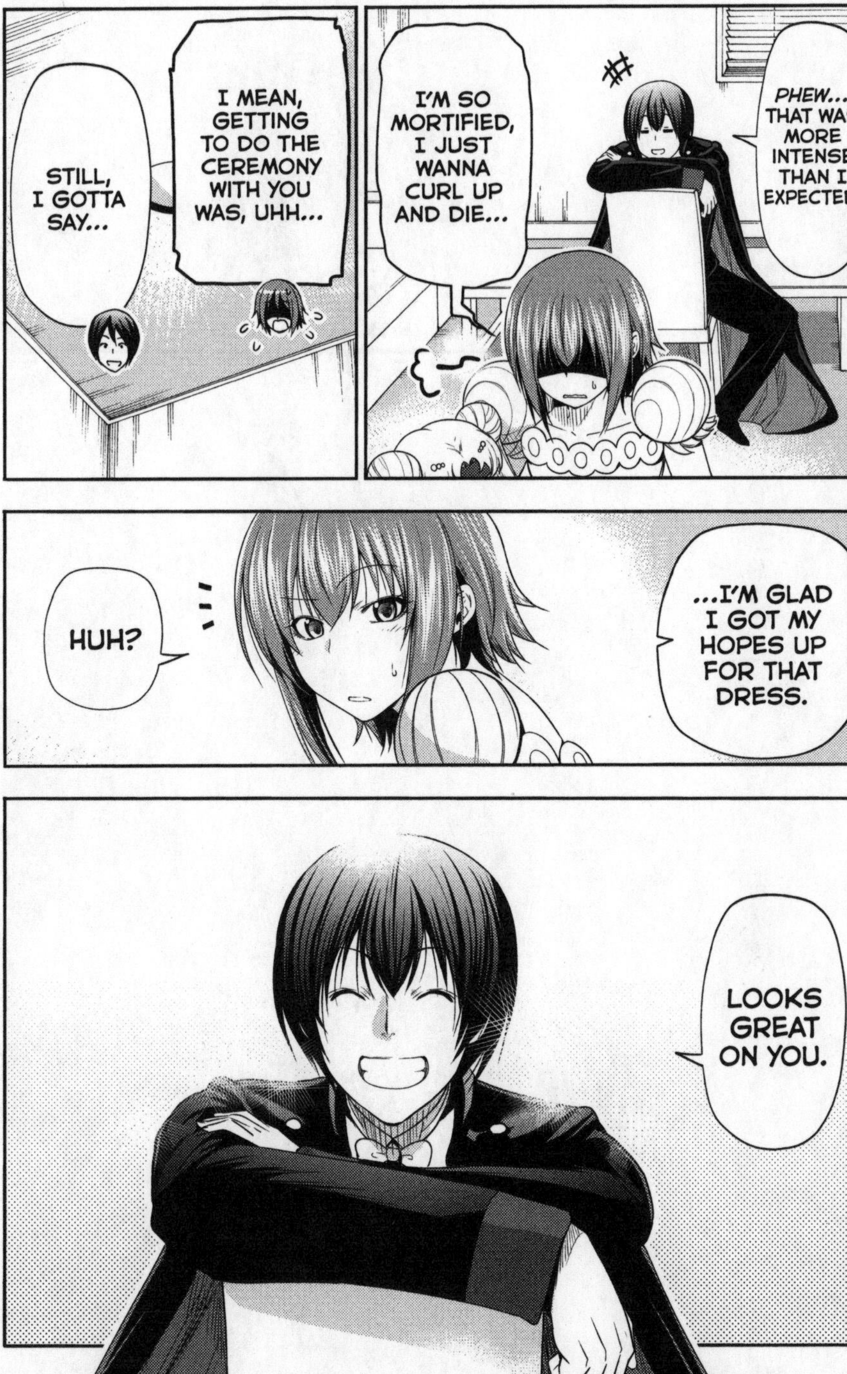
PHEW... THAT WAS MORE INTENSE THAN I EXPECTED.
I'M SO MORTIFIED, I JUST WANNA CURL UP AND DIE...
I MEAN, GETTING TO DO THE CEREMONY WITH YOU WAS, UHH...
STILL, I GOTTA SAY...
...I'M GLAD I GOT MY HOPES UP FOR THAT DRESS.
HUH?
LOOKS GREAT ON YOU.

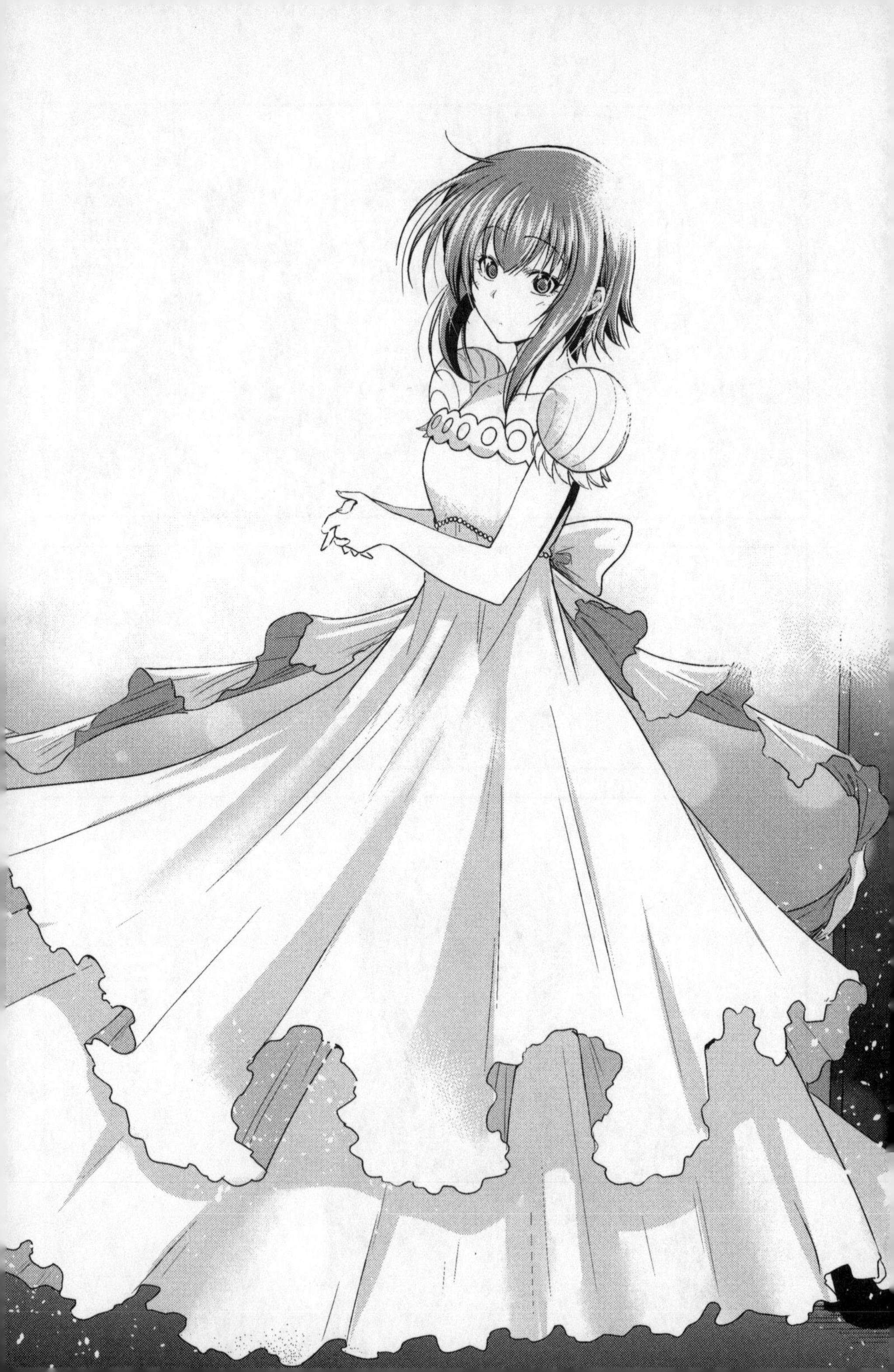

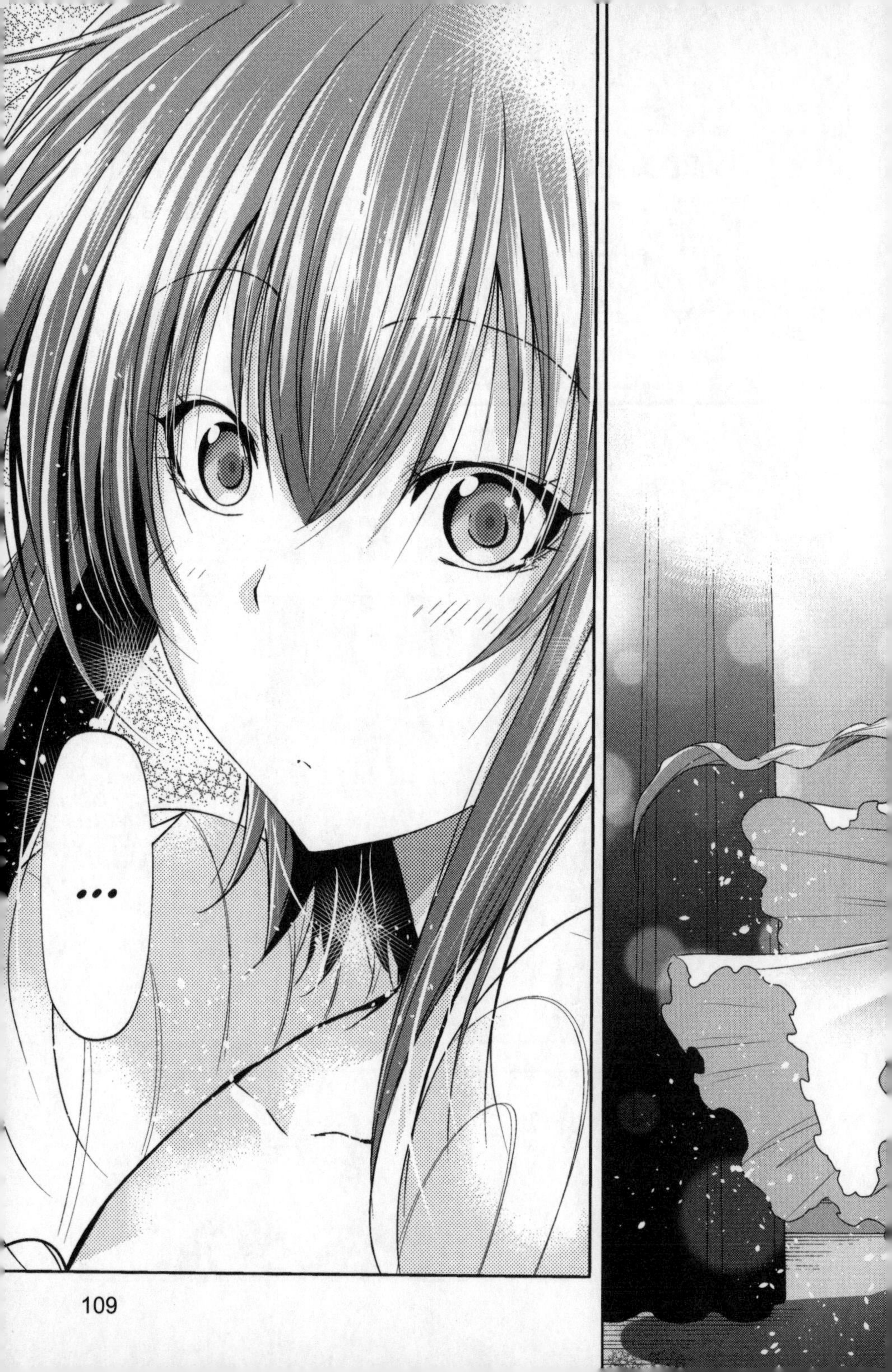
...

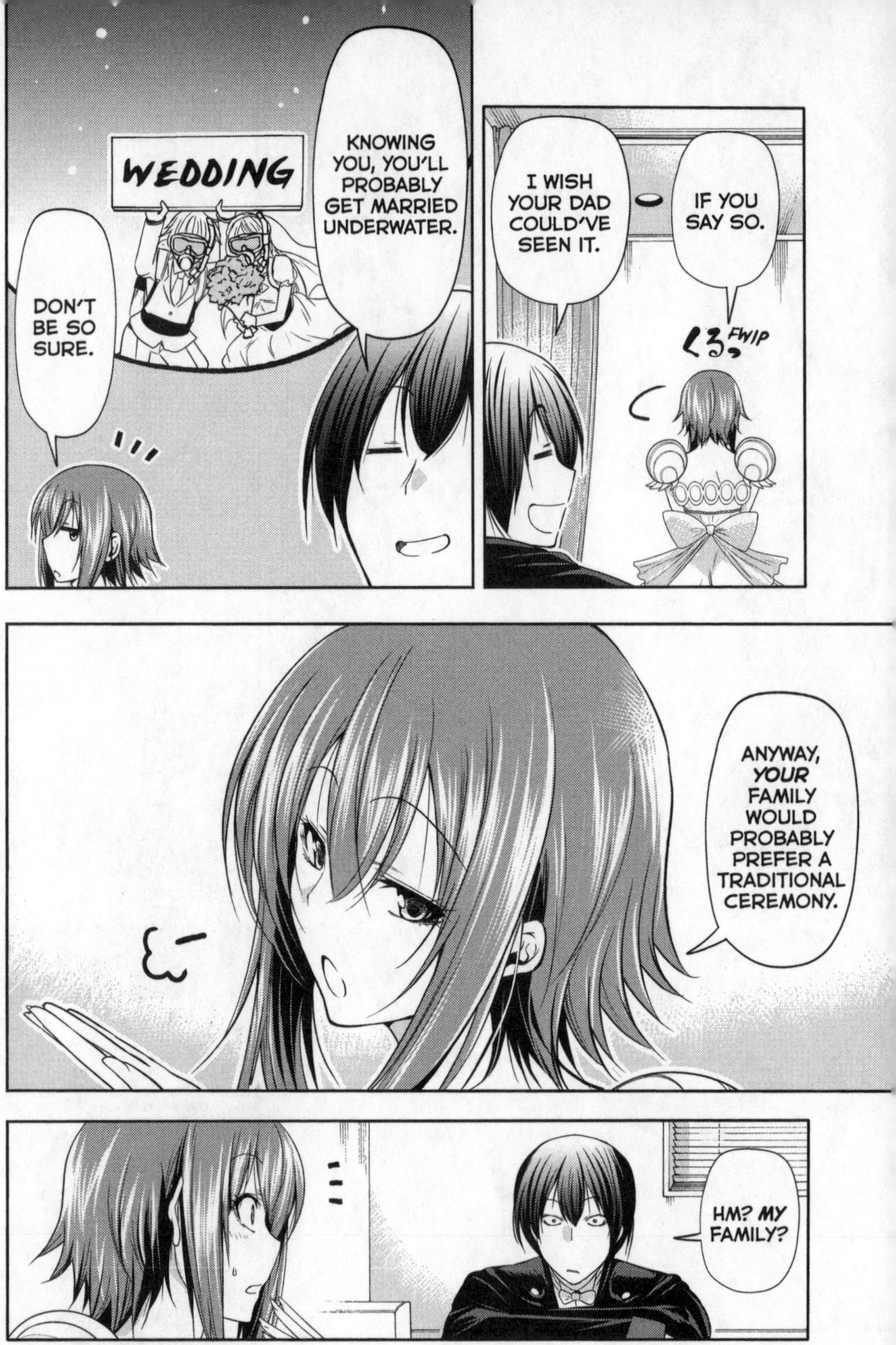
IF YOU SAY SO.
I WISH YOUR DAD COULD'VE SEEN IT.
くるっ FWIP
KNOWING YOU, YOU'LL PROBABLY GET MARRIED UNDERWATER.
WEDDING
DON'T BE SO SURE.
ANYWAY, *YOUR* FAMILY WOULD PROBABLY PREFER A TRADITIONAL CEREMONY.
HM? *MY* FAMILY?

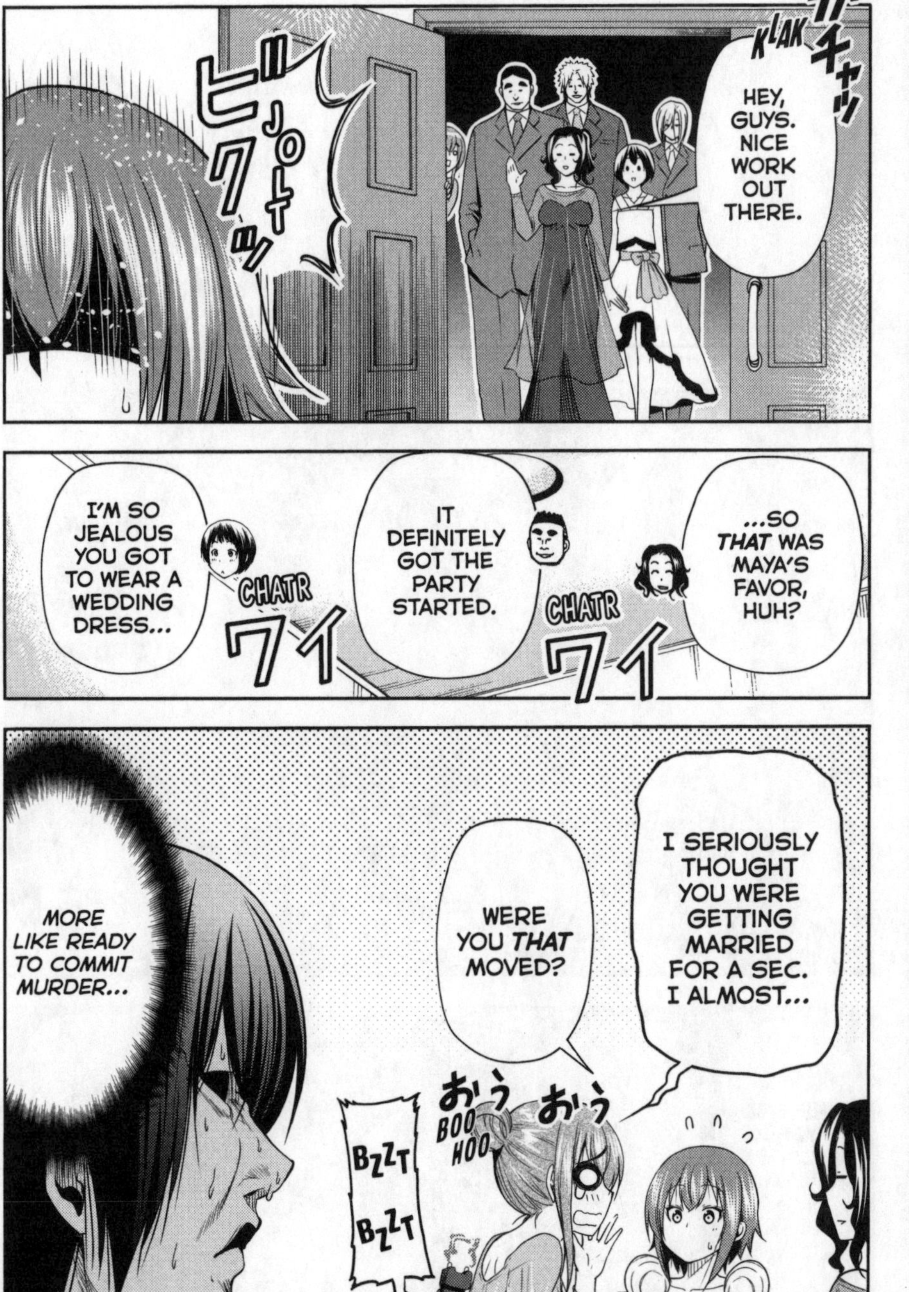

ガチャッ
KLAK
HEY, GUYS. NICE WORK OUT THERE.
ビクゥッ
JOLT
...SO THAT WAS MAYA'S FAVOR, HUH?
ワイ
CHATR
IT DEFINITELY GOT THE PARTY STARTED.
ワイ
CHATR
I'M SO JEALOUS YOU GOT TO WEAR A WEDDING DRESS...
I SERIOUSLY THOUGHT YOU WERE GETTING MARRIED FOR A SEC. I ALMOST...
おう
WERE YOU THAT MOVED?
おう
BOO HOO
BZZT
BZZT
MORE LIKE READY TO COMMIT MURDER...

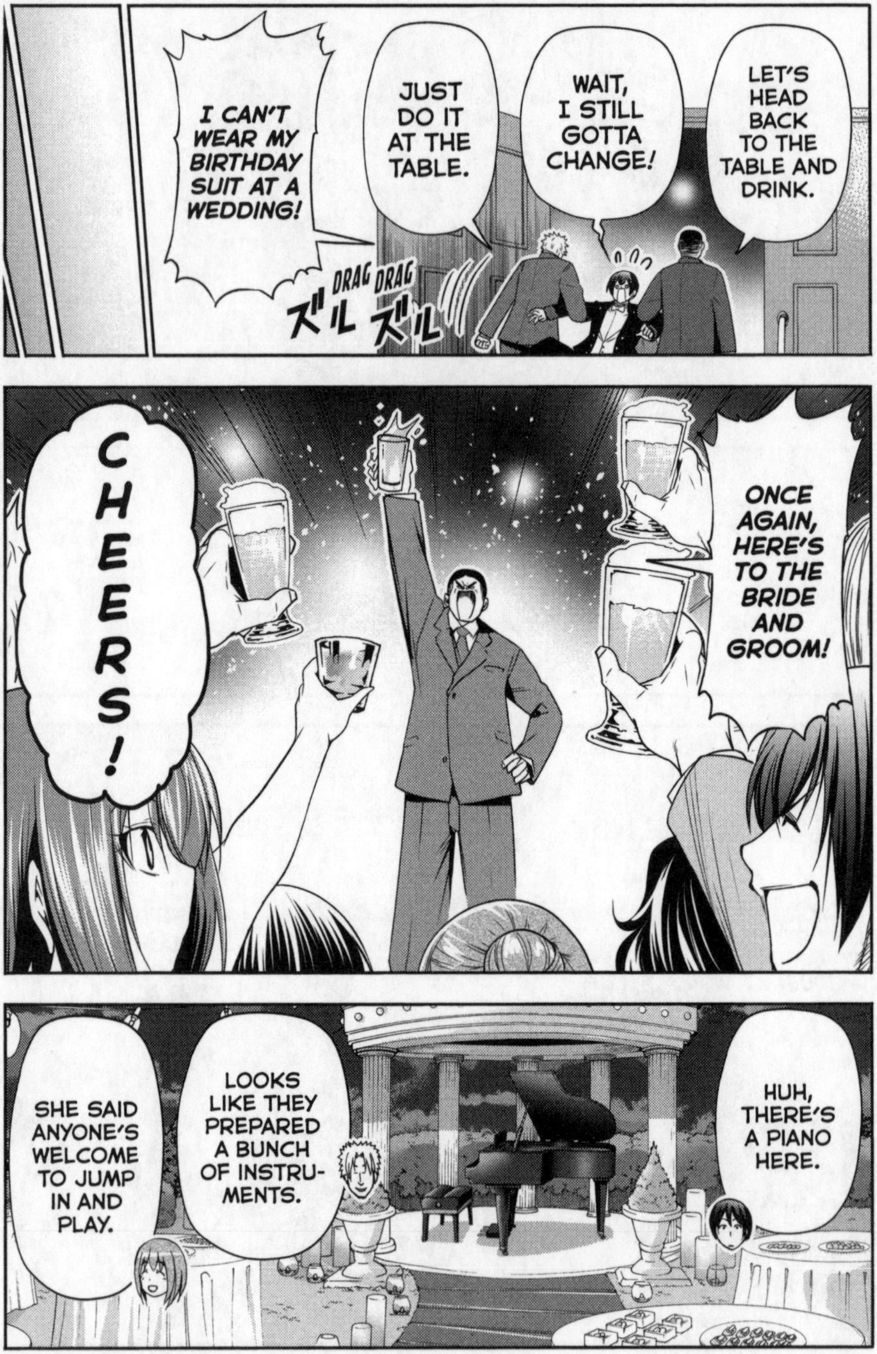
LET'S HEAD BACK TO THE TABLE AND DRINK.
WAIT, I STILL GOTTA CHANGE!
JUST DO IT AT THE TABLE.
I CAN'T WEAR MY BIRTHDAY SUIT AT A WEDDING!
ズル DRAG ズル DRAG
ONCE AGAIN, HERE'S TO THE BRIDE AND GROOM!
CHEERS!
HUH, THERE'S A PIANO HERE.
LOOKS LIKE THEY PREPARED A BUNCH OF INSTRU-MENTS.
SHE SAID ANYONE'S WELCOME TO JUMP IN AND PLAY.

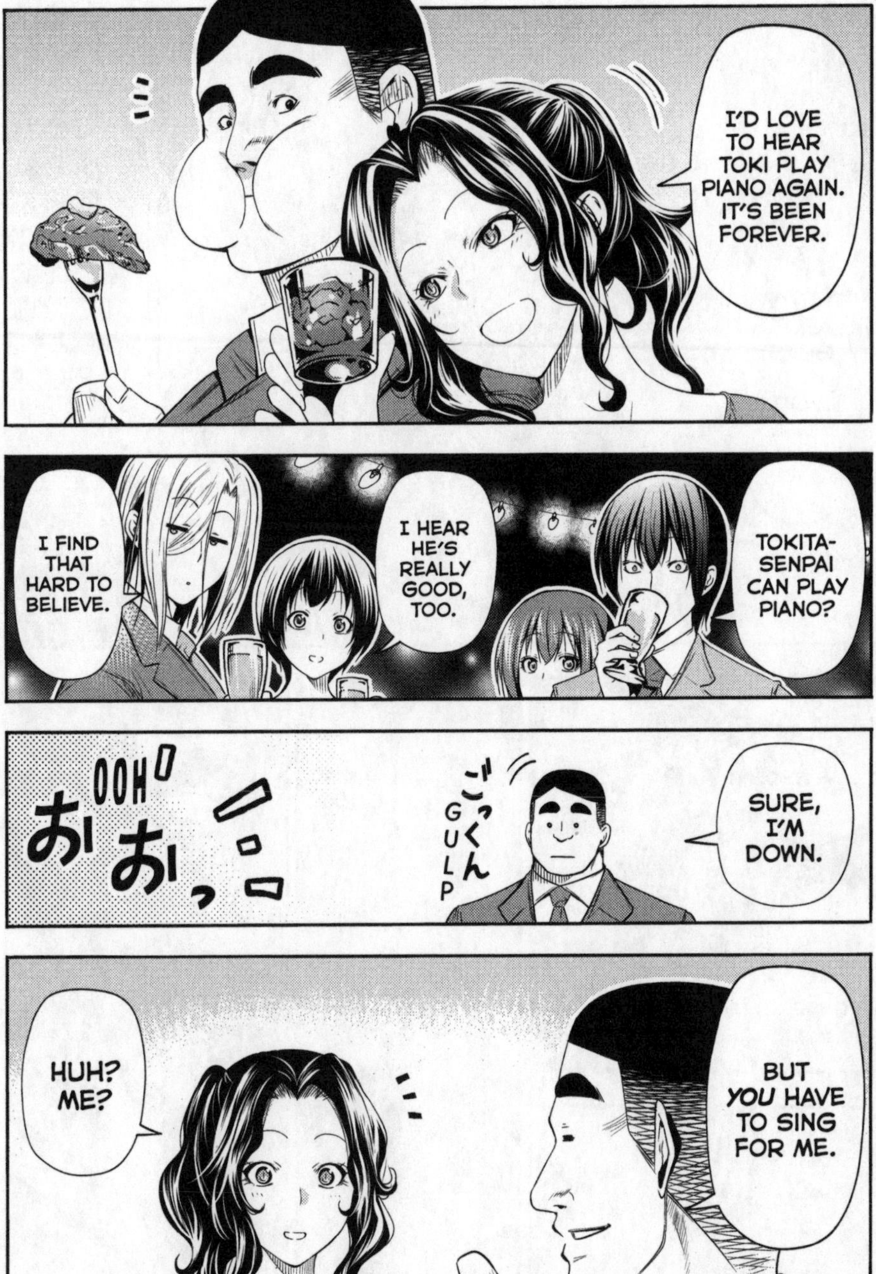
I'D LOVE TO HEAR TOKI PLAY PIANO AGAIN. IT'S BEEN FOREVER.
TOKITA-SENPAI CAN PLAY PIANO?
I HEAR HE'S REALLY GOOD, TOO.
I FIND THAT HARD TO BELIEVE.
SURE, I'M DOWN.
ごっくん
GULP
おおっ
OOH
BUT *YOU* HAVE TO SING FOR ME.
HUH? ME?

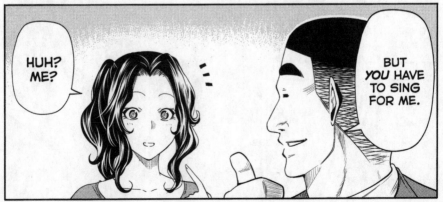

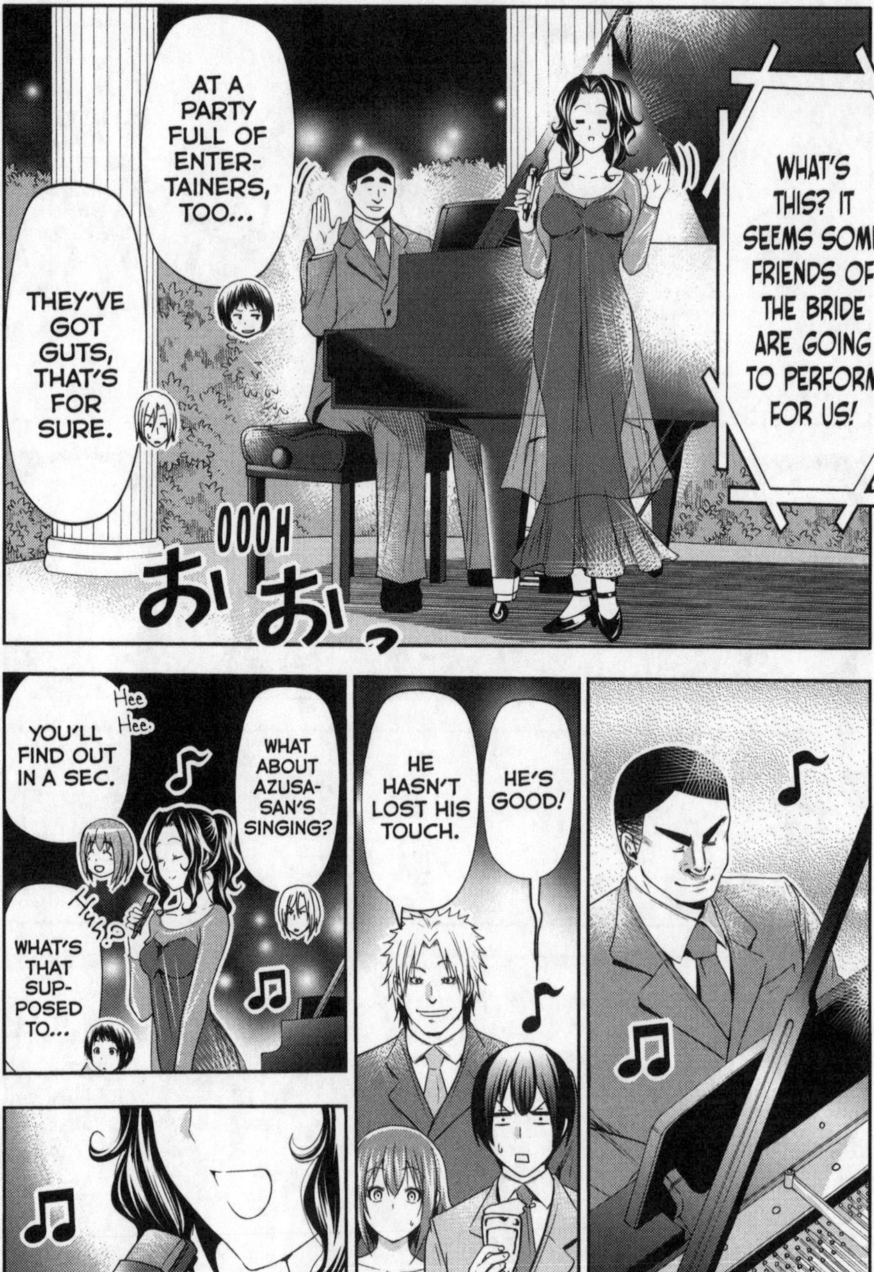
WHAT'S THIS? IT SEEMS SOME FRIENDS OF THE BRIDE ARE GOING TO PERFORM FOR US!
AT A PARTY FULL OF ENTER-TAINERS, TOO...
THEY'VE GOT GUTS, THAT'S FOR SURE.
OOOH
おおっ
HE'S GOOD!
HE HASN'T LOST HIS TOUCH.
WHAT ABOUT AZUSA-SAN'S SINGING?
Hee Hee.
YOU'LL FIND OUT IN A SEC.
Huh?
WHAT'S THAT SUP-POSED TO...

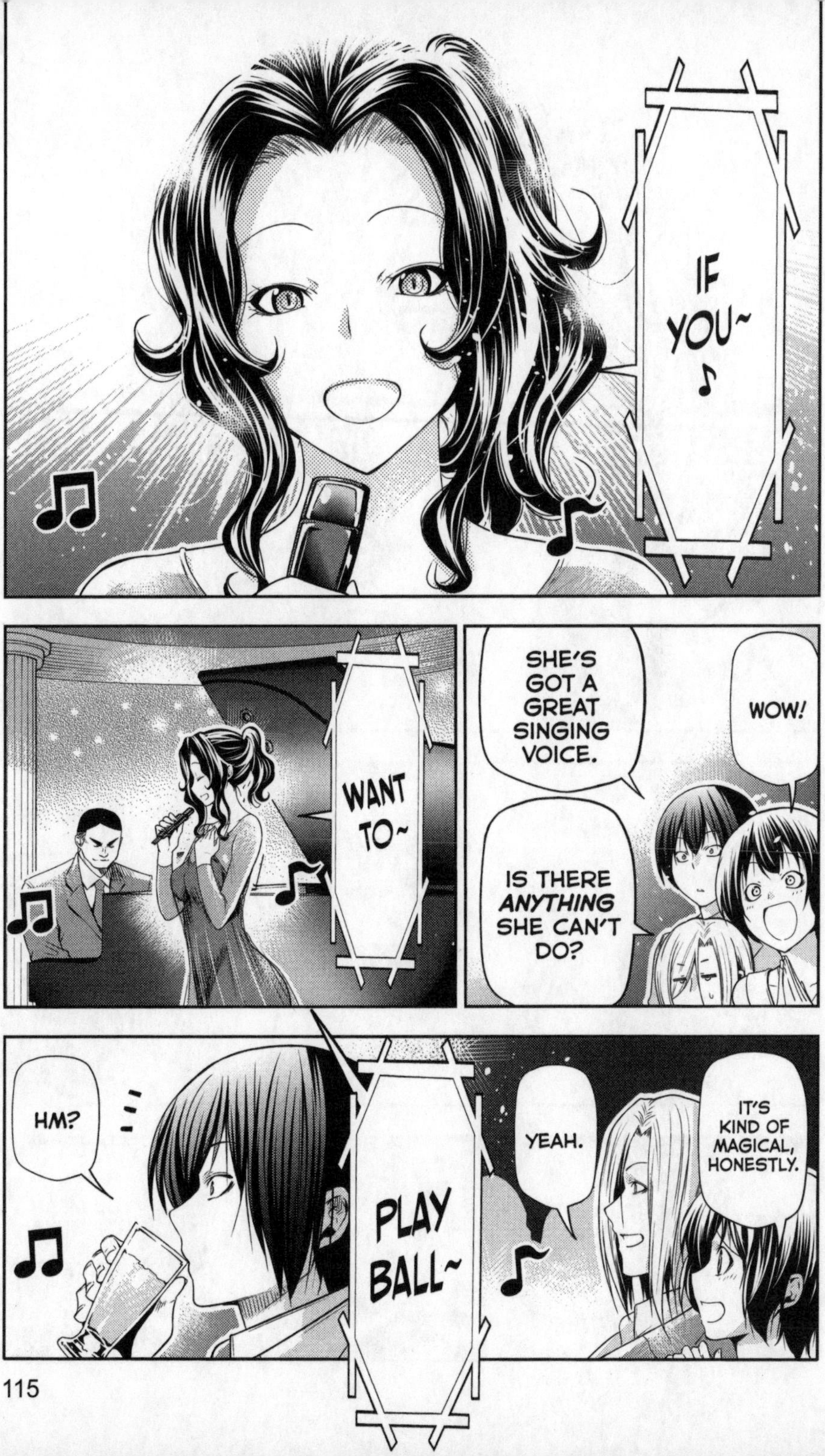
IF YOU~ ♪
WOW!
SHE'S GOT A GREAT SINGING VOICE.
IS THERE *ANYTHING* SHE CAN'T DO?
WANT TO~
IT'S KIND OF MAGICAL, HONESTLY.
YEAH.
PLAY BALL~
HM?

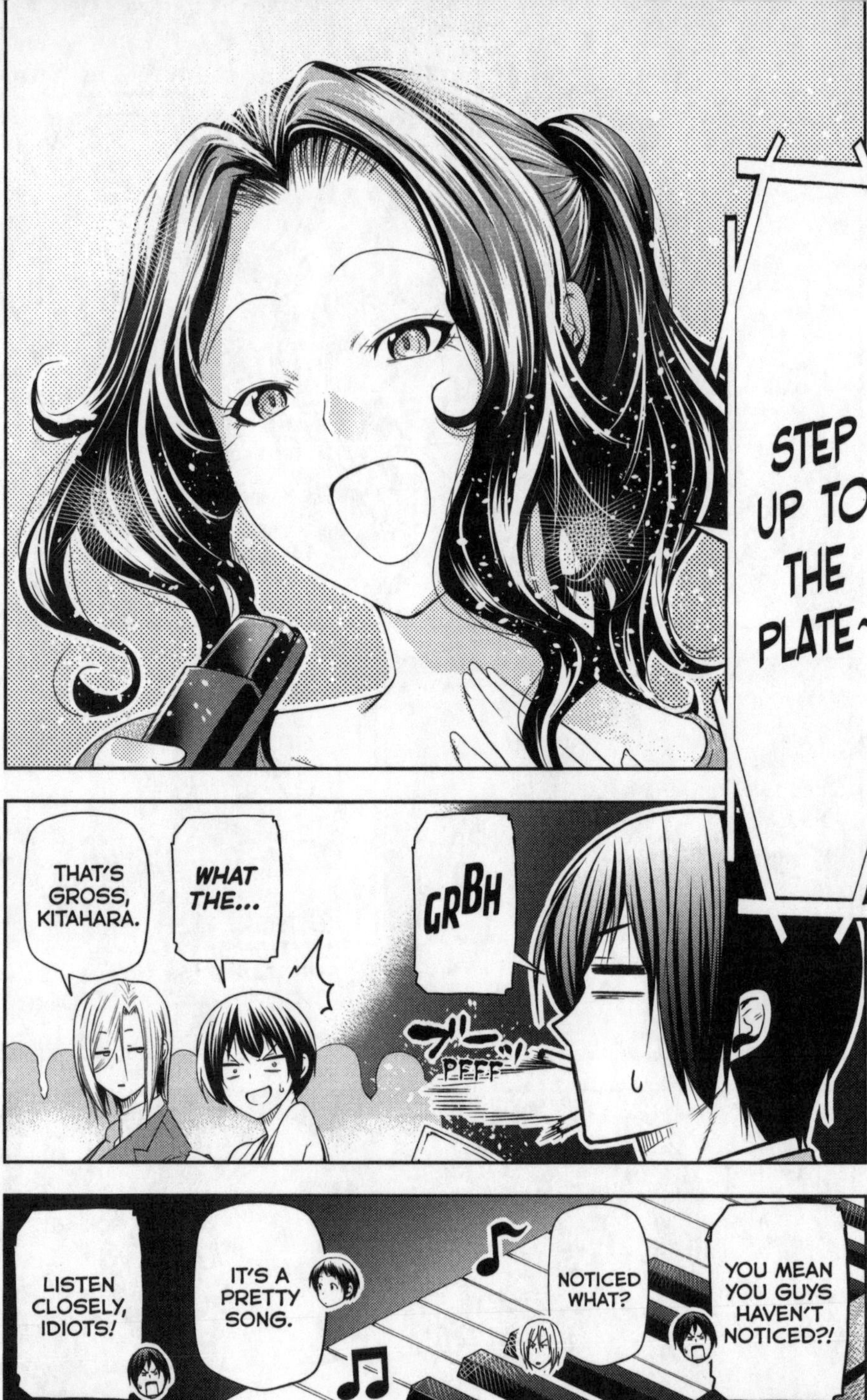
STEP UP TO THE PLATE~
GRBH
PFFF
WHAT THE...
THAT'S GROSS, KITAHARA.
YOU MEAN YOU GUYS HAVEN'T NOTICED?!
NOTICED WHAT?
IT'S A PRETTY SONG.
LISTEN CLOSELY, IDIOTS!

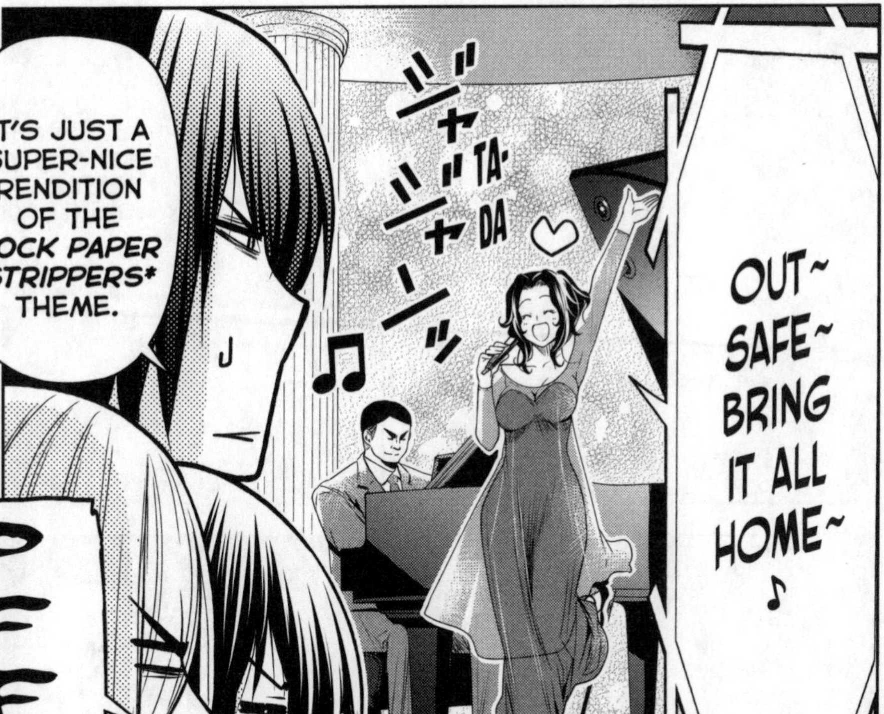
OUT~ SAFE~ BRING IT ALL HOME~ ♪
ジャジャーンッ
TA-DA
IT'S JUST A SUPER-NICE RENDITION OF THE *ROCK PAPER STRIPPERS** THEME.
PFFFT

*A PARTY GAME SOMETIMES FEATURED IN JAPANESE VARIETY SHOWS AND ADULT COMPUTER GAMES.

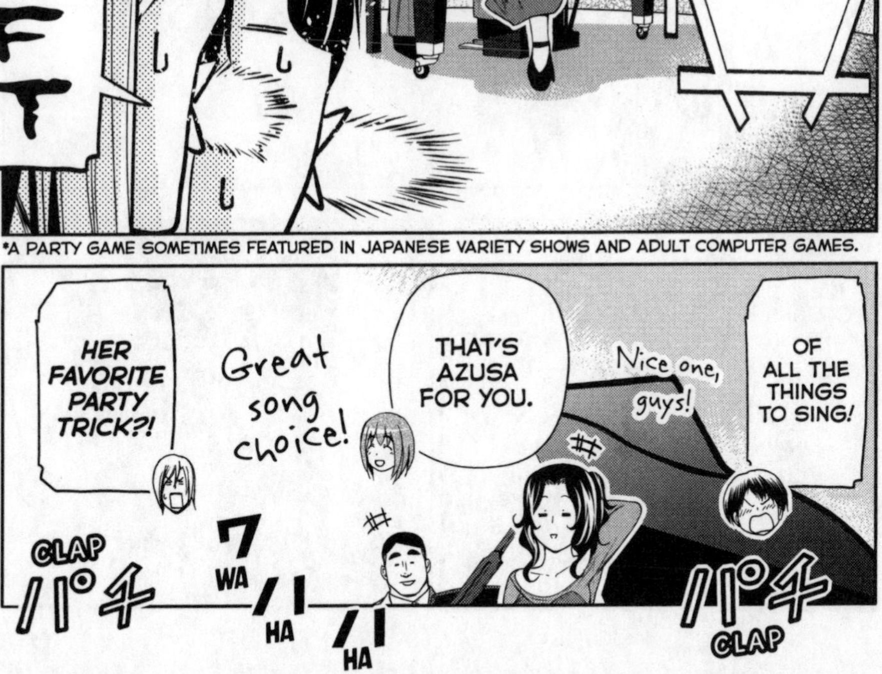
OF ALL THE THINGS TO SING!
Nice one, guys!
THAT'S AZUSA FOR YOU.
Great song choice!
HER FAVORITE PARTY TRICK?!
パチ
CLAP
ワハハ
WA HA HA
パチ
CLAP

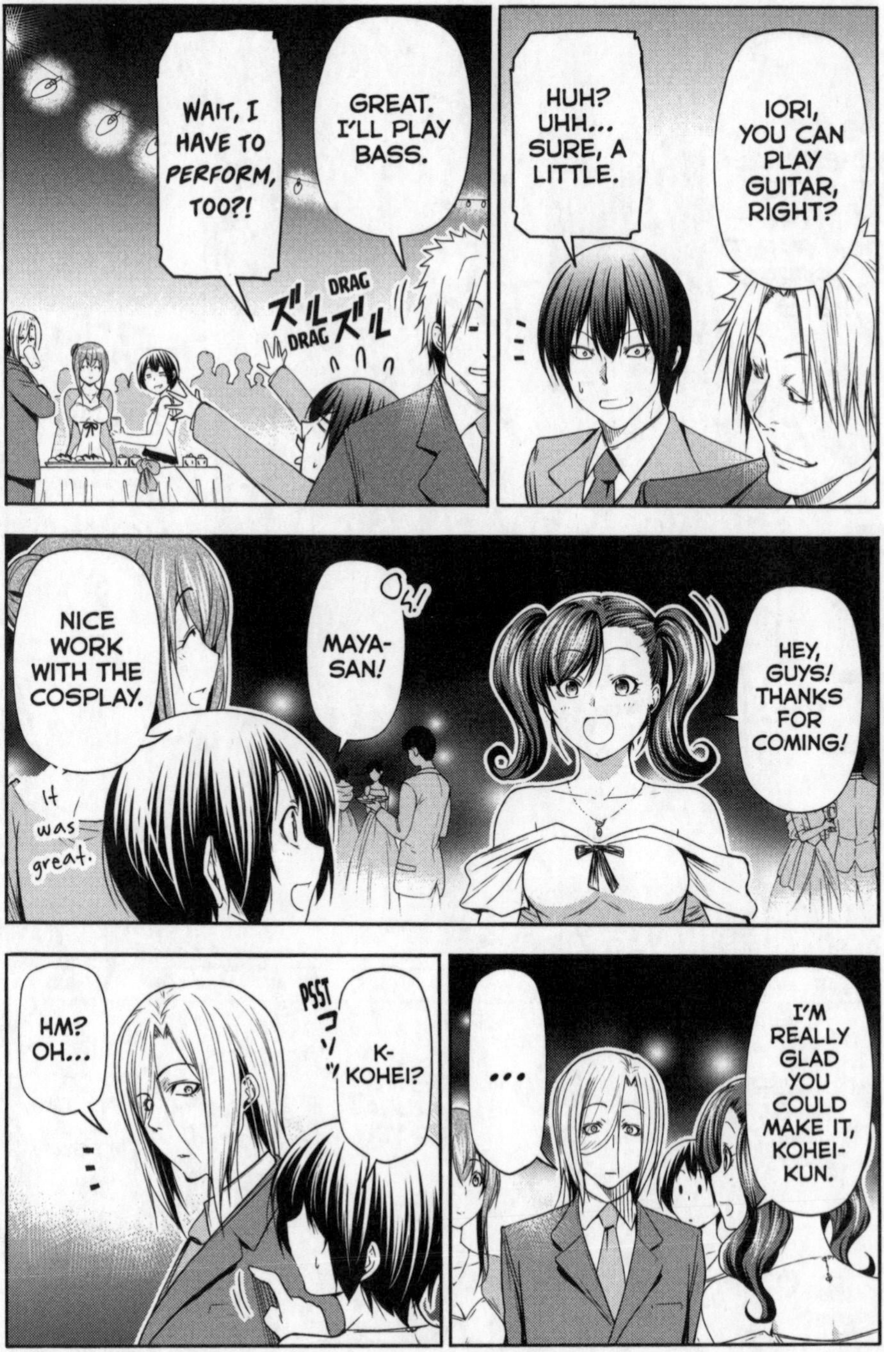
IORI, YOU CAN PLAY GUITAR, RIGHT?
HUH? UHH... SURE, A LITTLE.
GREAT. I'LL PLAY BASS.
ズルズル
DRAG DRAG
WAIT, I HAVE TO PERFORM, TOO?!
HEY, GUYS! THANKS FOR COMING!
Oh!
MAYA-SAN!
NICE WORK WITH THE COSPLAY.
It was great.
I'M REALLY GLAD YOU COULD MAKE IT, KOHEI-KUN.
...
コソッ
PSST
K-KOHEI?
HM? OH...

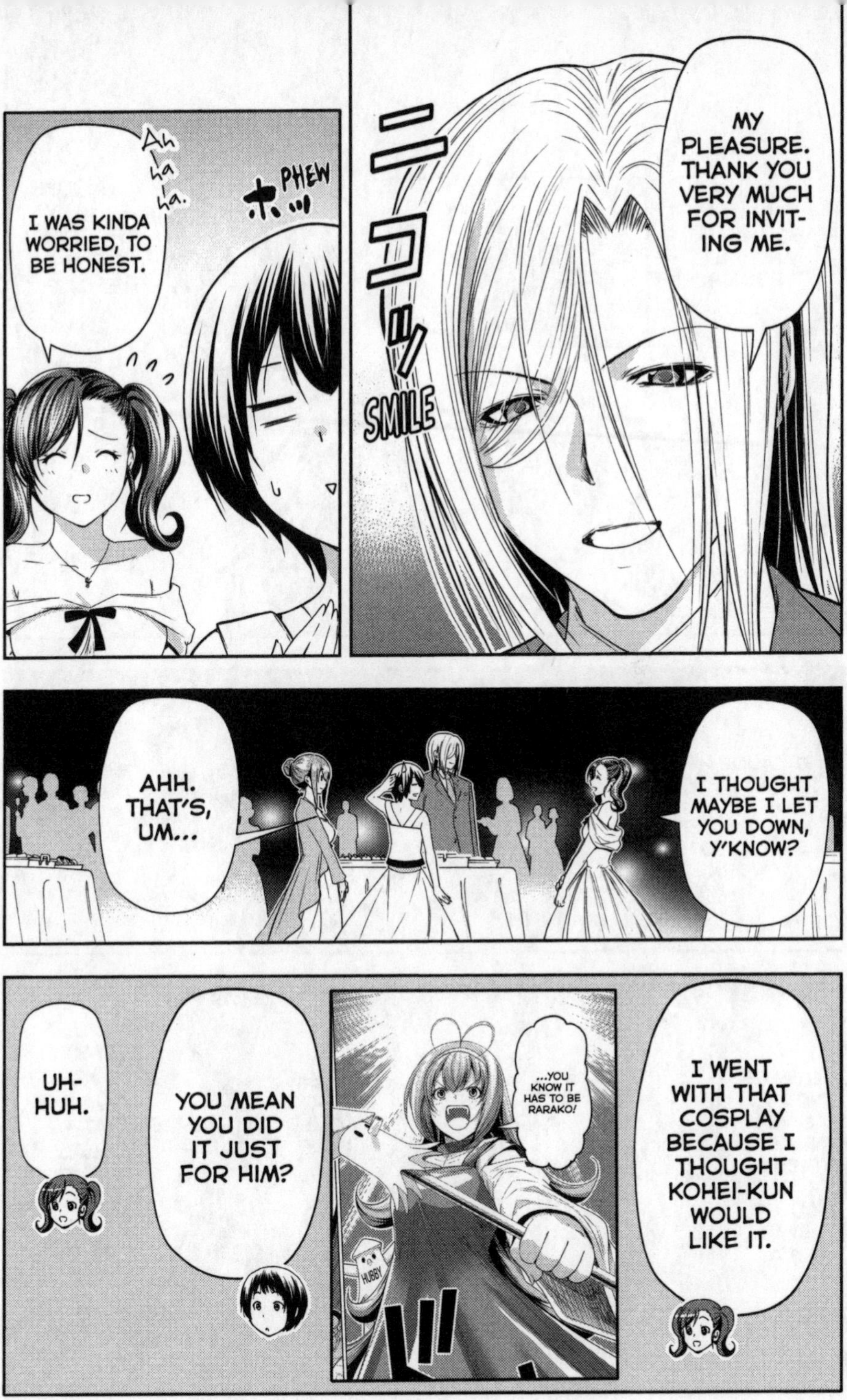
MY PLEASURE. THANK YOU VERY MUCH FOR INVIT- ING ME.
ニコッ
SMILE
ホッ
PHEW
Ah ha ha.
I WAS KINDA WORRIED, TO BE HONEST.
I THOUGHT MAYBE I LET YOU DOWN, Y'KNOW?
AHH. THAT'S, UM...
I WENT WITH THAT COSPLAY BECAUSE I THOUGHT KOHEI-KUN WOULD LIKE IT.
...YOU KNOW IT HAS TO BE RARAKO!
HUBBY
YOU MEAN YOU DID IT JUST FOR HIM?
UH- HUH.

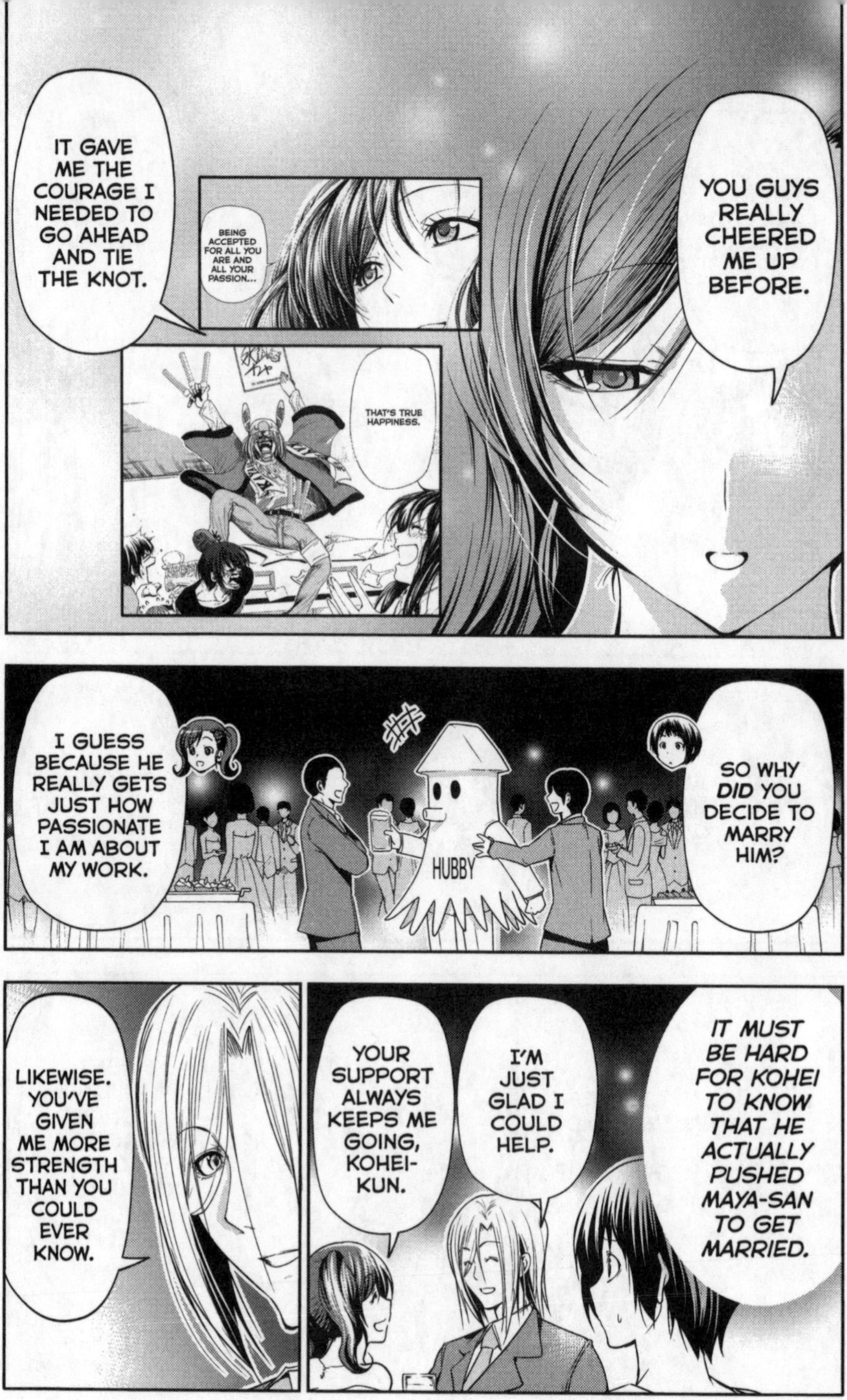
YOU GUYS REALLY CHEERED ME UP BEFORE.
BEING ACCEPTED FOR ALL YOU ARE AND ALL YOUR PASSION...
THAT'S TRUE HAPPINESS.
IT GAVE ME THE COURAGE I NEEDED TO GO AHEAD AND TIE THE KNOT.
SO WHY *DID* YOU DECIDE TO MARRY HIM?
HUBBY
I GUESS BECAUSE HE REALLY GETS JUST HOW PASSIONATE I AM ABOUT MY WORK.
IT MUST BE HARD FOR KOHEI TO KNOW THAT HE ACTUALLY PUSHED MAYA-SAN TO GET MARRIED.
I'M JUST GLAD I COULD HELP.
YOUR SUPPORT ALWAYS KEEPS ME GOING, KOHEI-KUN.
LIKEWISE. YOU'VE GIVEN ME MORE STRENGTH THAN YOU COULD EVER KNOW.

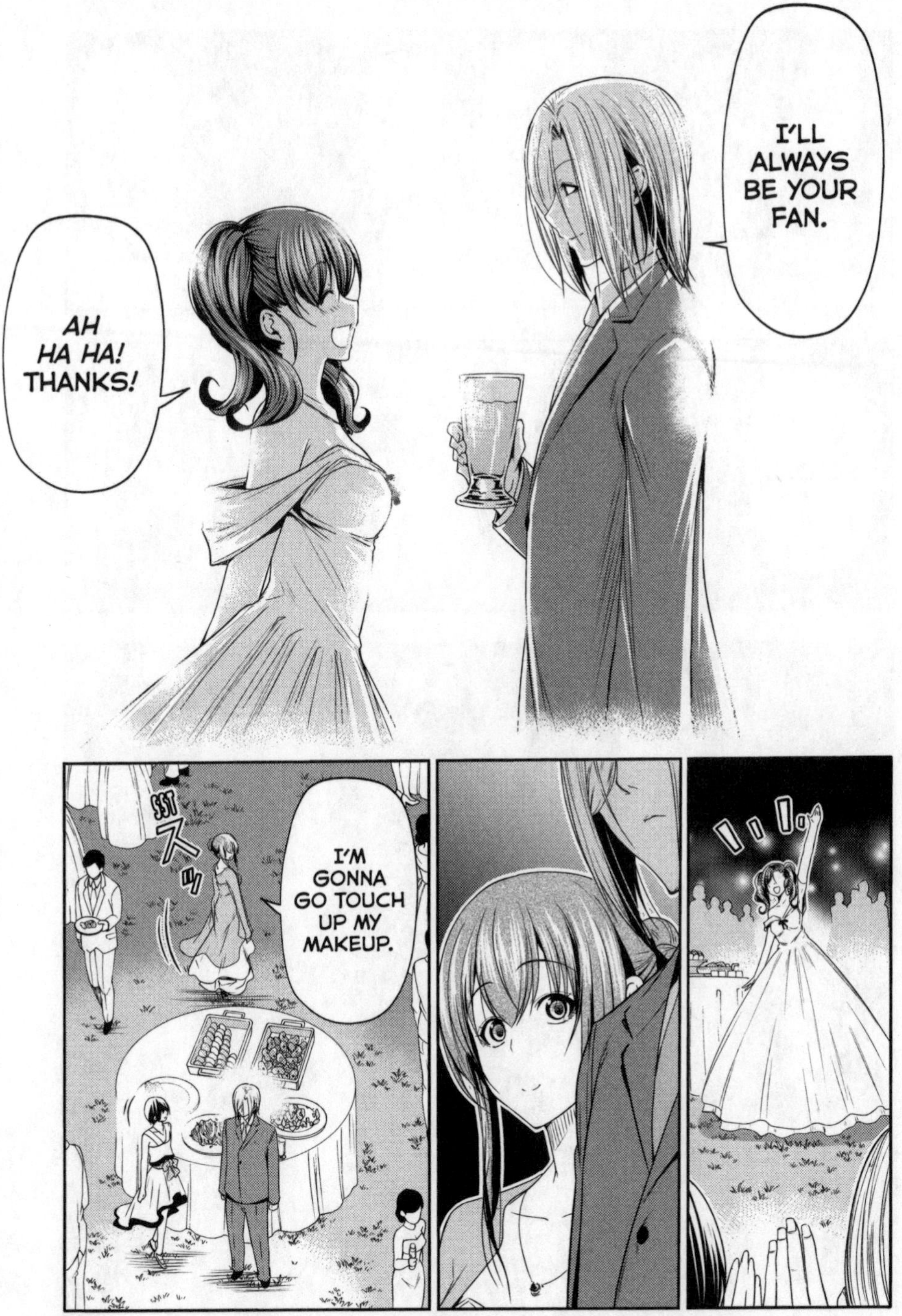
I'LL ALWAYS BE YOUR FAN.
AH HA HA! THANKS!
SST
I'M GONNA GO TOUCH UP MY MAKEUP.

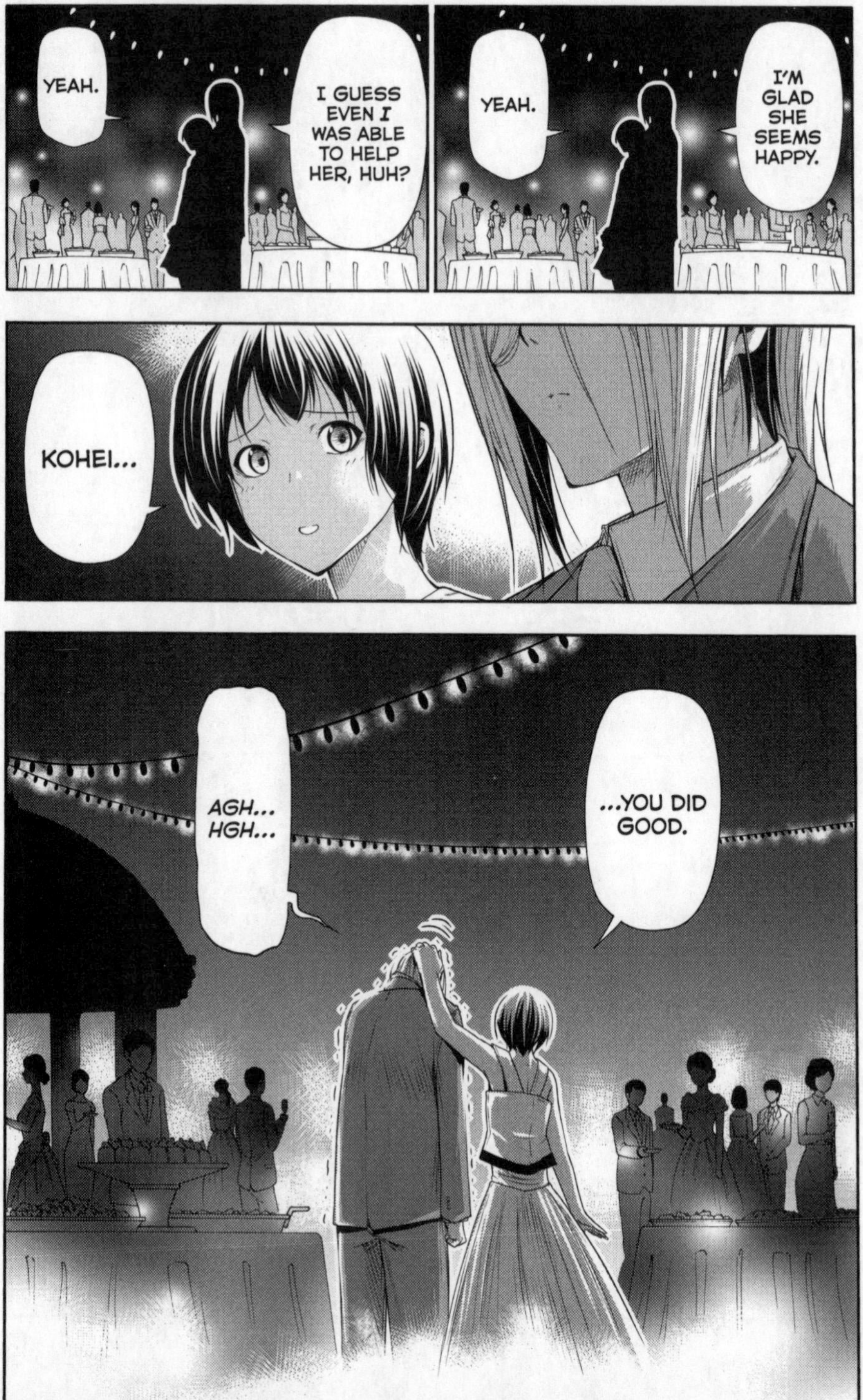
I'M GLAD SHE SEEMS HAPPY.
YEAH.
I GUESS EVEN I WAS ABLE TO HELP HER, HUH?
YEAH.
KOHEI...
...YOU DID GOOD.
AGH... HGH...

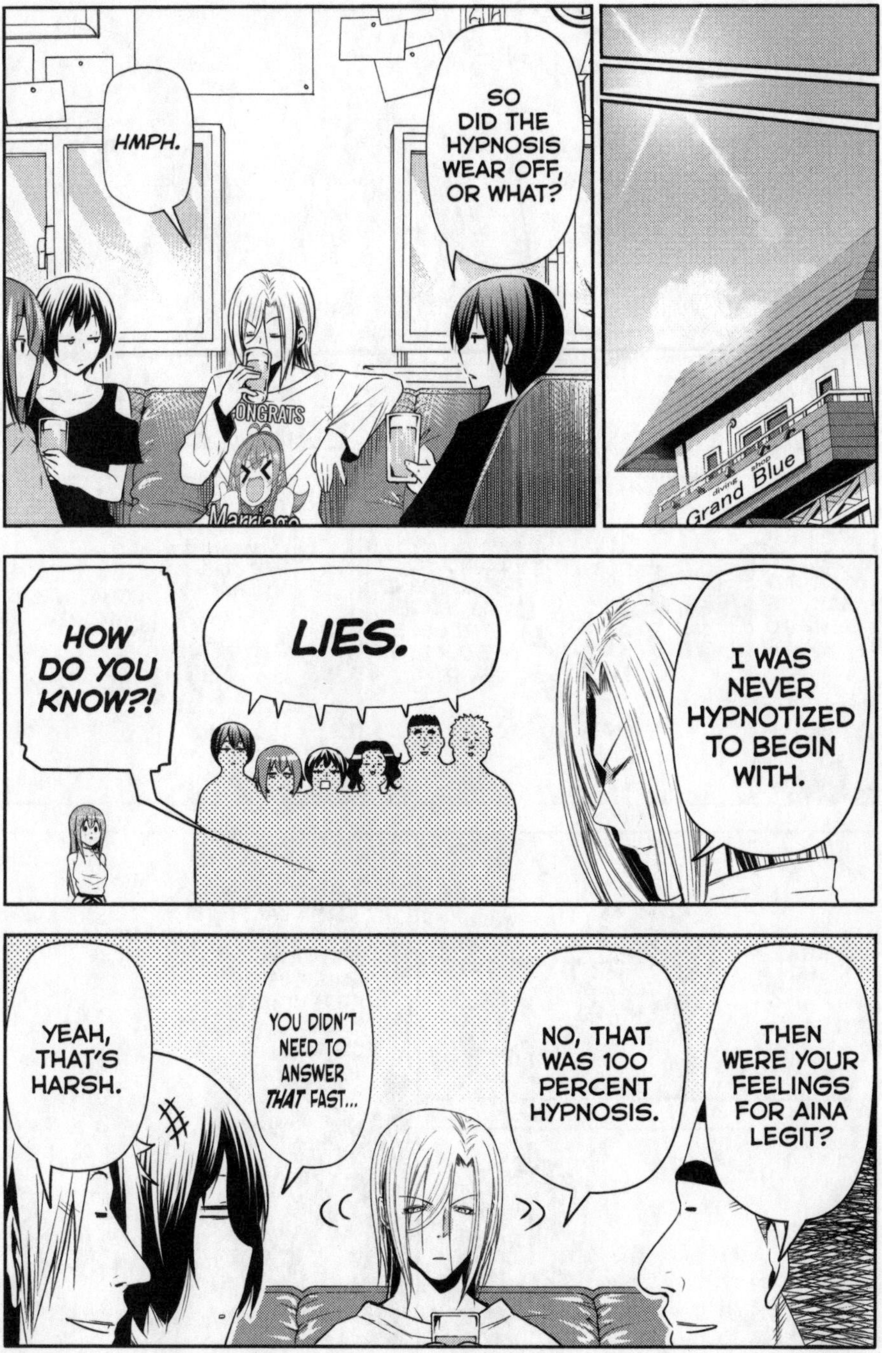
diving shop
Grand Blue
SO DID THE HYPNOSIS WEAR OFF, OR WHAT?
HMPH.
I WAS NEVER HYPNOTIZED TO BEGIN WITH.
LIES.
HOW DO YOU KNOW?!
THEN WERE YOUR FEELINGS FOR AINA LEGIT?
NO, THAT WAS 100 PERCENT HYPNOSIS.
YOU DIDN'T NEED TO ANSWER *THAT* FAST...
YEAH, THAT'S HARSH.

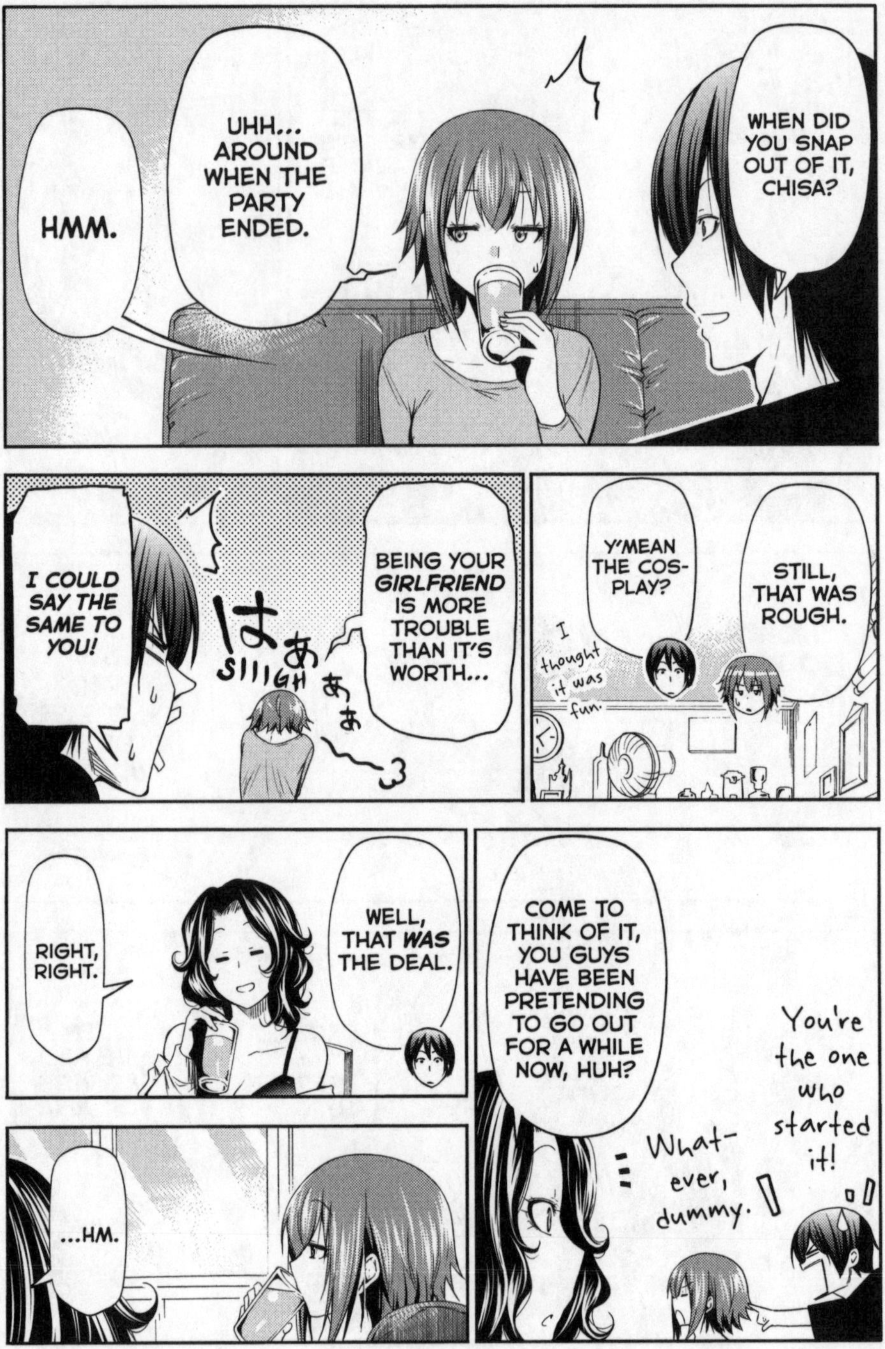

WHEN DID YOU SNAP OUT OF IT, CHISA?
UHH... AROUND WHEN THE PARTY ENDED.
HMM.
STILL, THAT WAS ROUGH.
Y'MEAN THE COS-PLAY?
I thought it was fun.
BEING YOUR *GIRLFRIEND* IS MORE TROUBLE THAN IT'S WORTH...
はあああ~
SIIIGH
I COULD SAY THE SAME TO YOU!
COME TO THINK OF IT, YOU GUYS HAVE BEEN PRETENDING TO GO OUT FOR A WHILE NOW, HUH?
You're the one who started it!
Whatever, dummy.
WELL, THAT *WAS* THE DEAL.
RIGHT, RIGHT.
...HM.

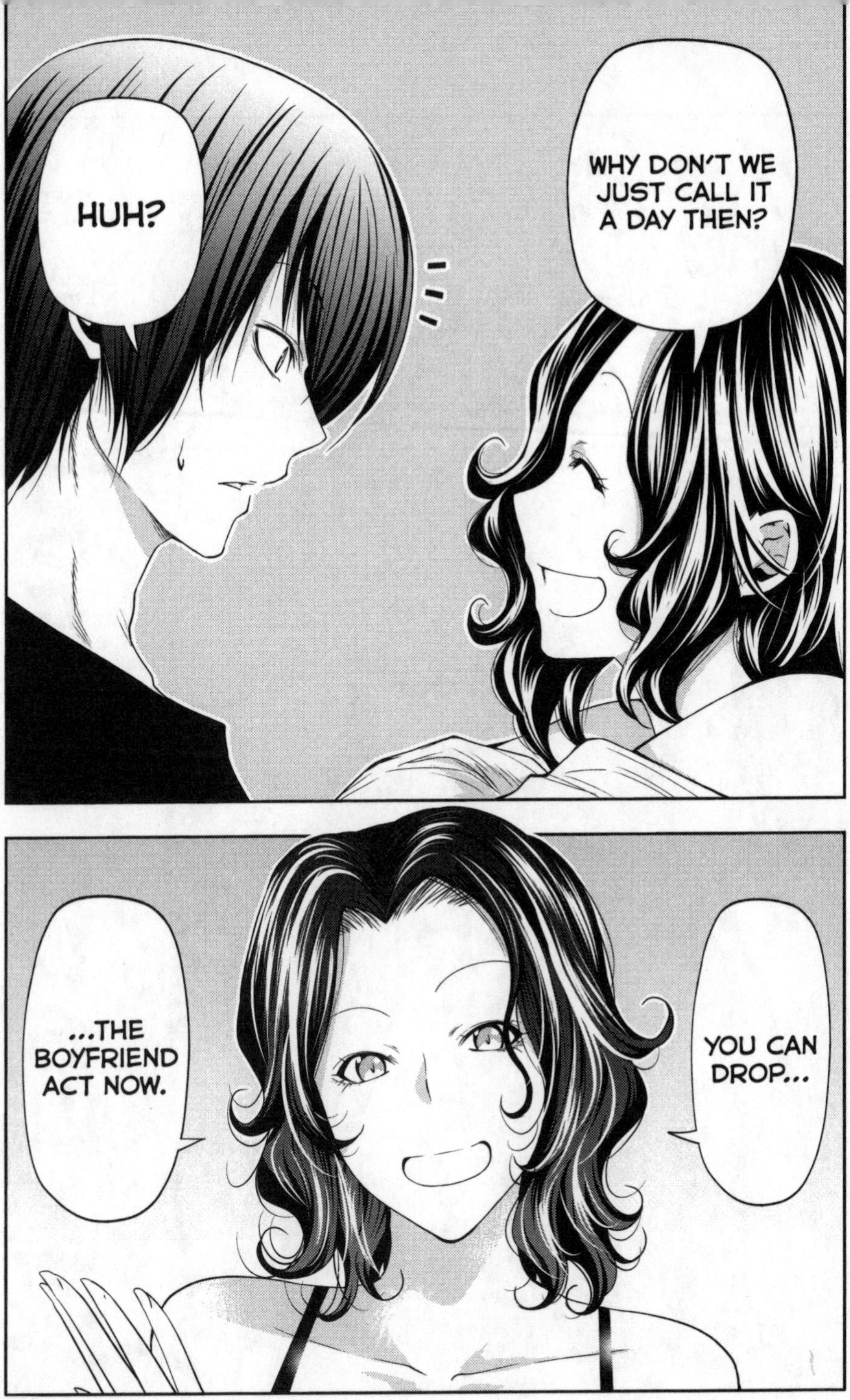
WHY DON'T WE JUST CALL IT A DAY THEN?
HUH?
YOU CAN DROP...
...THE BOYFRIEND ACT NOW.

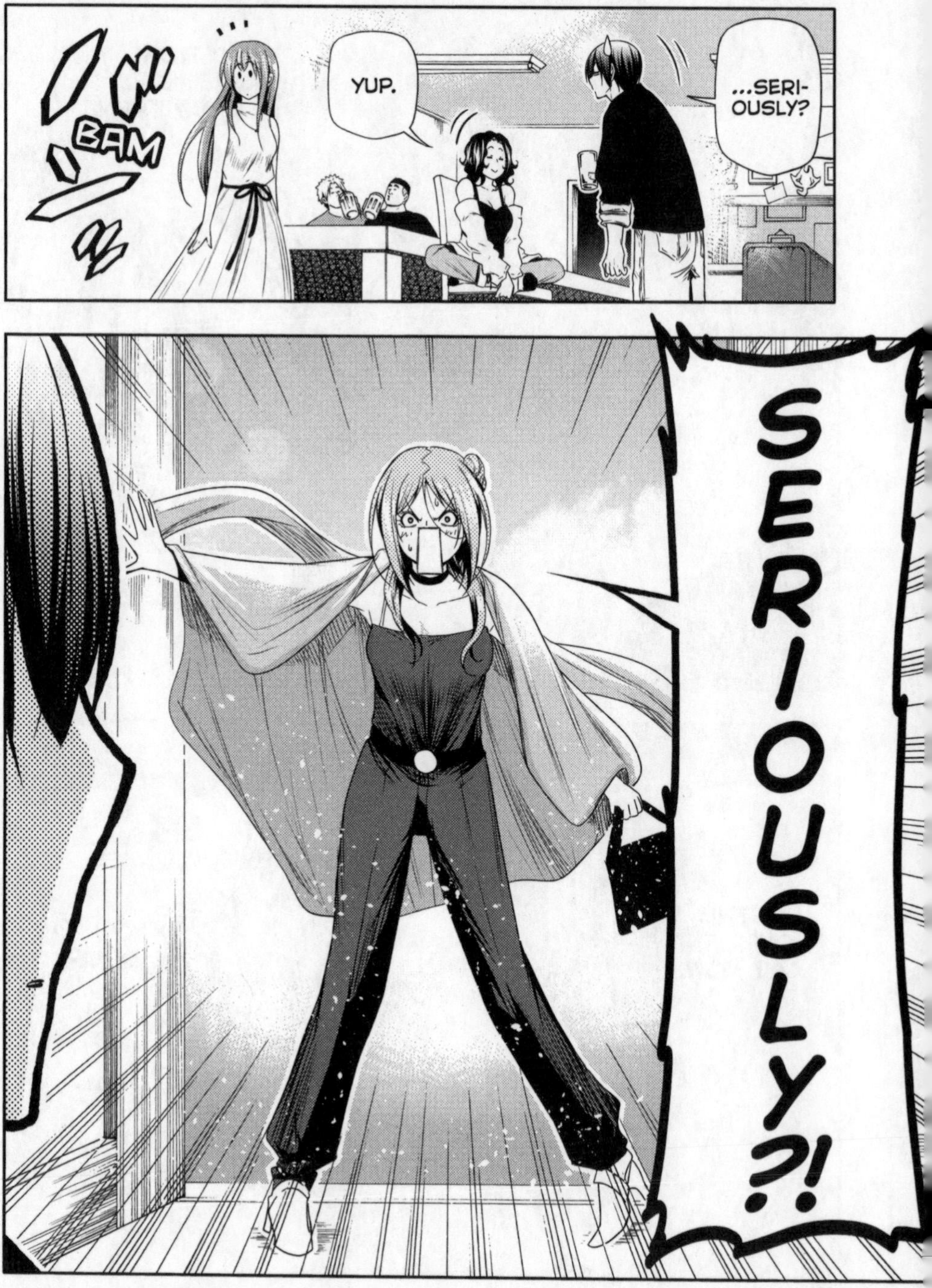
...SERI-OUSLY?
YUP.
...
BAM
SERIOUSLY?!

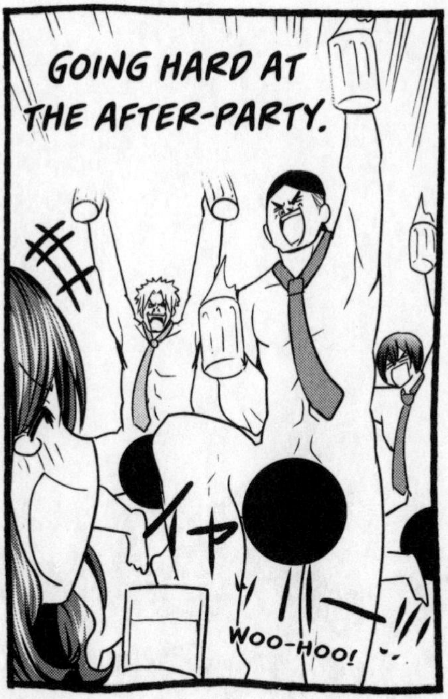
GOING HARD AT THE AFTER-PARTY.
WOO-HOO!

Grand Blue Dreaming

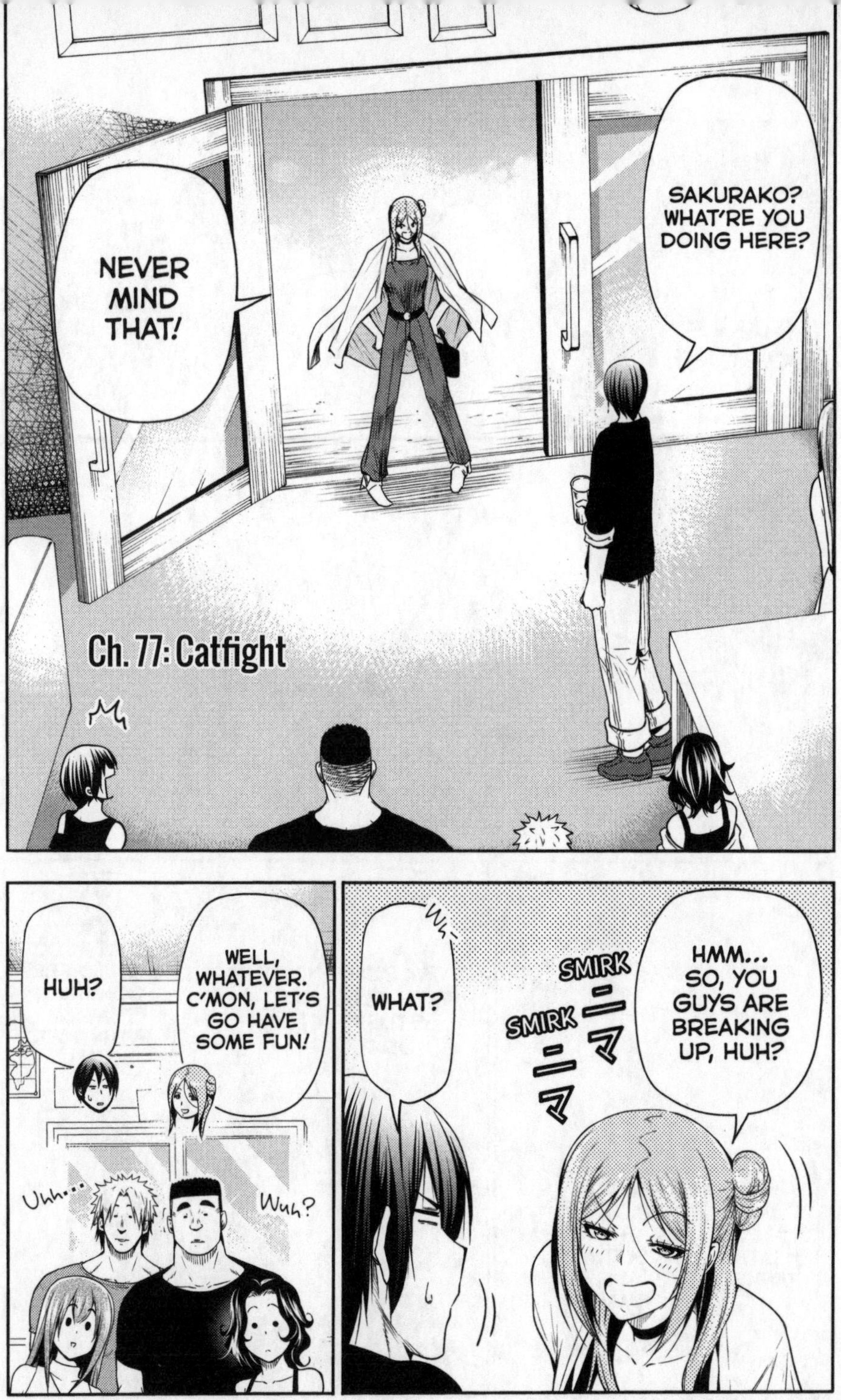
SAKURAKO? WHAT'RE YOU DOING HERE?
NEVER MIND THAT!
Ch. 77: Catfight
HMM... SO, YOU GUYS ARE BREAKING UP, HUH?
SMIRK ニマ
SMIRK ニマ
WHAT?
WELL, WHATEVER. C'MON, LET'S GO HAVE SOME FUN!
HUH?
Wuh?
Uhh...

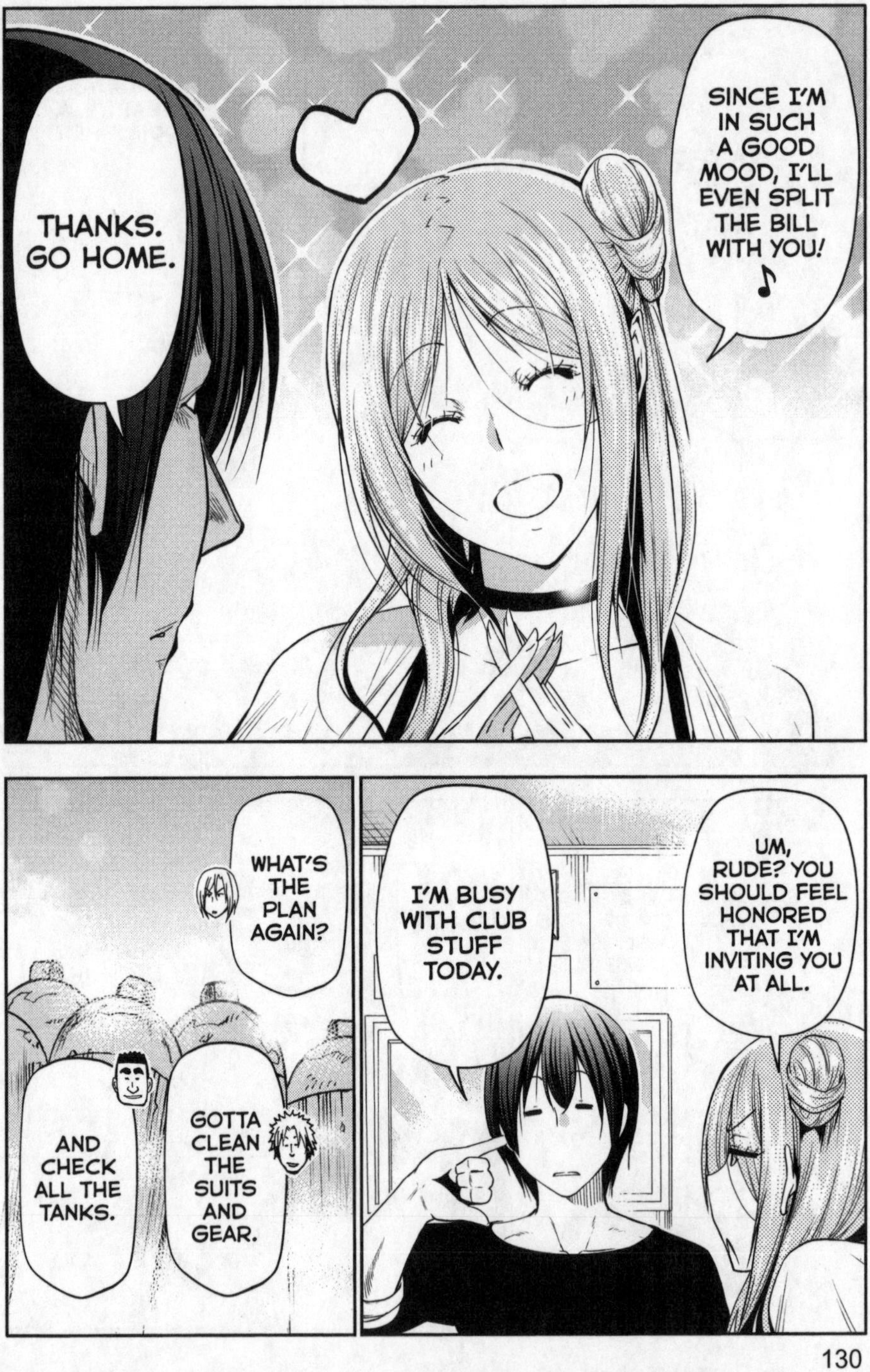
SINCE I'M IN SUCH A GOOD MOOD, I'LL EVEN SPLIT THE BILL WITH YOU! ♪
THANKS. GO HOME.
UM, RUDE? YOU SHOULD FEEL HONORED THAT I'M INVITING YOU AT ALL.
I'M BUSY WITH CLUB STUFF TODAY.
WHAT'S THE PLAN AGAIN?
GOTTA CLEAN THE SUITS AND GEAR.
AND CHECK ALL THE TANKS.

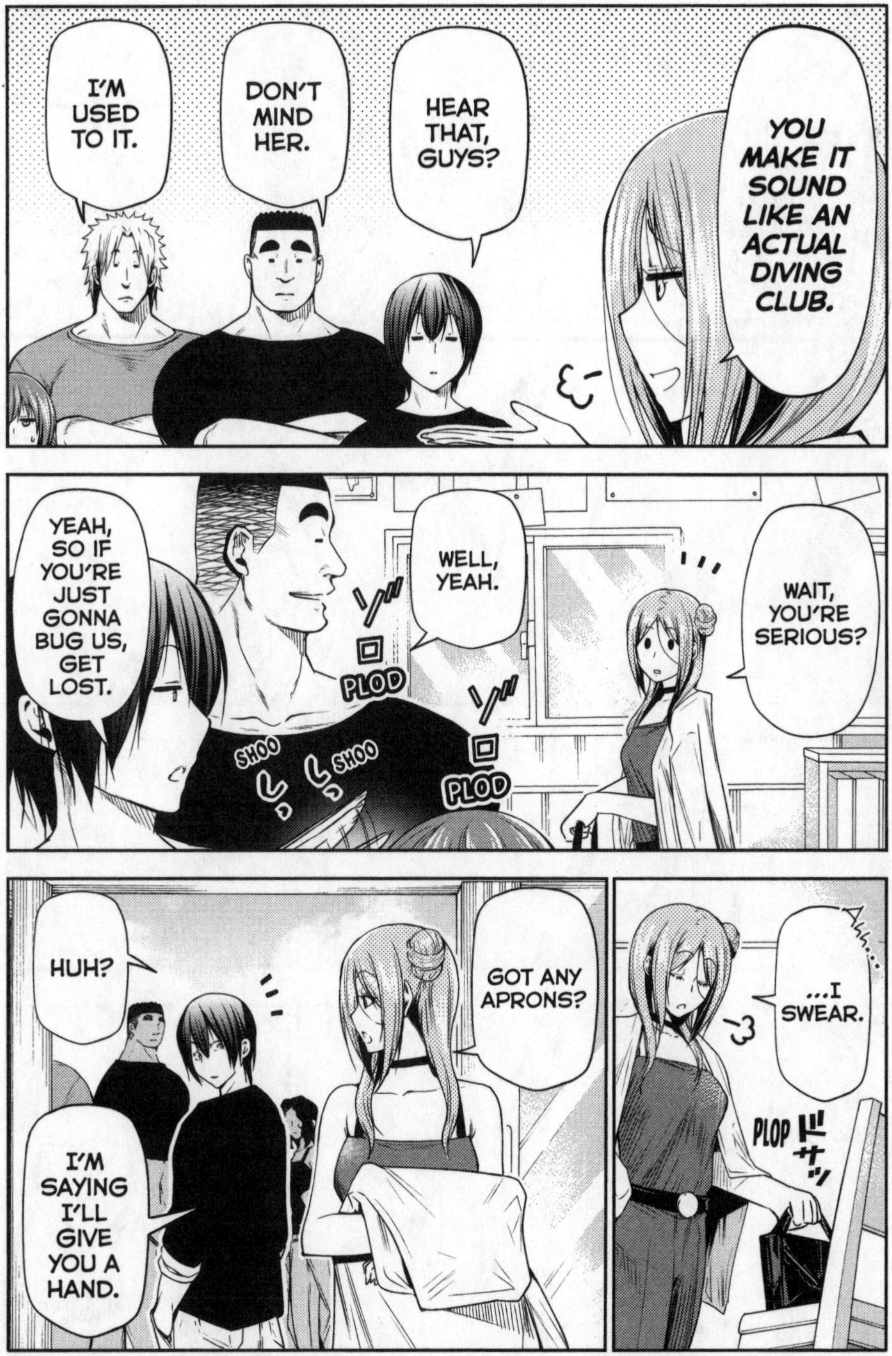
YOU MAKE IT SOUND LIKE AN ACTUAL DIVING CLUB.
HEAR THAT, GUYS?
DON'T MIND HER.
I'M USED TO IT.
WAIT, YOU'RE SERIOUS?
WELL, YEAH.
PLOD
PLOD
YEAH, SO IF YOU'RE JUST GONNA BUG US, GET LOST.
SHOO
SHOO
...I SWEAR.
PLOP
GOT ANY APRONS?
HUH?
I'M SAYING I'LL GIVE YOU A HAND.

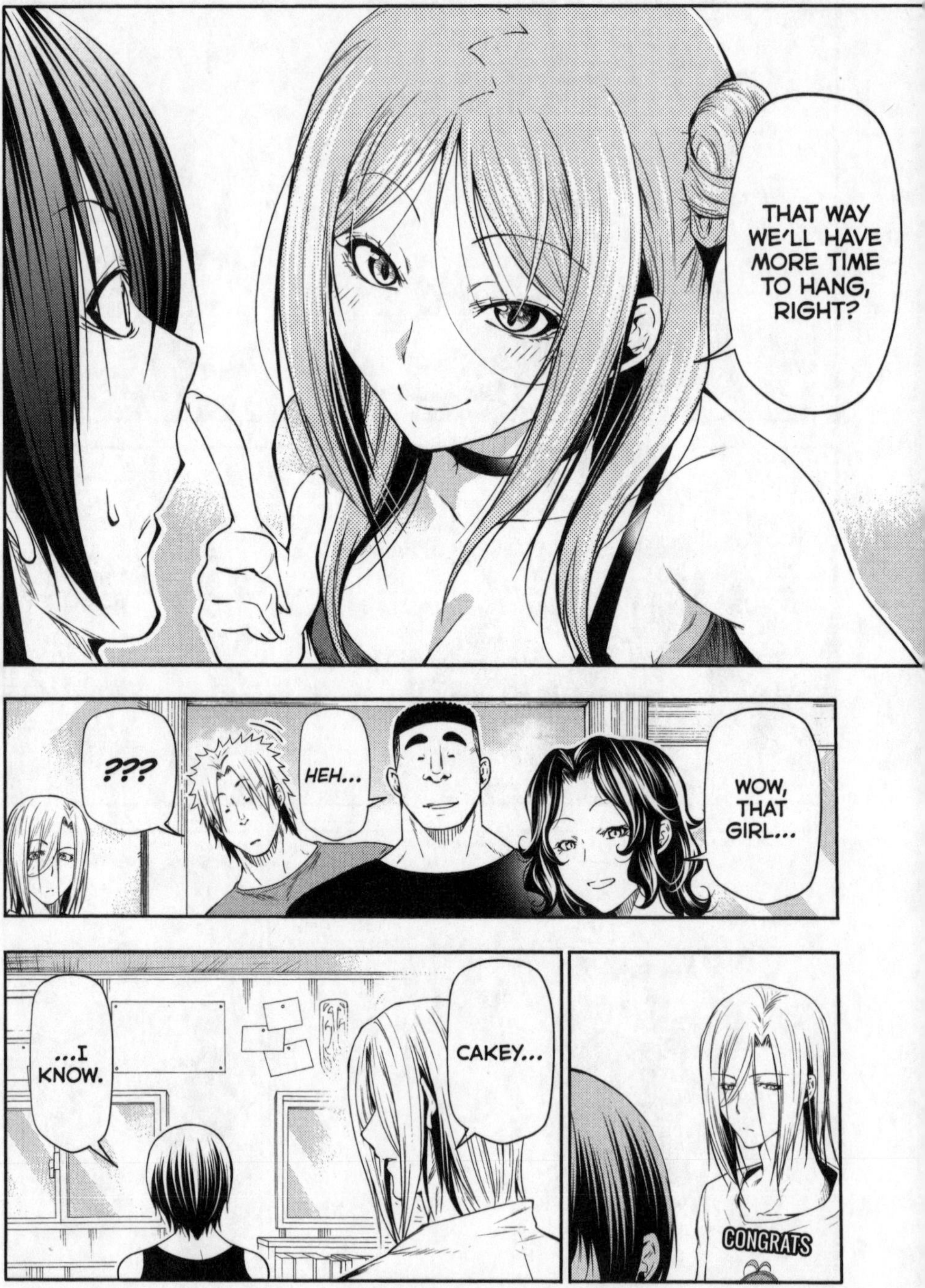
THAT WAY WE'LL HAVE MORE TIME TO HANG, RIGHT?
WOW, THAT GIRL...
HEH...
???
CONGRATS
CAKEY...
...I KNOW.

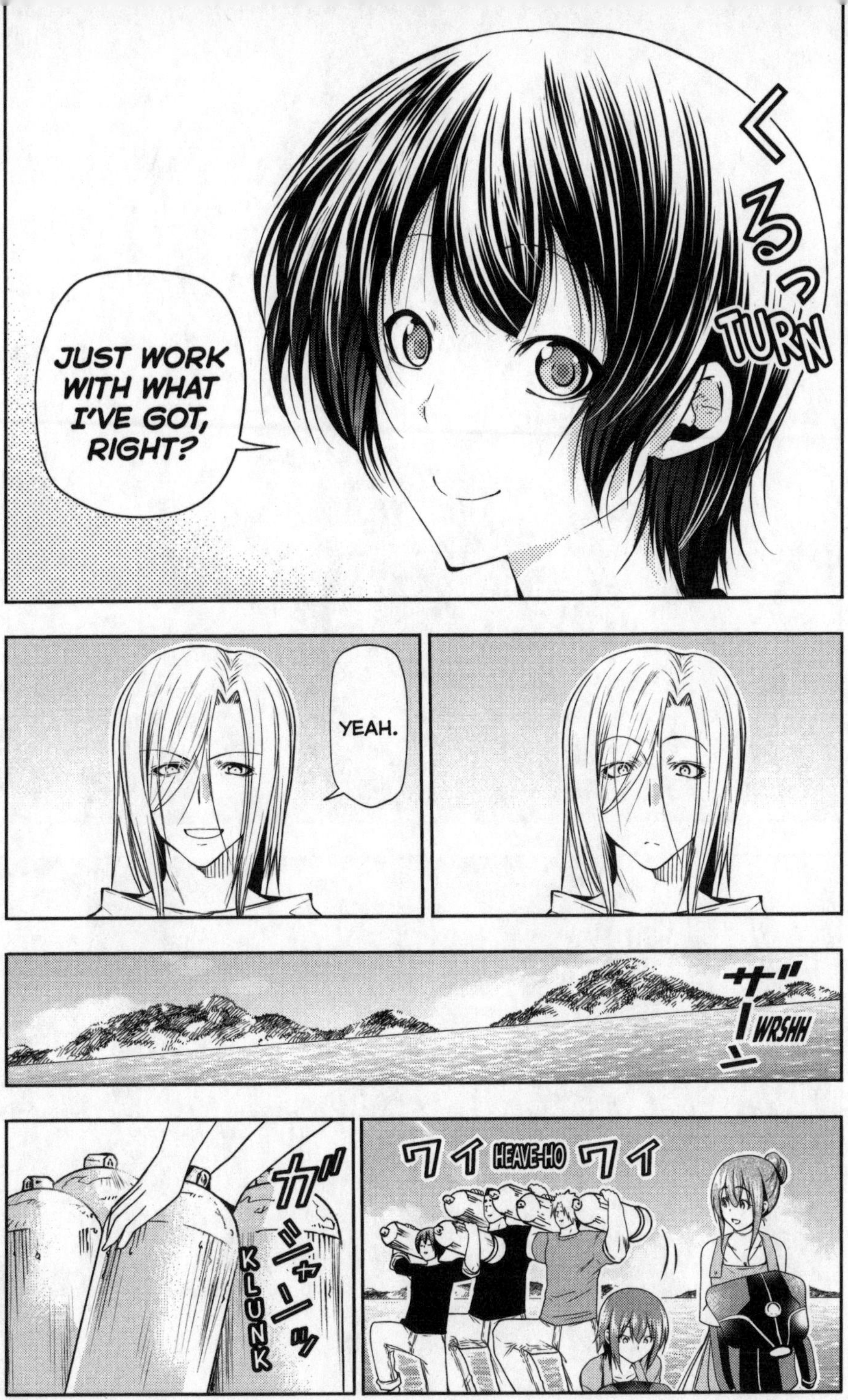
くるっ
TURN
JUST WORK WITH WHAT I'VE GOT, RIGHT?
YEAH.
ザーー
WRSHH
ワイ
HEAVE-HO
ワイ
ガシャーンッ
KLUNK

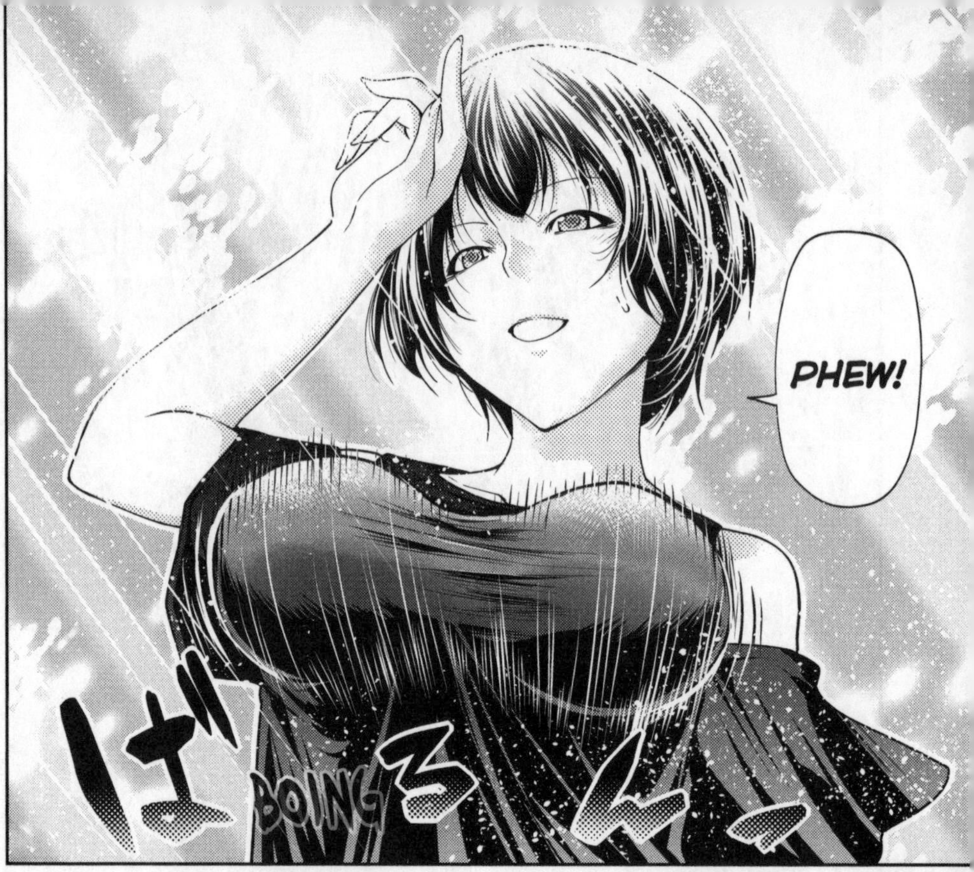
PHEW!
BOING

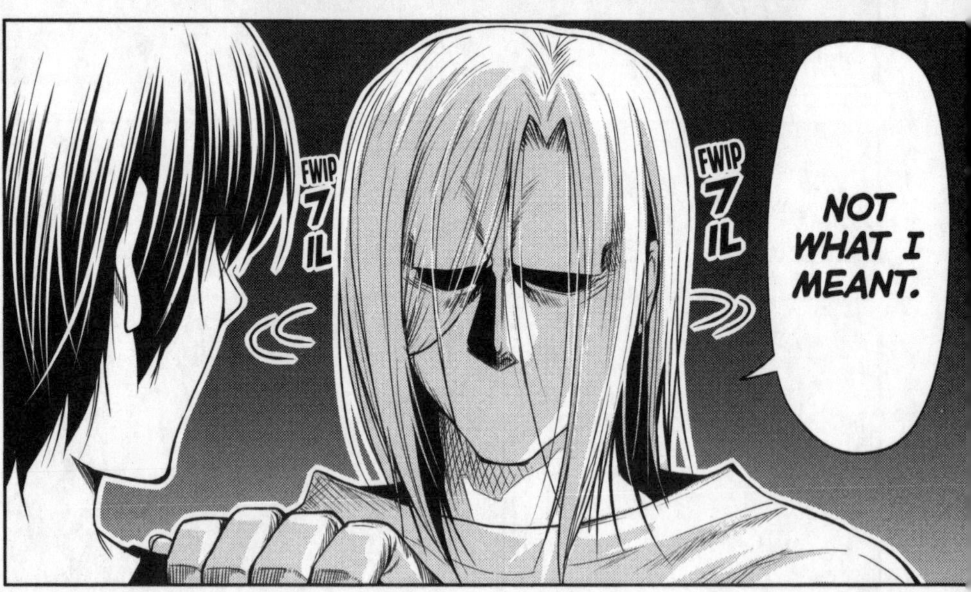
NOT WHAT I MEANT.
FWIP
FWIP

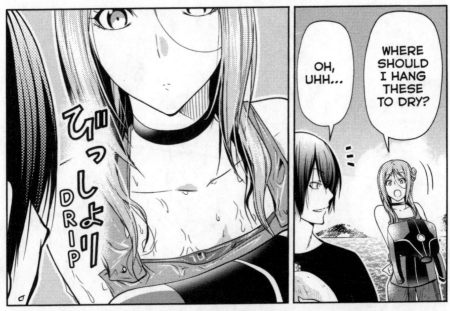

WHERE SHOULD I HANG THESE TO DRY?
OH, UHH...
びっしょり
DRIP
HEY, YOU SURE YOU'RE COOL WITH THAT?
Your clothes, I mean.
HM?
Oh...
NOT MUCH I CAN DO ABOUT IT, RIGHT?
OR WOULD YOU PREFER IT IF I WORE *JUST* THE APRON?
STOP! YOU'RE BRINGING UP BAD MEMORIES!
カッ
FLASH
どぉ
DA-DUM
WELCOME BACK, YOU TWO.

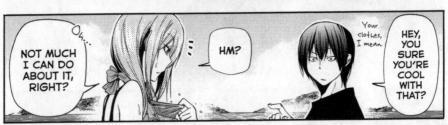

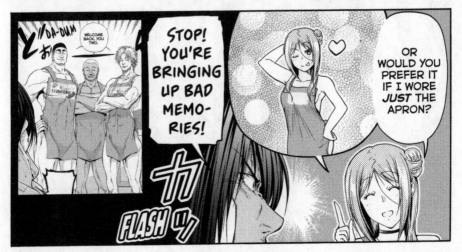

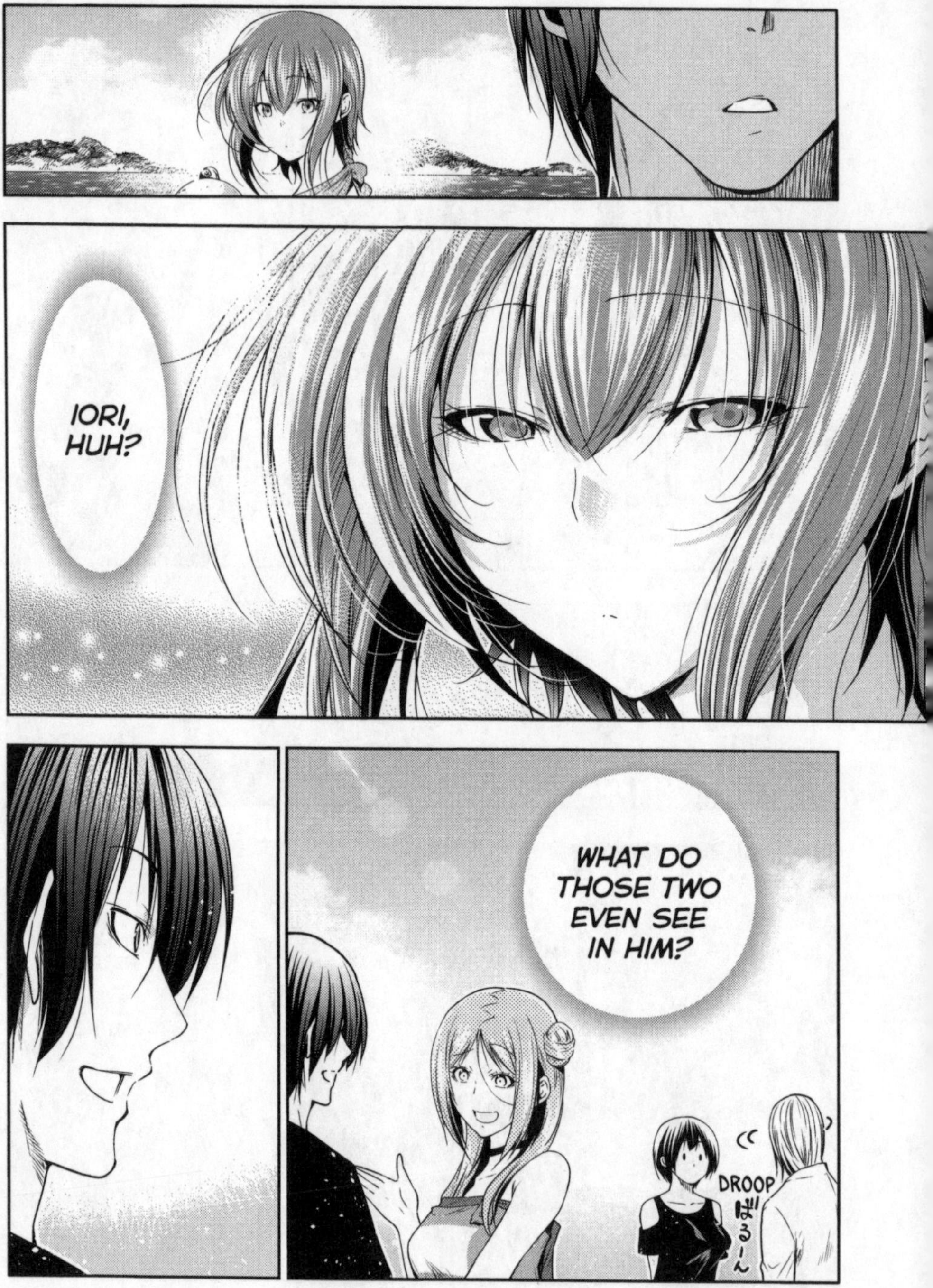
IORI, HUH?
WHAT DO THOSE TWO EVEN SEE IN HIM?
DROOP
ぼるーん

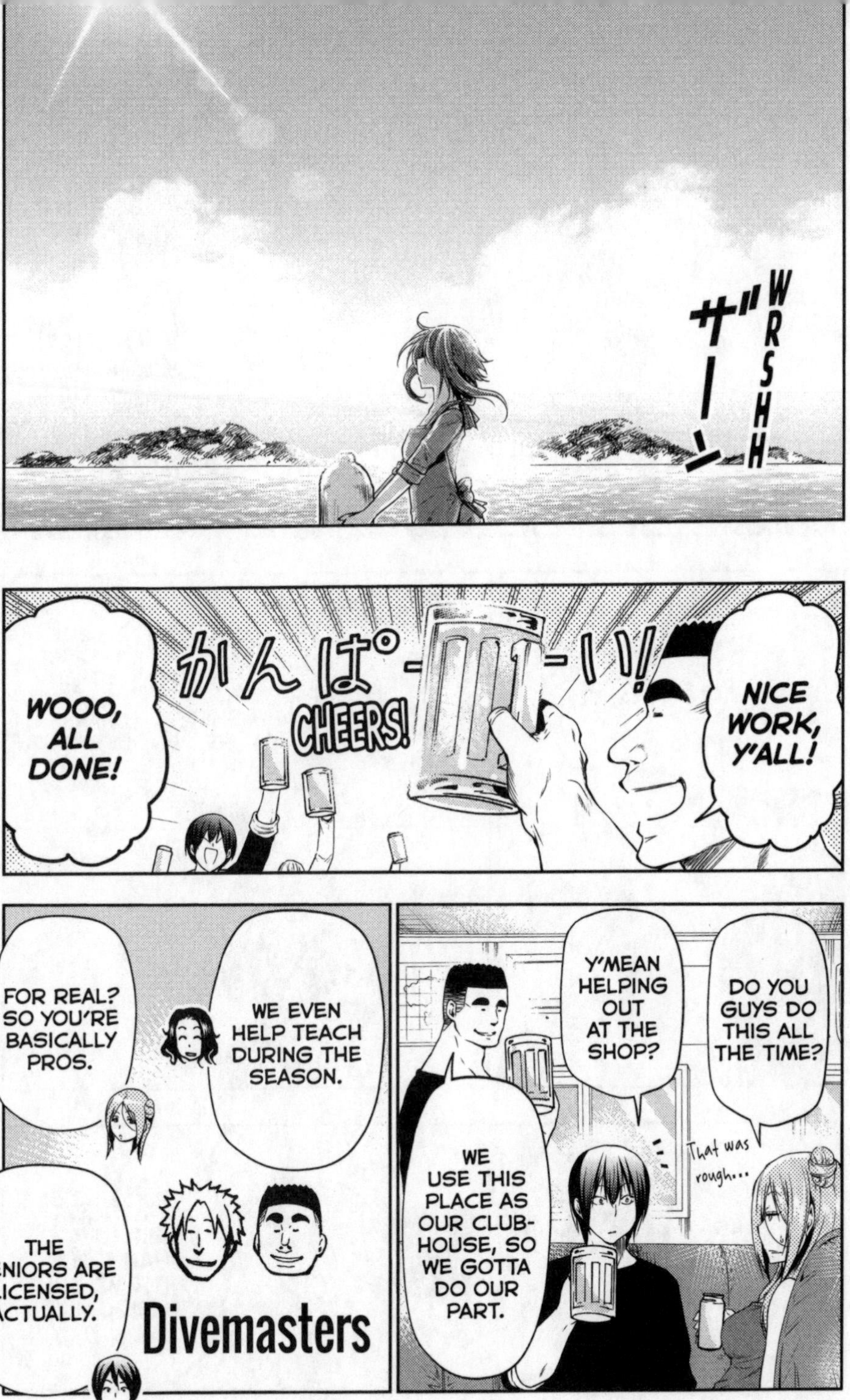
ザーー
WRSHH
NICE WORK, Y'ALL!
かんぱーーい!!
CHEERS!
WOOO, ALL DONE!
DO YOU GUYS DO THIS ALL THE TIME?
That was rough...
Y'MEAN HELPING OUT AT THE SHOP?
WE USE THIS PLACE AS OUR CLUB-HOUSE, SO WE GOTTA DO OUR PART.
WE EVEN HELP TEACH DURING THE SEASON.
FOR REAL? SO YOU'RE BASICALLY PROS.
THE SENIORS ARE LICENSED, ACTUALLY.
Divemasters

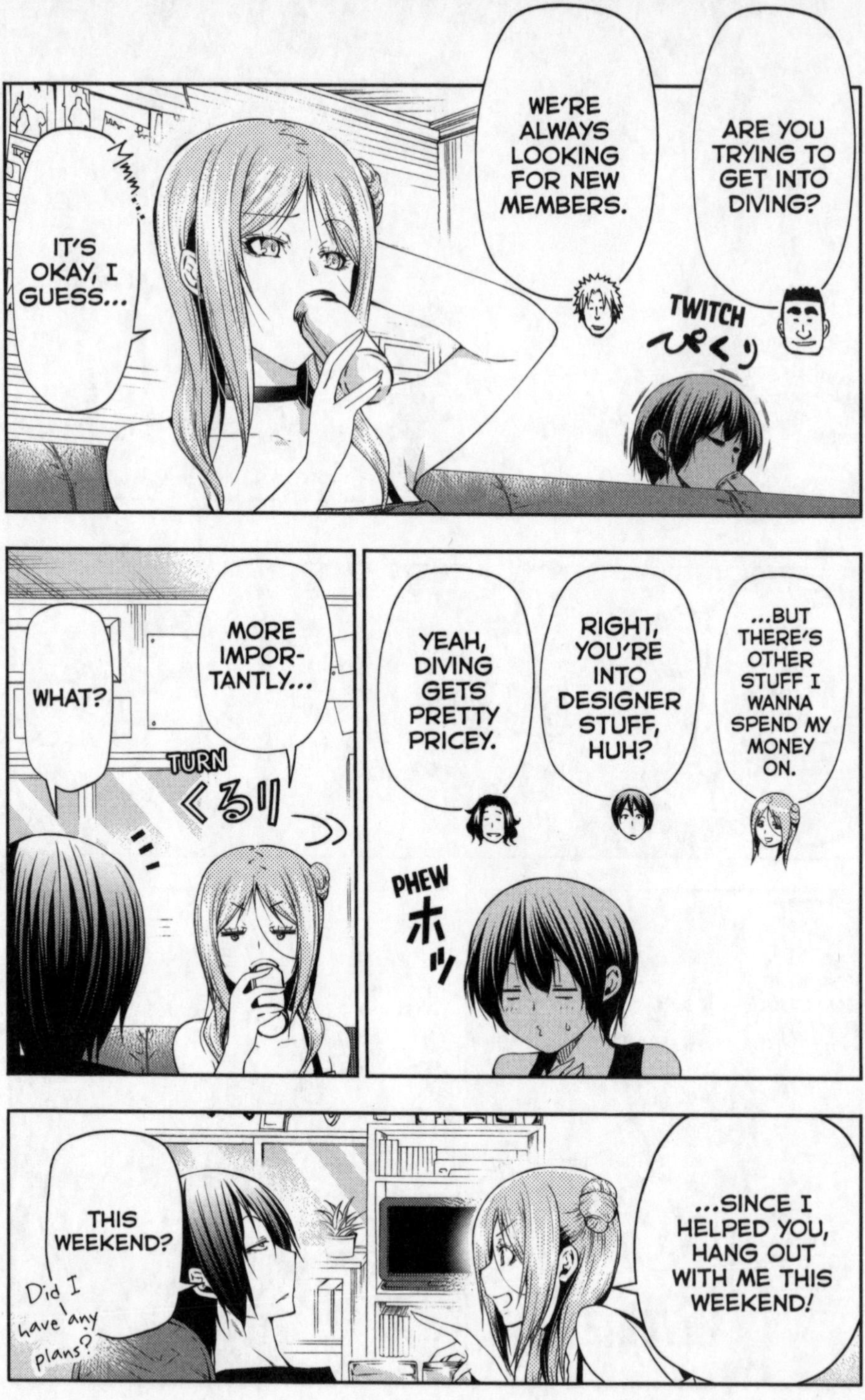
ARE YOU TRYING TO GET INTO DIVING?
WE'RE ALWAYS LOOKING FOR NEW MEMBERS.
TWITCH
ぴくり
Mmm...
IT'S OKAY, I GUESS...
...BUT THERE'S OTHER STUFF I WANNA SPEND MY MONEY ON.
RIGHT, YOU'RE INTO DESIGNER STUFF, HUH?
YEAH, DIVING GETS PRETTY PRICEY.
PHEW
ホッ
MORE IMPORTANTLY...
TURN
くるり
WHAT?
...SINCE I HELPED YOU, HANG OUT WITH ME THIS WEEKEND!
THIS WEEKEND?
Did I have any plans?

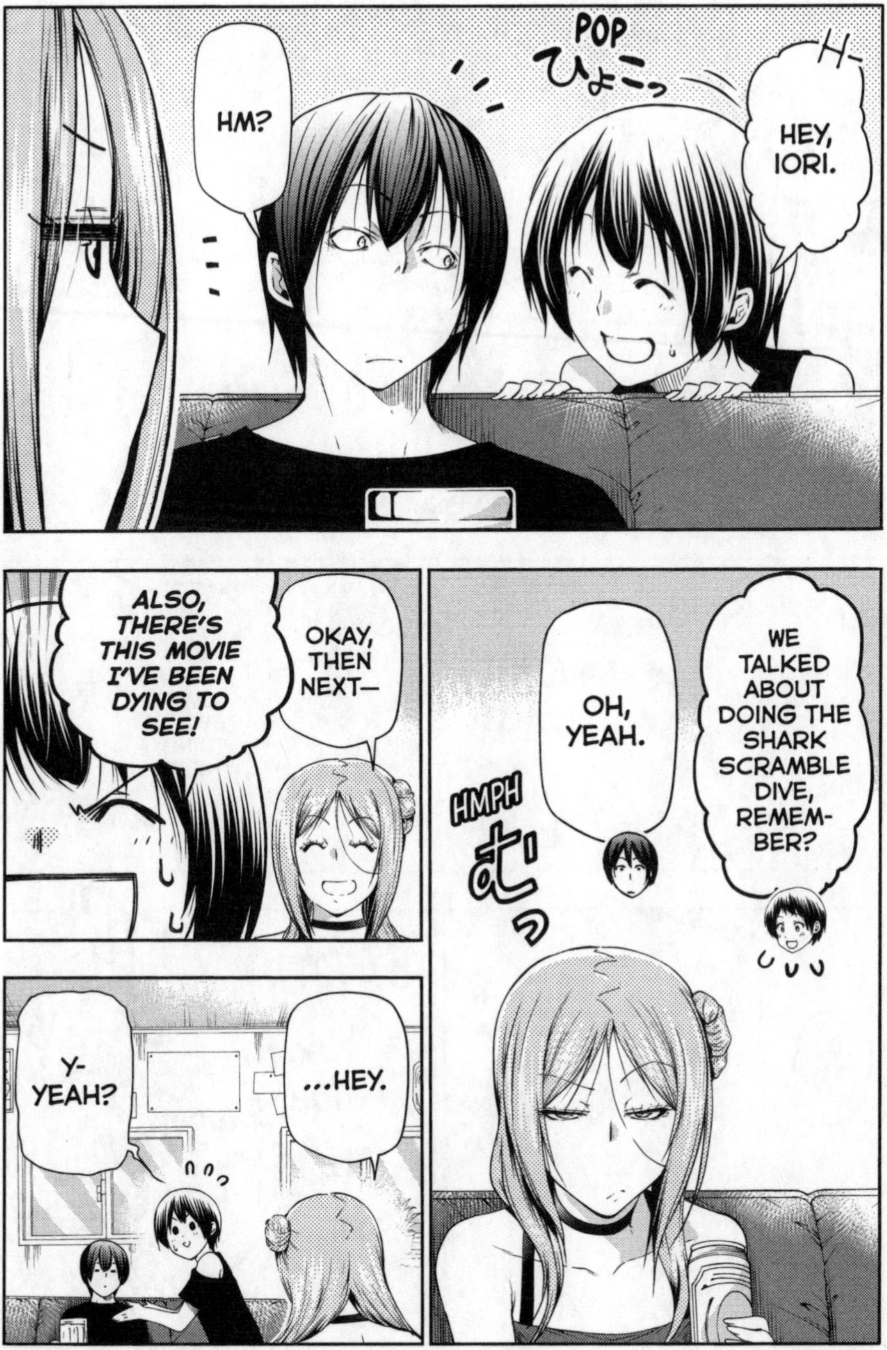
HEY, IORI.
POP
ひょこっ
HM?
WE TALKED ABOUT DOING THE SHARK SCRAMBLE DIVE, REMEMBER?
OH, YEAH.
HMPH
むっ
OKAY, THEN NEXT—
ALSO, THERE'S THIS MOVIE I'VE BEEN DYING TO SEE!
...HEY.
Y-YEAH?

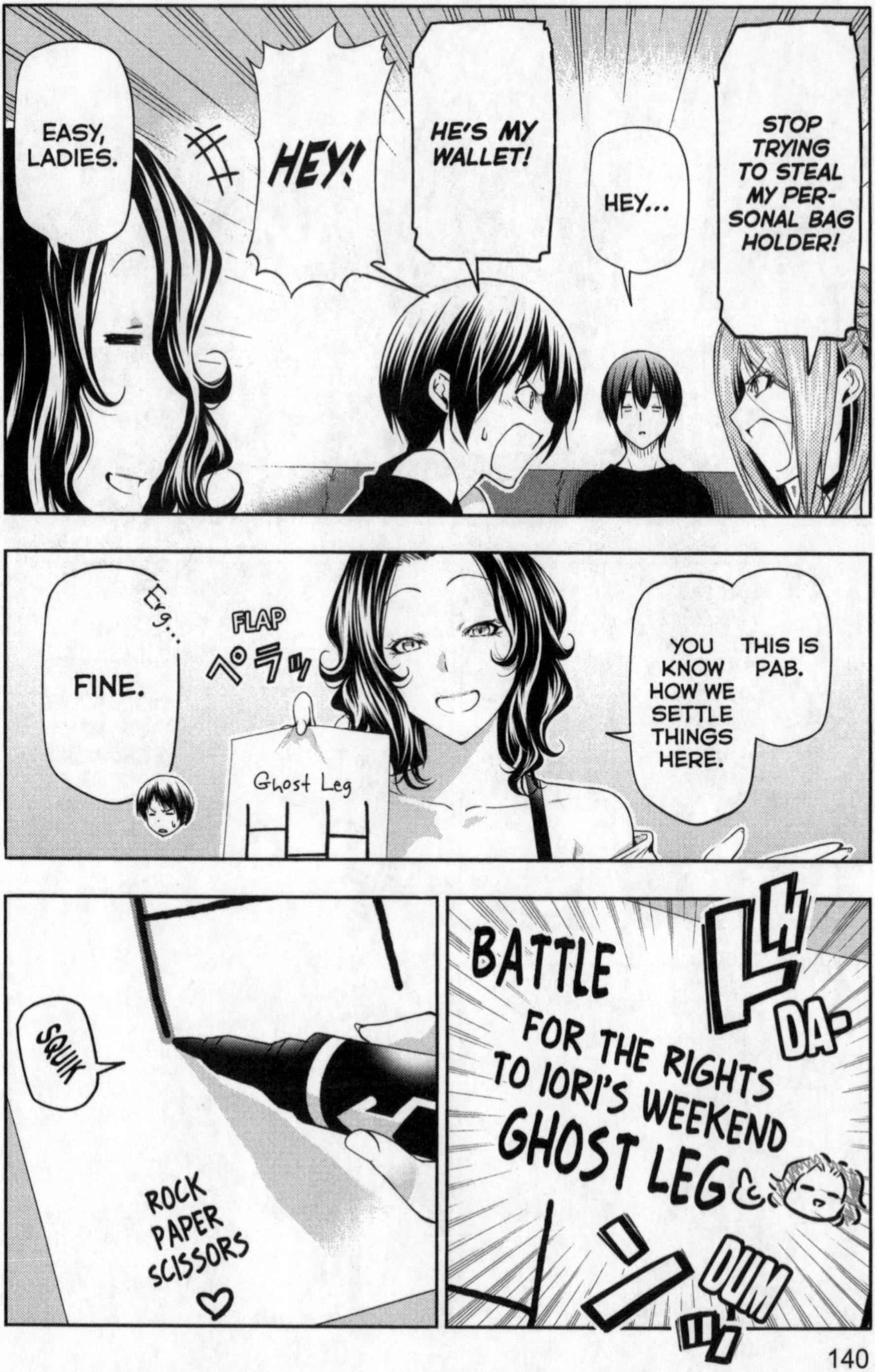
STOP TRYING TO STEAL MY PER-SONAL BAG HOLDER!
HEY...
HE'S MY WALLET!
HEY!
EASY, LADIES.
THIS IS PAB.
YOU KNOW HOW WE SETTLE THINGS HERE.
FLAP
ペラッ
Ghost Leg
Erg...
FINE.
BATTLE FOR THE RIGHTS TO IORI'S WEEKEND GHOST LEG
DA-
DUM
SQUIK
ROCK PAPER SCISSORS ♡

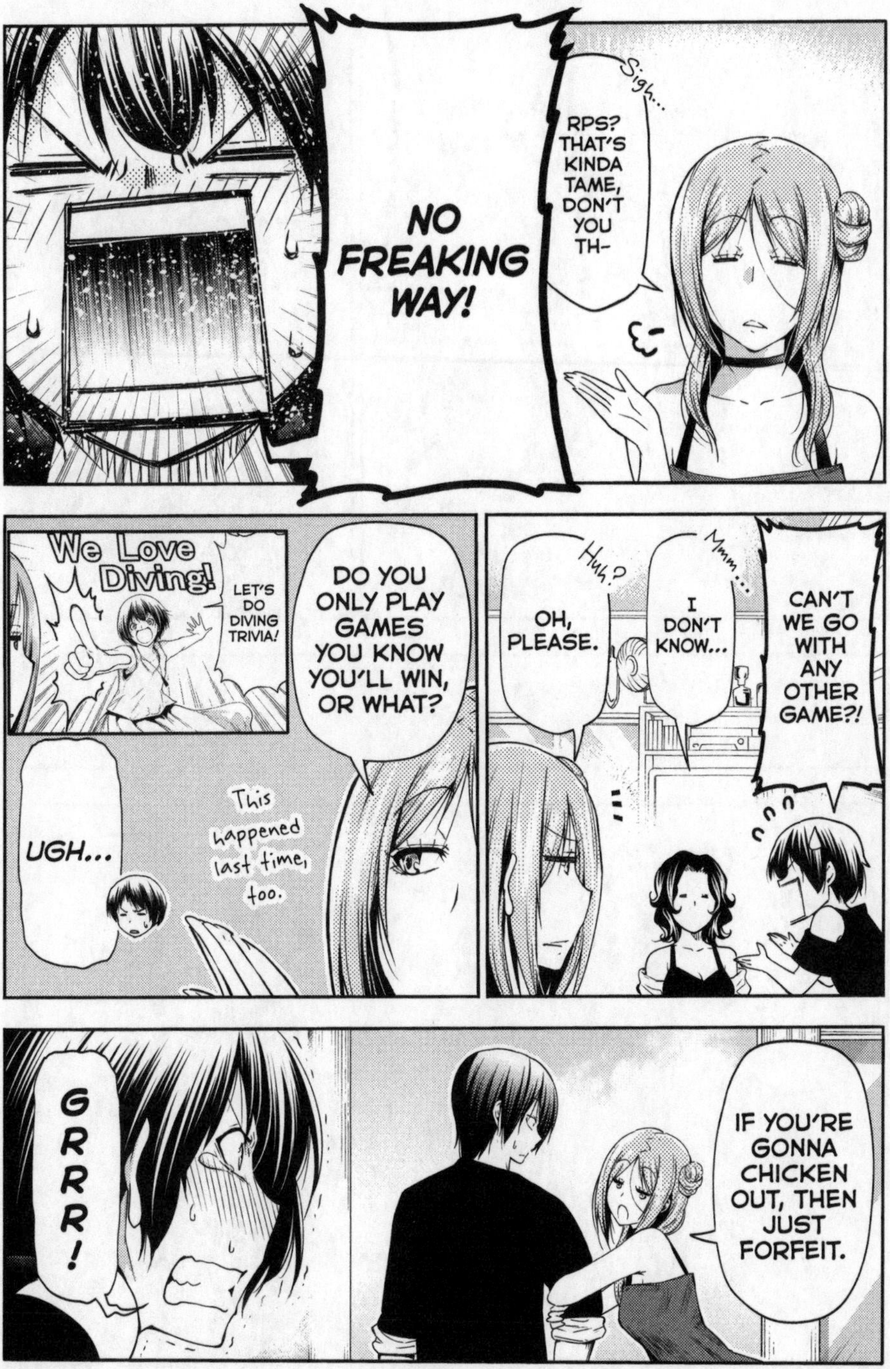
Sigh...
RPS? THAT'S KINDA TAME, DON'T YOU TH-
NO FREAKING WAY!
Mmm...
CAN'T WE GO WITH ANY OTHER GAME?!
I DON'T KNOW...
Huh?
OH, PLEASE.
DO YOU ONLY PLAY GAMES YOU KNOW YOU'LL WIN, OR WHAT?
We Love Diving!
LET'S DO DIVING TRIVIA!
This happened last time, too.
UGH...
IF YOU'RE GONNA CHICKEN OUT, THEN JUST FORFEIT.
GRRR!

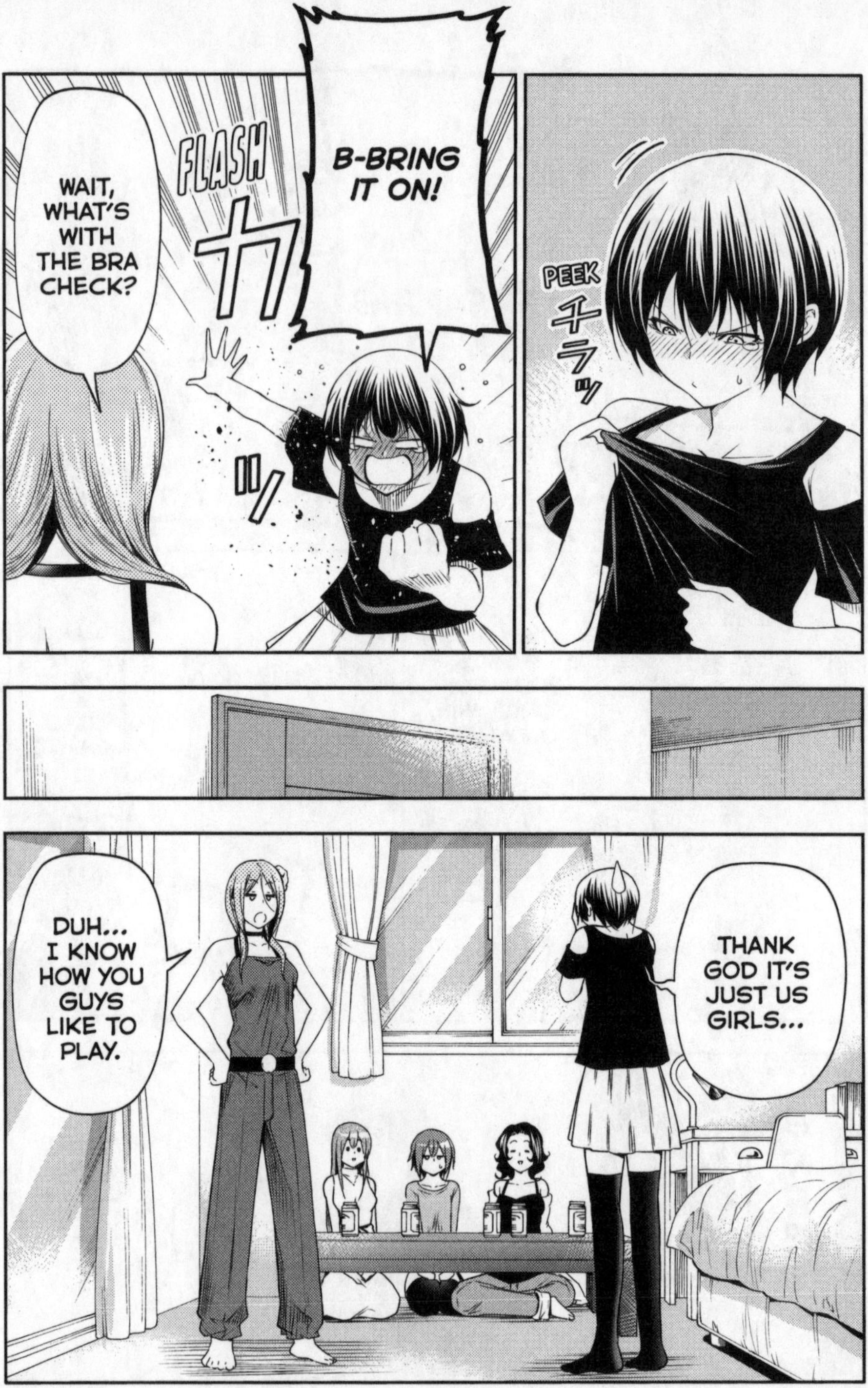
PEEK
チラッ
B-BRING IT ON!
FLASH
カ
WAIT, WHAT'S WITH THE BRA CHECK?
THANK GOD IT'S JUST US GIRLS...
DUH... I KNOW HOW YOU GUYS LIKE TO PLAY.

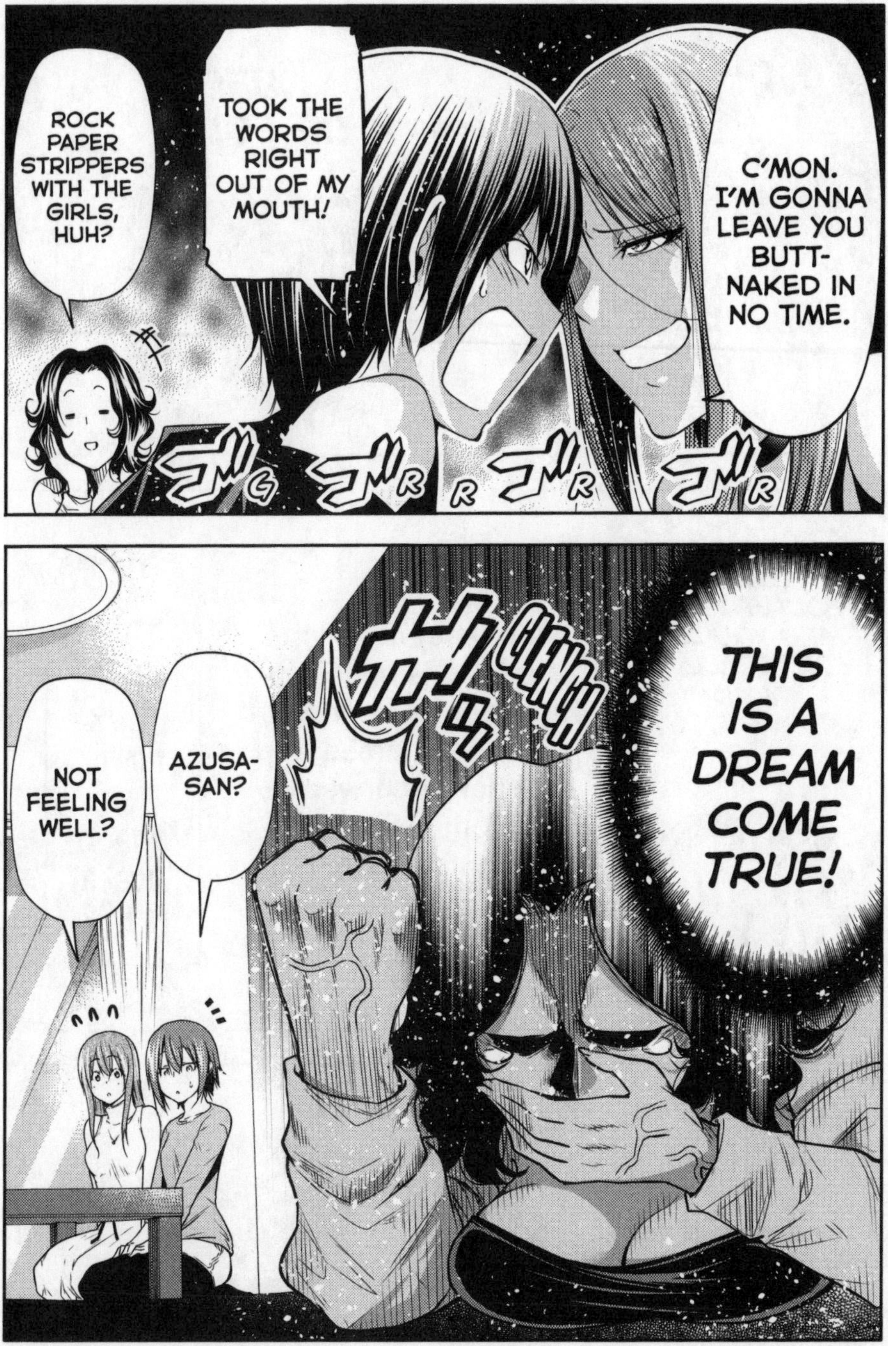
C'MON. I'M GONNA LEAVE YOU BUTT-NAKED IN NO TIME.
TOOK THE WORDS RIGHT OUT OF MY MOUTH!
ROCK PAPER STRIPPERS WITH THE GIRLS, HUH?
GRRRR
THIS IS A DREAM COME TRUE!
CLENCH
AZUSA-SAN?
NOT FEELING WELL?

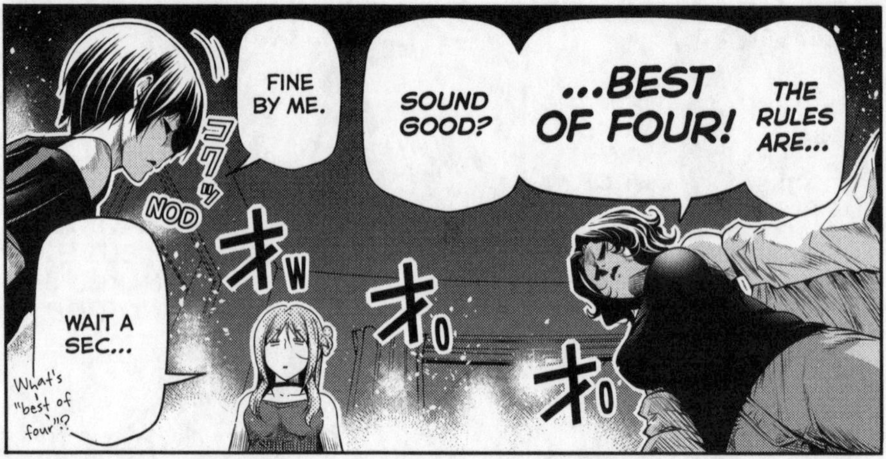
THE RULES ARE...
...BEST OF FOUR!
SOUND GOOD?
FINE BY ME.
NOD
W
O
O
WAIT A SEC...
What's "best of four"!?

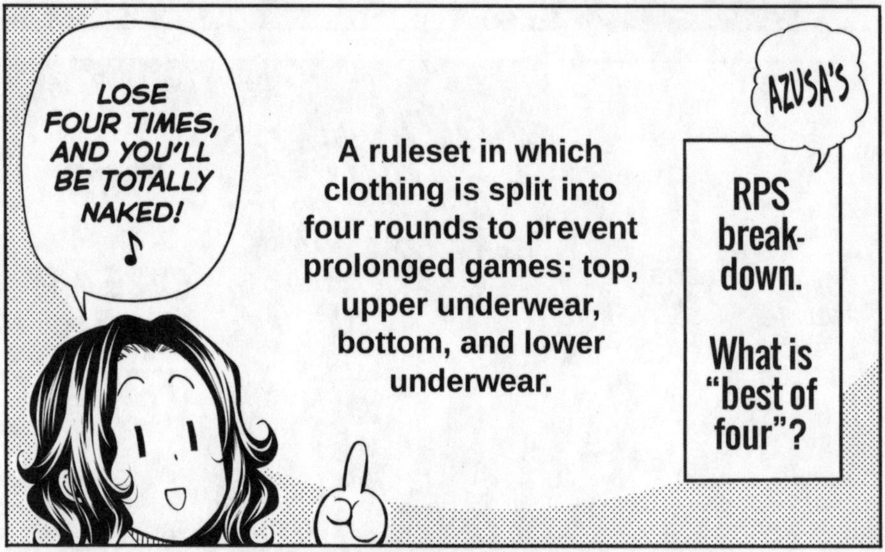
AZUSA'S
RPS break-down.
What is "best of four"?
A ruleset in which clothing is split into four rounds to prevent prolonged games: top, upper underwear, bottom, and lower underwear.
LOSE FOUR TIMES, AND YOU'LL BE TOTALLY NAKED! ♪

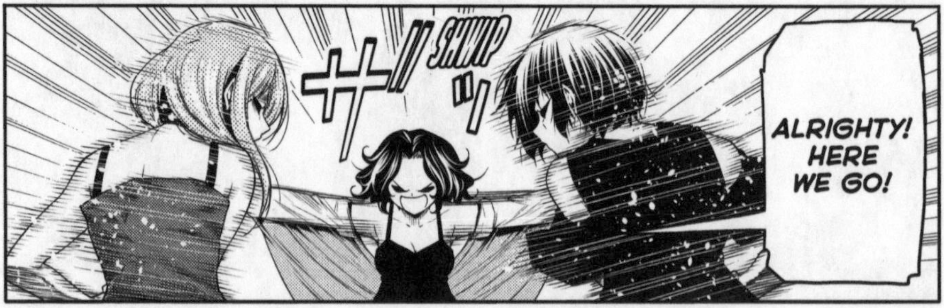
ALRIGHTY! HERE WE GO!
SHWIP

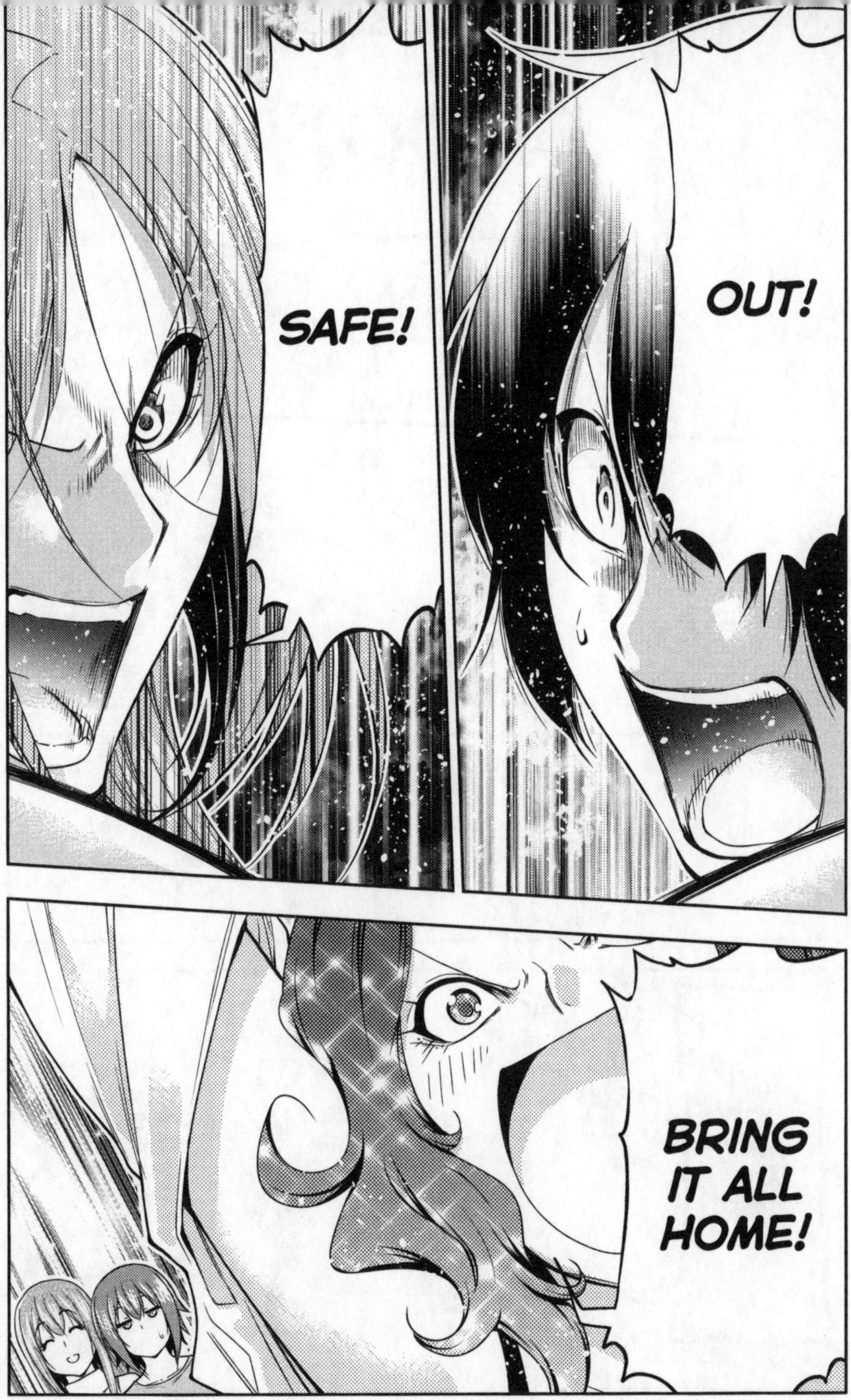
OUT!
SAFE!
BRING IT ALL HOME!

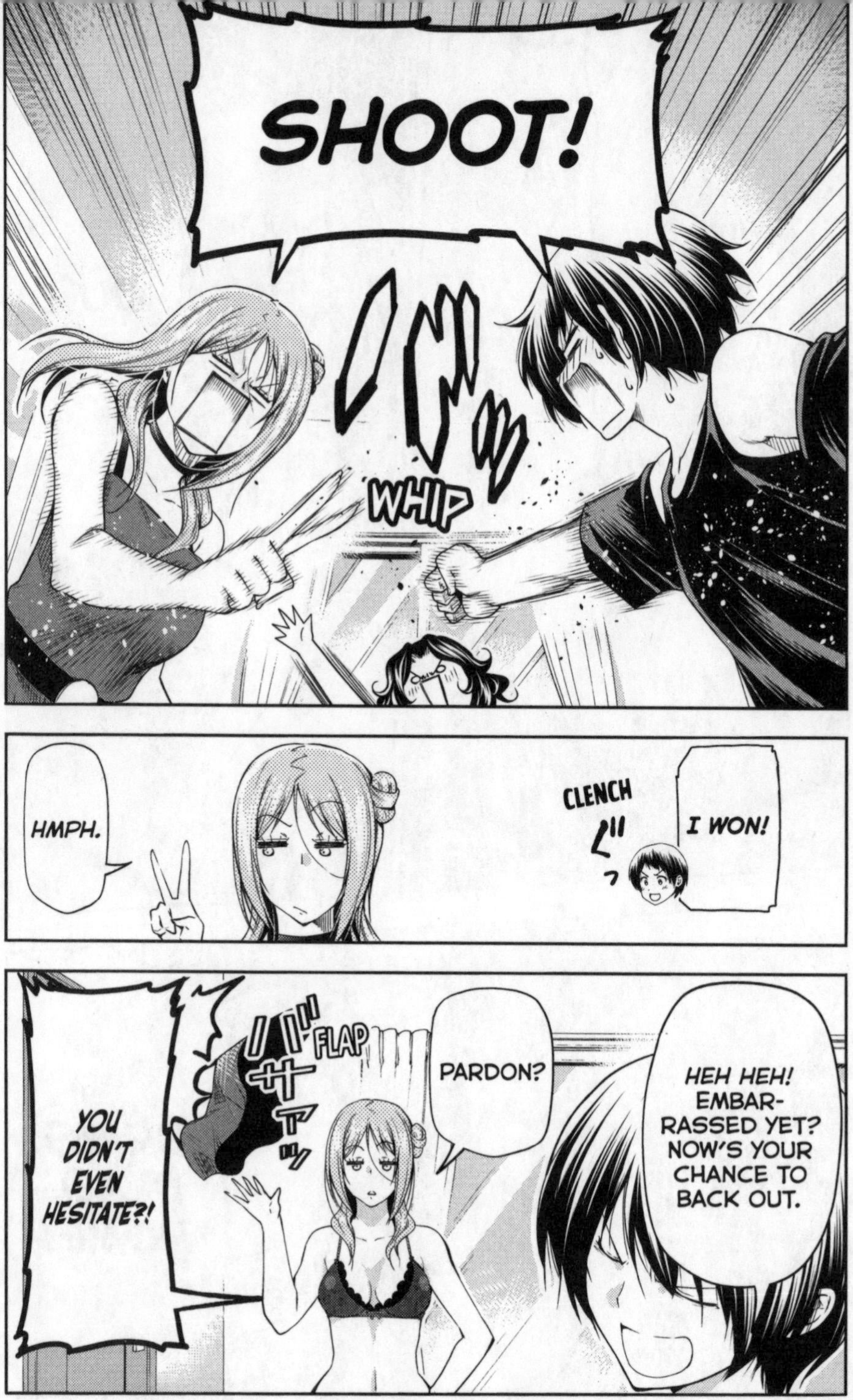
SHOOT!
WHIP
I WON!
CLENCH
HMPH.
HEH HEH! EMBARRASSED YET? NOW'S YOUR CHANCE TO BACK OUT.
PARDON?
FLAP
YOU DIDN'T EVEN HESITATE?!

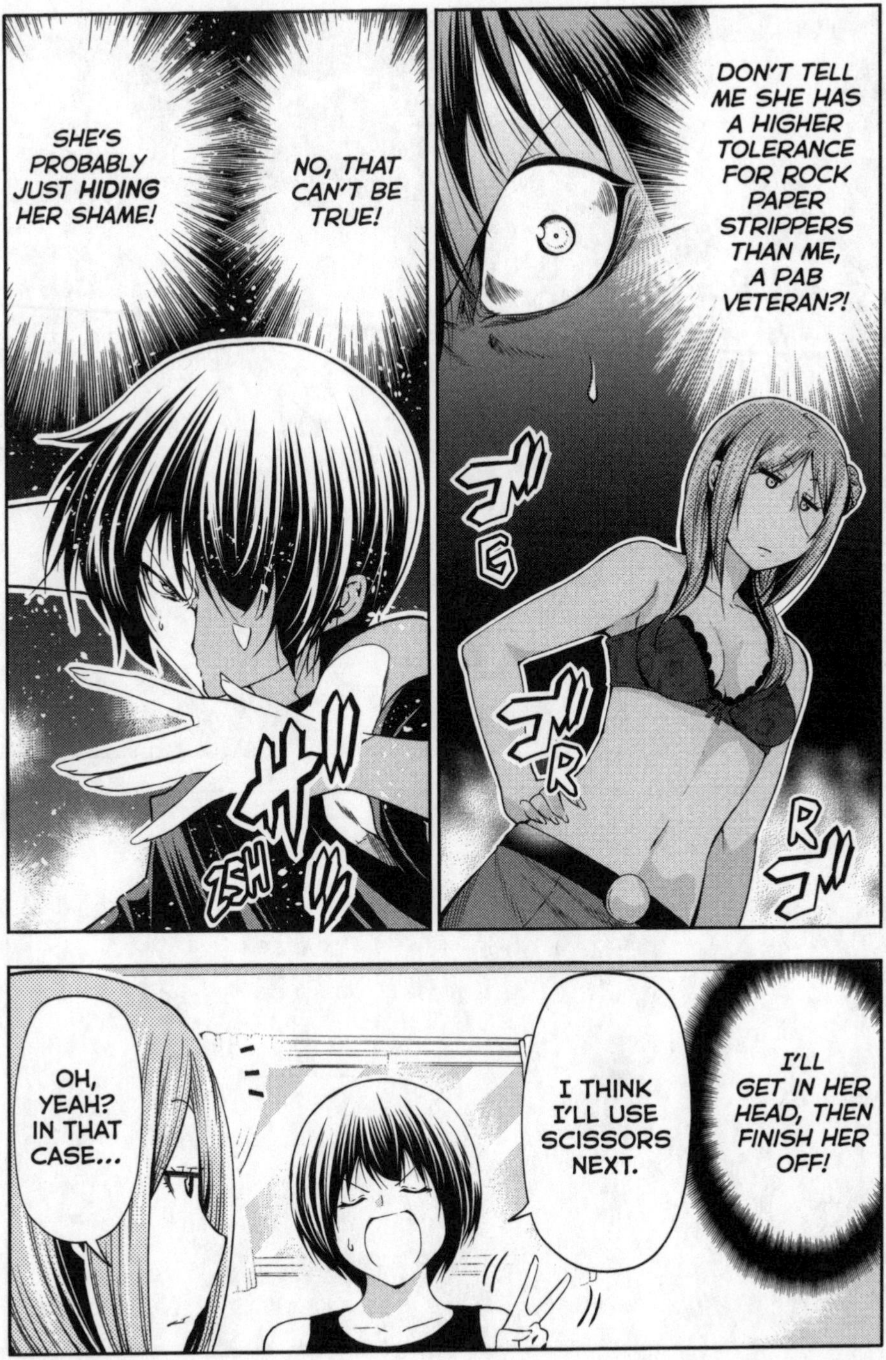
DON'T TELL ME SHE HAS A HIGHER TOLERANCE FOR ROCK PAPER STRIPPERS THAN ME, A PAB VETERAN?!
G
R
R
NO, THAT CAN'T BE TRUE!
SHE'S PROBABLY JUST HIDING HER SHAME!
ZSH
I'LL GET IN HER HEAD, THEN FINISH HER OFF!
I THINK I'LL USE SCISSORS NEXT.
OH, YEAH? IN THAT CASE...

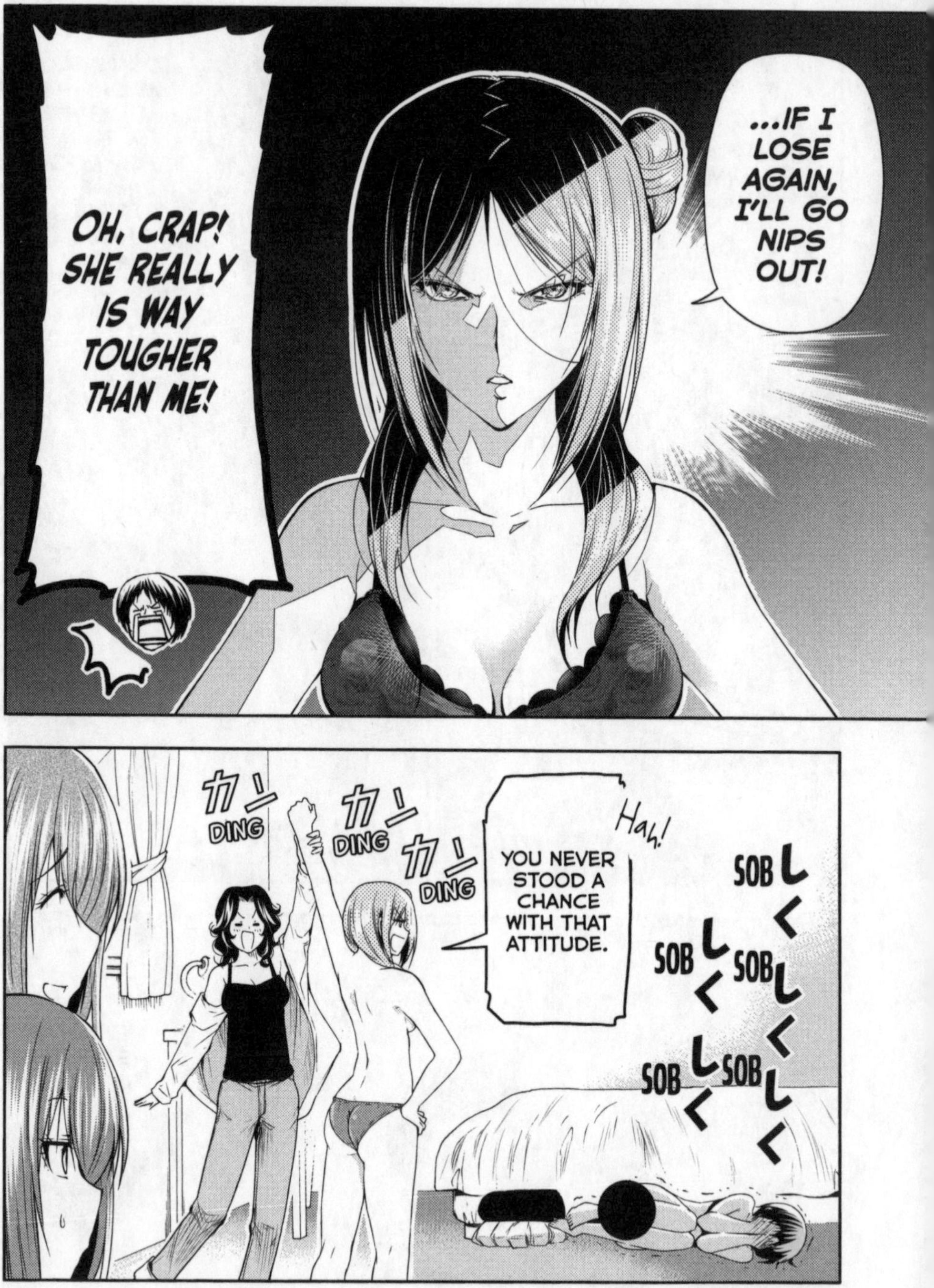
...IF I LOSE AGAIN, I'LL GO NIPS OUT!
OH, CRAP! SHE REALLY IS WAY TOUGHER THAN ME!
SOB しく
SOB しく
SOB しく
SOB しく
SOB しく
Hah!
YOU NEVER STOOD A CHANCE WITH THAT ATTITUDE.
カン DING
カン DING
カン DING

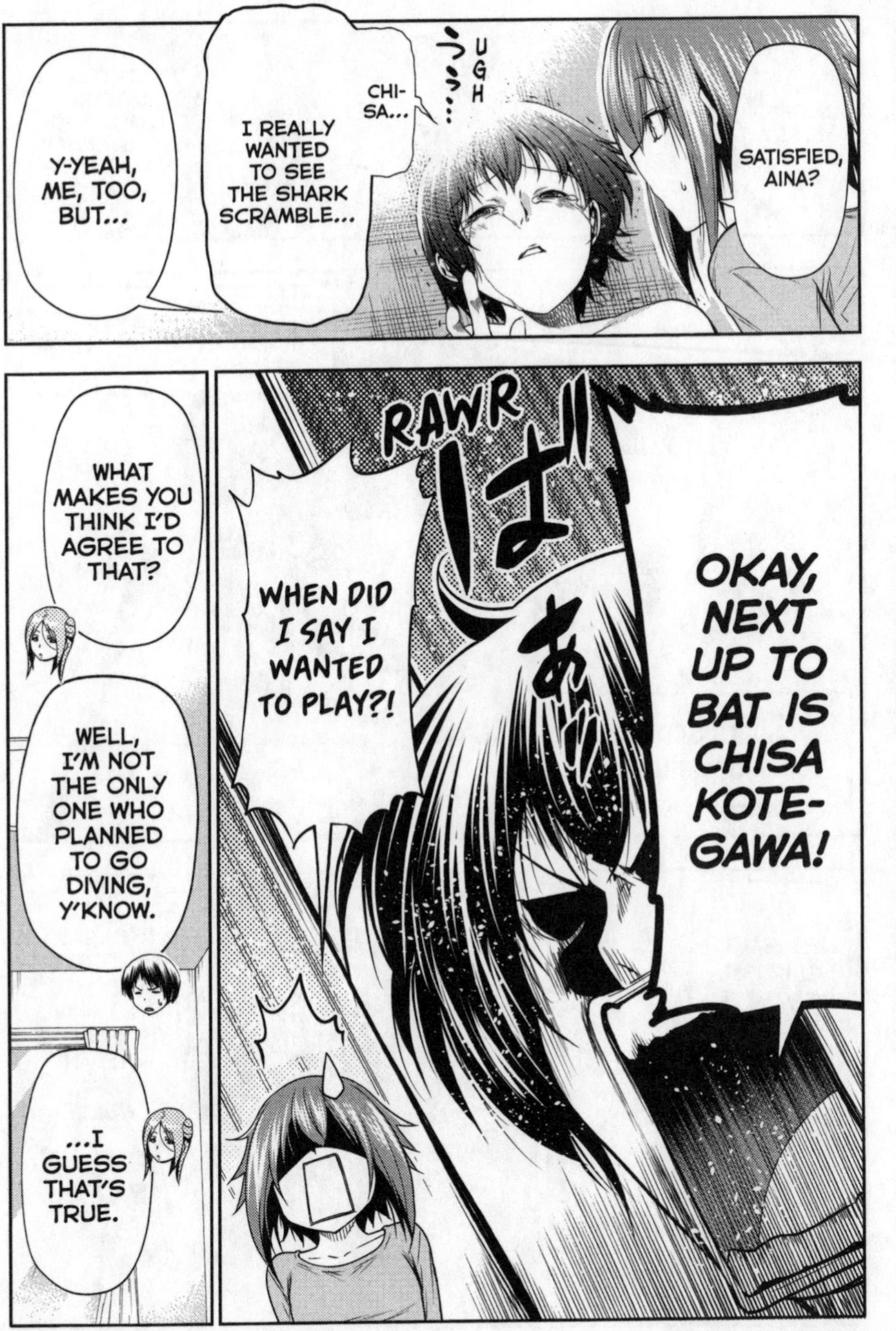
SATISFIED, AINA?
UGH
CHI-SA...
I REALLY WANTED TO SEE THE SHARK SCRAMBLE...
Y-YEAH, ME, TOO, BUT...
OKAY, NEXT UP TO BAT IS CHISA KOTE-GAWA!
RAWR
は
あ
WHEN DID I SAY I WANTED TO PLAY?!
WHAT MAKES YOU THINK I'D AGREE TO THAT?
WELL, I'M NOT THE ONLY ONE WHO PLANNED TO GO DIVING, Y'KNOW.
...I GUESS THAT'S TRUE.

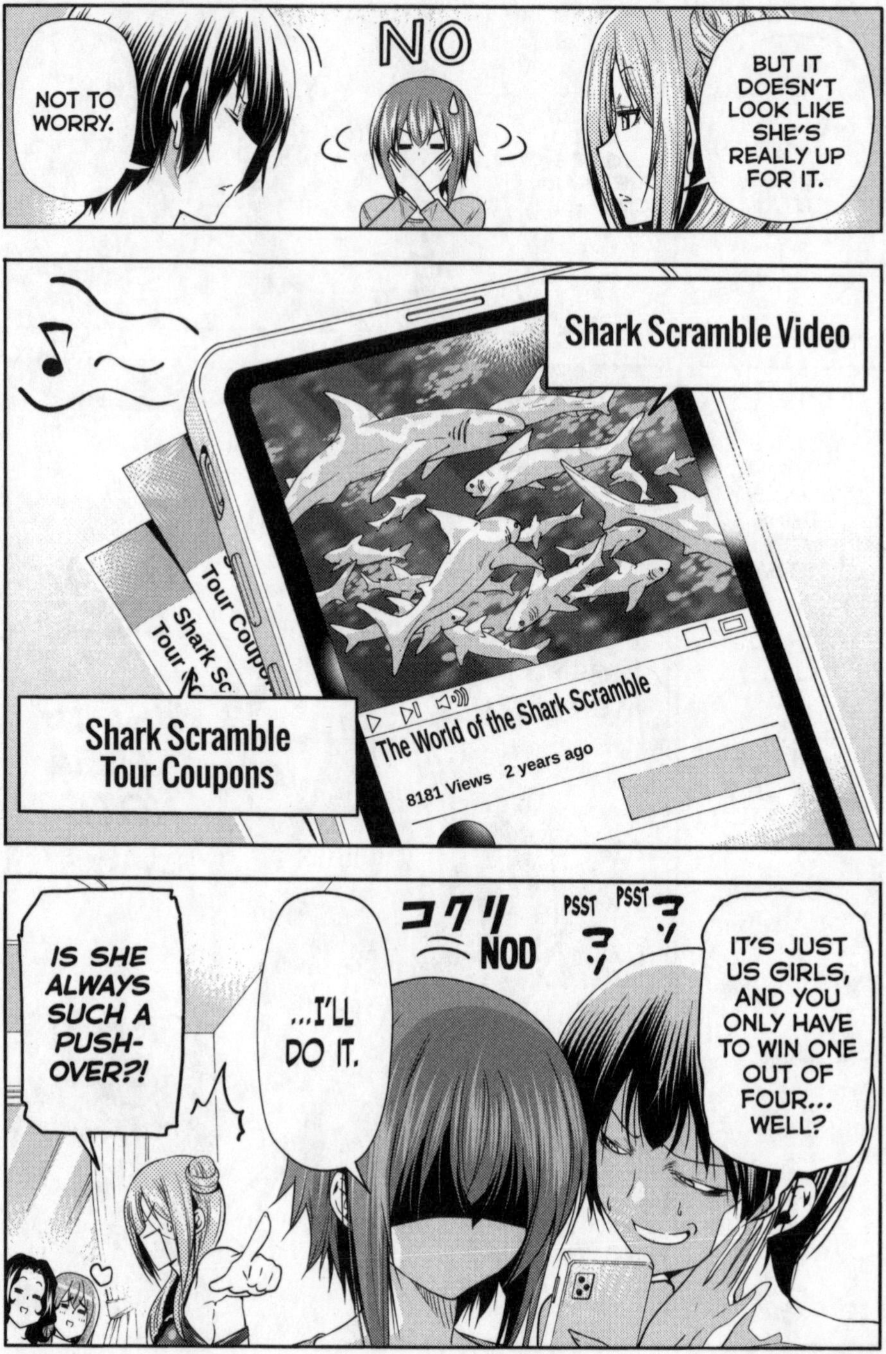
BUT IT DOESN'T LOOK LIKE SHE'S REALLY UP FOR IT.
NO
NOT TO WORRY.
Shark Scramble Video
The World of the Shark Scramble
8181 Views 2 years ago
Shark Scramble Tour Coupons
IT'S JUST US GIRLS, AND YOU ONLY HAVE TO WIN ONE OUT OF FOUR... WELL?
PSST PSST
コクリ NOD
...I'LL DO IT.
IS SHE ALWAYS SUCH A PUSH-OVER?!

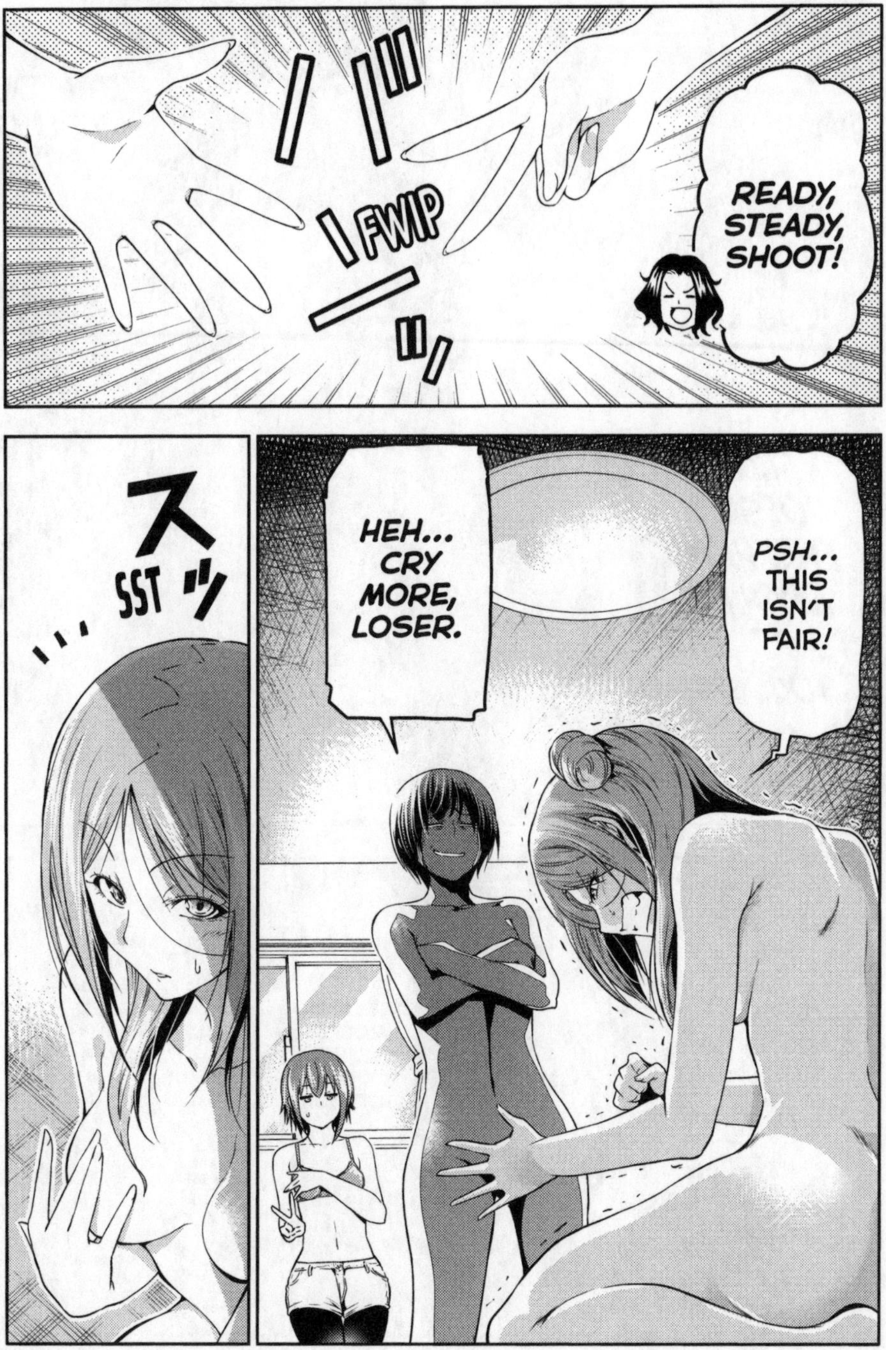
READY, STEADY, SHOOT!
FWIP
PSH... THIS ISN'T FAIR!
HEH... CRY MORE, LOSER.
SST
...

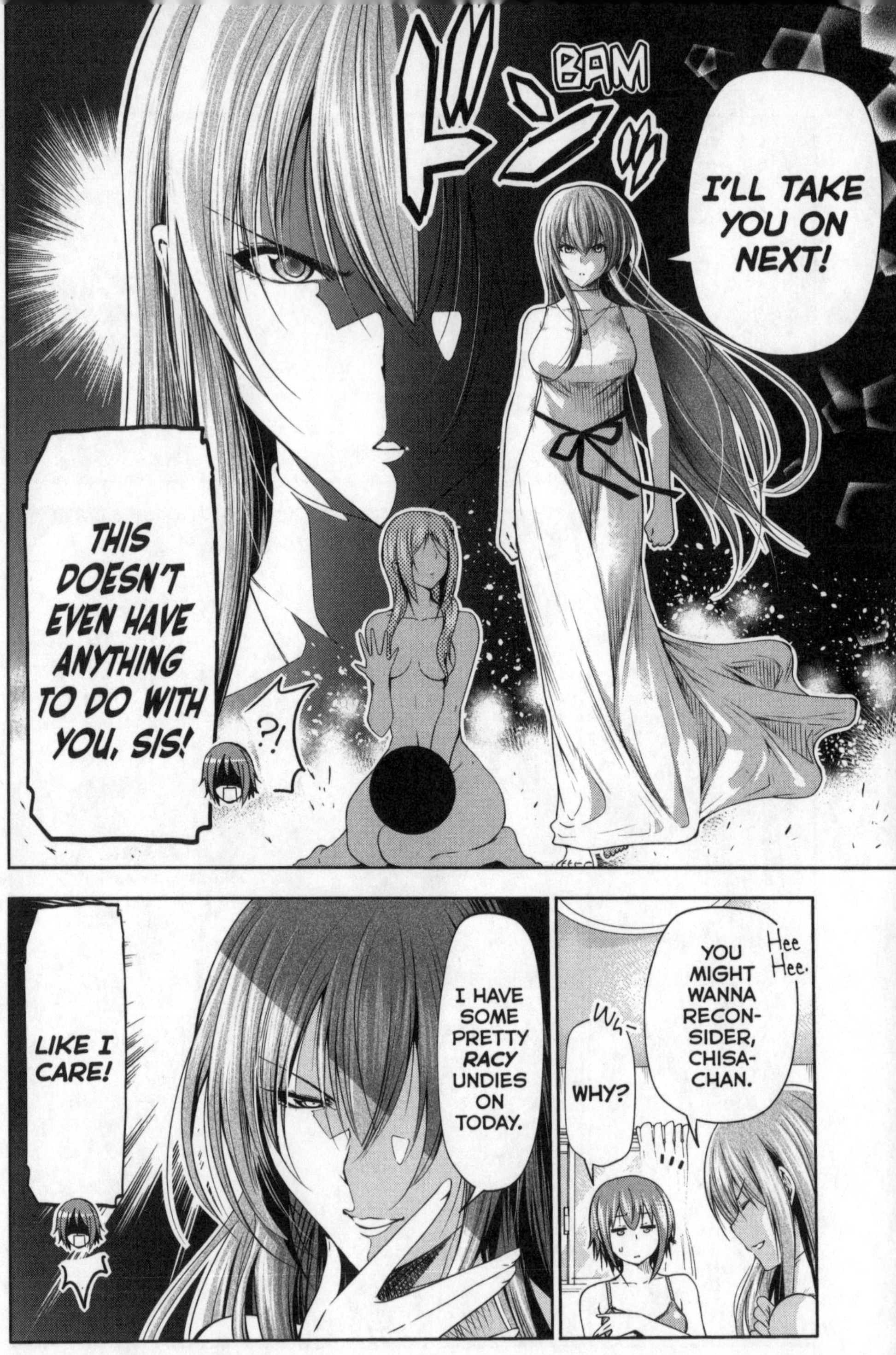
BAM
I'LL TAKE YOU ON NEXT!
THIS DOESN'T EVEN HAVE ANYTHING TO DO WITH YOU, SIS!
?!
Hee Hee.
YOU MIGHT WANNA RECONSIDER, CHISA-CHAN.
Wh-
WHY?
I HAVE SOME PRETTY RACY UNDIES ON TODAY.
LIKE I CARE!

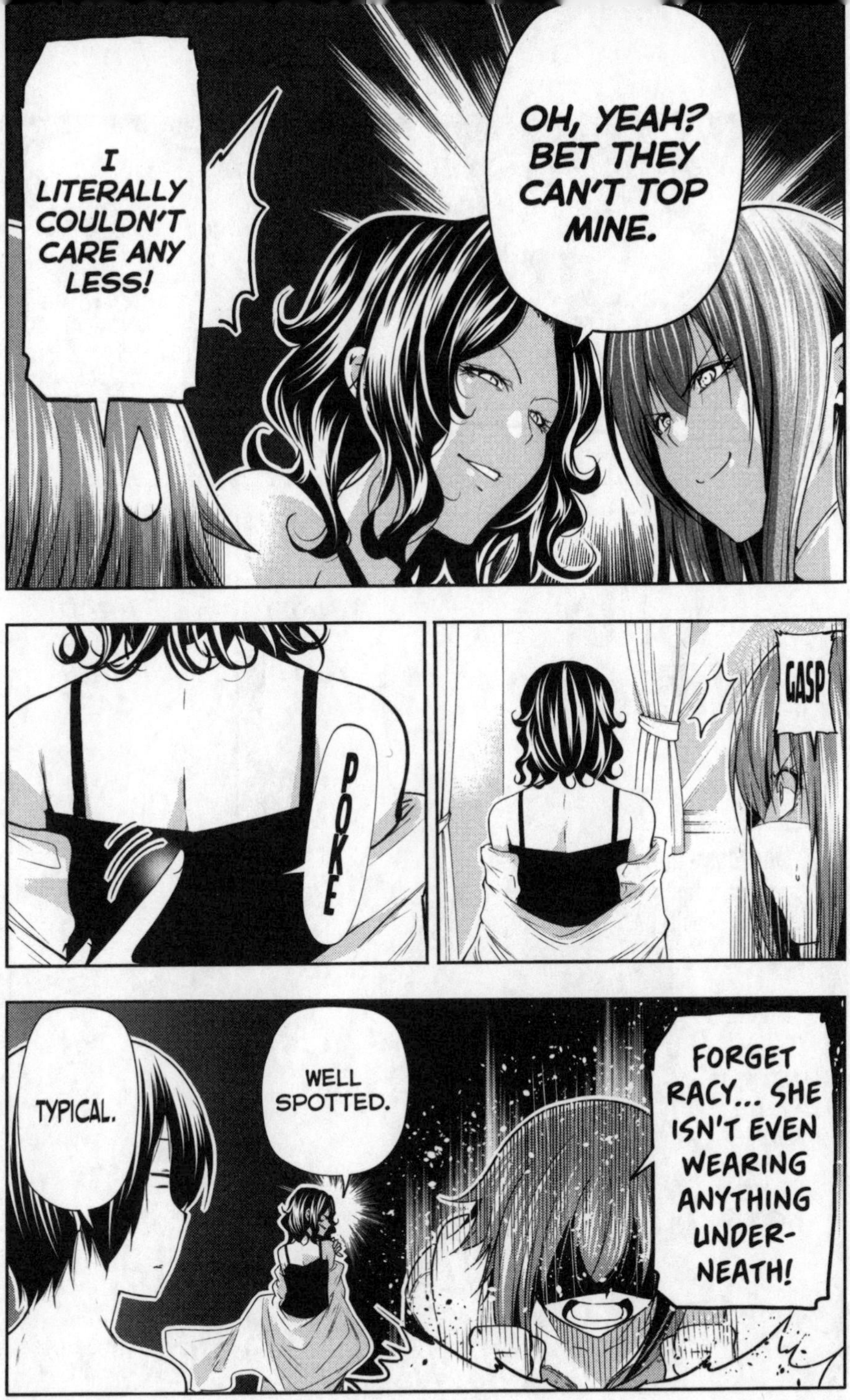
OH, YEAH? BET THEY CAN'T TOP MINE.
I LITERALLY COULDN'T CARE ANY LESS!
GASP
POKE
FORGET RACY... SHE ISN'T EVEN WEARING ANYTHING UNDER-NEATH!
WELL SPOTTED.
TYPICAL.

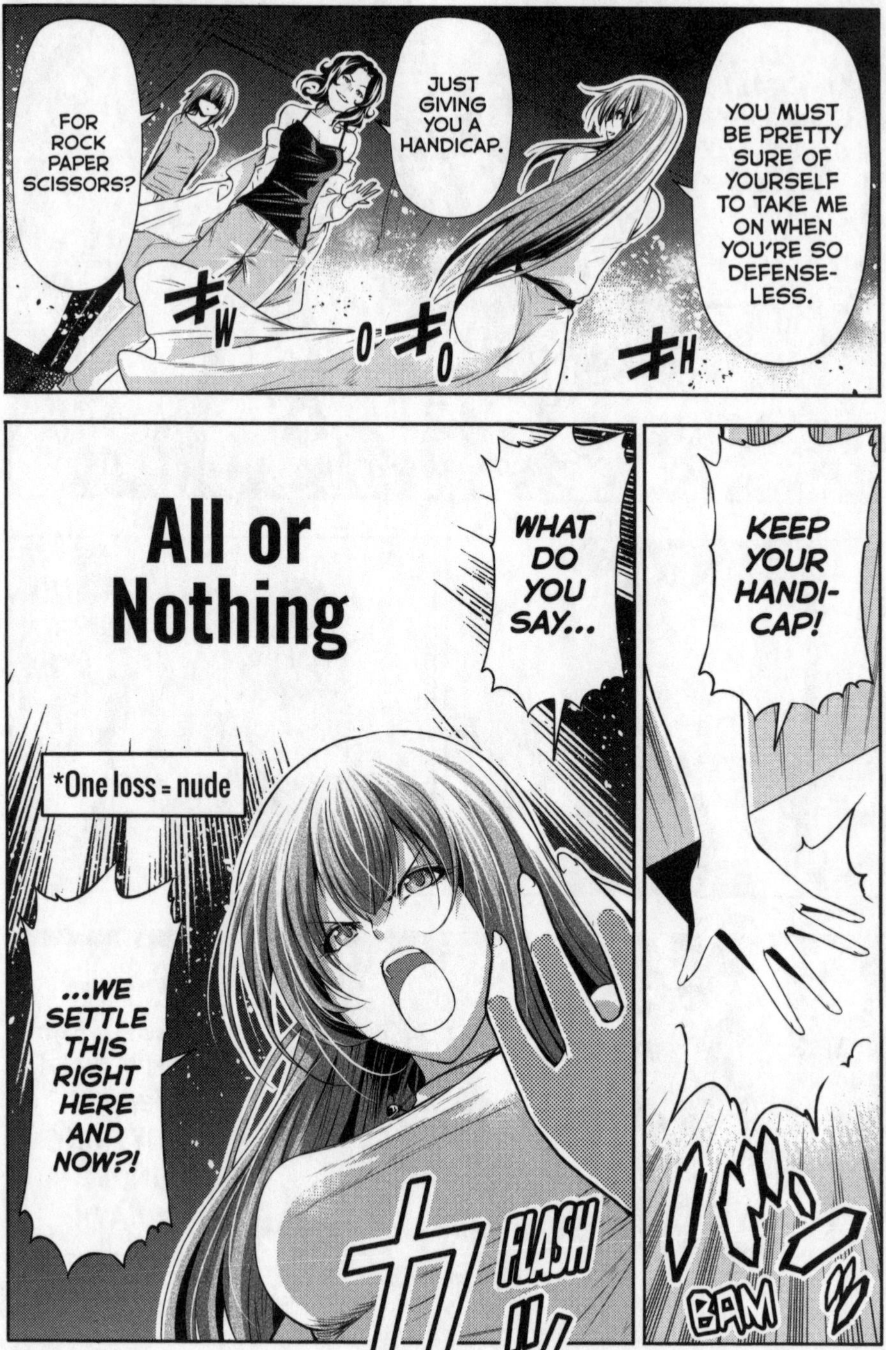
YOU MUST BE PRETTY SURE OF YOURSELF TO TAKE ME ON WHEN YOU'RE SO DEFENSE-LESS.
JUST GIVING YOU A HANDICAP.
FOR ROCK PAPER SCISSORS?
W
O
O
H
KEEP YOUR HANDI-CAP!
BAM
WHAT DO YOU SAY...
All or Nothing
*One loss = nude
...WE SETTLE THIS RIGHT HERE AND NOW?!
FLASH

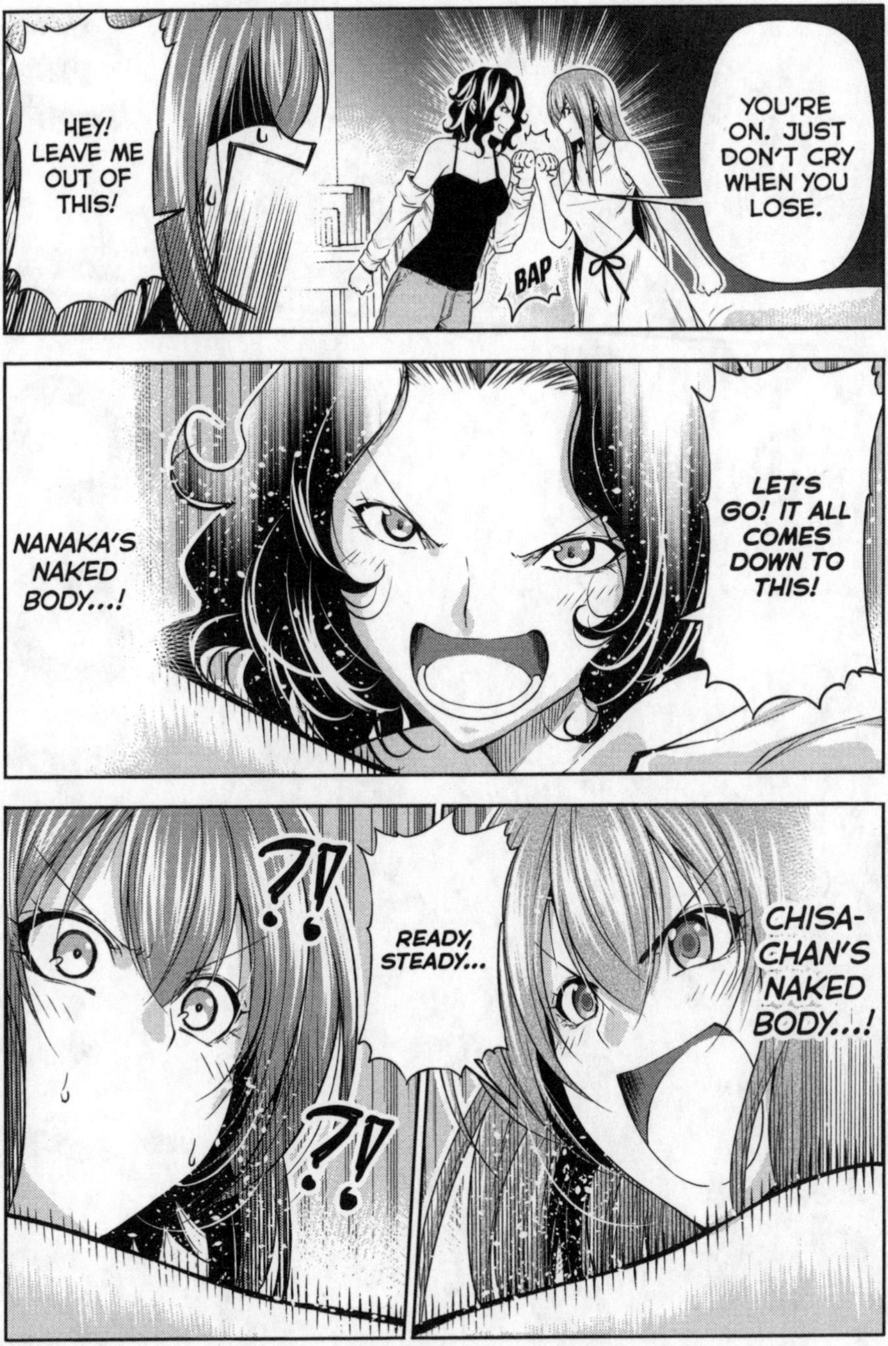
YOU'RE ON. JUST DON'T CRY WHEN YOU LOSE.
BAP
HEY! LEAVE ME OUT OF THIS!
LET'S GO! IT ALL COMES DOWN TO THIS!
NANAKA'S NAKED BODY...!
CHISA-CHAN'S NAKED BODY...!
READY, STEADY...
?!
?!

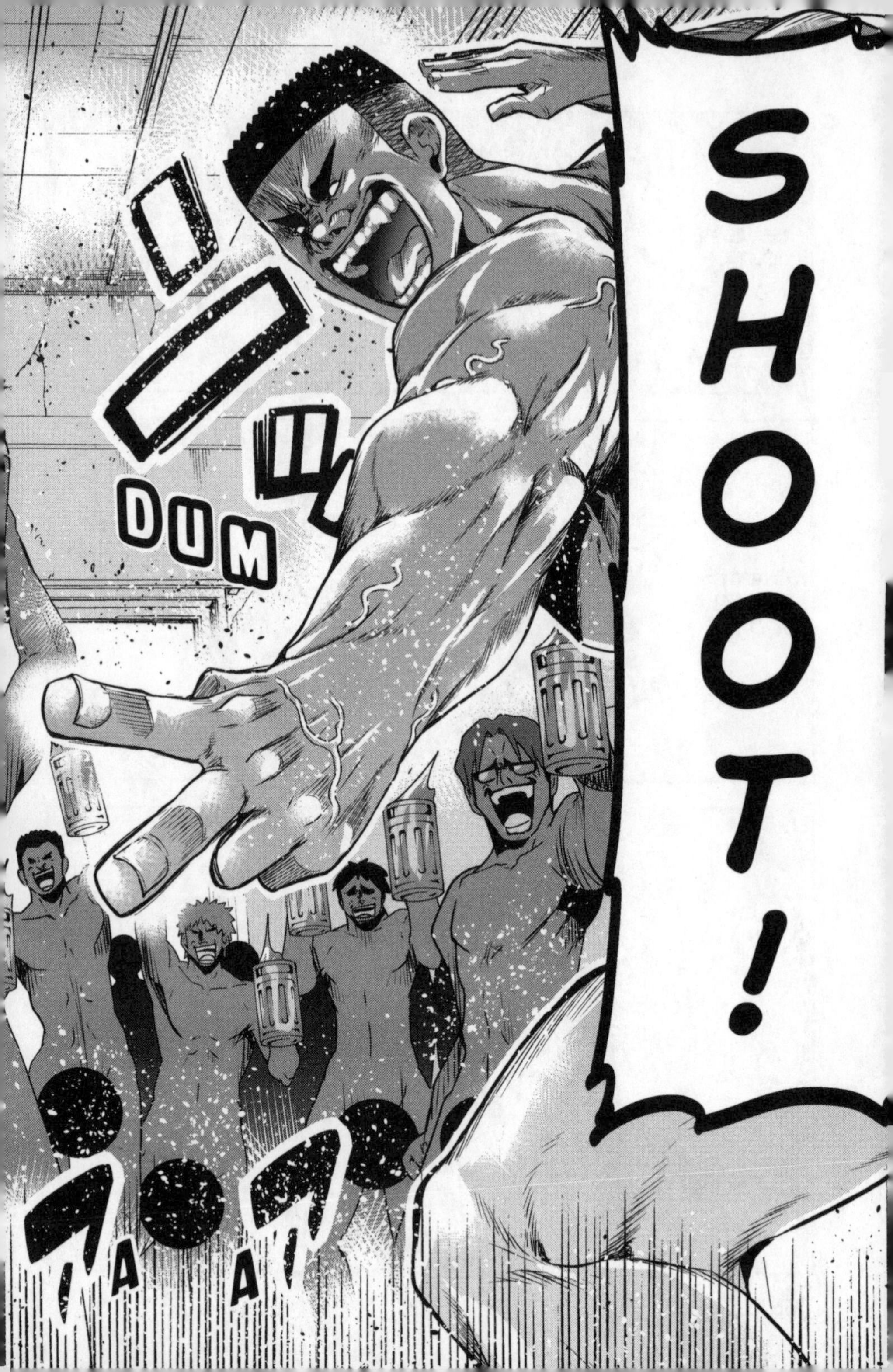
SHOT!
DUM

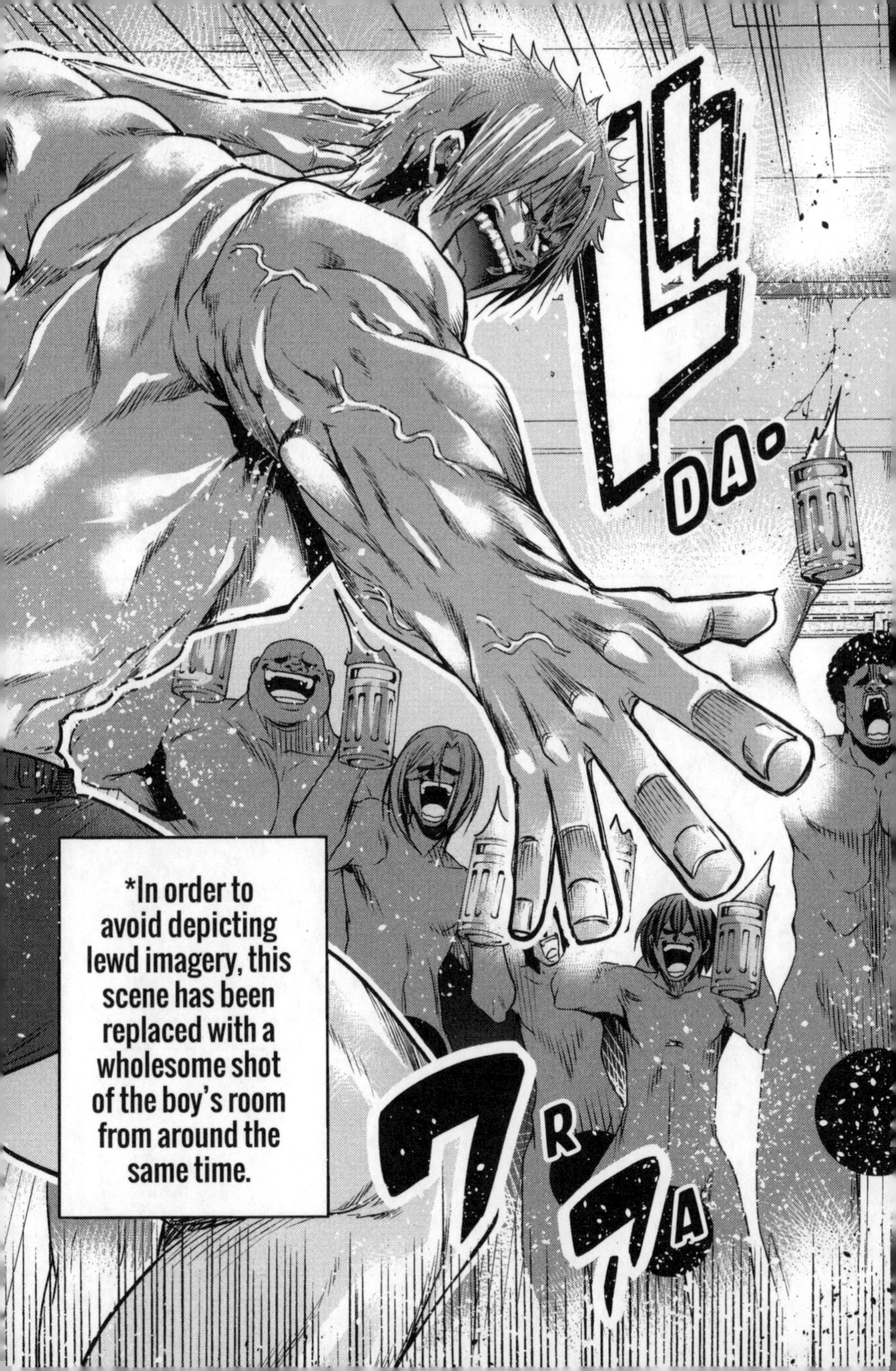
DA-
*In order to avoid depicting lewd imagery, this scene has been replaced with a wholesome shot of the boy's room from around the same time.
R
A

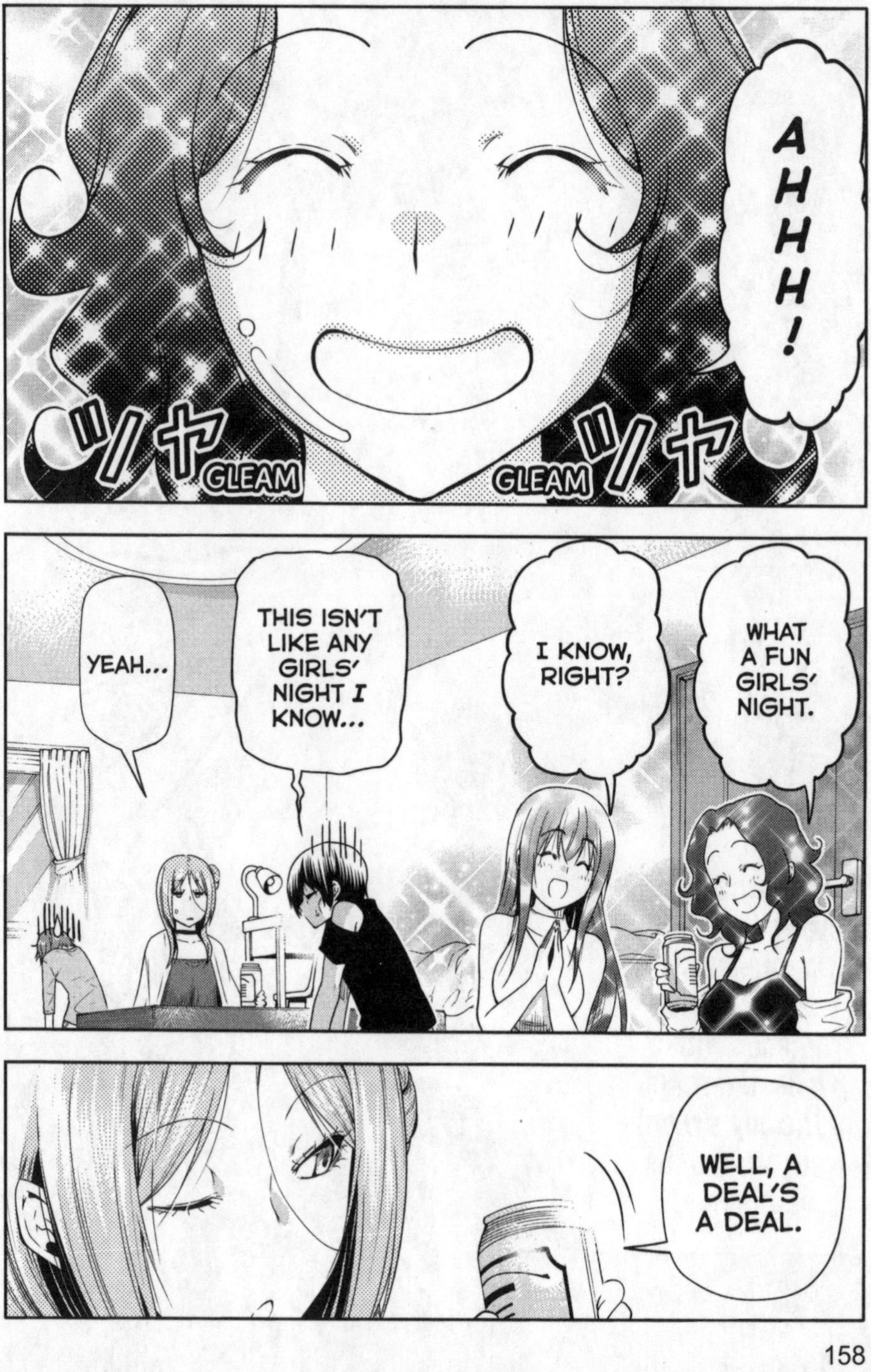
AHHH!
ツヤ GLEAM
ツヤ GLEAM
WHAT A FUN GIRLS' NIGHT.
I KNOW, RIGHT?
THIS ISN'T LIKE ANY GIRLS' NIGHT *I* KNOW...
YEAH...
WELL, A DEAL'S A DEAL.

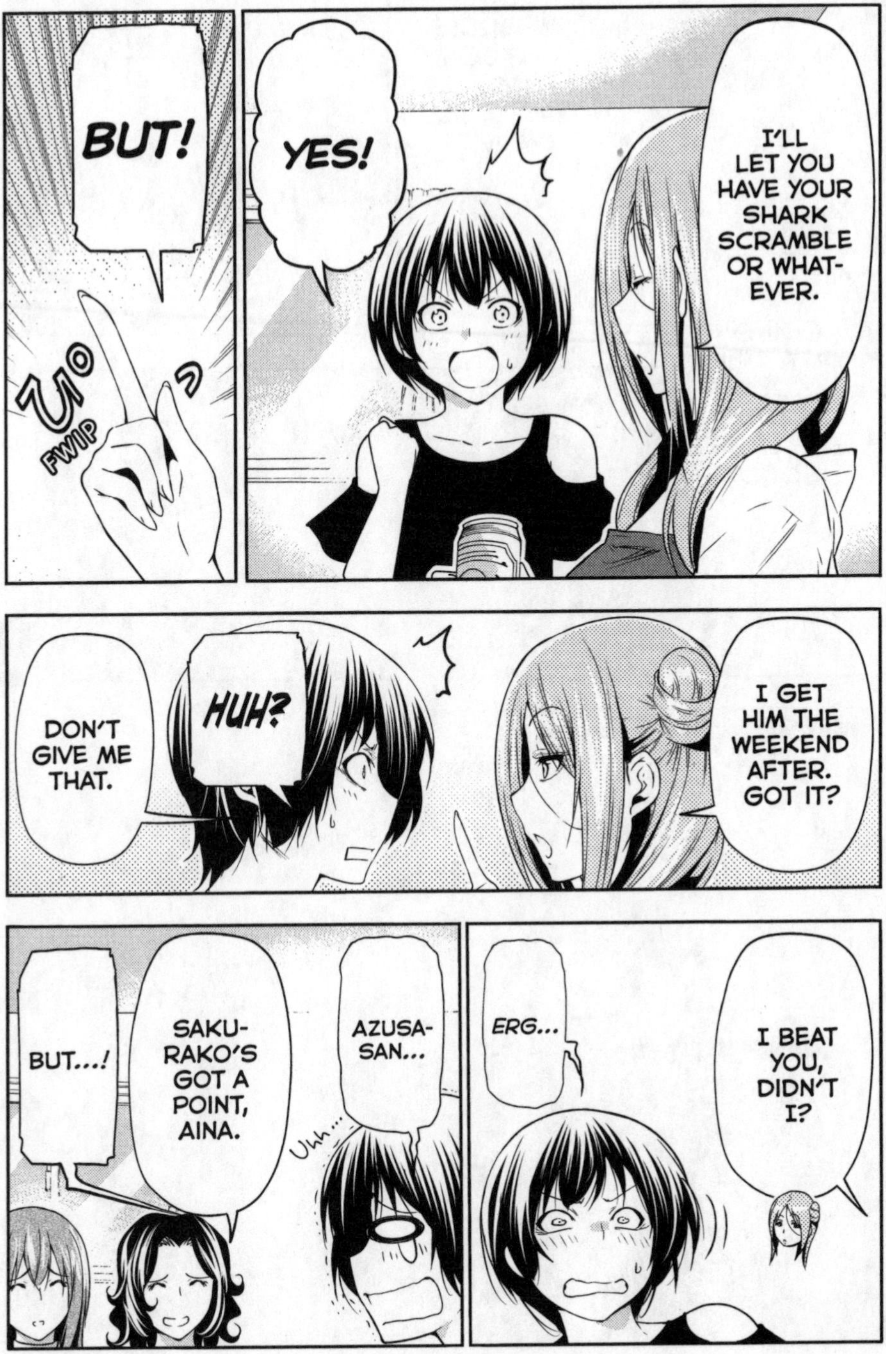
I'LL LET YOU HAVE YOUR SHARK SCRAMBLE OR WHATEVER.
YES!
BUT!
FWIP
I GET HIM THE WEEKEND AFTER. GOT IT?
HUH?
DON'T GIVE ME THAT.
I BEAT YOU, DIDN'T I?
ERG...
AZUSA-SAN...
Uhh...
SAKU-RAKO'S GOT A POINT, AINA.
BUT...!

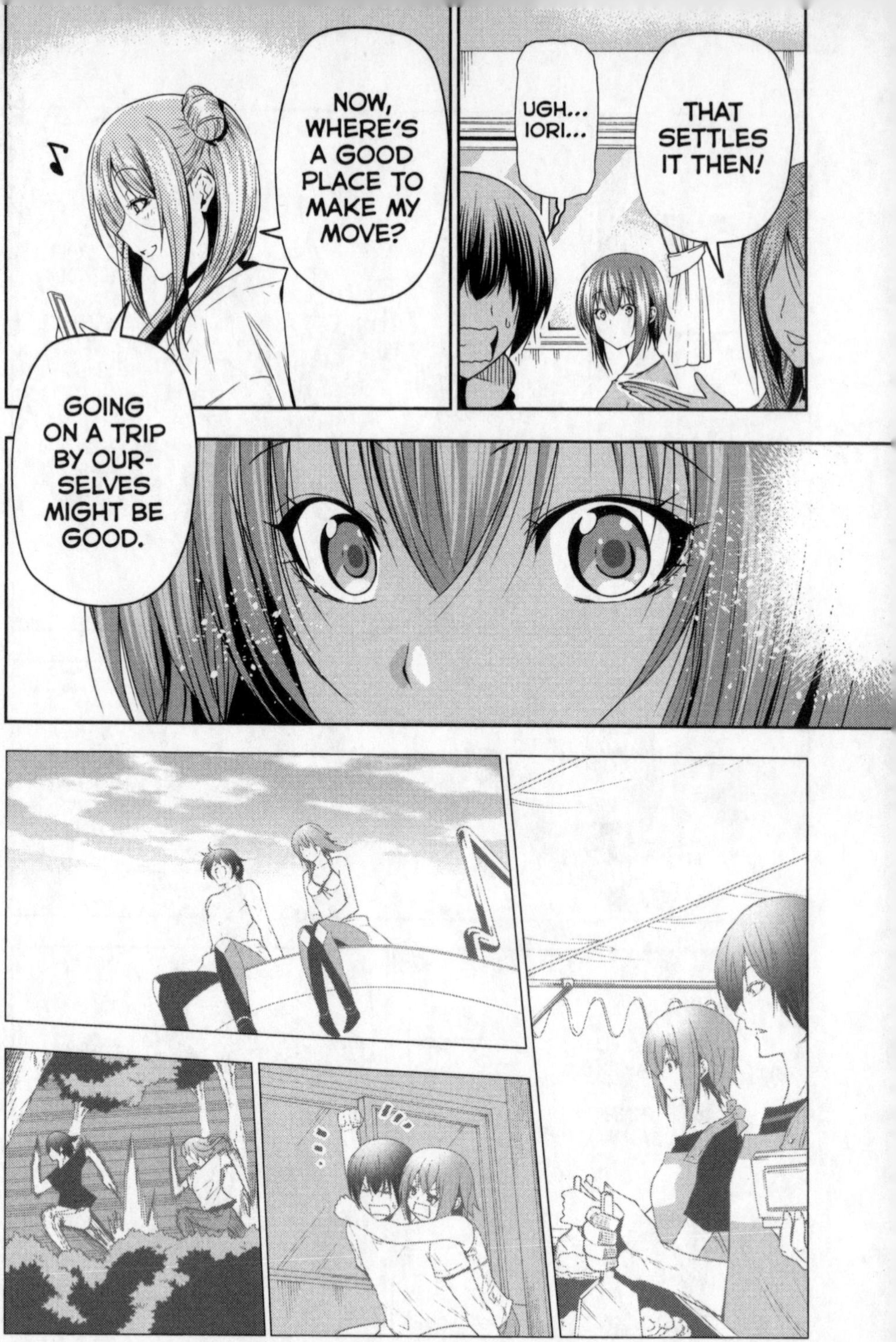
THAT SETTLES IT THEN!
UGH... IORI...
NOW, WHERE'S A GOOD PLACE TO MAKE MY MOVE?
GOING ON A TRIP BY OUR-SELVES MIGHT BE GOOD.

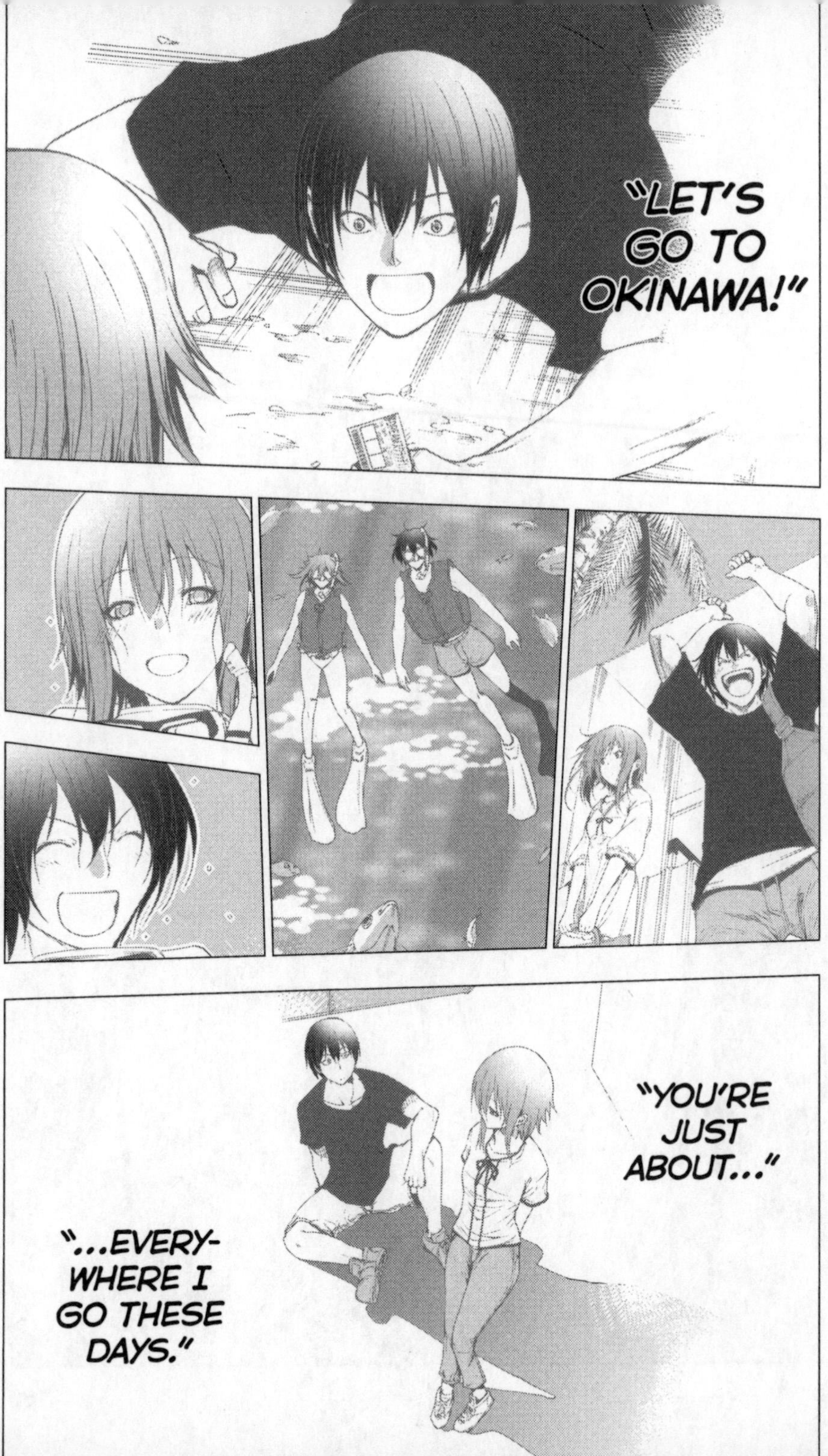
"LET'S GO TO OKINAWA!"
"YOU'RE JUST ABOUT..."
"...EVERY-WHERE I GO THESE DAYS."

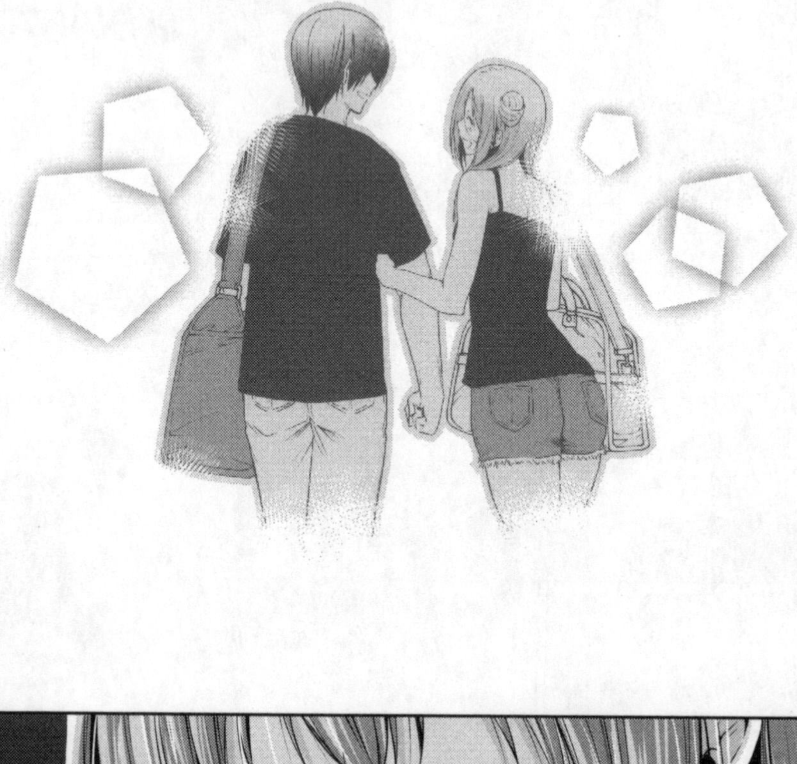

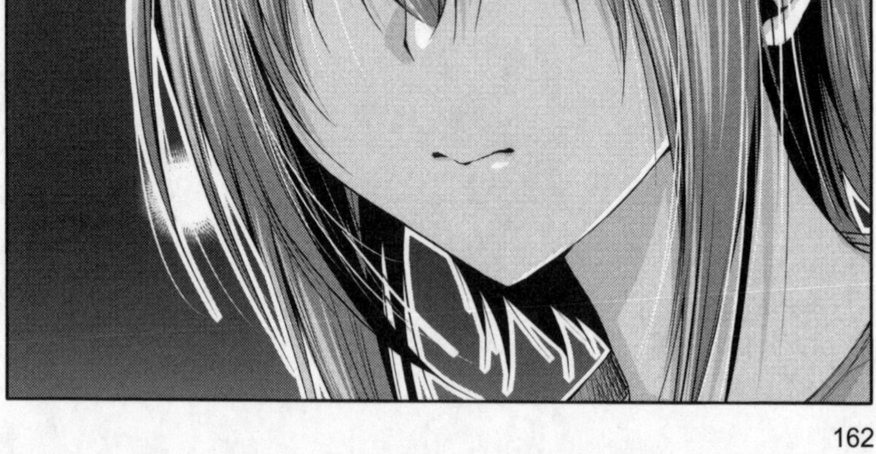

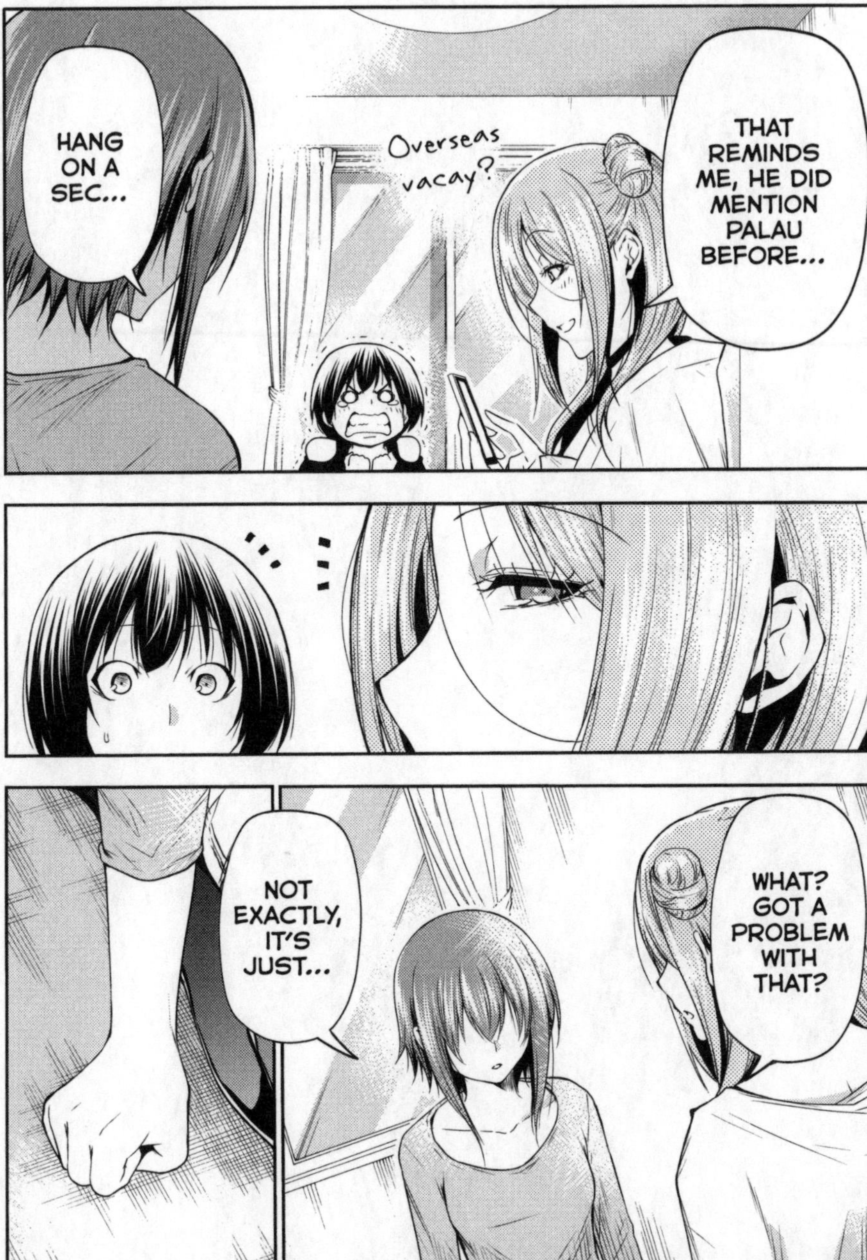
THAT REMINDS ME, HE DID MENTION PALAU BEFORE...
Overseas vacay?
HANG ON A SEC...
WHAT? GOT A PROBLEM WITH THAT?
NOT EXACTLY, IT'S JUST...

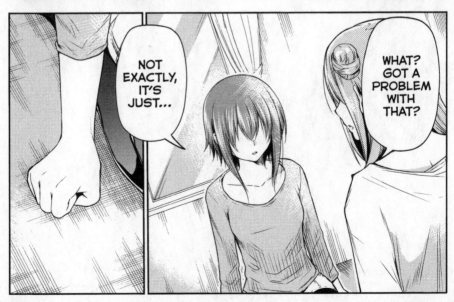

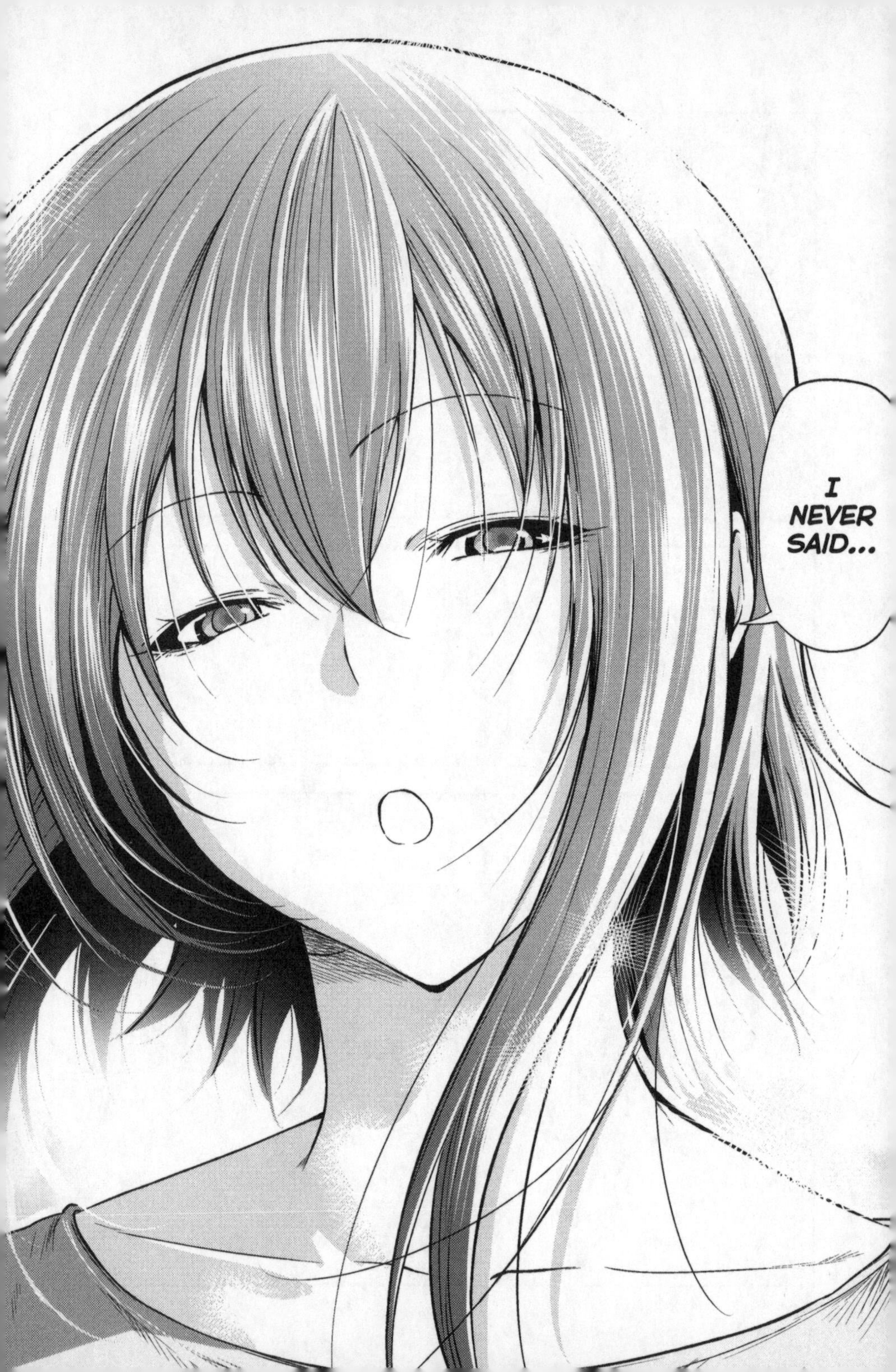
I NEVER SAID...

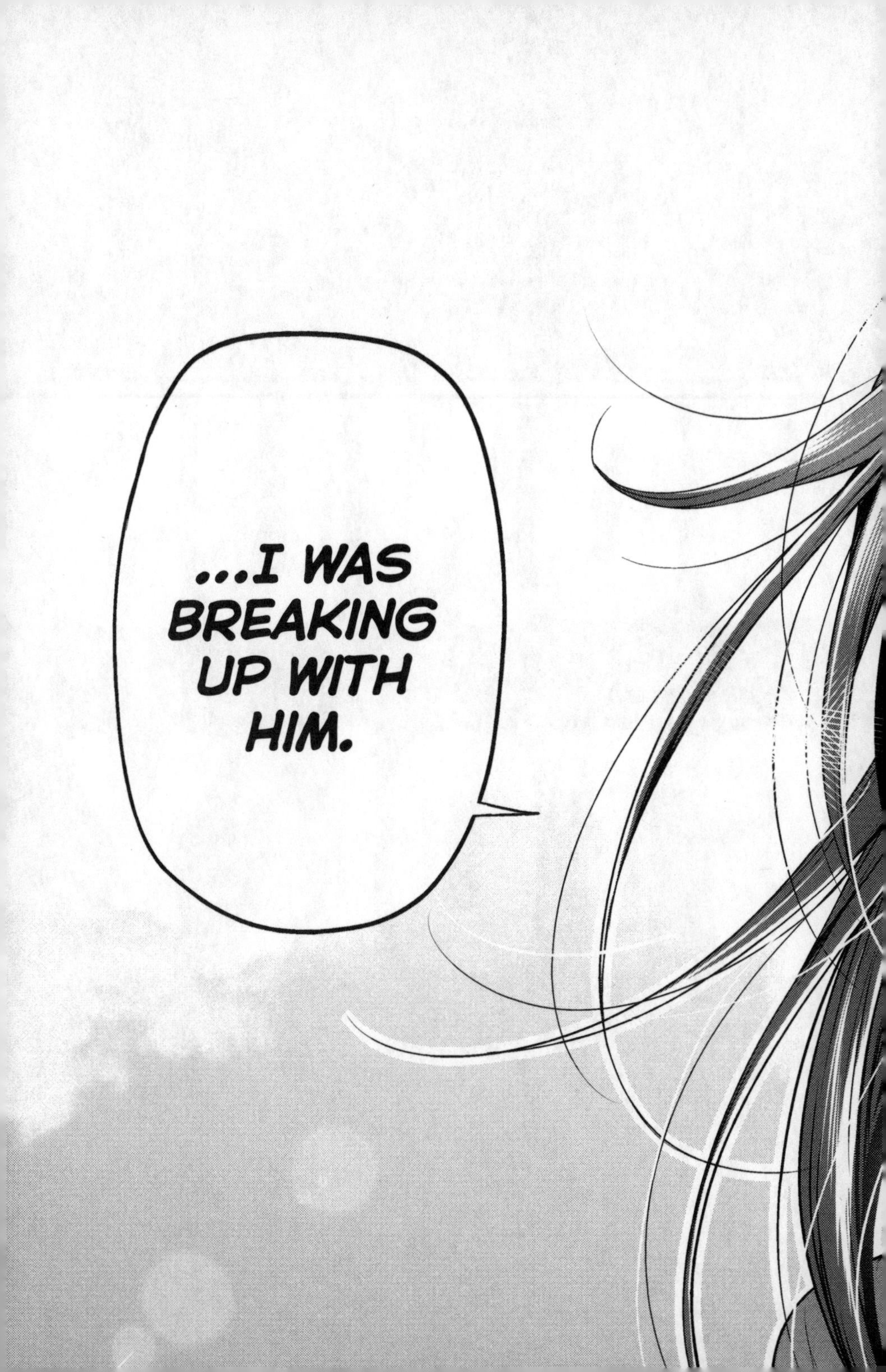
...I WAS BREAKING UP WITH HIM.

BONUS STORY

じーわ
SIZZZ
じーわ
SIZZZ
IT'S TOO HOT...
YES
じーわ
SIZZZ
じーわ
SIZZZ
Bonus Story: The Passion of Ichiro Yamamoto

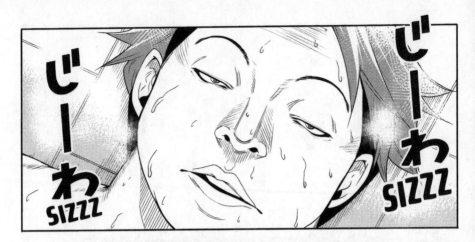

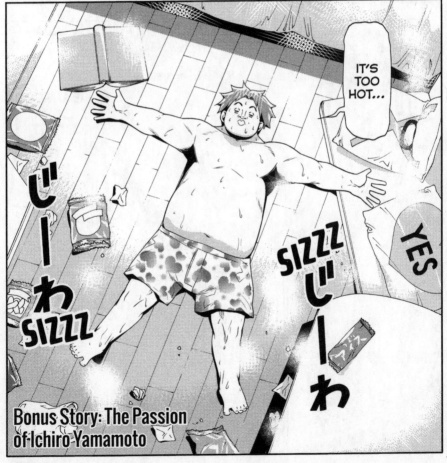

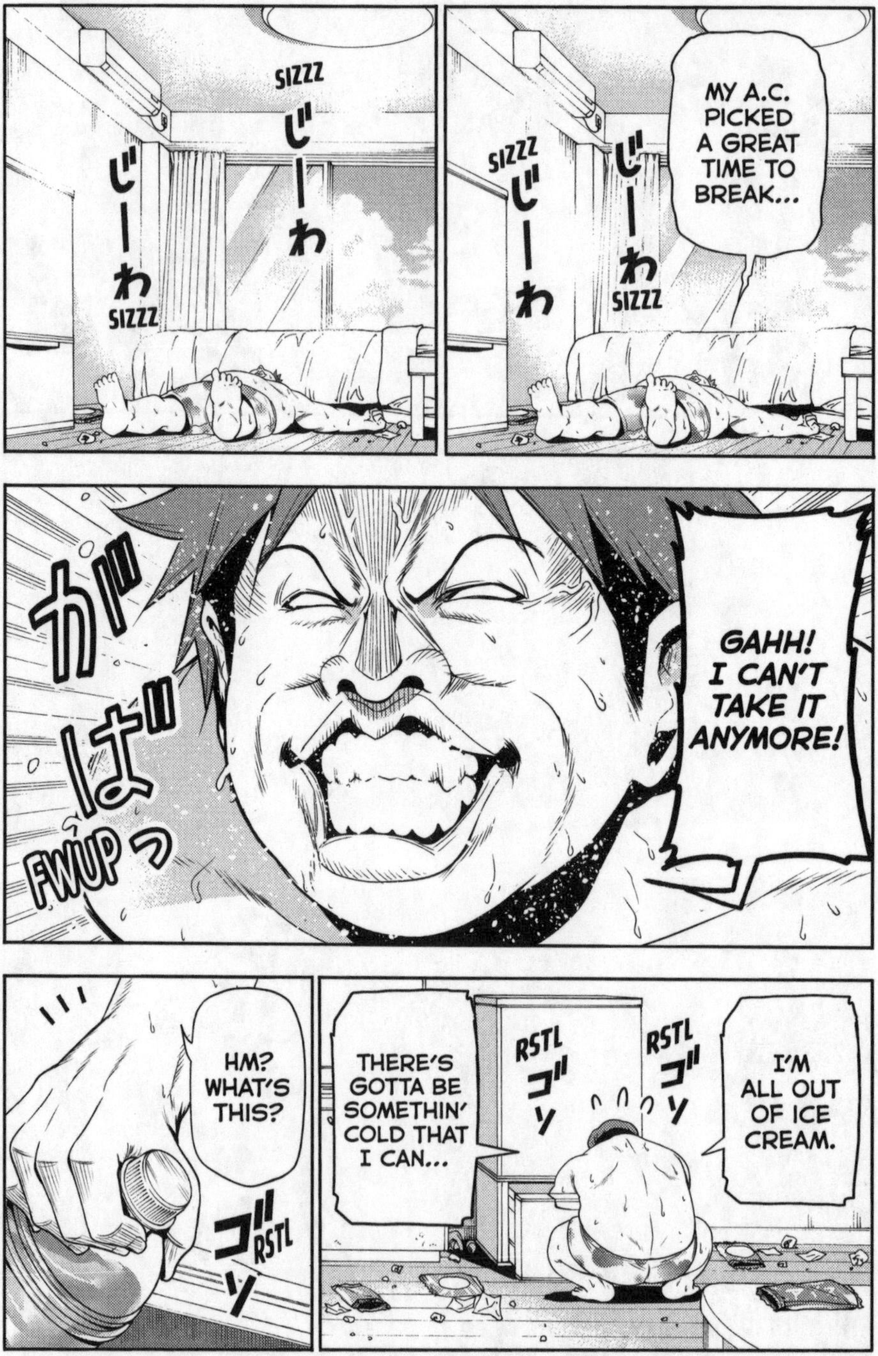
MY A.C. PICKED A GREAT TIME TO BREAK...
SIZZZ じーわ
じーわ SIZZZ
SIZZZ じーわ
じーわ SIZZZ
GAHH! I CAN'T TAKE IT ANYMORE!
がばっ FWUP
I'M ALL OUT OF ICE CREAM.
RSTL ゴソ
RSTL ゴソ
THERE'S GOTTA BE SOMETHIN' COLD THAT I CAN...
HM? WHAT'S THIS?
ゴソ RSTL

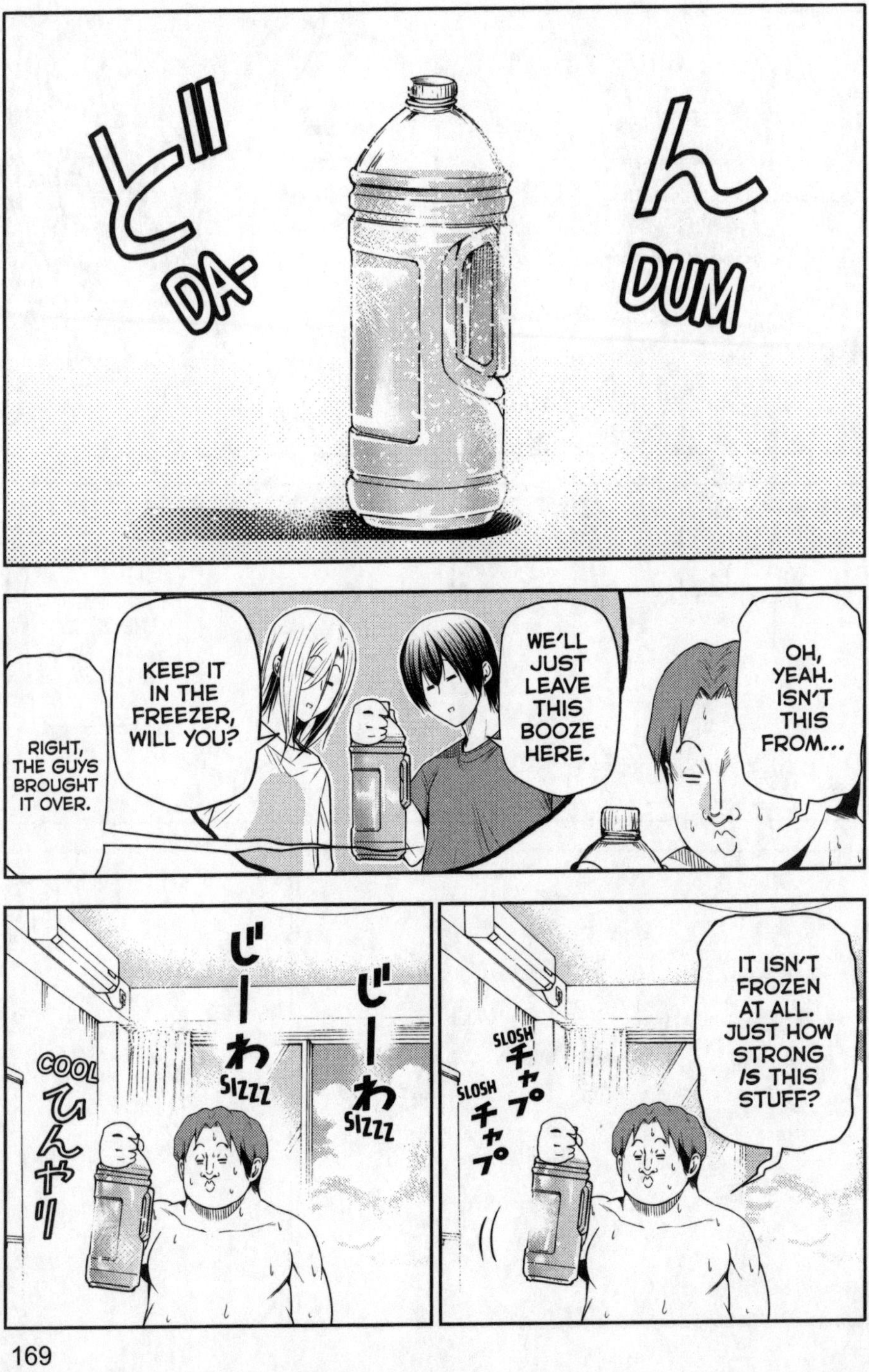
どん
DA-DUM
OH, YEAH. ISN'T THIS FROM...
WE'LL JUST LEAVE THIS BOOZE HERE.
KEEP IT IN THE FREEZER, WILL YOU?
RIGHT, THE GUYS BROUGHT IT OVER.
SLOSH チャプ
SLOSH チャプ
IT ISN'T FROZEN AT ALL. JUST HOW STRONG *IS* THIS STUFF?
じーわ SIZZZ
じーわ SIZZZ
COOL ひんやり

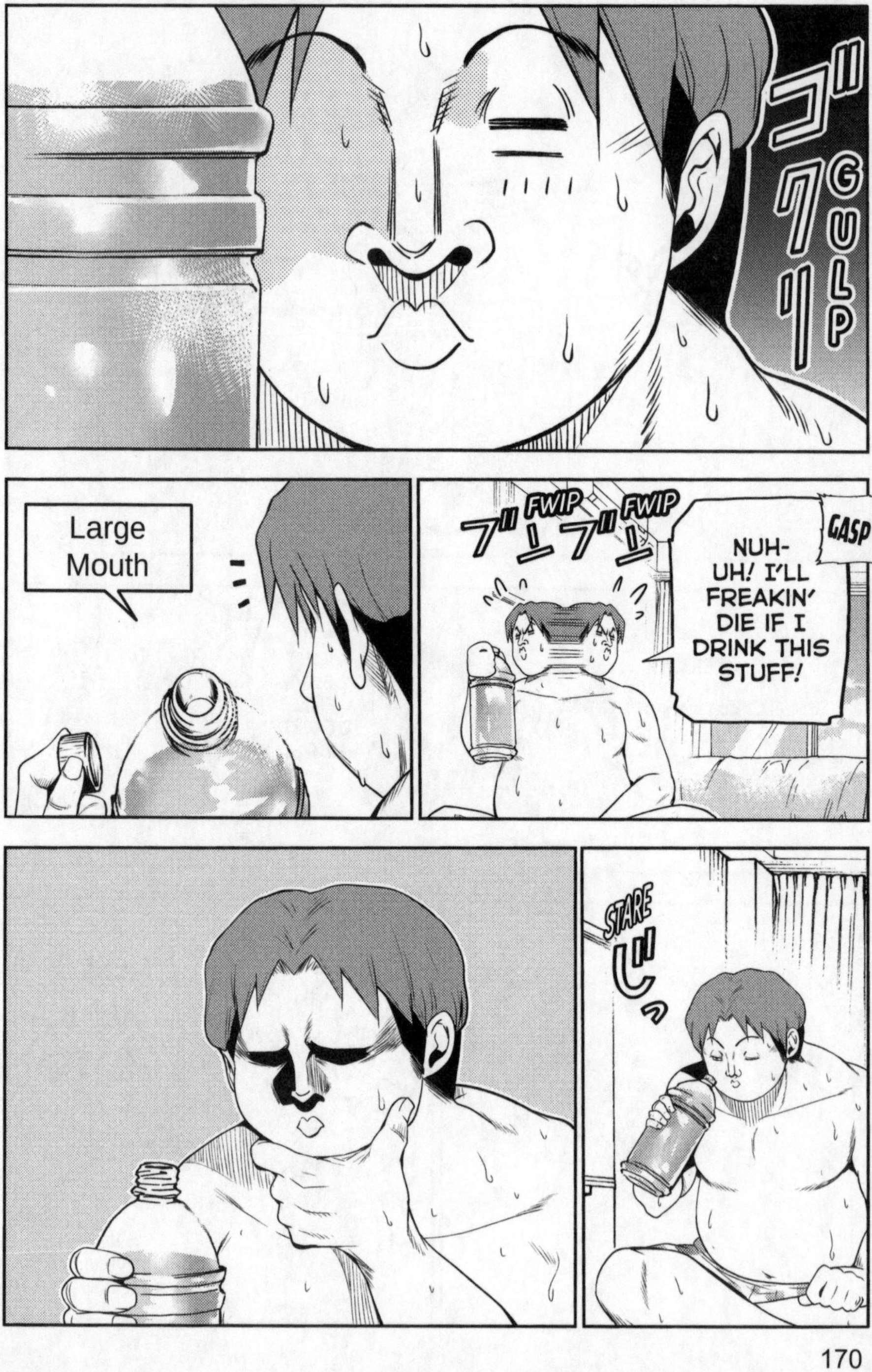
GULP
FWIP FWIP
GASP
NUH-UH! I'LL FREAKIN' DIE IF I DRINK THIS STUFF!
Large Mouth
STARE

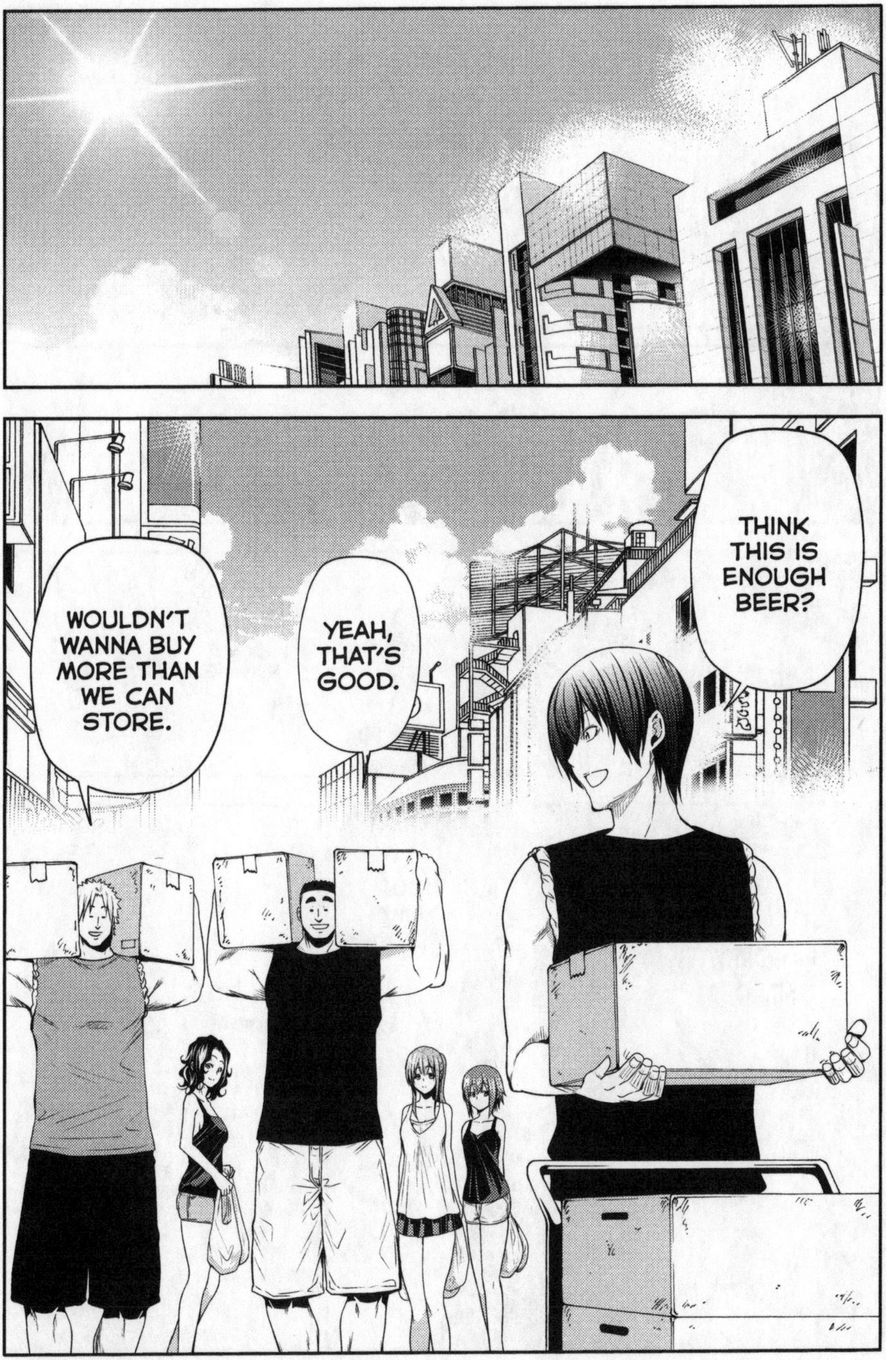
THINK THIS IS ENOUGH BEER?
YEAH, THAT'S GOOD.
WOULDN'T WANNA BUY MORE THAN WE CAN STORE.

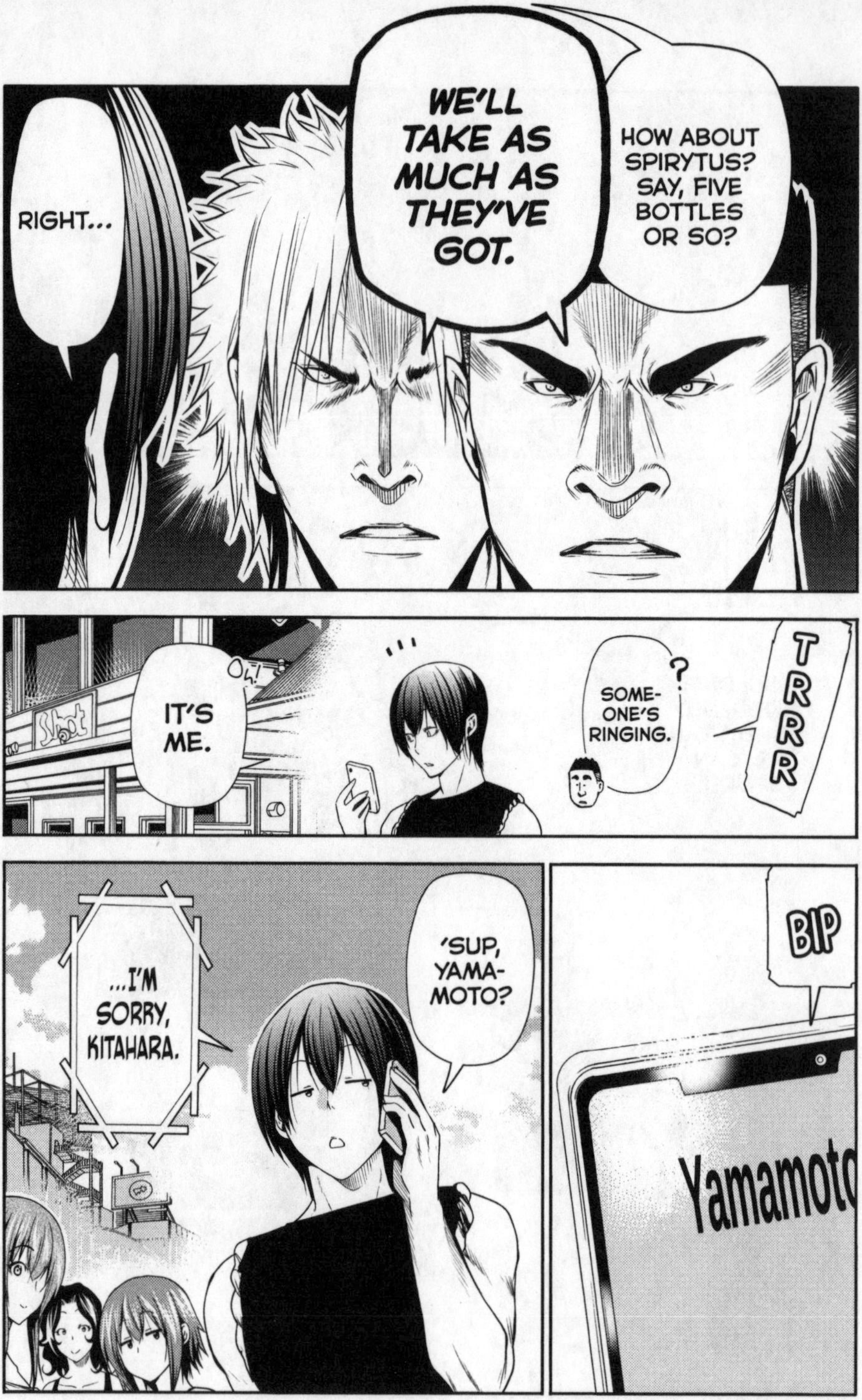
HOW ABOUT SPIRYTUS? SAY, FIVE BOTTLES OR SO?
WE'LL TAKE AS MUCH AS THEY'VE GOT.
RIGHT...
TRRR
?
SOME-ONE'S RINGING.
Oh!
IT'S ME.
BIP
Yamamoto
'SUP, YAMA-MOTO?
...I'M SORRY, KITAHARA.

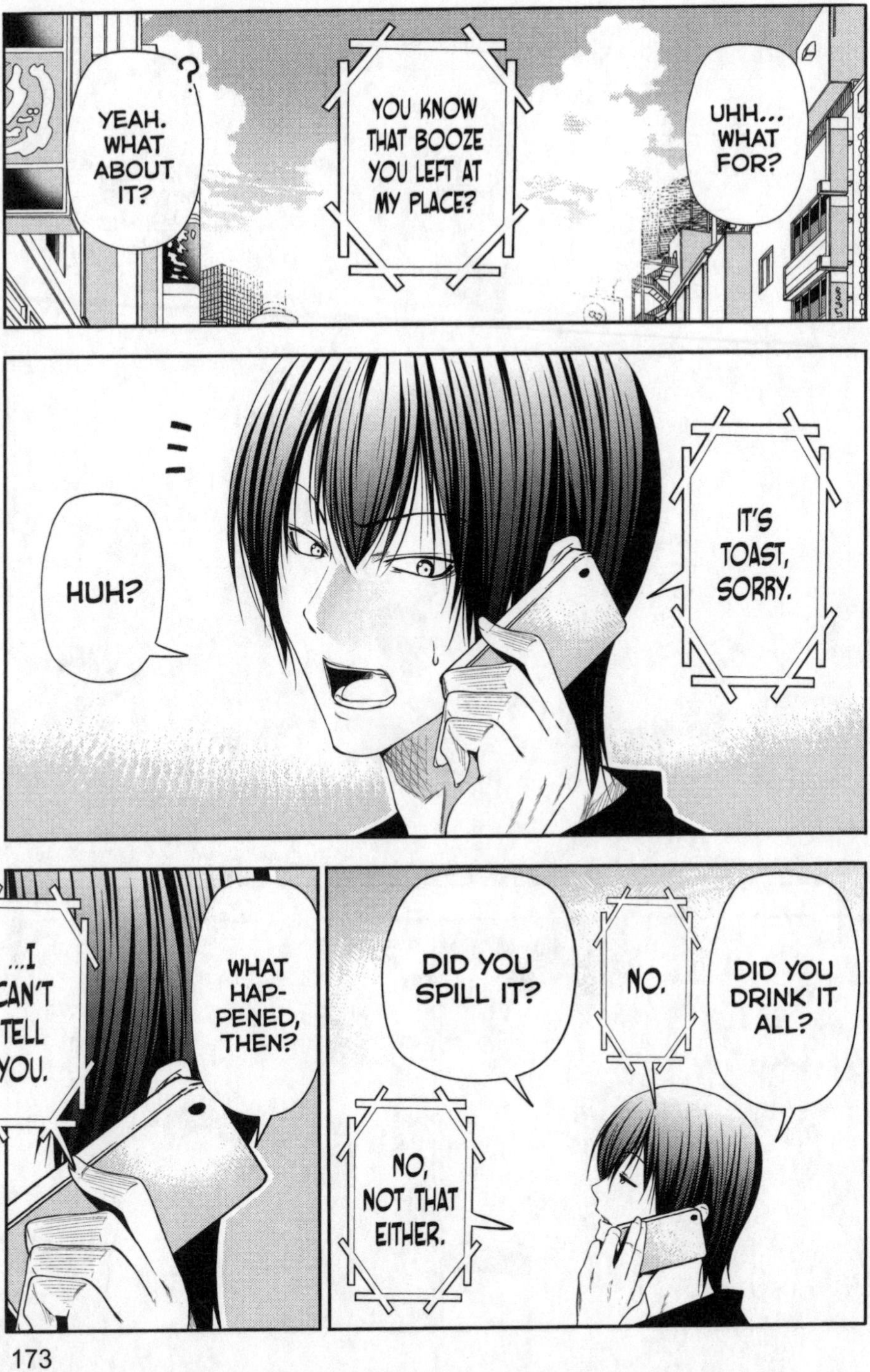
UHH... WHAT FOR?
YOU KNOW THAT BOOZE YOU LEFT AT MY PLACE?
? YEAH. WHAT ABOUT IT?
IT'S TOAST, SORRY.
HUH?
DID YOU DRINK IT ALL?
NO.
DID YOU SPILL IT?
NO, NOT THAT EITHER.
WHAT HAP-PENED, THEN?
...I CAN'T TELL YOU.

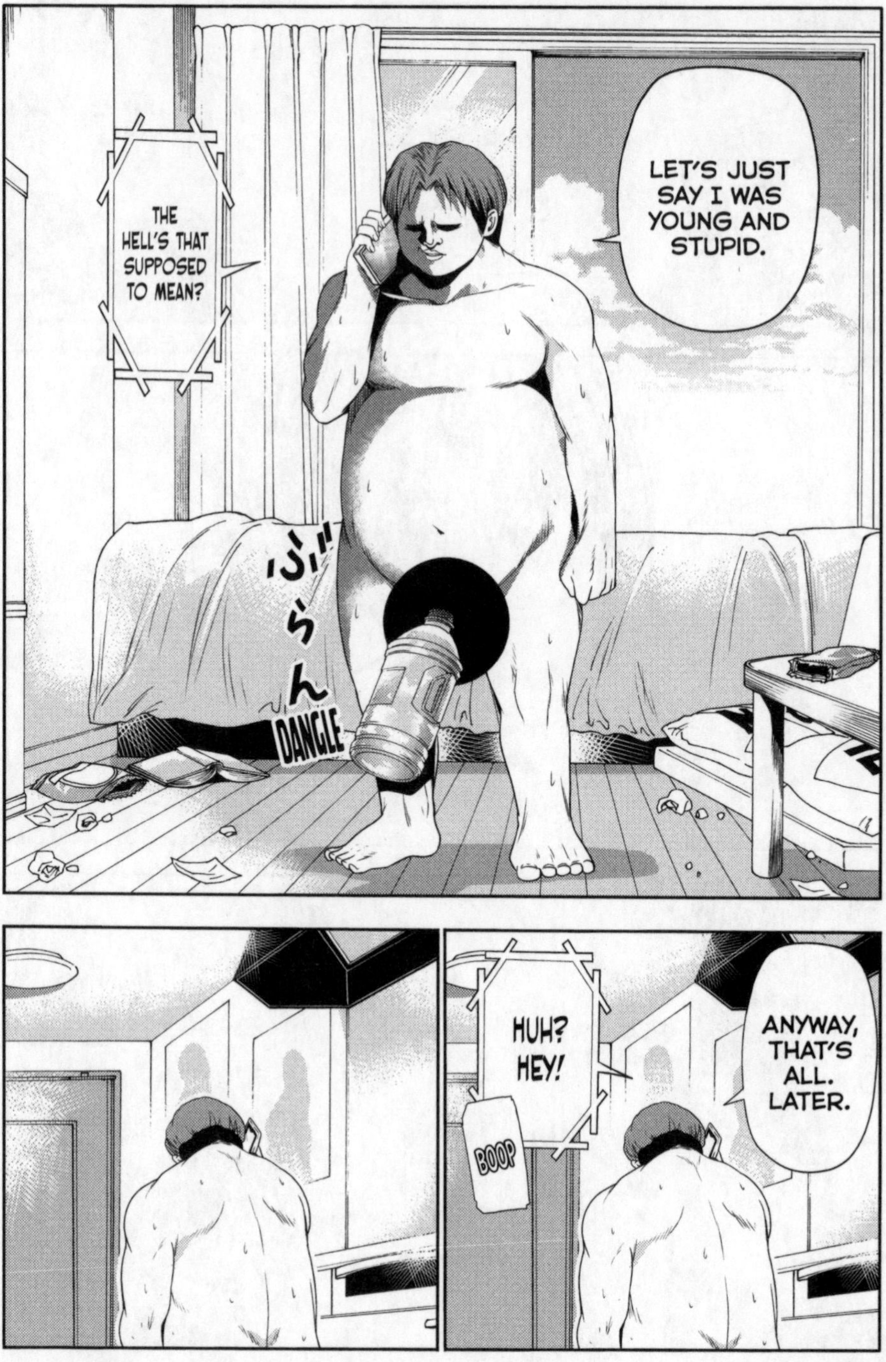
LET'S JUST SAY I WAS YOUNG AND STUPID.
THE HELL'S THAT SUPPOSED TO MEAN?
ぶらん
DANGLE
ANYWAY, THAT'S ALL. LATER.
HUH? HEY!
BOOP

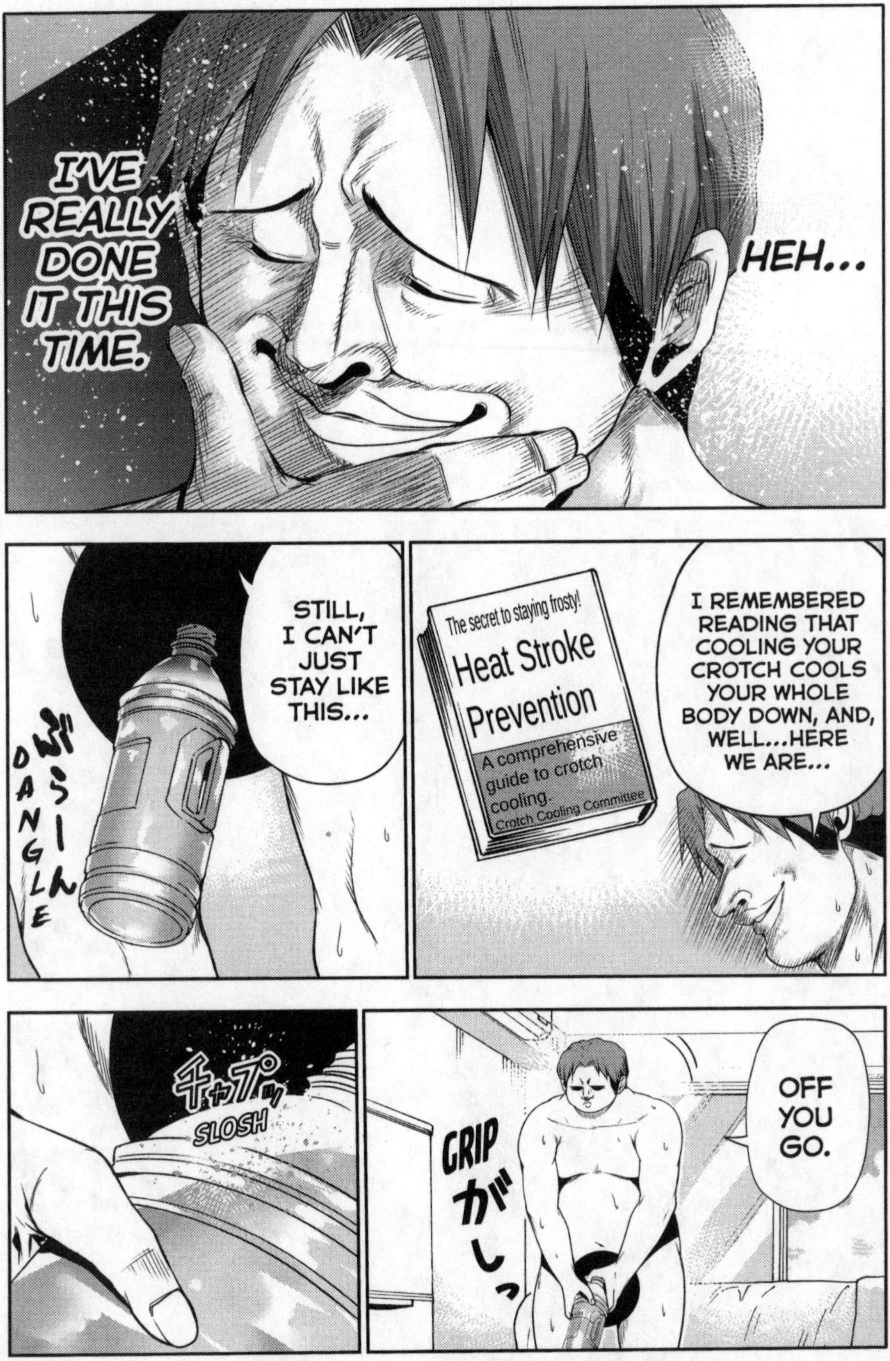
HEH...
I'VE REALLY DONE IT THIS TIME.
I REMEMBERED READING THAT COOLING YOUR CROTCH COOLS YOUR WHOLE BODY DOWN, AND, WELL...HERE WE ARE...
The secret to staying frosty!
Heat Stroke Prevention
A comprehensive guide to crotch cooling.
Crotch Cooling Committee
STILL, I CAN'T JUST STAY LIKE THIS...
ぶらーん
DANGLE
OFF YOU GO.
がしっ
GRIP
チャプッ
SLOSH

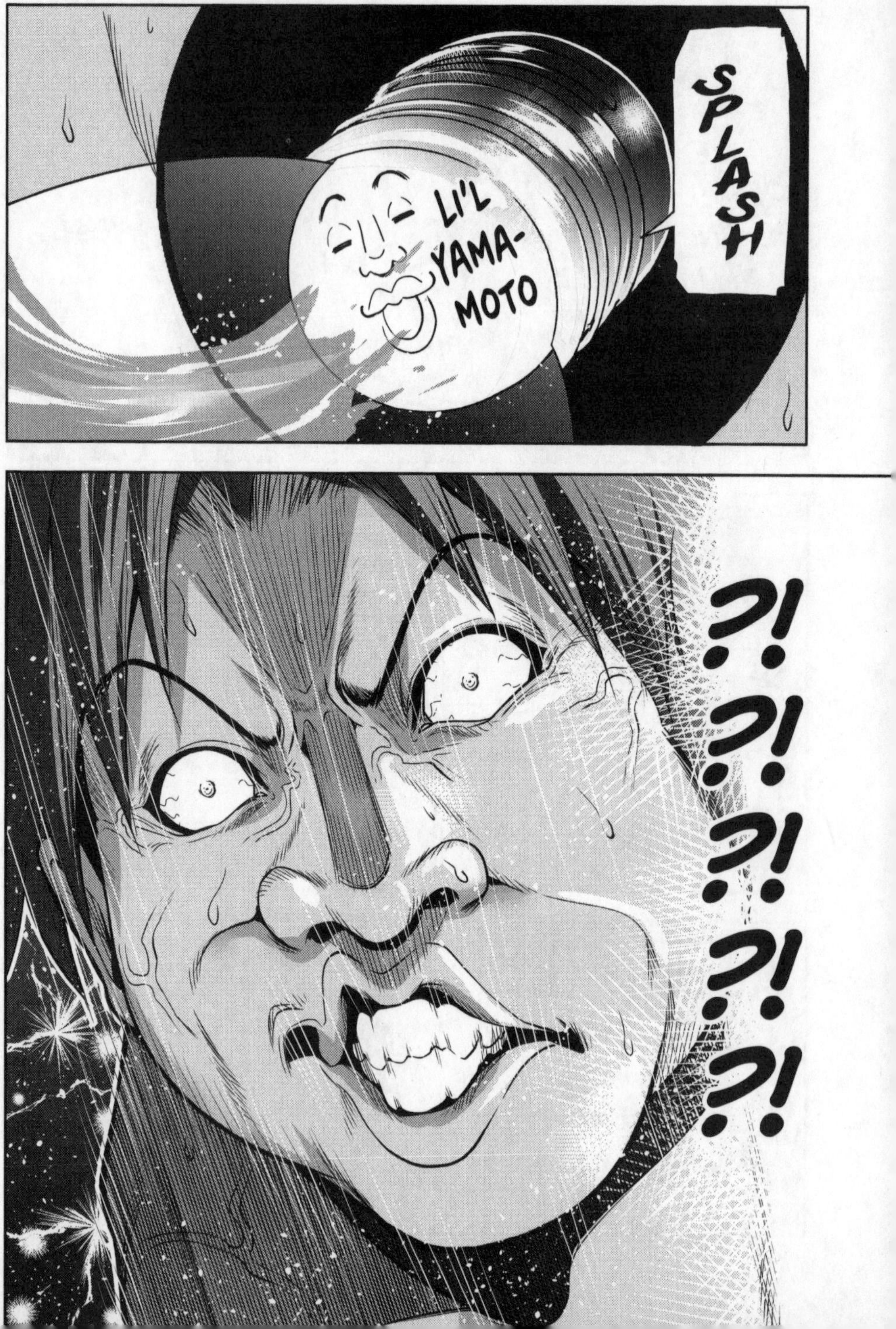
SPLASH
LI'L YAMA-MOTO
?!?!?!?!?!

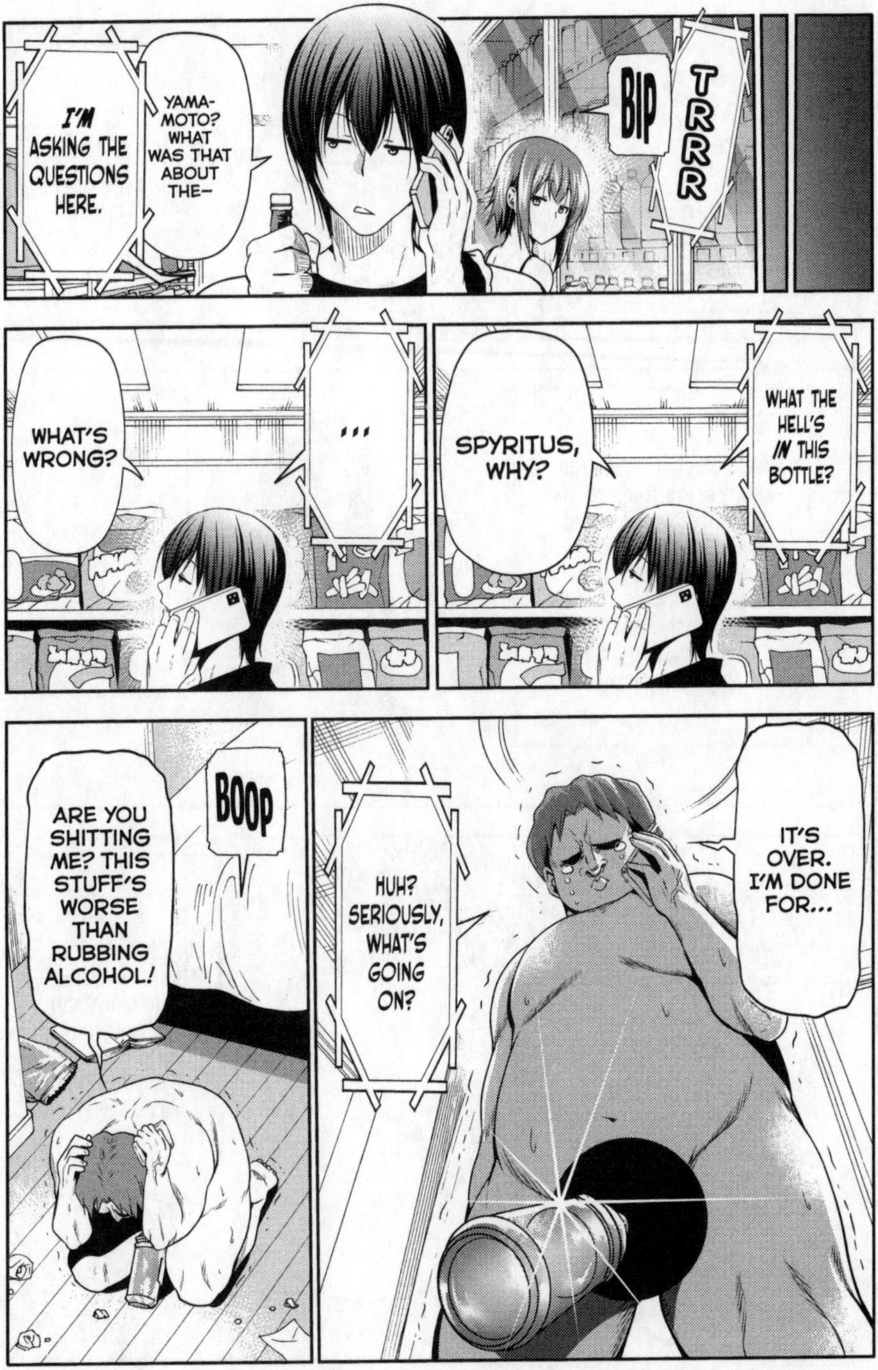
TRRR
BIP
YAMA-MOTO? WHAT WAS THAT ABOUT THE–
I'M ASKING THE QUESTIONS HERE.
WHAT THE HELL'S IN THIS BOTTLE?
SPYRITUS, WHY?
...
WHAT'S WRONG?
IT'S OVER. I'M DONE FOR...
HUH? SERIOUSLY, WHAT'S GOING ON?
BOOP
ARE YOU SHITTING ME? THIS STUFF'S WORSE THAN RUBBING ALCOHOL!

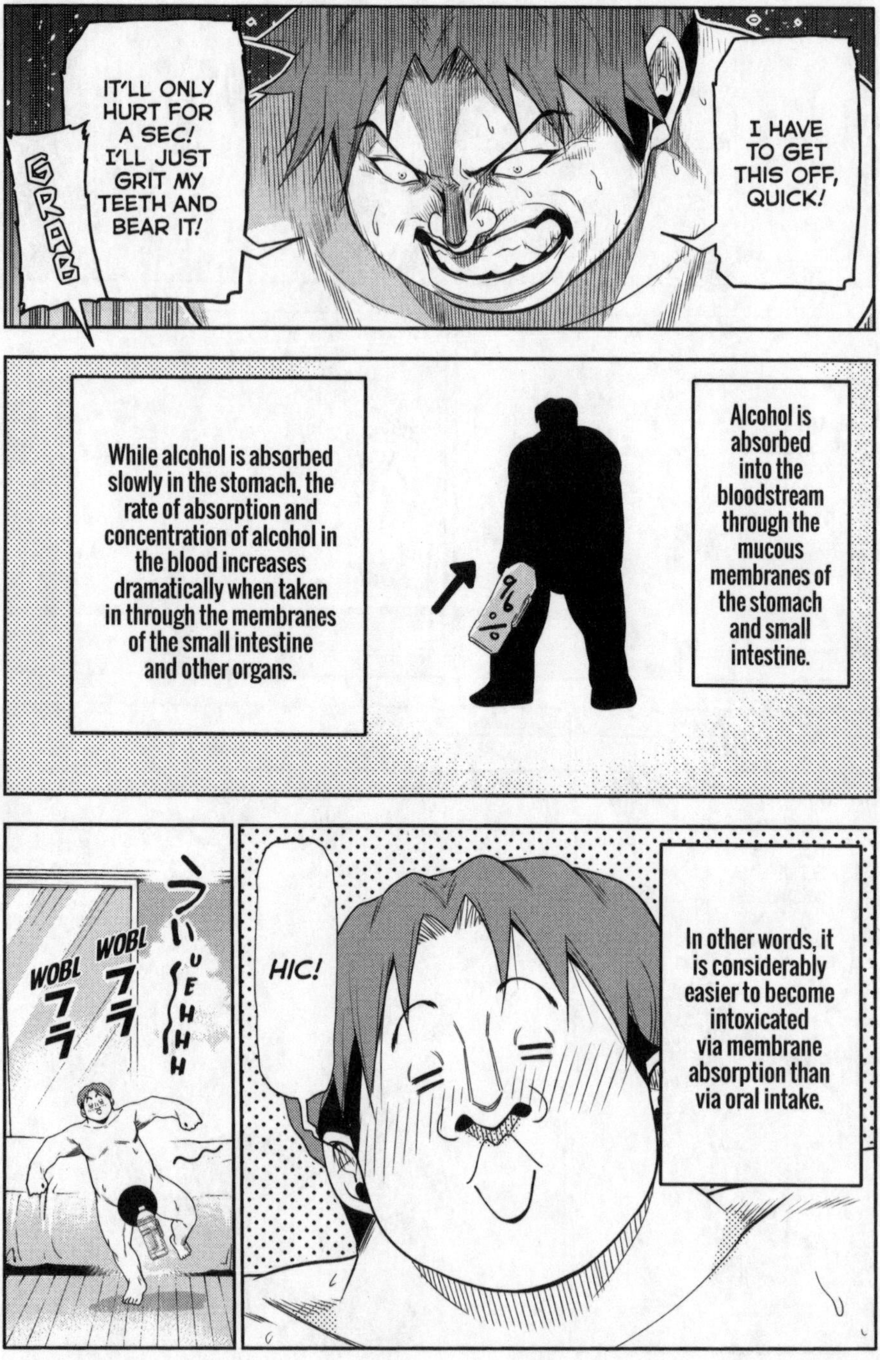
I HAVE TO GET THIS OFF, QUICK!
IT'LL ONLY HURT FOR A SEC! I'LL JUST GRIT MY TEETH AND BEAR IT!
GRAB
Alcohol is absorbed into the bloodstream through the mucous membranes of the stomach and small intestine.
While alcohol is absorbed slowly in the stomach, the rate of absorption and concentration of alcohol in the blood increases dramatically when taken in through the membranes of the small intestine and other organs.
%
In other words, it is considerably easier to become intoxicated via membrane absorption than via oral intake.
HIC!
うぃ～
UEHHH
WOBL
フラ
WOBL
フラ

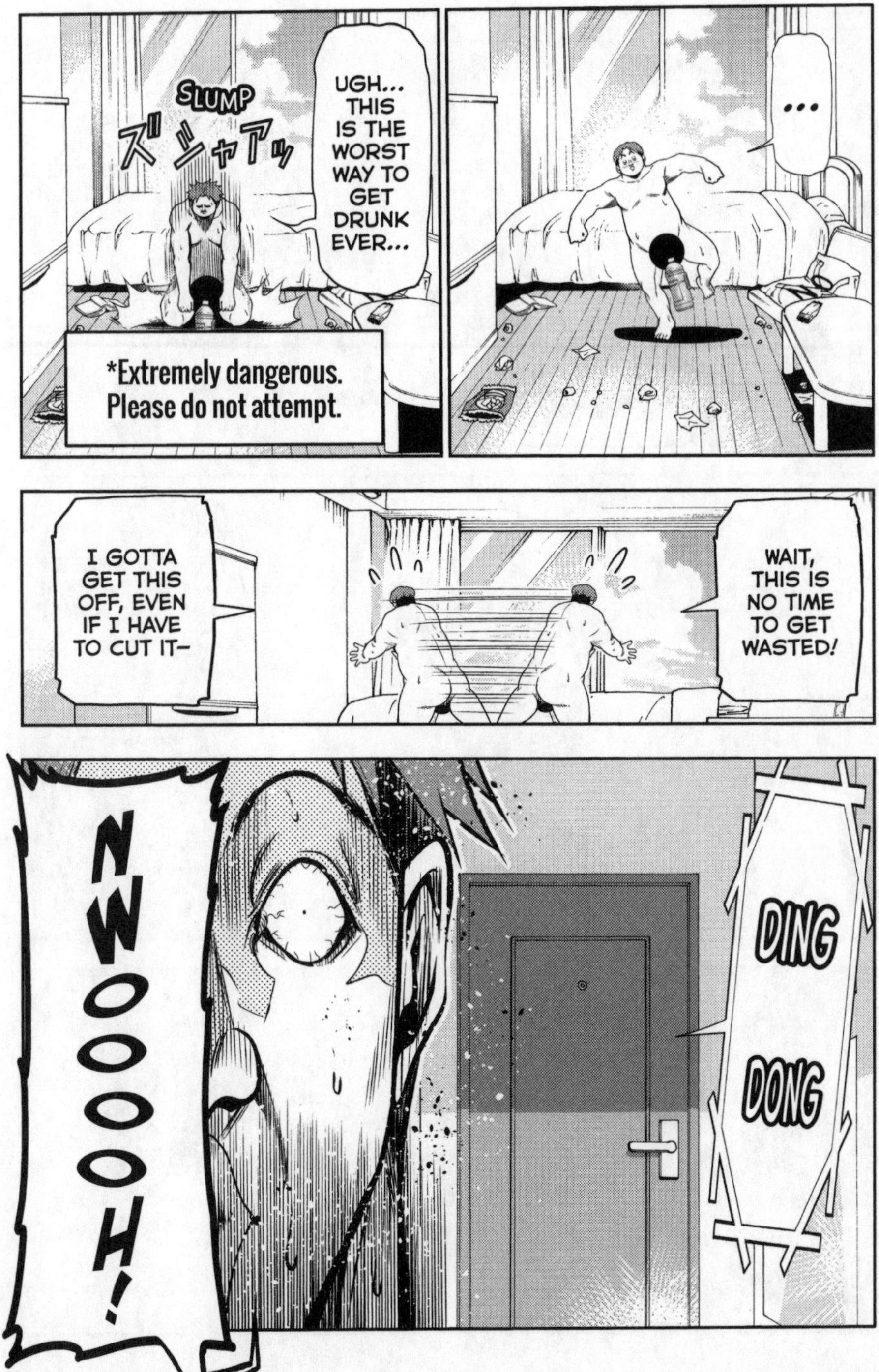
...
SLUMP
ズシャアッ
UGH... THIS IS THE WORST WAY TO GET DRUNK EVER...
*Extremely dangerous. Please do not attempt.
WAIT, THIS IS NO TIME TO GET WASTED!
I GOTTA GET THIS OFF, EVEN IF I HAVE TO CUT IT—
DING DONG
NWOOOOOH!

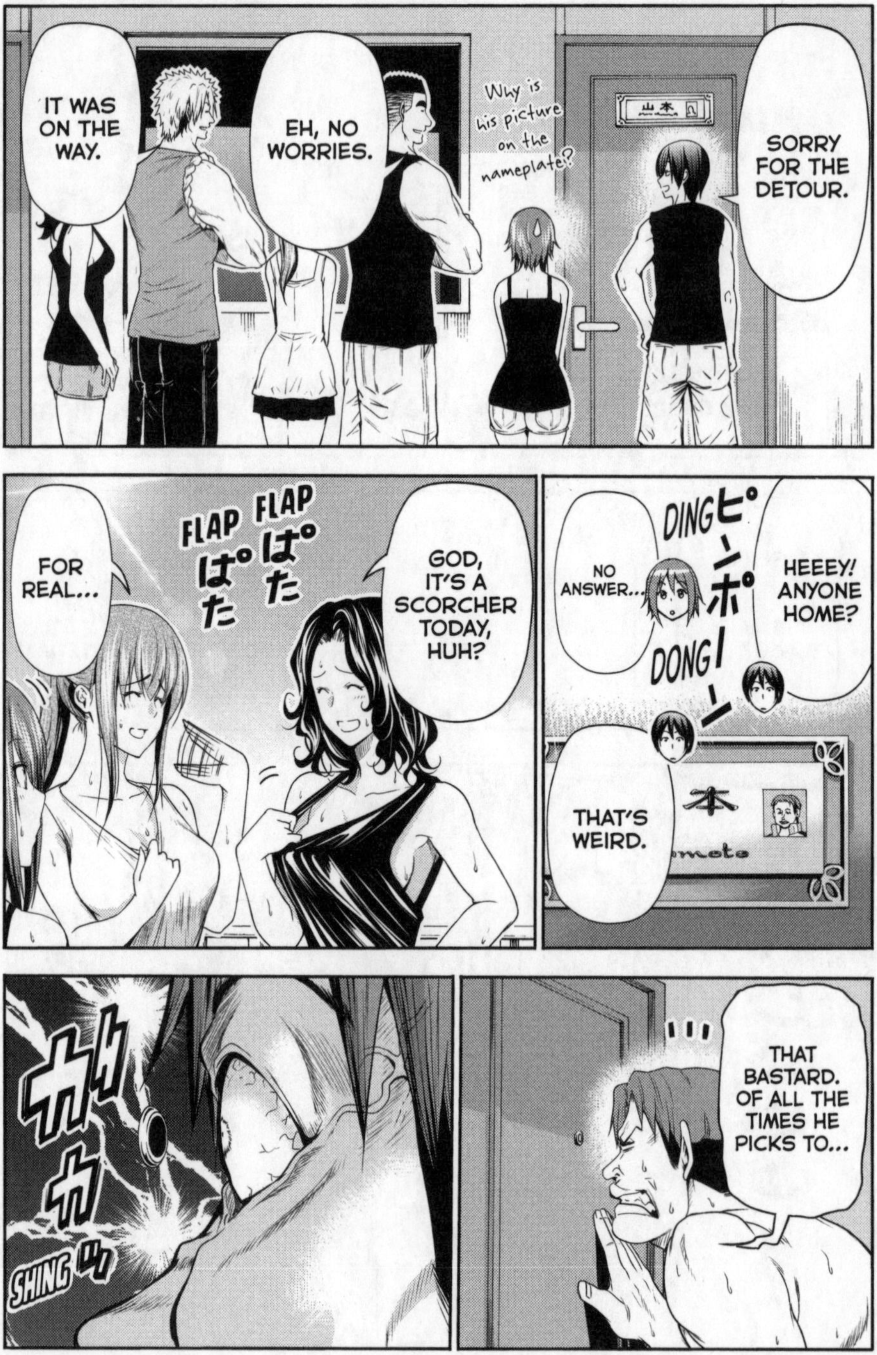
SORRY FOR THE DETOUR.
Why is his picture on the nameplate?
EH, NO WORRIES.
IT WAS ON THE WAY.
HEEEY! ANYONE HOME?
DING DONG
ピンポーン
NO ANSWER...
THAT'S WEIRD.
GOD, IT'S A SCORCHER TODAY, HUH?
FLAP FLAP
ぱた ぱた
FOR REAL...
THAT BASTARD. OF ALL THE TIMES HE PICKS TO...
SHING

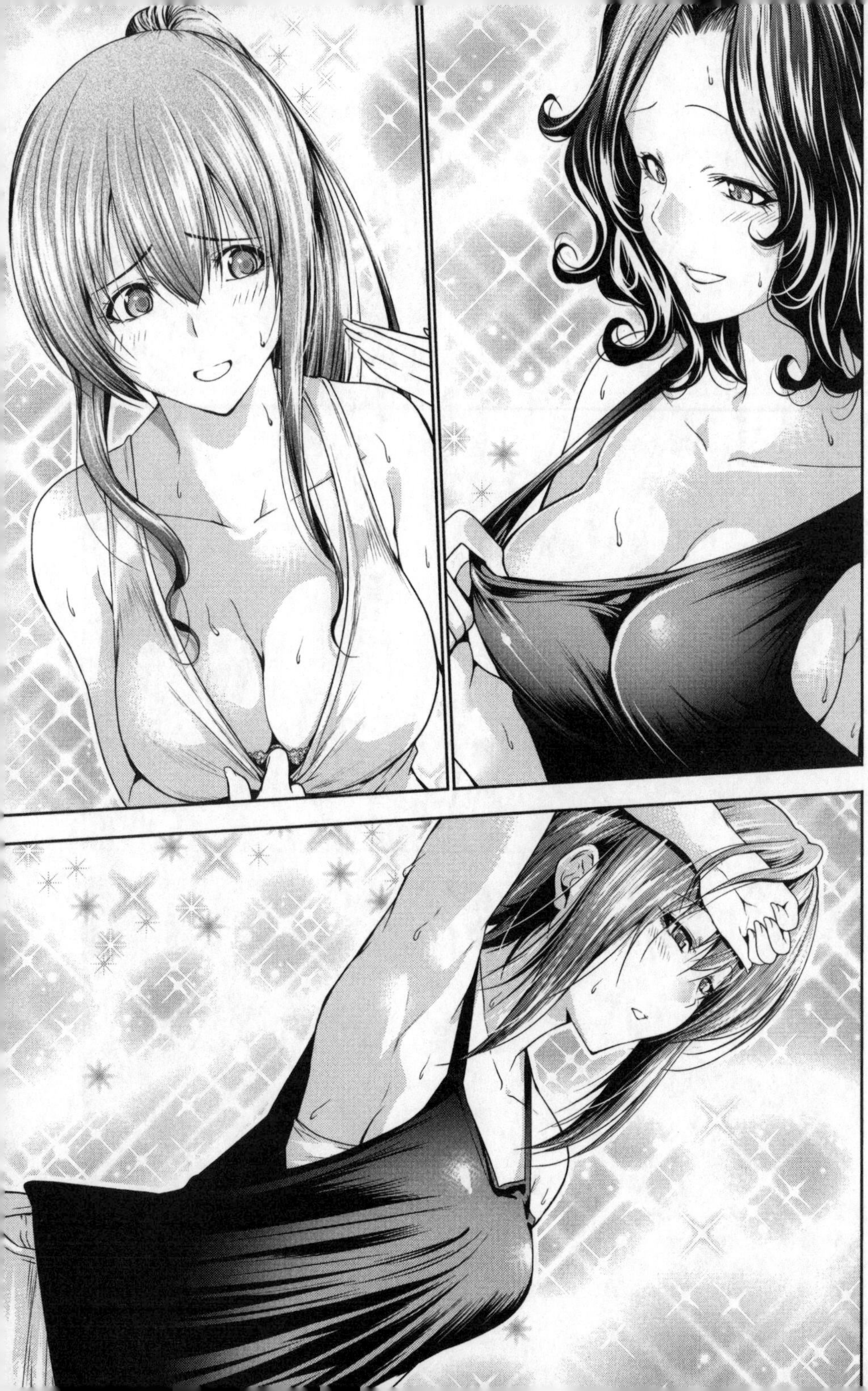

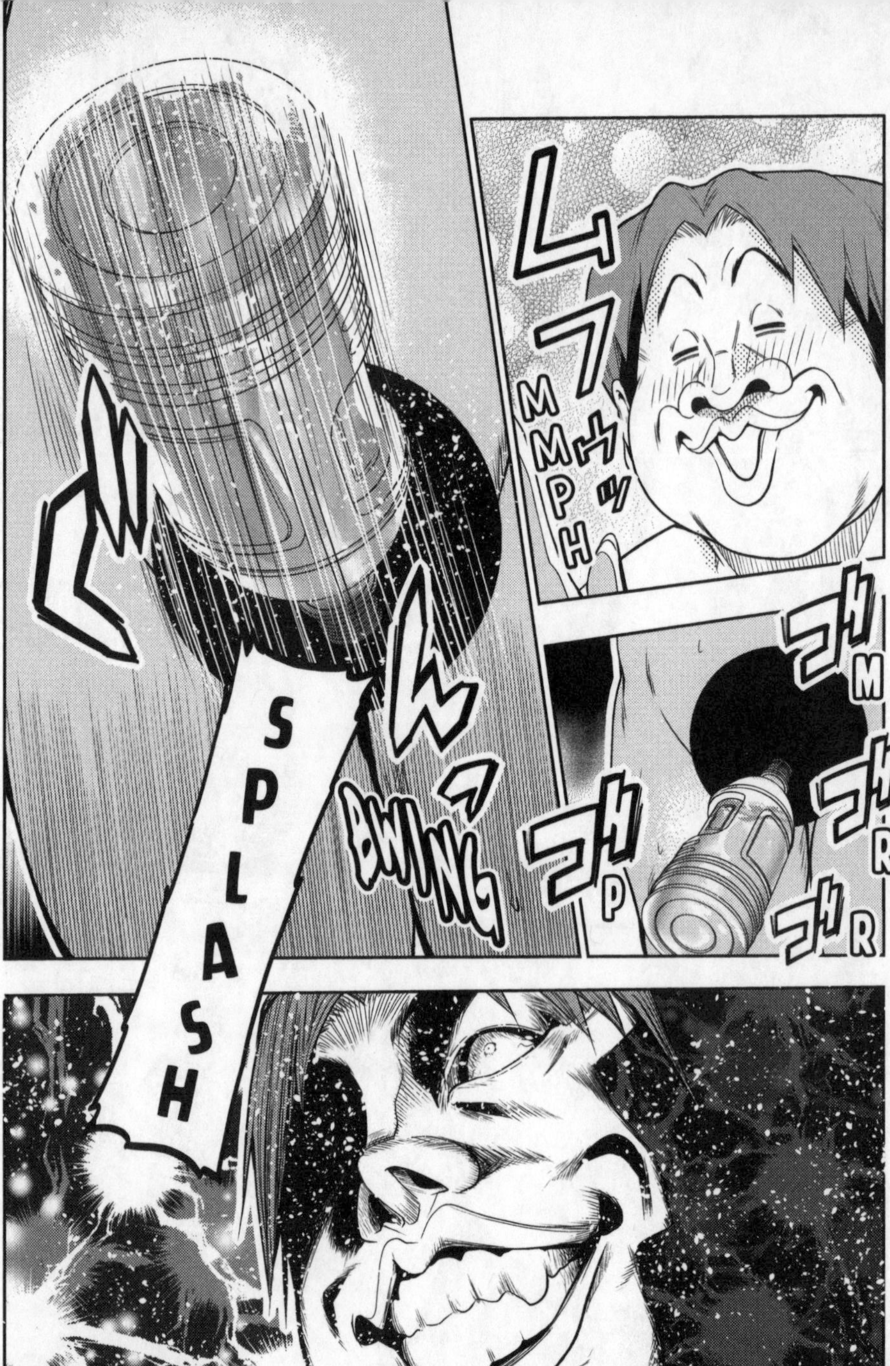
ムフゥッ
MMPH
M
R
R
P
BWING
SPLASH

I HEAR SOMEONE FLAILING AROUND INSIDE!

YOU ALL RIGHT, YAMA-MOTO?!

GAAAHHH!!

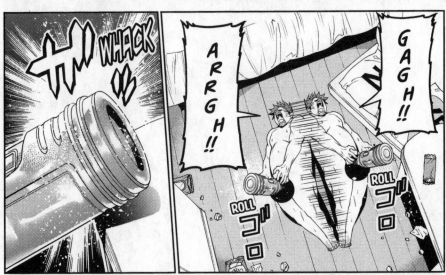

WHACK

ARRGH!!

GAGH!!

ROLL

ROLL

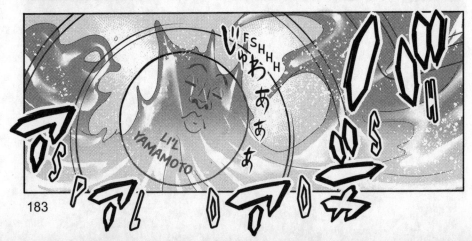

FSHHH

LI'L YAMAMOTO

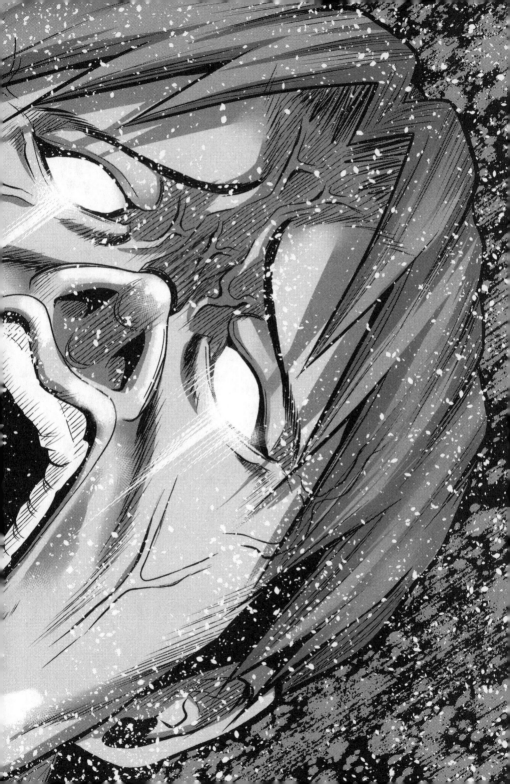

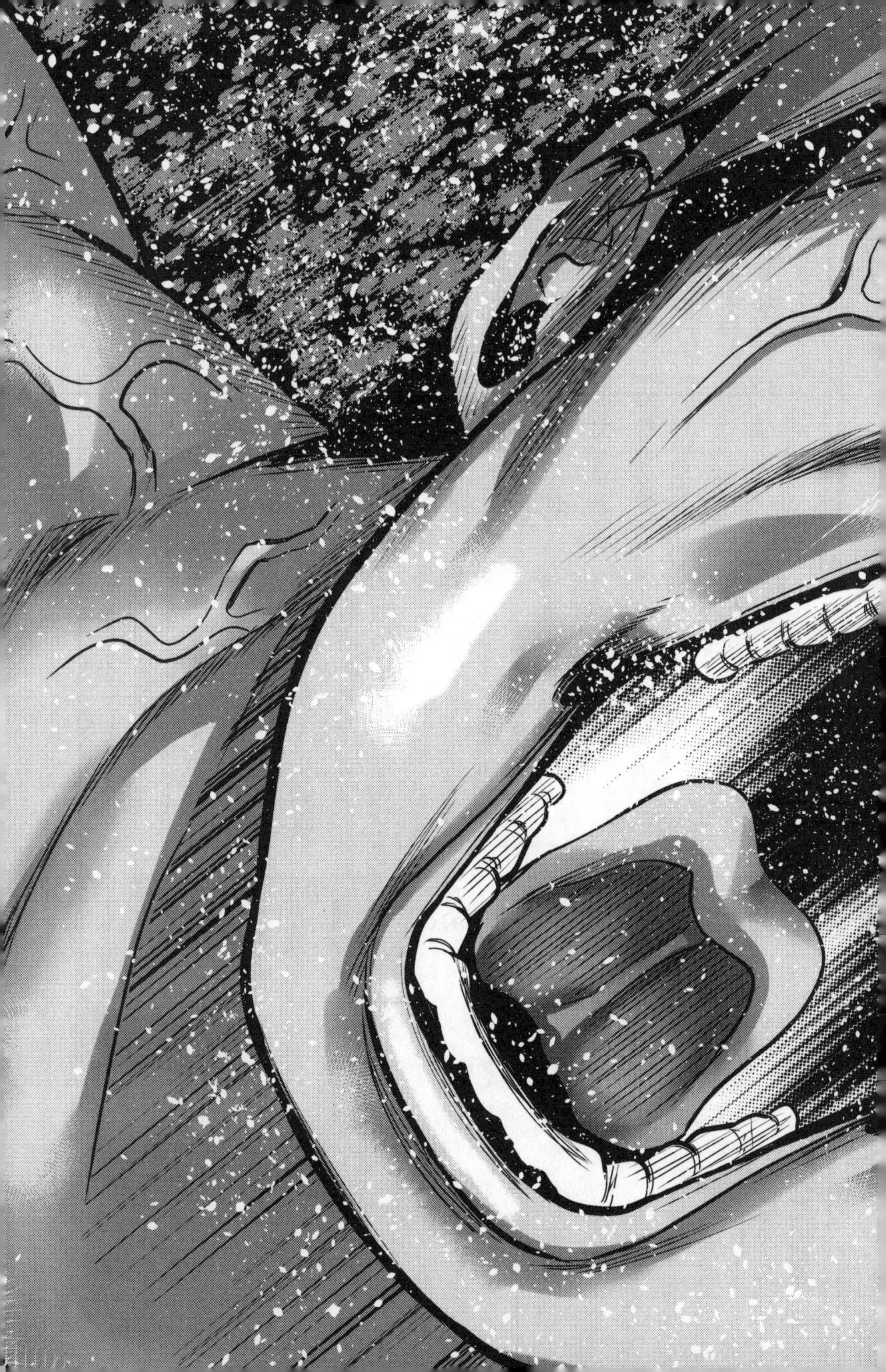

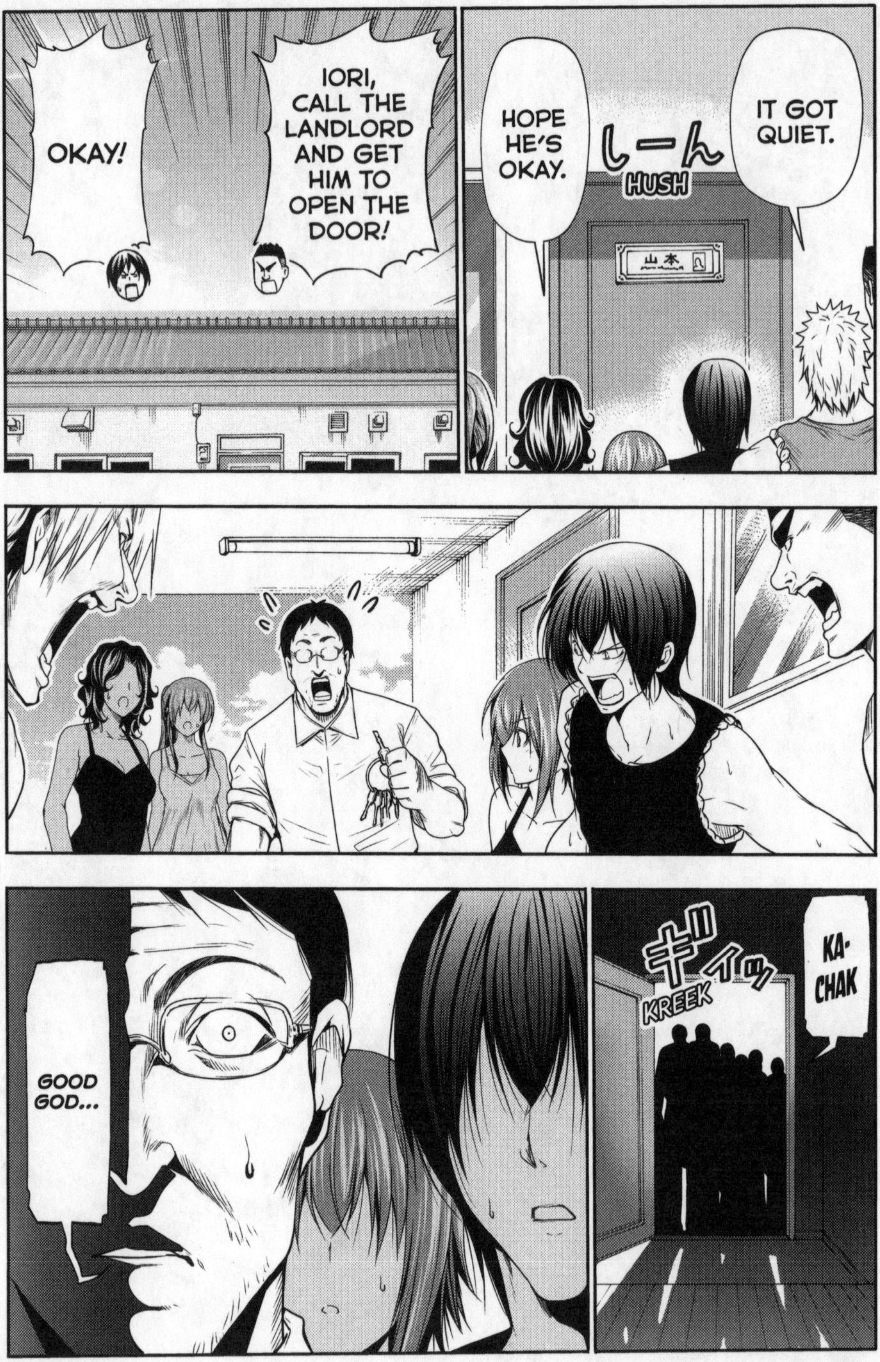

IT GOT QUIET.
しーん
HUSH
山本
HOPE HE'S OKAY.
IORI, CALL THE LANDLORD AND GET HIM TO OPEN THE DOOR!
OKAY!
KA-CHAK
ギィッ
KREEK
GOOD GOD...

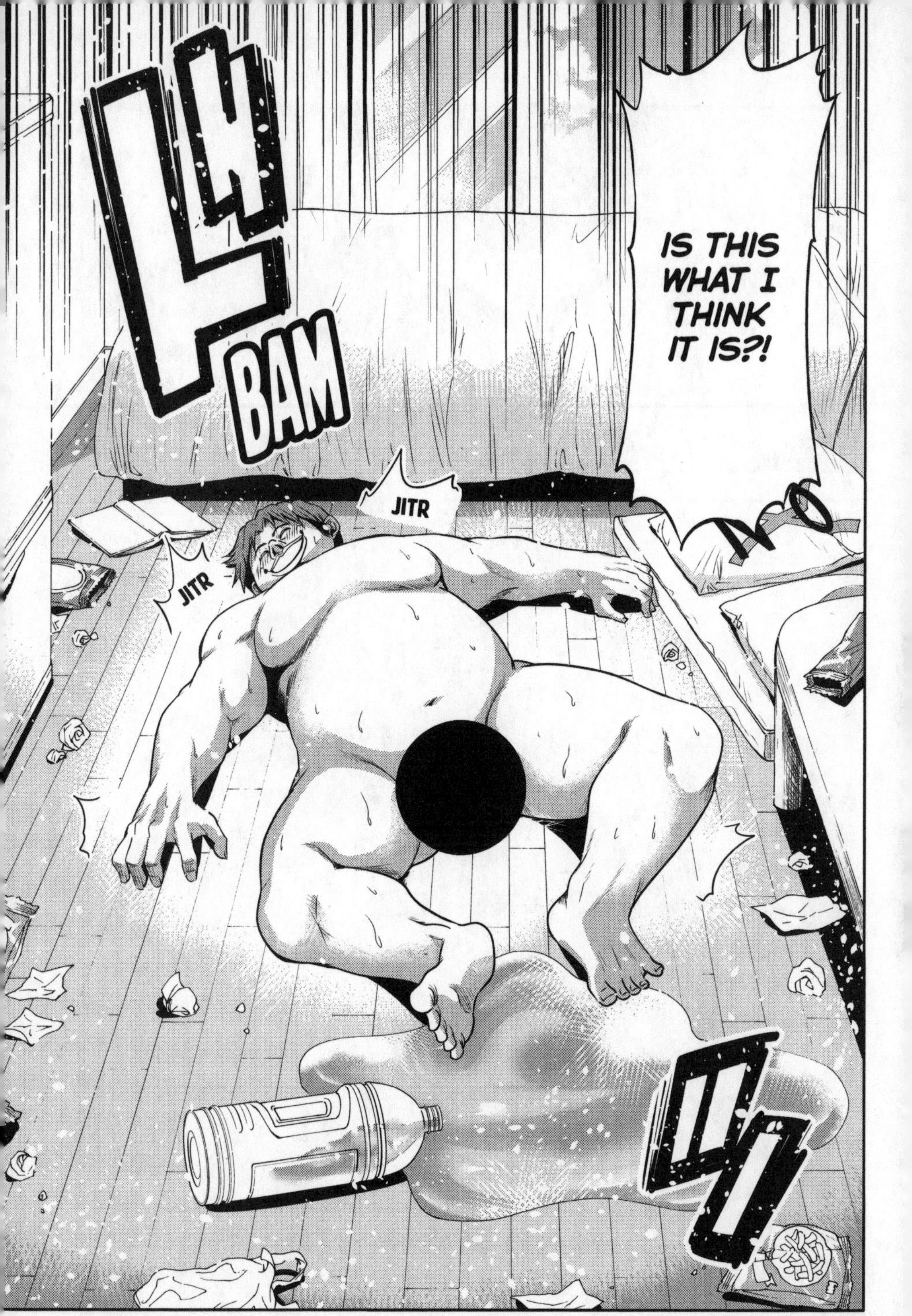
IS THIS WHAT I THINK IT IS?!
BAM
JITR
JITR

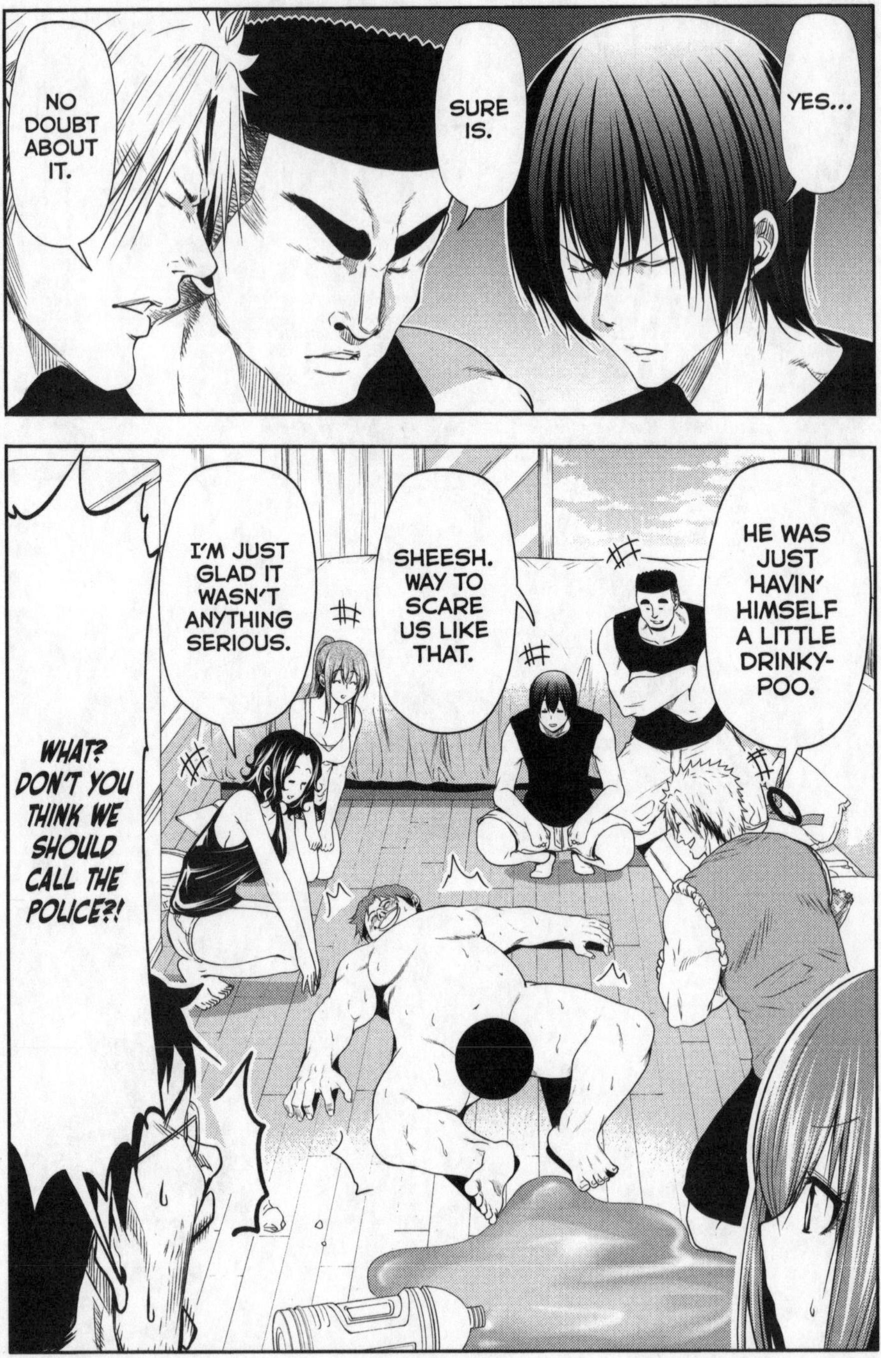
YES...
SURE IS.
NO DOUBT ABOUT IT.
HE WAS JUST HAVIN' HIMSELF A LITTLE DRINKY-POO.
SHEESH. WAY TO SCARE US LIKE THAT.
I'M JUST GLAD IT WASN'T ANYTHING SERIOUS.
WHAT? DON'T YOU THINK WE SHOULD CALL THE POLICE?!

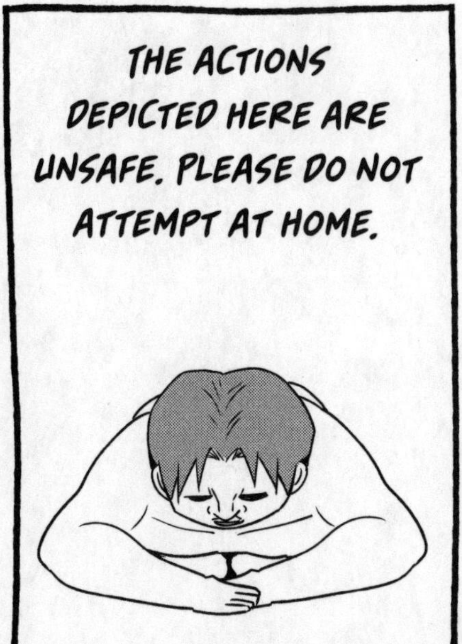

THE ACTIONS
DEPICTED HERE ARE
UNSAFE. PLEASE DO NOT
ATTEMPT AT HOME.

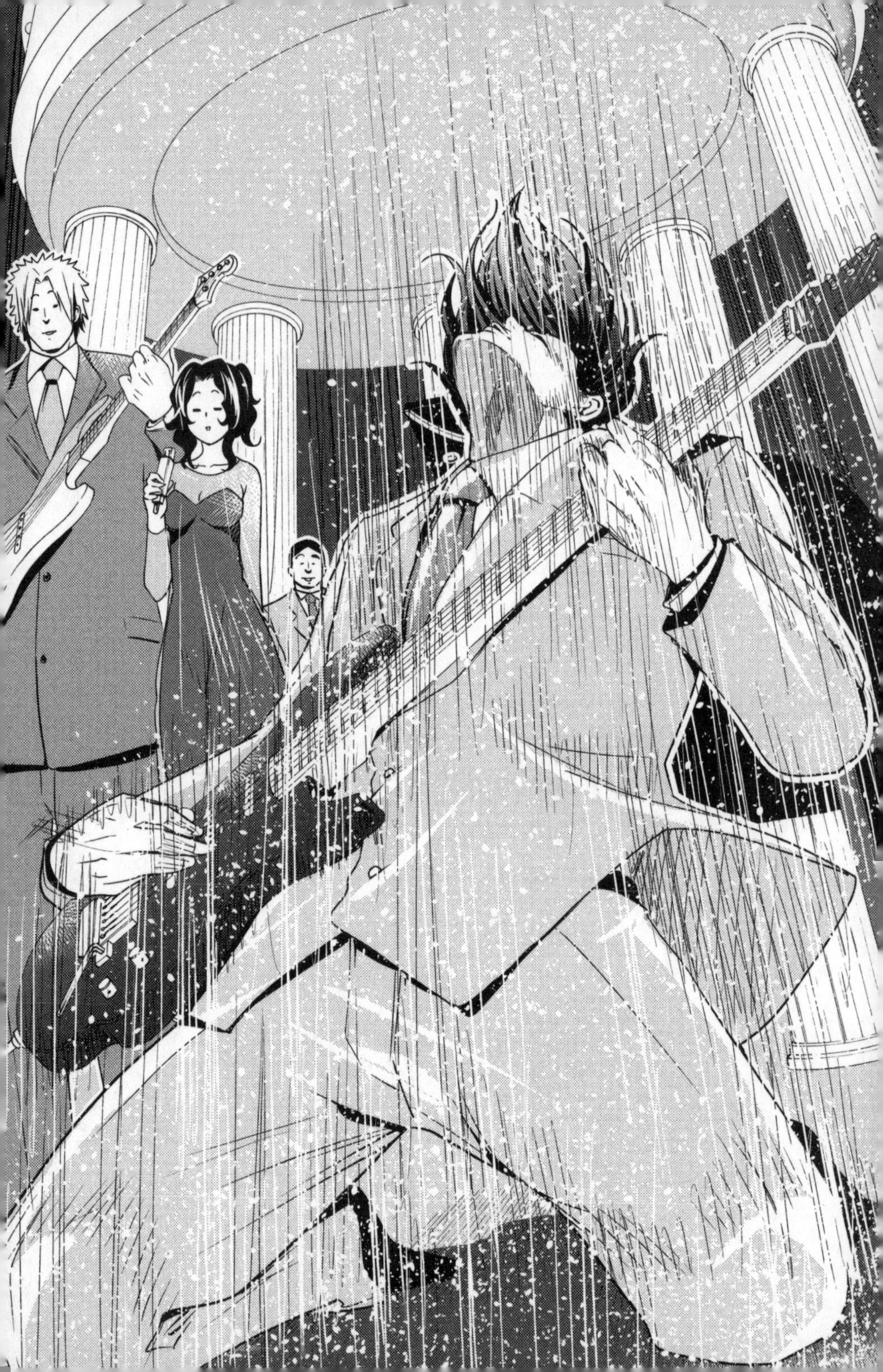

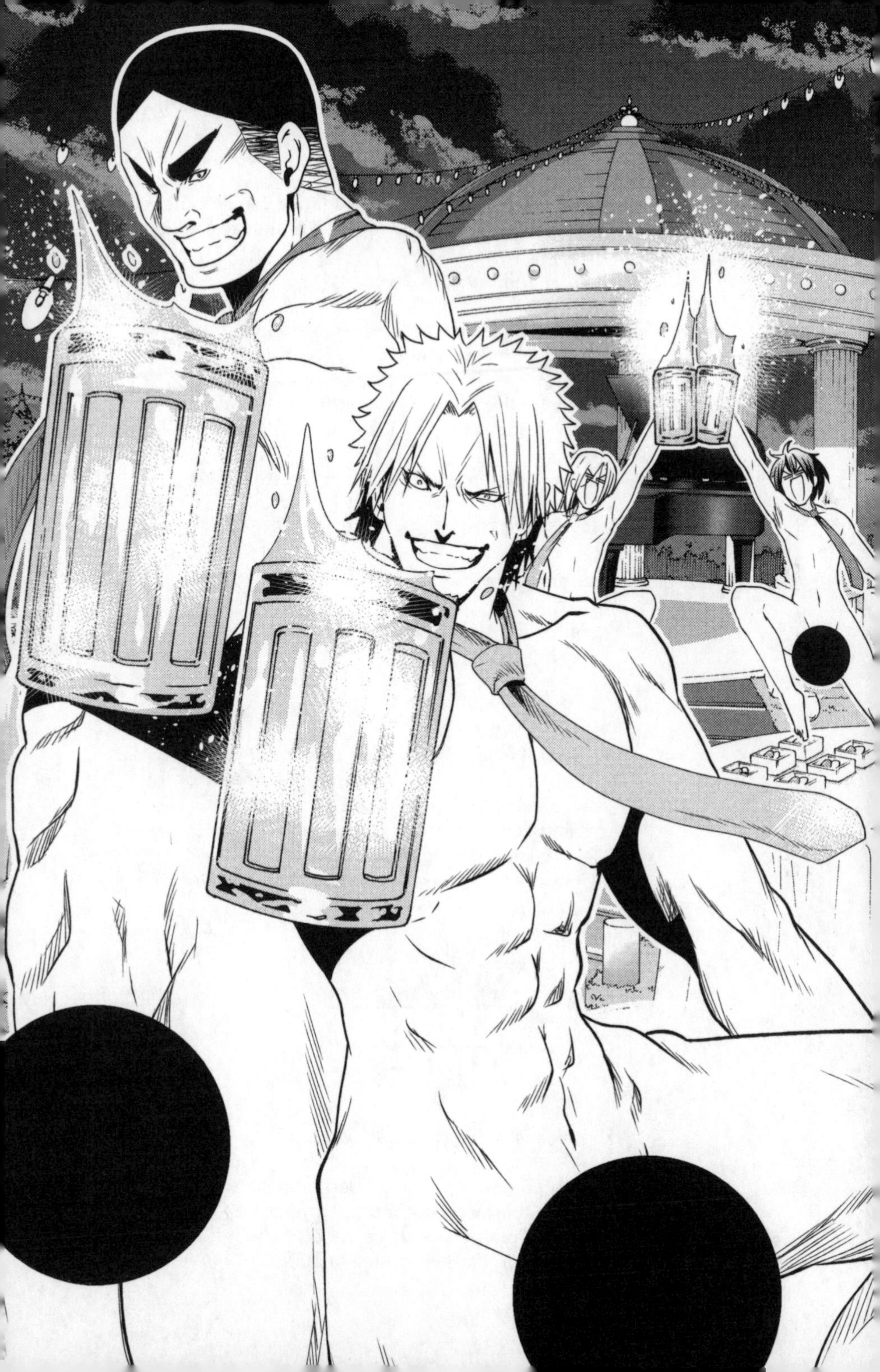

A Kodansha Comics Trade Paperback Original
Grand Blue Dreaming 19 copyright © 2022 Kenji Inoue/Kimitake Yoshioka
English translation copyright © 2023 Kenji Inoue/Kimitake Yoshioka

All rights reserved.

Published in the United States by Kodansha Comics, an imprint of Kodansha USA Publishing, LLC, New York.

Publication rights for this English edition arranged through Kodansha Ltd., Tokyo.

First published in Japan in 2022 by Kodansha Ltd., Tokyo.

ISBN 978-1-64651-700-8

Original cover design by YUKI YOSHIDA (growerDESIGN)

Printed in the United States of America.

www.kodansha.us

9 8 7 6 5 4 3 2 1
Original Digital Edition Translation: Adam Hirsch
Original Digital Edition Lettering: Jan Lan Ivan Concepcion
Editorial Assistance: YKS Services LLC/SKY Japan, INC.
Print Edition Lettering: Daniel Lee
Print Edition Editing: Andres Oliver
Kodansha Comics edition cover design by Phil Balsman

Publisher: Kiichiro Sugawara

Director of publishing services: Ben Applegate
Director of publishing operations: Dave Barrett
Publishing services managing editors: Alanna Ruse, Madison Salters, with Grace Chen
Production manager: Angela Zurlo